Third Edition

Quantitative Methods
for
Public Administration

Third Edition

Quantitative Methods
for
Public Administration

TECHNIQUES AND APPLICATIONS

SUSAN WELCH
Pennsylvania State University

JOHN COMER
University of Nebraska–Lincoln

WAVELAND

PRESS, INC.

Long Grove, Illinois

For information about this book, contact:
Waveland Press, Inc.
4180 IL Route 83, Suite 101
Long Grove, IL 60047-9580
(847) 634-0081
info@waveland.com
www.waveland.com

We dedicate this book to the memory of our late and good colleague and friend,
Robert D. Miewald, Professor of Political Science at the University of Nebraska.

Though Bob did not use many quantitative methods,
he is always associated in our minds with the study of public administration.
He viewed it as a high calling and helped thousands of students do so as well.

PREFACE

The continuing positive reception to the first and second editions of this book confirmed our belief that a strong need exists for a quantitative methods book designed for students of public administration and public policy. In this edition, as in the earlier versions, we provide numerous techniques, examples, and illustrations of methods relevant to these students.

This book is designed to cover materials required for research methods courses in MPA programs certified by the National Association of Schools of Public Affairs and Administration (NASPAA). It is also appropriate for traditional social science methods courses if the instructor wishes to use material focusing on examples and applications from the public policy area.

Users of the previous editions will find much of this edition familiar. But we have updated throughout, and substantially updated certain sections of the book. The speed of technological change meant that our previous discussion of computer use in data analysis, written in the mid-1980s, was of historical interest only. That treatment, focused in Chapter 4, has been replaced by an examination of the use of contemporary technology in data collection and analysis. Throughout the book, where relevant, we provide information about data and bibliographic sources on the Internet. The availability of substantial data archives on the Web, which we especially highlight in Chapter 3, is surely one of the major changes in the environment in which analysts work. In Chapter 3, we also provide additional information about computer-aided survey techniques which are now ubiquitous.

We also expanded our treatment of multivariate techniques in Chapter 10. Since the previous edition, logistic regression has become a much more common technique, and we describe it here. We also introduce students to regression-based event-history analysis, a frequently needed technique in policy analysis. The discussion of each of these techniques stands alone, as with other topics of the chapter (time series, causal modeling, and probit) so instructors may choose among them if they wish.

The text assumes no mathematics background. The statistics section starts with elementary material, such as how to construct a frequency table. Advanced students may be able to skim this material (Chapter 5) quickly, but we have found it useful in providing a background for and giving confidence to beginners and intermediate students, and even those advanced students who often can benefit from review.

In each chapter we have presented summaries of actual research projects, using the most important of the techniques discussed. The student will gain an understanding of how each technique has actually been used. Each chapter also contains problems and exercises, ranging from formulation of research designs and consideration of ethical questions to interpretation and calculation of statistics. Exercises for both computer calculations and "hand" calculation are provided.

In addition to descriptions of traditional social science research methods and statistical techniques, we also cover cost-benefit analysis and forecasting. Normally these are covered only in more specialized management texts. In many public administration programs, a research methods course may provide the students' only exposure to the jargon and techniques of cost-benefit analysis, which is an important analytic technique in management. The combination of traditional social service methods and management techniques in this book will be of value to instructors who choose to introduce their students to quantitative management techniques while continuing to emphasize research methods.

The plan of the book is similar to that of the previous edition. The introductory chapter explains the importance of knowing basic analysis techniques. The next two chapters introduce hypotheses, research design, measurement, and data collection, including an extensive inventory of data available on the Internet. Chapter 4 focuses on using the computer in data analysis. This chapter is placed after the research design section and before the statistics chapters because the process of organizing data for computer use logically comes after research design, but before analysis. However, the chapter stands alone and may be omitted or moved to another part of the course if the instructor does not want to introduce students to the computer at that point in the semester.

Chapters 5 through 10 cover statistical techniques, from simple univariate measures and cross-tabulation to multiple regression and other multivariate techniques. Statistical significance and hypothesis testing are dealt with in Chapter 7. The practical as well as the theoretical importance of statistical significance is emphasized with the use of concrete examples from the policy area. Chapter 11 introduces students to the logic and basic techniques of cost-benefit analysis, and points out the benefits and limitations of this mode of analysis. The final chapter discusses the role of policy research in public organizations. We stress the ethical considerations in doing policy research, and describe how policy research can be made useful in public decision making.

Before concluding, we would like to thank the many people who have assisted us in this project. We are grateful to the Literary Executor of the late Sir Ronald A. Fisher, F.R.S., to Dr. Frank Yates, F.R.S., and to Longman Group Ltd., London, for permission to reprint Tables III and IV from their book *Statistical Tables for Biological, Agricultural and Medical Research* (6th Edition, 1974). Joe Blankeneau assisted with the preparation of many of the

Research in Practice features. Our students have served willingly as guinea pigs for much of the material in the book, and we have appreciated their reactions and suggestions. Faye Moulton gave us especially good suggestions in the earlier versions of the book. As reviewers, Timothy Almy, Douglas G. Feig, Gordon P. Whitaker, Michael A. Maggiotto, and Philip A. Schrodt made many useful suggestions. We would also like to acknowledge the many helpful comments and suggestions we received from professors who reviewed this text. They are John Collins, Seattle University; Frank L. Davis, Lehigh University; John A. Hamman, Southern Illinois University; Laurence F. Jones, Angelo State University; and Leslie A. Leip, Florida Atlantic University. Marie Straka provided valuable assistance in preparation of the manuscript.

Susan Welch
John Comer

ABOUT THE AUTHORS

Susan Welch received her A.B. and Ph.D. degrees from the University of Illinois. Formerly the Carl Happold Professor of Political Science at the University of Nebraska-Lincoln, Welch is now Professor of Political Science and Dean of the College of the Liberal Arts at The Pennsylvania State University. She has published widely in the areas of urban and minority politics, women and politics, and public policy. Recent coauthored books include *Affirmative Action and Minority Enrollment in Medical and Law School* (1998); *Black Americans' View of Racial Inequality* (1991); *Women, Elections, and Representation,* second edition (1994); *American Government* (1999).

John Comer received his A.B. degree from Miami University, his M.A. from Kent State, and his Ph.D. from The Ohio State University. He is a professor of political science at the University of Nebraska-Lincoln. In addition to a graduate seminar in research methods, he teaches in the field of American politics, including public opinion, political parties, and interest groups. He is coauthor of a textbook on American politics.

TABLE OF CONTENTS

LIST OF TABLES

LIST OF FIGURES

I

INTRODUCTION

This book is directed toward students and practitioners in public administration and public policy, political science, and sociology, and at other social science students who are interested in how research methods and statistics are relevant to social and political problems.

Surveys of students in master's degree programs in public administration revealed that the research methods courses were among those found least valuable. Why is this? One reason is that traditional social science methods courses focus on examples that students of policy and administration do not see as relevant or useful. Often these texts do not clarify how techniques derived from the study of voting behavior, social stratification, demography, and other social science topics can be useful in assessing how effective the health care services are in a community or in deriving valid tests for personnel assignments. Methods courses may also be seen as ineffective because the study of methods, especially statistics, is viewed by many students as difficult, unexciting, and alien to their career preparation and interests.

We probably cannot make methods and statistics exciting. But we do hope to show students how methods and statistics are relevant to problems they will face in public agencies. We will do that throughout the book by using examples and exercises relevant to policy problems and by including selected "research in practice" demonstrations of how a method or statistic can be applied to policy and administrative situations.

This book is not a complete statistics book. Rather we have introduced a variety of methods and statistics that students will find useful. We hope that many students will become interested in research methods and statistics and will continue to develop their research and analytical skills. We do not expect students who complete this book to be statisticians. But it is reasonable to expect them to be able to compute useful statistics involving one or two variables, to understand the logic and be able to interpret some of the more commonly used multivariate statistics, as well as to develop the ability to converse knowledgeably with researchers about problems encountered in the research process.

We will also introduce the student to quantitative methods useful to managers, methods not normally treated in statistics books. We will examine some quantitative procedures utilized in cost-benefit analysis, in planning, and in other aspects of management. In each instance we will show the usefulness of systematic methodology for answering questions that managers, evaluators, and administrators encounter in their daily routines.

The Usefulness of Methods and Statistics to Public Administration and Policy

Whether in universities, police departments, or health agencies, bureaucracies increasingly rely on statistics and quantitative measures for information about the scope and success of their programs. University administrators calculate enrollment and credit-hour statistics to justify moving funds from departments of education to those of information technology; police administrators gather and process crime data to convince the public that the police department needs a larger budget; health planning administrators use statistics to justify their decision that no new hospitals should be built in a community. Both administrators and social scientists have used statistics to persuade federal courts that policies relating to such issues as school finance, integration, affirmative action, jury selection, and so forth are unconstitutional. In each of these cases, policy decisions are based at least in part on the results of quantitative analyses.

Furthermore, low- and middle-level bureaucrats are constantly pressed to collect, maintain, and present data to show their departments' productivity and problems. Often questions arise that may be answered using statistical data. How many miles of highway were built in 1999? How many mental health clients were treated last year? How many participants in alternative-sentencing programs committed another crime? How many applicants for drivers' licenses had to wait more than one hour? Descriptive measures such as these are crucial to agencies in justifying their existence and budget to taxpayers, policymakers, and clients.

Moreover, among service professionals, benchmarking has become endemic. **Benchmarking** is comparing some aspect of your agency's operation to that of other agencies or institutions of your type. Benchmarking can focus on measures of service, such as days to process a client's application for benefits, measures of output, or measures of resources, such as the number of employees per client.

The following are specific examples illustrating some common situations where quantitative methods are crucial.

1. A local United Way agency wants to find out if its distribution of United Way funds meets with community approval, if there are unmet needs which the community favors meeting, and if the United Way appeal is efficiently reaching likely donors. To answer these questions

someone in the agency must be aware of the appropriate quantitative methods. Agency personnel who would likely contract out this project to a survey research firm must be sophisticated enough in quantitative methodology to be able to frame the questions to be answered and to evaluate critically the data collection procedures and results presented to them by the survey research consulting firm.

2. The governor decides to launch a total quality management (TQM) initiative (sometimes called Continuous Quality Improvement [CQI]). The director of your social service agency wants to know how your agency compares in service efficiency with similar state agencies in your region in dealing with applicants for job training. Knowledge of quantitative methods and basic survey techniques will help you ask the right questions and be able to interpret the answers in this benchmarking project.

3. A new police chief joins a local force and discovers that a large proportion of uniformed officers are stationed in the downtown area directing traffic. The police chief decides that a better use of these uniformed personnel would be to scatter them throughout various neighborhoods in proportion to the crime rates of each area. As the head of the unit charged with making recommendations for deployment of the force, you can more readily respond to the chief's decision if you have a knowledge of the data sources available to examine crime rates and of analysis techniques appropriate to that data. You could provide alternative allocation choices for the chief.

4. Many states and localities are setting up economic development programs by providing tax incentives for businesses wishing to relocate or expand in their areas. Your local council is considering such a program, but wonders if the benefits outweigh the costs of lost tax revenue. As the head of the economic development agency, you know that assessing this requires an understanding of appropriate ways to quantify costs and benefits and an ability to choose sound criteria for comparing programs that your community might use.

Clearly, familiarity with statistics is necessary to survive and be successful in bureaucracies. Some of you will be the ones who actually collect the statistics; others will be responsible for evaluating and making decisions on the basis of those statistics. Still others of you may not go into public administration at all but will be involved as citizens in evaluating governmental or educational programs. Whichever of these roles you will fill, it is clear that you will have to understand some of the basics of quantitative data: how it should be collected, computed, and interpreted. It is important to all citizens, not just those working in public agencies, that they not automatically flinch and turn to the next page when a chart, table, or graph appears in a report or newspaper article. You do not need to love statistics, but you should learn to live with them comfortably. To make informed decisions, it is important to be able to critically evaluate information presented to you in quantitative form, neither standing in awe of the statistics nor simply ignoring them.

This latter point is worth reiterating. One of the nice things about having a familiarity with methods and statistics is that you will know when not to take them seriously; you will be able to recognize when the information being presented to you is likely to be invalid and meaningless. Knowing how to spot conclusions based on worthless data is just as important as being able to draw valid conclusions from appropriate data.

This can be crucial to a public manager. If you contract with an evaluation firm or a survey research consulting group to carry out work for your agency, you have to be able to critically analyze the results presented to you by your consultants. Were the procedures valid? Was the statistical analysis appropriate to the data and correctly done? Were the statistics interpreted correctly? In other words, have you been presented with gold or garbage? Your ability to evaluate these kinds of factors will determine whether your agency will be a victim of fraud and shoddy work done by incompetent or dishonest consultants or be the recipient of useful information.

The same is true for a citizen who is not a part of a public agency. These same skills can be used in evaluating news reports of polls, in serving as a member of citizen advisory boards to public and private agencies, or in evaluating newspaper and journal reports of studies done of public agencies. In each of these roles, informed and reasoned judgment requires the ability to understand statistics and quantitative methods. Members of boards of directors of private firms are also called upon to exercise these kinds of judgments. What you learn here should be useful to you no matter what career you choose.

POLICY EVALUATION

Before the 1960s, legislatures and citizens interested in the quality of programs tended to look at the way the program operated. They collected quantitative data, but it was of a descriptive kind: How many clients did the program have? What was the staff-to-client ratio? What kinds of financial and other resources were available to program administrators? Accreditation reviews of universities were typical of this kind of program assessment. Review teams would judge the quality of a university's program by the size of its library, the proportion of its faculty holding Ph. D.s, the ratio of faculty to students, the financial base of the institution, and its other resources.

More recent analyses of programs often focus on the processes by which programs deal with their clients. Focus on processes is particularly obvious in total quality management or continuous quality improvement initiatives. In these projects, one objective is to improve customer or client service by streamlining processes. Thus, it is important to have quantitative data to measure these processes. For example, how long clients have to wait to see counselors, the number of people a client might have to see to receive needed services, the time lapsed between receipt of a bill and payment, and other indicators of the way the program actually operates.

When social scientists speak of **program or policy evaluation** (we use the terms interchangeably), they are usually speaking of assessments of programs that focus on outcomes. The question to be answered is not how many resources a program has, nor how the program runs, but whether or not the program has met its goals. Does a drug program actually succeed in helping clients to become drug-free? Does a family-planning program reduce the number of unplanned births among its clients? Does a mandatory jail term for drunken driving reduce the number of alcohol-related traffic deaths? Does the death penalty reduce homicide? These kinds of questions force analysts to focus on the success of the program in achieving its goals. Is the program doing what its funders and supporters think it is supposed to do? It is now very common for funding agencies, private or public, to require program evaluations.

Policy evaluation that focuses on outcomes relies heavily on social science methodology. Such methods can help answer the specific and applied questions of policy analysts as well as the general and theoretical questions of other social scientists. Social science methods are useful to policy evaluation research because they:

1. Permit the framing of a question in a way that it can be answered (hypothesis formulation).
2. Suggest strategies for how to collect evidence to provide answers to the question (research design).
3. Provide guidelines on what kinds of information will answer the question and how to collect it (measurement and data collection).
4. Provide appropriate analysis techniques for the data (statistical analysis).

Each of these aspects of methods will be examined as we proceed through the text.

Thus, evaluating the outcomes of programs requires special kinds of methodological skills. For example, suppose that you are an administrator in a state welfare office. Your task is to evaluate the success of a workfare program that has been in place in your state for two years. Workfare programs, now required by federal law, are those designed to give job training and employment skills to recipients of welfare. Often they use private companies to provide training. At first glance, one might think that evaluating such a program would be easy. After all, one needs only to know whether the people who went through the program were able to get off welfare or not. However, a good policy evaluation is much more complicated than that. It is not enough to find out if the individual left the welfare rolls. That is because most welfare recipients do not stay on the rolls long; only a small minority are permanent recipients. But one can leave the rolls for reasons other than getting a good job. Some people die, for example. Less morbidly, others have children who leave home, so they are no longer eligible. Some remarry and lose eligibility or they exhaust their eligibility period. So a meaningful evaluation of the workfare program must not only look at the names on the rolls, but at the actual employment record of those who received training. What proportion of the women participating in the program have steady employment six months or a year following their training?

Further, not only must the analyst find out what happened to people in the workfare program, he or she must determine whether their employment record is better than if they had not participated in the program. In other words, are they better off than they would have been in the absence of a program? This is a key question. After all, in any group of people, some who are unemployed today will be employed next year, regardless of whether they are enrolled in job training programs, just as some drivers arrested for drunk driving will never be arrested again for that offense even if they are not sent to jail or to rehabilitation. In the absence of a workfare program, many people leave the rolls because they get a job. So, the tricky part of program evaluation is trying to determine whether what happened to the clients of the program was different than would be expected if no such program existed.

Here is where methods training is useful. Obviously, no one can say for sure what any particular person would have done if he or she had not been in a program such as workfare. But one can determine how other, similar people who did not have the program behaved. To make that determination, one has to compare individuals who went through the program with other similar individuals who did not. Only after comparing the program recipients to others who resemble them can one reach a conclusion about the success of the program. Learning how to determine what appropriate comparison groups are and how to go about collecting data from them are important aspects of research methodology.

Thus, policy evaluation requires special kinds of methodological skills. It is necessary to know how to handle descriptive data on agencies, programs, and clients, and how to plan research strategies that allow you to try to answer the question: Are the clients of the program any different after having the program than they would have been in its absence? Thus, program evaluators must have a good understanding not only of statistical analysis, but also of research designs and data collection procedures.

THE PLAN OF THE BOOK

Before you can (or should) collect data and compute statistical measures, you need to think about what it is you want to know. If you are the head of the streets department and are interested in finding out how successful the department is in keeping the number of potholes to a minimum, you must first formulate the information you need more specifically. That is, are you interested in its success in one part of the community compared to another? Or are you more interested in its success this year compared with last year and the year before? Or are you mainly interested in the cost to the city of different ways of repairing potholes? Each of these different questions requires a different research design and different data. Therefore, before gathering information, you must formulate your questions and plan your data collection and analysis procedures.

This book is organized to help you do this step by step. Chapter 2 presents information on research design, while in Chapter 3 we discuss problems of data collection and measurement. In Chapter 4 we survey the use of information technology in data collection and analysis. We will focus on such questions as how to collect data for easy conversion to computer usage, how to code and store the data, and what kinds of options are available for analysis. We will also survey some of the kinds of programs available for other management tasks, such as data management and financial analysis.

Chapter 5 will show you how to use simple displays of data to provide useful summary information. We will present some measures of central tendency. Further, we will discuss how to construct basic quantitative techniques of frequency distributions and visual tools, such as charts and graphs, and when to use them. These techniques are very useful when you are summarizing information in reports and tables.

In Chapter 6 we continue the discussion of data analysis. While often a good deal of information can be conveyed using one-variable measures, such as means and medians, sometimes it is necessary to analyze the relationship between two conditions. For example, you might want to see if urban counties spend more per capita on schools than do rural counties. Or you might want to examine relative mortality rates among whites and African Americans. Chapter 6 presents some ways to show relationships among two or three variables; we discuss tools such as cross-tabulation and measures of association. The concept and techniques of sampling can be very important to the public manager. Managers are often called upon to provide information where it is impossible to garner measurements on all of the objects of interest, whether they are participants in a workfare program, beneficiaries of United Way monies, or neighborhoods within a local community. Sampling is a way to collect information on a subset of the total population, and it allows the manager to draw conclusions within a specified range of error regarding characteristics of the population. In Chapter 7 we discuss sampling and procedures for estimating and testing hypotheses about populations.

In Chapters 8 and 9 you will learn about correlation and regression, two of the most common statistical techniques found in consultant and agency reports as well as in scholarly policy articles. These techniques are very appropriate in policy evaluation. For example, regression allows you to estimate how much impact an auto inspection program has on highway fatalities while taking into account the other factors that influence highway fatalities, such as miles driven, speed limits, urban density, and so forth. We will introduce you to the underlying logic of correlation and regression and how to interpret and display regression results to a lay audience. A thorough study of Chapters 8 and 9 should allow you to interpret and use simple and multiple regression.

Chapter 10 will focus on some more advanced techniques for analysis of three or more variables. Causal modeling and time series analyses are discussed. Then we will look at some analytic techniques for the analysis of data that do not meet the requirements for ordinary regression.

Chapters 2 through 10, then, deal with the research process as it relates to the public manager from data collection to statistical analysis, from research design to computer use. Chapter 11 introduces cost-benefit analysis, a widely used and much discussed technique for estimating relative costs of alternative ways of reaching a given agency goal. In the chapter you will be given an overview of the method, and the pros and cons of cost-benefit analysis as a tool will be extensively discussed.

Finally, Chapter 12 reviews the relationship of policy research to policy making. A consideration of the ethics of research is also presented.

We are trying to provide a rather comprehensive yet simple introduction to quantitative methods for the policy analyst and the public manager. In teaching our own classes, we have found that policy and administration students tend to fear quantitative methods, yet when the subjects are presented in the right way, students do grasp the importance of learning about them. We believe that a knowledge of these methods is crucial to the modern manager and the informed citizen. Our hope is that when you finish this book you will be a knowledgeable consumer and an adventuresome user of statistical methods.

KEY TERMS

Benchmarking
Program or policy evaluation

2

PLANNING POLICY RESEARCH:
HYPOTHESES AND RESEARCH DESIGN

A policy researcher frequently wants to answer questions relating to the effectiveness of a policy. Do gun control laws reduce crime? Do health maintenance organizations provide better health care than fee-for-service plans? Will a decrease in speed limit reduce traffic fatalities on a city street? Does mainstreaming exceptional children cost less than special programs? Will the establishment of a twenty-four-hour-per-day help line reduce suicides? These questions are similar in form to, though different in substance from, questions asked by pure researchers: Does television news influence attitudes about politics? Do issues influence voting behavior more than party loyalties do? Does household crowding cause crime and aggression?

HYPOTHESES AND VARIABLES

Implicit in each of these questions, whether policy related or not, is the notion of a **dependent variable** and an **independent variable**. By variable we simply mean something that can take on different values. The independent variable can be thought of as a potential cause, the dependent variable as the effect. The dependent variable is that which is being affected; the independent variable is something that is assumed to be causing the effect. For example, will lowered speed limits reduce traffic fatalities? Traffic fatalities is the dependent variable, the thing to be affected (lowered, we hope) by the independent variable, the speed limit. Another example: Does team policing reduce crime? Here the dependent variable is crime, the independent variable is team policing. The assumption is that team policing (independent variable) will affect crime (the dependent variable).

Team policing   ⟶   Crime

(Independent variable)   (Dependent variable)

The policy researcher then will want to test to see if this relationship is in fact true. Notice that the relationship may be true or false: team policing may reduce crime, it may increase crime, or it may have no effect at all. A statement predicting that a relationship exists between an independent variable and a dependent variable is called a **hypothesis**. Examples of some hypotheses are:

H1: Decreasing the speed limit will decrease traffic fatalities.
H2: Changing from at-large to district city council elections will increase minority representation.
H3: Increasing the number of police on the street will decrease the crime rate.
H4: Providing tax breaks for new industry will increase the formation of new jobs.

Each of these statements implies a causal relationship: an independent variable (speed limit, type of election, number of police, tax breaks) is hypothesized to produce changes in a dependent variable (fatalities, minority representation, crime rate, new jobs). In policy research the independent variable is usually the policy; the dependent variable is something the policy is expected to affect. In some cases the researcher might want to analyze the effects of a particular condition on some sort of social disorder that might be alleviated by a new policy. What effect does unemployment have on juvenile crime? What effect do cyclamates have on cancer rates? In these cases neither the dependent variable nor independent variable are policies. Some hypotheses are stated in null terms; that is, the independent variable is hypothesized to have no effect on the dependent variable. This is called the **null hypothesis**. This form of hypothesis formulation is useful in testing for statistical significance, as we will see in Chapter 7.

Whichever way the hypothesis is stated, it must be possible, at least in principle, to verify or disconfirm it. It must be stated in such a way that it can be shown to be either true or false in a given instance. Statements that cannot be verified or disconfirmed are not really hypotheses.

In applied research, hypotheses are not always stated explicitly. But it is essential in planning policy research that you have the question you want to answer clearly in mind. If you have not specified such questions, then stop until you do. Failure to specify precisely what question you want to answer will waste time and other resources because it will not be clear to you what information you want to collect.

EXERCISES

2-1 A university administrator is interested in studying the relationship between class size and knowledge obtained by students. Formulate a hypothesis. Which is the dependent variable and which is the independent variable?

2-2 A member of Congress is interested in the utilization of the food stamp program. She asked her aide to compare counties in her district to determine if utilization is related to the educational, income and racial status of residents of these counties. Formulate two hypotheses, and specify the dependent and independent variables.

2-3 The absence of right-of-way designations (stop signs) at intersections on county roads is suspected to increase traffic accidents. Determine the dependent and independent variables and state the hypothesis in null terms.

UNIT OF ANALYSIS

The **level** or **unit of analysis** is another important concept. Units of analysis are the objects being studied, e.g., individuals, groups, geographical units: anything on which information can be gathered. The independent and dependent variables are, of course, measures of some property of the units; education, income, and age are measures of individual characteristics. Level of analysis refers to the same thing; when our research is on individuals, we speak of the individual level of analysis. With groups or geographical units, we often speak of the aggregate level or aggregate analysis.

The idea of unit or level of analysis is not a difficult one, but do not confuse unit with variable. Variables are properties of units. For example, years of formal education (a variable) is a property of an individual (unit of analysis). Total population (a variable) is a property of a city (unit of analysis). Be aware that the same hypothesis can be examined with different units or at different levels of analysis. For example, we might hypothesize that support for tax-cutting referenda is related to education. To test this, we could survey individuals to compare their education to their opinions on tax cuts, or we could employ aggregate data dealing with referenda support and median level of education, using, for example, the county as the unit of analysis.

Guard against drawing conclusions about one level of data using data relating to another. This misstep is called the **ecological fallacy**. In other words, based on county level data showing that counties with the most college graduates had the highest level of support for a tax-cutting referendum, it is invalid to conclude that among individuals, education is positively related to support for this referendum. It may be that within many counties, the greatest support comes from the less educated. There are techniques for drawing inferences across levels, but they need not concern us here. For the beginning student, our recommendation is to determine the most appropriate and feasible unit, or level, of analysis before beginning your research.

EXERCISE

2-4 Specify the unit, or level, of analysis for each of the problems in Exercises 2-1, 2-2, and 2-3.

CONTROL VARIABLES

Hypothesis testing is simply determining whether data you have collected supports your hypothesis. Many times, however, the hypothesis you are testing may appear to be valid only because of the effects of other variables. For example, assume you were testing the hypothesis that African Americans are more likely to be elected to city councils in cities with district rather than at-large elections. Your data then showed this to be true. But, before accepting the hypothesis, you would need to look further to affirm that it was really the impact of district elections causing the increase in African American representation. Perhaps cities with high percentages of African Americans in the population were more likely to adopt district election plans. One would naturally expect more African American representation when there are more black people in the city's population. Thus it is possible that the large number of African Americans in the population rather than district elections themselves are producing increased representation. So the relationship in Figure 2-1B might be a more accurate portrayal than that in Figure 2-1A.

The relationship between district elections and African American representation might then be considered a **spurious relationship.** The proportion of African Americans in the population must be considered in testing the original hypothesis; it is an obvious alternate cause of increased black representation.

In the analysis, the proportion of African Americans in the population is called a **control variable,** a factor that must be accounted for in testing for the strength of the hypothesized relationship. You can incorporate the impact of African American population into the original hypothesis, as in H1 or H2, to make it clear that you are taking this obvious fact into account.

H1: For cities with approximately the same percentage of African American population, there will be greater black city council representation in those cities with district elections than in those with at-large elections.

H2: Alternatively, controlling for the percentage of black population, there will be more African American city council representation in those cities with district elections than in those with at-large elections.

In Chapters 6 through 9 we will discuss several ways of "controlling" for factors that may affect the relationship between independent and dependent variables. Sometimes this can be done in your research design; at other times statistical manipulations must be used.

For any hypothesis there are potentially hundreds of controls. How do you decide which to use? In making the choice, ask what factors are most likely to be related to both the independent variable and the dependent variable. Your knowledge of the subject will suggest factors to be controlled. The following are some to consider.

FIGURE 2-1   Causal Relations

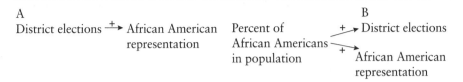

1. Demographic Characteristics of the Individual, State, or Locality

Differences in educational level, urbanization, social class, ethnicity, age, sex, and so on are often related to differences in the kind of outcomes you are exploring (i.e., crime rates or reading levels or use of public services). Thus you must ask yourself which, if any, demographic characteristics are plausibly related to changes in your independent and dependent variables. For example, in testing the hypothesis that gun regulation laws reduce homicide rates, you would want to consider other factors that are related to homicide rates and might also be related to the adoption of gun regulation laws: urbanization, the age distribution of the population, and the poverty rate, for example. Each of these factors independently affects homicide rates and might also be related to the adoption of gun regulation laws; thus their impact must be controlled for in making an assessment of gun control laws.

2. Historical Trends

If you compare states with gun registration laws to those without, you might find that those without have lower homicide rates. You would then want to find out whether this has been true over a long period of time, perhaps even before the adoption of the gun control laws, or whether relative rates of homicide changed coincident with adoption of the new laws. If possible, before concluding that a policy had an impact, always look at the historical patterns, the rate of activity before the policy change, as a control variable.

3. Political and Economic Factors

Are there policies or political and economic circumstances beyond the policy you are examining that might affect the dependent variable and also be related to the policy? For example, again using the gun control case, perhaps other crucial economic or political factors affect homicide and differentiate the states which have or do not have gun control legislation. Perhaps one group of states has higher unemployment than the other group. Since unemployment is related to crime, this could distort the relationship being examined. Or perhaps one group of states has more strict sentencing or a different kind of legal system than the other group. Or a change in police administration or a turnover in the mayor's or governor's office could result in changes in policy, administration, enforcement, expenditures, and other factors potentially influencing the relationship. These kinds of factors must be considered when planning your research, even though you might eventually decide that they are not important enough to be incorporated into the analysis.

4. *Other Factors*

Consider whether there are other factors potentially related to the independent variable that might influence the dependent variable. Many kinds of behavior are influenced by such simple and seemingly random things as weather or changes in seasons. So you would not want to compare traffic accidents or crime rates in December of one year with July of the next in assessing the impact of some policy. Changes in technologies or lifestyles might be other factors to consider in accounting for changes in the dependent variable.

seasonality and technological changes

EXERCISE

2-5 List three possible control variables necessary to test each of the hypotheses you stated in Exercises 2-1, 2-2, and 2-3. Justify why each variable should be controlled.

OPERATIONALIZING THE HYPOTHESES

In order to test a hypothesis, we must know precisely what is being stated. Let's look at one of our examples: Do gun control laws reduce crime? Or stated as a hypothesis: "The presence of gun control laws will result in lower crime rates." On the surface this looks straightforward. However, closer inspection will reveal that the hypothesis has not been defined in **operational terms, that is, in terms that make it clear what is being tested**. First, what does the term "gun control law" mean? In order to test the hypothesis, you must specify more carefully what kind of law is being considered. You could mean laws outlawing handguns; you could mean laws requiring owners of guns to register; or you could mean laws requiring gun owners to pass tests concerning firearms safety and use. Let's assume that what you would like to test is whether laws requiring registration of guns have an impact on crime rates. So a restatement of your hypothesis might be:

> Laws requiring registration of guns result in lower crime rates.

Examine this hypothesis more closely. We see yet another term that is ill-defined: crime. What is meant specifically by "lower crime rates"? Probably you do not believe that gun registration laws reduce auto theft, violations of drug laws, or shoplifting. Rather, you probably think that gun registration laws reduce the incidence of homicide, armed robbery, assault with a deadly weapon, and other crimes of violence. Therefore you must further specify the hypothesis to be tested. For example:

H1: Laws requiring registration of guns will result in a reduced homicide rate.

H1A: Laws requiring registration of guns will result in a reduced rate of armed robbery.

and so forth.

Thus, operationalizing the variables in a hypothesis is putting them into such a form that another person reading the hypothesis would know immediately what is being hypothesized. Operationalizing your variables is useful because it forces you to carefully think through exactly what it is you are trying to measure. An operationalized hypothesis cannot have unclear terms in it. Examples of hypotheses that are not in operational form include:

H1: Training in group dynamics will increase employee cooperation in the State Department of Community Affairs.

H2: The introduction of zero-based budgeting will make the budget process more efficient.

H3: Staggered work hours for employees will improve employee morale and efficiency.

What is wrong with these hypotheses? Each contains terms that are so vague they are subject to a wide variety of interpretations. Each hypothesis has the potential for being made operational, but as is, none is operational. For example, what does it mean to increase employee cooperation? Before such a hypothesis could be tested, you would have to be much more specific about what is being measured. It could be anything from management-employee relations or fights on the premises to increased productivity by work groups. Likewise "efficient" is a word that is practically meaningless until further defined. What does "A more efficient budget process" mean? That budget increments from year to year will increase more slowly? Or decrease? Or that the budget will take less staff time to put together? These three hypotheses also offer examples of other nonoperational terms that you should be able to spot.

In other words, propositions such as these are a result of unclear thinking. They are unmeasurable and could not be tested in their present form. They must be defined so that they could be tested in a meaningful way. If the relationship is not stated in such a way that another policy researcher could read the hypothesis and know what it is you are examining, then the statement is not fully operational.

EXERCISES

2-6 Look again at your hypotheses in Exercises 2-1, 2-2, and 2-3. Are they operational? If not, put them in operational terms.

2-7 Operationalize the following hypothesis in two different ways: As compared with prison terms, supervised probation for young offenders is more efficient and does not increase criminal tendencies.

2-8 Operationalize the following hypothesis in two different ways: Giving tax breaks to expanding businesses will help economic development in this state.

PLANNING THE RESEARCH: RESEARCH DESIGN

A research design is a plan to allow you to test the validity of your hypotheses, taking into account the factors you believe might affect the relationship between the dependent and independent variables. A research design is simply the way that you propose to go about testing your hypothesis. There are many kinds of research designs. Most seek to approximate the "experimental" design. In this section, therefore, we will describe the experimental design, discuss why it is considered the best design, and then present some of its weaknesses insofar as it applies to policy research. We will then describe and evaluate five other designs that incorporate only part of the true experimental design. Though often policy researchers will not be able to carry out an experimental design, it is important to understand why it is the ideal, and how to compensate if you are unable to set up an experimental design.

EXPERIMENTAL DESIGNS

Experimental designs, used most often in laboratory studies of animal and human behavior, seek to control the impact of extraneous factors on the hypothesized relationship by randomization, measurement at more than one point in time, and the use of "control" groups. We can illustrate these procedures and demonstrate their usefulness by examining the following example. Suppose you want to test the following hypothesis:

> The verbal abilities of children who have completed a year of a Head Start program will be greater than those of children not participating in such a program.

Assume for the purposes of this illustration that we have adequate agreement on how one measures "verbal abilities;" assume we can use an agreed-upon standardized test. Assume further that we have some consensus on what a Head Start program is in terms of abilities stressed, techniques used, and time involved. We therefore will move to the question of how one designs a research effort to test this hypothesis. A first thought would simply be to test children before and after entering the program to measure their expected increased verbal abilities.

This simple, but unfortunately too simple, strategy means that whatever our findings are, the wastebasket is the most appropriate place to file them! This is because there are important **threats to internal validity** of our research. An internally valid experiment is one where all sources of change other than the program itself have been controlled for or taken into account. We can have little confidence in findings from studies that do not deal with threats to internal validity.

What are the threats to internal validity of an experiment that simply measured children before and after their participation in a program?

1. Maturation

The plan does not take into account any increase in verbal abilities due to normal maturation. Normal children increase their verbal abilities as they age. Thus, any group of young children might improve their verbal abilities over several months, even in the absence of any program.

2. Selection

Even if you took into account maturation by comparing children in the program with other children of the same age, your plan does not take into account any self-selection of the children into the program. Perhaps children who are enrolled in the program have parents who are more concerned about their children's education than are other parents. Or perhaps the parents themselves have greater verbal abilities which they pass along to their children. Thus, the increase in the children's scores may have little to do with the Head Start program at all.

3. Sample Mortality

By sample mortality, we mean that some people drop out of experiments before they are complete. This may bias the results. Over the course of a year's Head Start program, for example, some children will have moved to another city, others will have lost interest, still others may find the program not to their liking, and some may have dropped out due to illness or family problems. You cannot assume that the verbal abilities of those who dropped out are like those who did not. It is very plausible that most of those who dropped out are lower in verbal abilities than those who stayed in. If this is so, a posttest on the remaining participants would yield a higher mean score than the pretest on all the participants, even if the children who remained in the program did not increase their scores at all! Thus, one must take steps to understand and try to correct the effects of sample mortality on the experiment.

4. Testing

Perhaps the children "learned" how to take the posttest simply by taking the pretest and thus were more familiar with the format of the test and possibly even some of the test items. This would, of course, raise the posttest scores.

5. *Instrumentation*

It could be that the scores rose because the test changed in some subtle way. Perhaps the test giver read the directions more slowly, provided extra time, gave special encouragement, or even provided clues to the answers. Perhaps the test items were easier. These kinds of changes are changes in instrumentation, the nature of the test and test-taking experience.

6. *History*

Maybe, during the time of your study, external conditions changed in some way affecting the children. For example, maybe there was a national campaign to combat illiteracy and encourage reading, with special daily television programs designed to help children acquire verbal skills. Perhaps there was a special program instituted in your community to reach teenage mothers and provide them with extra resources to help in child raising. These kinds of external influences could affect your results.

7. *Regression*

If the original scores were low, a normal process called regression toward the mean (or Galtonian regression, to distinguish it from the statistical procedure we will examine in Chapters 8 and 9) leads to a high probability that the scores would increase. If scores are high, the same process leads to the probability of decreasing scores. This may be a harder concept to grasp than the first six, but a simple illustration will help. If Johnny got a 0 on the first test, chances are, even if he learned nothing in the course, he will get higher than a 0 the second time. Simple probabilities of randomly guessing one or two right would lead to a higher score. And, there is no way he could get a lower score. There is nowhere to go but up for Johnny. Jenny, on the other hand, got a 100 on the first test. She is likely to get a lower score the second time. For her, there is a zero probability she will do better, since she received the highest score possible. There is some probability that she will miss an item, perhaps misreading it or simply not knowing one particular answer. For her, there is no way to go but down.

To overcome these threats to internal validity, you will want to create an experimental design by taking the following measures. Before the program starts for a given year, compile a list of all children eligible for this program. These would obviously be based on criteria such as age, parents' income, and perhaps other characteristics of the children or their household. From that list, *randomly* assign (by drawing lots or other sampling techniques discussed later) half the children to be enrolled in the program (called the **treatment**, or **experimental, group**), and half to serve as a **control group** (a group that will not get the program).

TABLE 2-1   **Experimental Design**

	RANDOMLY CHOSEN EXPERIMENTAL GROUP	RANDOMLY CHOSEN CONTROL GROUP
Pretest (time 1)	0_1	0_1
Treatment (the program)	x	
Posttest (time 2)	0_2	0_2
Researcher compares	Posttest score minus pretest score	Posttest score minus pretest score

Following the assignment of each child, give a **pretest** of verbal abilities to both groups. Assuming a random selection of children, the pretest scores of the groups should be approximately equal. Now the treatment group will participate in the program, the control group will get no program. At the end of one year of the program (or whenever appropriate), a **posttest** will be given to both groups. Because the two groups have similar scores at the pretest (time 1), differences in scores at time 2, the posttest, can be attributed to the effects of the program. Simply subtract the mean pretest score of each group from the mean posttest score of each group, and use a simple test (see Chapter 7) to see if any differences between the two groups are statistically significant. Table 2-1 illustrates this process.

Let's assume that the control group averaged 65 on a pretest, the experimental group averaged 70. After a year the control group averaged 82, the treatment group 90. The gain for the control group was 17 (82-65), the gain for the treatment group 20 (90-70). Intuitively the difference between 17 and 20 does not seem very large; statistical tests would probably show it not to be significant (see Chapter 7), so you might conclude that the program had little effect. Note that if you simply looked at the before and after scores of the treatment group, you would see a gain of 20 and perhaps be impressed. But the control group gives you a baseline against which to compare changes in your experimental group. Note, too, that if you are interested in more significant long-term gains, you could test each group at some point following time two in order to see if the children retained what they learned during the year.

The experimental design we have outlined is widely used in medical experiments (such as when testing new drugs), animal experiments, and psychological experiments. It controls for the various threats outlined above by random selection, a control group, and a pre- and posttest. Random selection ensures that both the experimental and the control group are equivalent to begin with, which eliminates selection bias. Randomization also checks regression effects. History, maturation, and instrumentation are checked by the existence of a control group. For example, both the experimental and the control group will be exposed to the same history (outside influences that might produce a change from pre-to posttest).

The experimental design does not control for the effect of testing itself. It is possible, for example, that both groups will increase their verbal scores by the second testing date simply because they have learned to take the test. A further refinement of the experimental design, therefore, is to assign the children randomly to four rather than two groups. Two groups will be treatment groups, but only one will receive a pretest; the other will receive only a posttest. Similarly, in the two control groups only one will receive both a pretest and posttest, the other a posttest only. This form of experimental design is called a **Solomon four-group design** and is illustrated in Table 2-2.

With this four-group design, you can compare the gains made by groups one and three, but you can also compare the posttest scores of groups one and three with those of groups two and four to see how much of the gain was due to testing itself. If the posttest score of group one was 82 and group three was 90, but groups two and four were only 75 and 72, respectively, we might conclude that part of the gain of the first two groups was simply a learning process from the testing itself. This would increase our awareness of the potential of the program in increasing students' verbal abilities.

Further complexities can also be introduced into the design. For example, researchers have often found that just the fact that a treatment is being applied to a group in a social setting will bring about short-term changes no matter whether the treatment is really effective or not. This is called the **Hawthorne effect**. An analogy in medical research is the phenomenon of patients feeling better after taking medicine even though, unknown to them, the medicine is a sugar pill, a placebo. In social research just the fact that a group thinks a public agency is paying attention to them may change their behavior.

Thus, when experimenting on the effectiveness of new drugs, researchers give all subjects something, whether or not they are in the experimental group. It might be the drug being tested or simply a placebo, a sugar pill. The improvement rate of patients on placebos can be compared with that of patients taking the drug being tested. In social research you could give control groups a "program" unrelated to the real program. For example, in the Head Start experimental design, you might want to have a control group of children engage in some sort of group recreational activity unrelated to verbal learning. In that way you could control for the effects of group interaction itself in improving verbal ability.

The experimental design does not take into account sample attrition. In our example, children who are initially a part of either the control or the experimental group will leave town, lose interest, be ill, or dropout of the study for some other reason. How do you deal with that problem? You must keep a careful record of the dropouts. Who were they? What groups did they come from? What were their pretest scores? If equal numbers drop from the control and the experimental groups and their scores were similar, then probably not much distortion has occurred. But if the dropouts from one group are primarily high-scorers and dropouts from another group are low-scorers, posttest results will be biased. You must either remove their scores from the pretest or in

TABLE 2-2   Solomon Four-group Experimental Design

	RANDOMLY CHOSEN CONTROL GROUP 1	RANDOMLY CHOSEN CONTROL GROUP 2	RANDOMLY CHOSEN EXPERIMENTAL GROUP 3	RANDOMLY CHOSEN EXPERIMENTAL GROUP 4
Pretest (time 1)	0_1		0_1	
Treatment (the program)			X	X
Posttest (time 2)	0_2	0_2	0_2	0_2

some way approximate their predicted results on the posttest; for example, you could give each the average score of other children with the same score on the pretest. At any rate you should not simply leave their scores in the pretest group and compute the changed scores on that base.

The experimental design is a flexible tool for evaluating the effects of a given policy or program and comparing it to other programs while accounting for the effects of various threats to validity. The randomization process and the before-after measures provide a control for the possible relationship of social and other characteristics to the dependent variable. However, our example should also illustrate some of the real difficulties with the experimental design in policy research. These drawbacks are considerable and have greatly diminished the use of this design in the policy field. Some of the problems occur because of randomization. It is difficult, and sometimes impossible, for a public servant or agency to deny a service to a person who is legally entitled to it even though that service may or may not have any positive value. It is both a legal and ethical problem to tell parents that their children are not going to receive a program because they are going to be put into a control group. Parents will ask why their neighbor's children can get into a program while theirs cannot. The agency opens itself up to public criticism and lawsuits. Thus in many cases randomization will not be possible because of these concerns.

Another problem is that some people will not want to participate in a program (or would not want their children to). A government or private agency cannot force people to participate in a voluntary program. It can provide incentives for participation, but that could lead to selection bias. Reluctance to participate would not be a problem if the nonparticipants were identical to the participants. However, to continue with our example, it is probably true that parents who want their children to participate in Head Start are different in some respects from those who do not want their children to participate or who do not care. There may be differences of education, background, income, race, motivation to learn, and so forth. If children who enroll come from different kinds of homes than children who do not enroll, then it is difficult to attribute differences in their learning to the program rather than to their social background. So with many public programs, you cannot use an experimental design because of the problem of exclusion of some who would like to be in the program coupled with the unwillingness to participate on the part of other eligible people.

Another problem with the experimental design is that it assumes that a program has a finite beginning and end and that the program is relatively constant. Yet most programs are ongoing; relatively infrequently will you have the opportunity to set up an experimental program. And programs are normally modified continuously. If administrators identify aspects of a program that are not working, they will change them if possible. Good results obtained from one technique of teaching verbal skills may diffuse to other programs before the end of the formal experiment. This is rational behavior from the point of view of agency administrators, but it makes it difficult to determine the impact of a program, since the "program" may be three or four different programs over the space of a few months or a year. These problems limit the utility of an experimental design, which assumes a certain constancy.

Finally, generalizability might be a problem. While design weaknesses that limit your ability to establish a causal connection between an independent and a dependent variable pose threats to internal validity, problems that limit your ability to generalize across categories or classes of individuals and across settings pose threats to **external validity**. Experimental designs particularly can pose problems of external validity. Experiments done on college students, for example, may not be valid or apply to older adults. Similarly, findings about the virtues of Head Start in Urbana, Illinois, might not apply to Chicago. The extent to which findings from an experiment (or any research, for that matter) are generalizable to other people or settings depends on the population from which the sample is drawn. While generalizability may not be a concern in some very applied research, policy researchers should be aware and sensitive to it.

However, do not automatically exclude the possibility of using an experimental design in doing policy research. An enterprising evaluation researcher may be able to design a policy experiment without coercion, exclusion, or ignoring the realities of ongoing agency programs. We will report three such examples from an excellent article by R. Conner.[1] A fourth example is highlighted in Research in Practice 2A.

In one example, the researcher tested whether, in the case of moving traffic violations, giving tickets payable by mail, tickets requiring court appearances, or tickets only warning the driver would be equally or more effective than the standard ticket requiring the driver to go to the city clerk's office and pay a fine. The problem was to randomly assign arrested drivers to these four categories. The researchers were able to avoid a bias against certain drivers and assure randomness by giving each patrol officer a book containing only one type of ticket. These rotated each day. Thus Officer A received on Monday

---

[1] R. Conner. "Selecting a Control Group," *Evaluation Quarterly*, March 1977, pp. 195–244.

Research in Practice 2A

AN EXPERIMENTAL DESIGN

Almost all states authorize the use of work release programs for prisoners. This type of program allows a prisoner to leave prison for all or part of the day in order to hold a job. How effective are such programs in reducing recidivism? One investigation used an experimental design to try to answer that question.

The Florida Division of Corrections permitted a random assignment of inmates to a work release group and a non-work release group. Two-thirds were given work release; one-third were placed in the control group. Those in the control group continued their normal activities within the prison. The random procedure yielded two groups that were in fact similar on all characteristics thought important (demographic characteristics, prior record, and so forth). The work release group worked for six to twenty-four months, as their sentences allowed.

The researchers used eighteen different measures of recidivism in order to test for the effects of the program, including measures of further arrests, bookings, convictions, incarcerations, and crime severity. No difference occurred between those on work release and the control groups in the probability of being arrested, convicted, or incarcerated, or in the seriousness of the crime.

The researchers concluded that the program itself appeared to have neither a negative nor positive effect on recidivism. They then examined whether the length of time in the program made any difference, speculating that perhaps those involved in work release the longest might be less likely to re-enter a life of crime. But after dividing the work release group into those who participated less than eighty-two days and those who participated more than eighty-two days, the researchers found no differences in the two groups. Nor did they find that work release made a greater difference for African Americans than for whites, those highly educated than for those less educated, or for any other group of prisoners.

The researchers concluded that if their research is indicative, the program of work release must be justified on economic or humanitarian grounds rather than on its greater efficiency in rehabilitating convicted felons.

SOURCE: Gordon P. Waldo and Theodore G. Chiricos, "Work Release and Recidivism," *Evaluation Quarterly*, February 1977, pp. 87–107.

a book with only warning tickets; on Tuesday, a book with only $20-fine tickets. Officer B received on Monday a book with tickets requiring court appearances; on Tuesday, a book with warning tickets; and so on. In that way the officers had no discretion (assuming the violation fell within the defined class of violations appropriate to the experiment), nor was there discrimination against drivers in one part of town versus another.

Another researcher used a similar system in assessing the effectiveness of fines, probation, or education programs in reducing the number of DWI (driving while intoxicated) offenses. In that project the researcher gained the cooperation of the chief judge in the city. A fixed schedule was set so that on certain days of the month, DWI offenders were given one kind of punishment, on other days, a second kind of punishment. Unfortunately for the success of the experiment, judges were allowed to deviate in exceptional cases. And it turned out that there were many exceptional cases, occurring disproportionately among those who had lawyers to defend them and who would have received the educational program sentence. Thus the design was severely violated, probably contaminating the results.

The American Heart Association's Nutrition Education Project in Chicago is a third example. Here the researcher solicited volunteers who were randomly assigned to one of five groups: a control group or one of four education groups where the individual was taught about nutrition in different ways. Researchers told members of the control group that they would receive the actual program at the end of the experimental period, but meanwhile they would receive no program. In this way most stayed with the project and then later received the benefits of the program.

These three examples provide some useful, practical examples of ways experimental designs can be used in real settings. In some cases treatment of a subject can be delayed while he or she serves in a control group. This would seem perfectly proper in cases where the capacity of the facilities is not great enough to handle at one time all who want a program. In the Head Start example, it might be that some children could be enrolled in the program in January; others who had volunteered might be delayed until a later time. Obviously this kind of decision must depend on the availability of the resources of the program, the necessity for the group to have the program without delay, and other needs of the target groups.

Sometimes a random design can be achieved because the "clients" have no discretion, as in the DWI and moving-violations examples discussed. The keys to the success of these projects were to win the cooperation of those officials administering the program and to allow them little discretion in the random assignment. Discretion leads to bias even though it is not necessarily conscious bias.

Suppose, however, that you cannot use an experimental design to test program effects. What are the alternatives? Remember what a design must accomplish: it must allow you to isolate, as best you can, the effects of the independent variable on the dependent variable from the possible effects of other factors, including various threats to internal and external validity. The experimental design does this by random selection of experimental and control groups and by pre- and post-measures of the dependent variable. Alternative designs provide other ways to control for these extraneous factors, but are not as thorough in protecting from threats to internal validity.

Some of the alternative designs have been called "**quasi-experimental**." We will look at two quasi-experimental designs: time series and before and after with controls. Then we will discuss three other designs that are less satisfactory but may be adequate when used with care and insight.

Quasi-experimental Designs

The **time series design.** In using a time series (longitudinal) design, you attempt to isolate the effect of the program from the other extraneous factors (the control variables) by taking numerous measures of the dependent variable over a long period of time before and after the program is implemented. Campbell has labeled these "reforms as experiments." A change in a policy allows you to see if your dependent variable also changes. Suppose, for example, you were trying to test the effect on traffic fatalities of a state's raising its speed limit from 55 to 65. Many states made this change after 1987 federal legislation allowing states to raise the speed on rural interstates to 65 miles an hour. If you used a longitudinal design, you would record traffic fatalities over several years before and after the speed limit was changed. Perhaps you would start with fatalities in 1980 and record them annually until 2002. The point of recording fatalities before the changed speed limits is to establish a trend line in order to see if the passage of the law affected preexisting rates of fatalities. The fatality rate before the change of the speed limit is a sort of control in looking at fatalities after the change.

Figure 2-2 illustrates what a trend line might look like for this example. The figure shows an increase in accidents after 1987. However, we do not know if this is meaningful until we see what the trend was before 1987. In our hypothetical example, we see that the fatalities had been going down before 1987, indicating that the increase in the speed limit likely had an effect.

However, had the pre-1987 line looked anything like any of the three patterns in Figure 2-3, our conclusion would have been different. Path A shows that traffic fatalities had been increasing since 1980; the post-speed-law trend only continued the pre-speed-law trend. Thus, if path A were the true trend line, we would have to say the law had no effect. Path B indicates that speed laws were in fact increasing before 1987 but that this increase accelerated after the passage of the speed law. The law had an effect although not as dramatic as in Figure 2-2. Path C shows that fatalities had been subject to regular ups and downs before 1987 and that the post-1987 pattern could just be part of the regular cyclical trend of traffic fatalities. The pattern evidenced in C is a good example of why as many years (or other time points) as possible should be traced in a longitudinal study; what looks like a dramatic effect might only be part of an ongoing regular cyclical pattern. A longer time series, then, protects against regression effects.

FIGURE 2-2   **Hypothetical Effect of Time on Fatalities**

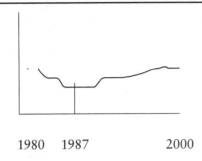

1980   1987   2000

FIGURE 2-3   **Alternative Pre-1975 Trends**

Traffic fatalities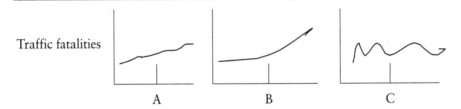

A   B   C

Suppose, however, that the pattern illustrated in Figure 2-2 was the one you found in your analysis. How would you know if the traffic fatalities were really affected by the speed law? One threat to the validity of your conclusions is history. Maybe other things happened around 1987 that could affect traffic fatalities. Perhaps the miles driven increased, which would cause increased fatalities. Suppose you discover that miles driven did increase, but that the fatality rate per mile also increased. This gives you more confidence in your original conclusions.

Another common threat to validity of time series designs is instrumentation. Perhaps the State Patrol changed the definition of traffic fatalities to include deaths resulting from traffic accidents but occurring within a year rather than immediately. This would affect the measurement of your dependent variable in potentially serious ways. You would have to try to obtain the raw data that would allow you to sort out traffic deaths by using the same criteria over time.

Another way to control for threats to internal validity in time series designs is to find a control group as we did in the experimental design. Perhaps the state you were analyzing also adopted more stringent seat belt laws at the same time it raised the speed limit. The effect of the changed speed limit would be complicated by this other policy change. One way to sort out the effects of the changed speed limits and the seat belt law is to find one or more neighboring states to serve as a control. A state that changed its speed limit but not its seat belt laws would be a good control. You then plot its fatality rates for the same years. What you would be most interested in is not its absolute rate but rather how it compares with your experimental state.

The latter design is called a longitudinal design with a control or **multiple time series.** Notice that you have not randomly divided your "subjects," in this case states. In seeking controls, try to find cases that match your "experimental" case as closely as possible on the relevant variables. For example, if your "experimental" state were Alabama, you might select Mississippi as a control. You probably would not select California. Differences in political culture, in income level, urbanization, population density, educational levels, weather (relevant to traffic fatalities) and so forth are all important to consider in choosing a control for a longitudinal study.

In choosing controls for studies of cities, the same kinds of factors should be considered. An example of the use of control groups in time series analysis is discussed in Research in Practice 2B.

You will learn more about time series analysis in Chapter 10.

The Before-and-after-with-control-group Design

Perhaps you are doing policy research where time series data are not available. Longitudinal data are, of course, most readily obtainable when you are working with governmental units rather than with individuals. What are your design alternatives then? Recall the Head Start example. By using another quasi-experimental design, we can come close to what we had attempted to do with our original experimental design, yet avoid some of the problems (though we do create new problems). This design is called the **before-and-after-with-control group.**

To carry out the design, we do not assume that we can divide children randomly into experimental and control groups (or four such groups). For example, if 100 children have enrolled in the program, we then try to find 100 children similar to those children who have not enrolled in the program. Since we know that children of different ages and sex have different rates of increasing their verbal ability, we would want to find a group of children with the same age and sex mix as our experimental 100 children. We also would probably want to match the children on socioeconomic variables, indirectly trying to control for parental interest in education and the child's verbal environment at home. There may be other factors to take into consideration too, such as ethnic background, place of residence, and so forth. Thus instead of random selection, in this design we must deliberately try to obtain a control group that matches as closely as possible those children in the program. In that way we can control reasonably well for many of the extraneous influences on verbal ability, social background, and maturation effects particularly.

After we obtain the control group, we carry out the testing just as we did in the experimental design. What has been gained and lost in contrasting this quasi-experiment with a true experimental design? What we have lost is the

Research in Practice 2B

A Time Series Design

One of the classic uses of the time series design was to measure the impact of a crackdown on speeders in Connecticut. After a very high Connecticut traffic death toll in 1955, attributed by some to excessive highway speed, the governor implemented a policy whereby all persons convicted of speeding would have their drivers' licenses suspended for thirty days for the first speeding violation, sixty days for the second, and indefinitely for the third. After six months of this program, traffic fatalities had been cut by 15 percent compared to the previous year, and suspensions for speeding had increased over twenty-fold. However, as the traffic fatalities rose over the next six months, questions were raised as to the effectiveness of the program.

Although the 1956 total was less than that of 1955, there were too many threats to the validity of the conclusions if these simple before-and-after measures were used. Perhaps 1956 had unusually good weather, or car models introduced that year were safer (effects of history). Perhaps the reduction in 1956 was part of a long-term trend toward reduction in traffic deaths due to better roads, better drivers' education, or some other cause unrelated to the crackdown (maturation). Perhaps the publicity surrounding the high rate of deaths in 1955 promoted driver safety by itself (testing). Perhaps 1955 had an all-time high death rate, and rates would be expected to return to normal levels without a program (regression effect). Or perhaps the reported drop in

assurance that because of random selection, the control group is identical in characteristics to the experimental group. It is always possible, when trying to match a control group to an experimental group as we must do in this quasi-experiment, that we have missed some important characteristics. There may be some element affecting the dependent variable, verbal ability, that we miss when we control only for a variety of socioeconomic variables. In other words, the very criteria that prompted some parents to enroll their children in the program and other parents not to enroll their children might be the crucial variable, and we have not controlled for that. In terms of threats to validity, we have probably done a pretty good job controlling for maturation, but perhaps we have not controlled adequately for self-selection and its relationship to other potential threats. What we gain in using the quasi-experimental design, however, is the ability to carry out a reasonably good design without depriving some children and their parents of a program they want. Further, in this instance we operate realistically on the assumption that some parents will not the death rate is a simple reflection of instability in the statistics. So a number of plausible hypotheses existed as to why the rate may have decreased.

To explore the validity of these alternative explanations, a time series design was used. Traffic fatalities in Connecticut were plotted for five years before and five years after the crackdown. Given that time series data, it could be seen that indeed there was a good deal of instability in Connecticut's traffic death rate, and in fact 1955 had been the highest on record. The drop between 1955 and 1956 did not appear to be unusual in light of the ten-year history of fluctuation in the rates.

To check further on the effect of the crackdown, time series data were also gathered from four neighboring states so that Connecticut's pattern could be compared with a control group. Here the differences showed that the crackdown did make a difference in Connecticut's death rate compared to the others, since Connecticut had the sharpest and most prolonged drop in the death rate even though the rates in all states showed fluctuations.

Other elements of the time series research design allowed the researchers to show that while speeding violations did decrease after the crackdown, driving with suspended licenses increased (as one would suspect), and interestingly the proportion of speeders found not guilty by the courts increased dramatically.

SOURCE: Donald T. Campbell and H. Laurence Ross, The Connecticut Crackdown on Speeding: Time Series Data in Quasi-Experimental Analysis," *Law and Society Review*, August 1968, pp. 33–53.

want to participate in this type of program and cannot and should not be forced to do so. We trade off "purity" for practicality, but the design is rigorous enough to give a good chance of accounting for extraneous factors that might lead to a wrong interpretation of the effects of the program. Except for selection bias, the design approximates the true experimental design in taking into account threats to internal validity.

The key to the success of this design is the choice of a control group. You would not try to match the controls to the treatment group on a one-to-one basis; rather you would try to obtain groups that in the aggregate matched on key variables (i.e., in our example, percent male, percent Anglo, percent with family incomes less than $10,000, and so forth). One possibility for obtaining a control group as much as possible like the treatment group if the program has an excess demand would be to use those who applied for the program and were rejected, assuming they met the criteria for eligibility. Of course if the program accepts all those who are eligible, then using the program rejects would be inappropriate because they would be different in some key respects from the participants. Sometimes you might use as a control group those in a program designed to accomplish the same ends as the program you are studying but one that uses different treatments. That is, in finding a control group for a new alcoholism treatment program, you might try to obtain controls from ongoing programs, such as Alcoholics Anonymous.

EXERCISE

2-9 Discuss how the time series designs and the before-and-after with-control-group designs compare to the experimental design in handling threats to internal and external validity.

Other Designs

None of the remaining three designs we will discuss provides the assurance that threats to internal validity are controlled. One is simply a **before-and-after-design**. Participants in the program are measured before and after their participation. We have already outlined all the threats to validity of this design. Would the participants have been equally well off (or worse off) if they had not participated? There is no way to know. If you choose to use this design, try to find people of similar characteristics against which to compare your subjects after they have participated. For example, if you used this design to study the Head Start students, try to compare them with other children of the same age. Perhaps you could compare their records in the first grade. Obviously there are even more problems than in the previous design in obtaining a comparable reference group. Nevertheless it is imperative to try, or else you will be interpreting in a vacuum the changes in your experimental group.

In this design you will have to use your creativity to try to define as many plausible alternative explanations as possible for the changes you have found (if any) in your treatment group. If you can find ways of disproving these explanations, then your hypothesis that the program had an effect will appear more valid. Whether or not you can disprove or cast doubt on the alternative explanations, at least consider and discuss them so that readers of the report are aware of them. So, for example, you would discuss in your report the likelihood that children of the same age group as your Head Start group would have made the gains they did in the absence of a program. Research in Practice 2-C illustrates this design.

Another very commonly used design is the **after-only-with-comparison**. In this design no pretest is given. Instead, participants are compared with a control group only after their participation in the program. Suppose you used this design with the Head Start program. You found that following the program, the children in the experimental group had verbal scores of 75 and in the control group, scores of 82. Does this mean the program had an impact?

Research in Practice 2C

BEFORE AND AFTER DESIGN

In recent years, both the courts and state legislatures have been concerned with equity in school financing, that is, how equal are individual school districts in the amounts they spend per pupil. The federal courts have indicated that educational quality should not be a function of the wealth of the school districts, and in many states, taxpayers and parents have challenged existing funding systems.

In most states, much of the financing for the public schools is provided by local governments. Naturally, there are large discrepancies from district to district influenced by the affluence of the district, the size of the tax base (created by the presence of business and industry as well as affluence), and the willingness of local citizens to tax themselves to support their schools. In most states, the state government also contributes to the support of local schools. States can provide equal support for every child, or they can give special help to the poorest districts.

In 1992, after state court action, Kansas changed its school tax and funding system in order to provide greater per pupil equity across the state and to give special help to the smallest districts. As in many states, the per pupil spending in Kansas had varied wildly, from a minimum of less than $3200 in some districts to more than $12,000 in others. This reflected both significant differences in property values and other wealth in the districts and the tax rate that localities imposed. The districts with the fewest pupils had the greatest variations.

One evaluator set out to see if the new school finance system made a difference in school spending in Kansas. There was no opportunity to use experimental techniques so she used a basic before and after design. She collected data on each school district in the state, including information on spending, property values, and school enrollment. She then compared a variety of measures of spending in 1991, before the changes were adopted, and in 1993, after the changes were adopted. She found that the amount of variation among districts did decrease after the new system was adopted. Moreover, smaller districts benefited the most from the change, as planned. Thus, even though there remained significant differences among districts, the objectives of the new policy were at least partially achieved.

After more time passes, future researchers might examine these data with a time series design to make sure that the before and after differences found here were not just one time, idiosyncratic changes.

SOURCE: Jocelyn M. Johnston, "Changing State-Local Fiscal Relations and School Finance in Kansas: Pursuing 'Equity,'" *State and Local Government Review* 30 (Winter, 1998): 26–41.

It is difficult to say. Perhaps students in the program were better to begin with than those not enrolling in the program. In that case the program had no positive impact at all. On the other hand, perhaps the children in the program really lagged behind their peers before they entered the program. If that were the case, the program might be seen as very successful.

Choosing between these alternative interpretations is difficult without a pretest to guide you. There are steps you can take in your interpretation, however. You can compare the two groups on other characteristics. If the two groups are similar in socioeconomic, age, and other characteristics, you can be more confident in the differences in test scores you find (though you cannot be too confident). You might also be able to compare your posttest scores of the children who have already gone through the program with the scores of other children about to enter the program. In other words, you have a pseudo pretest. You will have to be sure, however, that the children on whom you take a pretest are similar to those in your original group.

There are statistical techniques that are crucial when you have an after-only-with-comparison design (see Chapter 9). Sometimes you cannot avoid having to do an after-only-with-comparison study, particularly if you are called in to do an evaluation after the program is already started. In fact this design is probably the one most commonly used by political scientists and sociologists in their research. Controls for extraneous influences are introduced not in the design itself, but later by statistical manipulation.

Many types of survey research are examples of an after-only-with comparison design. Surveys allow comparisons among users and nonusers of public services, for example. If you were interested in the effectiveness of a neighborhood police officer-outreach program in improving citizen attitudes toward the police and awareness of police functions, a community survey would permit attitudinal and awareness comparisons between those who did and did not have contact with neighborhood police officers. You could further control for characteristics, such as age, race, and income, that may affect both attitudes and contact. Thus, with a specially chosen control group and appropriate statistical analysis, this can be a powerful design. See Research in Practice 2D for an example of an excellent after-only-with-comparison design.

The last design, the **after-only**, is in some ways the weakest we have discussed, yet it is quite common. The after-only study simply takes a measure after the treatment or program. There is no basis for comparison either with a pretest or with a control sample. Controls for factors influencing the dependent variable must be done statistically through an examination of differences within the experimental group. A common example of an after-only design is a user survey. Assume you polled users of the city parks to assess attitudes toward the city park system. This is essentially an after-only study where you ascertain which people used the park and then poll them to find out their attitudes toward it. Use of the park is the "treatment," and your survey is the posttest. You do not know if your users have more favorable attitudes than they did before, but perhaps this is not of primary interest to you. What you probably want to know is which kinds of users are more satisfied, which parks are the most and least satisfactory, and so forth. Using statistical procedures (see Chapters 6 through 9) which allow you to examine different kinds of respondents and compare them, you may be perfectly satisfied with the results of your after-only study.

But suppose you institute a change in the park system; let's say you install new playground equipment in the parks. An after-only study will not be able to tell you if the installation of the park equipment raised or lowered assessments of the parks. In order to do that, you would need before and after data.

Thus even though the after-only study is weak, for some kinds of questions it is perfectly adequate or is the best you can hope for. That is, it may be all right for policy research where you are not trying to assess changes. However, much policy research is trying to discover changes in people's attitudes and behavior. When that is your aim, try to design a study incorporating a time series or a before-and-after approach with as good a set of controls as possible.

EXERCISES

2-10 Which threats to internal validity are each of these research designs subject to: after-only, after-only-with-comparison, and before-and-after?

2-11 What is the most appropriate design to answer the following questions? What is an alternative design for each? What control variables seem more appropriate and why? How does your design take into account these necessary controls?

- a. What is the effect of district elections (as compared to at-large) on African American representation on city councils in urban communities?
- b. How successful is a particular educational program for alcohol abusers in reducing alcoholism?
- c. What impact do gun registration laws have on homicide rates?
- d. How have the payment limits for Medicare patients affected the health of senior citizens?

2-12 You are the research analyst in a countywide adult diversion program (ADP). The purpose of this program is to give first-time, nonviolent offenders an alternative to the regular criminal justice process. First-time offenders are screened by the county attorney. Those deemed suitable for the program by the nature of their offense are sent to your ADP agency. There you screen further and recommend acceptance or rejection based on the individual's attitudes and willingness to participate in the program. Once in the program, the charges against the individual are dropped, and the individual signs a contract to carry out an agreed-upon program of counseling, community service, and/or restitution. The nature of each contract varies from individual to individual.

Supporters of the program have argued that it is less expensive to treat first-time offenders in this way than in the normal process of the court system. Supporters also argue that those offenders who go through the program are less likely to commit second offenses than are other offenders. Now the program has been in operation for two years, and its budget is being scrutinized by the county board. The county board chair

Research in Practice 2D

An After-Only-With-Comparison Design

Several researchers were attempting to determine the cause of pedestrian fatalities: that is, what kinds of people tend to be victims of fatal accidents while walking. Although a profile of pedestrian fatalities could be compiled and compared with census data, the researchers felt that such a procedure would not be adequate. For example, if elderly people are more likely victims than younger ones, the researchers wanted to know if that was because elderly people walk more or because among those who walk, the elderly are disproportionately likely to be involved in fatal accidents. In order to make this determination, the researchers selected fifty of fifty-two cases of pedestrians eighteen years and older who died as a result of being hit by a motor vehicle in Manhattan over a six-month period. Information was collected on the characteristics of the victim and his or her injuries. The next problem was to find a control group of pedestrians with which to compare these victims. The researchers were ingenious in so doing. They went to each accident site on a subsequent date but always on the same day of the week and a time as close as possible to the exact time of the accident. Once there, they interviewed and obtained breath specimens (to test for alcohol) from the first four adult pedestrians of the same sex as the deceased person. This resulted in a comparison group of about 200 persons matched to the victims by accident site, time and day of accident, and sex. Almost all of the sites were visited within five weeks of the accident so as to control also for seasonal variation.

indicates that next year you will have to provide evidence that the program is working in order for it to be renewed. Your program director assigns you the task of carrying out the research to obtain and assess the relevant evidence about whether the program is in fact working.

Design a research plan to come up with the most appropriate evidence. Assume you have about six months' time to carry out the project. Make sure you are clear about the questions you are asking and the relationship of the research design to those questions. Defend your design in terms of its internal validity and practicality.

Now design a second way to produce the evidence needed.

In what ways does this second plan differ from the first? Which is more appropriate? Why?

2-13 You are a researcher in a state's department of health. One of the programs in the department is designed to improve neonatal care (care in the first few hours of a baby's life). The aims of the program are to reduce neonatal deaths. The program seeks to do this by providing expert assistance to hospitals seeking to improve their level of neonatal care and providing certification when the neonatal facilities and personnel in the

In order to obtain the "cooperation" of passing pedestrians, the aid of the police was enlisted, and a patrolman accompanying the research team asked the pedestrian to step aside and answer a few questions from the doctors. This method would be seen today as questionably ethical since respondents were not asked to give informed consent or told why they were being stopped. Only twelve did refuse, perhaps because of the presence of the patrolman. Respondents were told that their name was not to be known. The interview consisted of questions concerning residence, age, marital status, and occupation, while sex, race, appearance, sobriety and weather conditions were also noted. After finishing the interview, the subject was asked to blow into a bag for an alcohol test.

In comparing victims to the control group, the researchers found that those killed were more likely to be older (by an average of seventeen years) than the controls, more often foreign born, more often Manhattan residents, less often married, and more often of lower socioeconomic status. The victims were considerably more likely than the controls to have a high concentration of alcohol in their blood.

The procedure used in selecting this control group, then, allowed the researchers to make inferences about the difference between victims and those similarly at risk: those others who were not involved but who were pedestrians in the same place, day, and time as the victims.

SOURCE: William Haddon, Jr., Preston Valien, James R. McCarroll, and Charles J. Umberger, "A Controlled Investigation of the Characteristics of Adult Pedestrians Fatally Injured by Motor Vehicles in Manhattan," in *The Quantitative Analysis of Social Problems*, ed. Edward Tufte (Reading, Mass.: Addison-Wesley Publishing, 1970), pp. 126–52.

---

hospitals reach a prescribed adequate level. Hospitals are not required by law to be certified but receive some financial assistance when they are.

Your new health department director is looking for ways to cut the budget and inquires about the effectiveness of this particular program. You are given a month to provide an evaluation of the program's success.

Describe and discuss two alternative research designs that would allow you to evaluate the success of the program. What are the key questions you will ask, and how will your design allow you to answer these questions?

TABLE 2-3 Key Features of Research Designs

	Experimental	Time series	Before and after with controls	Before and after	After-only	After-only with controls
Random Selection of Sample(s)	Yes	No	No	No	Not usually	No
Pre- and Post-test Measurements	Yes	Repeated	Yes	Yes	No	No
Control Groups	Yes	Normally no, but could incorporate control feature	Yes	No	No	Yes
Degree of Threats to Internal Validity	Relatively low	Relatively low	Medium	Relatively high	Very high	Relatively high
Specific Threats						
Maturation	Low	Possible	Low	High	High	Possible
Selection bias	Low	High	High	High	High	High
Sample mortality	Medium	Low	Medium	High	High	High
Testing	Possible*	Depends	Low	High	Low	Low
Instrumentation	Low	High	Low	High	Possible	Low
History	Low	High unless control	Low	High	High	Low
Regression	Low	High unless controls	Low	High	Not applicable	Not applicable

*Solomon four-group design controls for this threat.

Key Terms

Independent variable
Dependent variable
Hypothesis
Null hypothesis
Unit of analysis
Level of analysis
Ecological fallacy
Spurious relationship
Control variable
Operational terms
Experimental designs
Threats to internal validity
  Maturation
  Selection
  Sample mortality
  Testing
  Instrumentation

History
Regression
Treatment, or experimental, group
Control group
Pretest
Posttest
Threats to external validity
Solomon four-group design
Hawthorne effect
External validity
Time series design
Multiple time series design
Before-and-after-with-control-group
  design
Before-and-after design
After-only-with-comparison design
After-only design

For Further Help

Babbie, Earl. *The Practice of Social Research,* 8th ed. Belmont, Calif.: Wadsworth, 1998. An excellent overview of research designs.

Campbell, Donald T., and Julian Stanley. *Experimental and Quasi Experimental Designs for Research.* Skokie, Ill.: Rand McNally, 1963. A classic, excellent brief source for help with design problems.

Cook, Thomas D., and Donald T. Campbell. *Quasi-Experimentation.* Skokie, Ill.: Rand McNally, 1979. A much more detailed examination of design and analysis problems.

Langbein, Laura I. *Discovering Whether Programs Work: A Guide to Statistical Methods for Program Evaluation.* Santa Monica, Calif.: Goodyear Publishing, 1980. Despite its title, this work largely is a guide to research designs rather than statistics, and it has good treatments on causation.

Nachmias, David, and Chava Nachmias. *Research Methods in the Social Sciences.* New York: St. Martin's Press, 1987. A somewhat more advanced discussion than the others cited.

Weiss, Carol. *Evaluation Research: Methods for Assuring Program Effectiveness.* Englewood Cliffs, N.J.: Prentice-Hall, 1972. An excellent short primer on setting up policy evaluation research.

3

MEASUREMENT AND DATA COLLECTION

Good measures can help turn abstract ideas into important, relevant findings, while poor measures render invalid seemingly meaningful findings. This chapter will provide you with an overview of some important considerations about levels of measurement and criteria for good measures. Then we will introduce some issues you will face in data collection, and methods for dealing with them. The focus of that discussion will be twofold. First, what kinds of data are appropriate to policy research? Second, how do you balance considerations about good measurement with the day-to-day needs of policy researchers who frequently need to produce data and show results quickly?

MEASUREMENT

LEVELS OF MEASUREMENT

In doing policy research, you will employ different levels of measurement. Unlike the natural sciences, where measures are often precise units such as meters, grams, or seconds, social science measurement is often imprecise, even crude. Measurement levels are called nominal, ordinal, interval and ratio. It is important to understand the differences among levels because each level requires different statistical procedures.

The **nominal level** of measurement is simply a classification. There is no sense of "order" in that level of measurement. Units (individuals, counties, states, or whatever) are simply classified into two or more categories. For example, type of household is a nominal measure. Households can be classified into a number of categories: married couples living by themselves, married couples living with dependent children, people living alone, non-relatives living together, married couples living with other relatives, and so forth. There is a classification, but there is no sense of order. If you were translating these classes into numerical values, it would not make any difference if you coded married couples living alone as 1 and individuals living alone as 2, or vice versa. Race is another nominal level of measurement. You can classify people into several categories on the basis of their race, but you do not imply that one category is larger than another even though you might assign African Americans a 1, whites a 2, Asians a 3, and others a 4. You could, as another example of the nominal level of measurement, classify states as to their primary economic base, such as primarily agricultural, industrial, mining, or mixed, or any number of other categories.

Nominal classifications can be very precise in their ability to sort units into one or another category. However, they do not communicate that one unit has more or less of some property than another, nor do they specify the precise amount of some property that a unit possesses. Thus, certain statistical procedures are inappropriate with nominal measures. In this sense, nominal measurement is a lower level of measurement than either ordinal or interval. For example, if we have classified types of households in a fourfold categorization where 1 = married couples living by themselves, 2 = married couples living with dependent children or other relatives, 3 = persons living alone, and 4 = other household types, it would not be appropriate to calculate the "mean" (see Chapter 5) type of household, since the numbers are arbitrarily assigned to each type.

While nominal measures only classify, ordinal measurements imply order. In an **ordinal measure**, you can say that X category is more than or less than Y category. For example, suppose you ask a random group of people about their attitudes toward nuclear power plants: "Do you favor building more nuclear power plants or not?" Possible responses might be: strongly favor, favor, depends, do not favor, strongly do not favor. This is an example of an ordinal measure. You can classify and order. We can say that Frank Gonzalez, who responded "strongly favor," is more supportive of building nuclear power plants than Betty Steinman, who responded "do not favor." There is an order from most in favor to least in favor. If we assigned numbers to these responses we would want to assign a 1 to strongly favor, 2 to favor, and so on, or a 5 to strongly favor, 4 to favor, etc. It would make no sense to assign a 3 to "favor," 5 to "depends," and a 1 to "strongly does not favor," because that would destroy the order implicit in the responses. Thus ordinal measures, as their name implies, are ordered.

Another example of a common ordinal measure is a scale. Suppose again that you are interested in attitudes toward nuclear power plants. Perhaps asking one question is not enough; the question about building nuclear power plants only gets at one aspect of the issue. So you devise four statements about nuclear power plants; for the sake of simplicity, let's say that those you question must answer "agree" or "disagree" to each one.

1. I favor building more nuclear power plants.
2. I do not favor closing those nuclear power plants that exist.
3. I believe we will solve the problem of nuclear waste.
4. I believe nuclear power plants are safe.

Each time an individual agrees, he receives 1 point; if he disagrees, he receives 0 points. If you sum the answers, individuals could receive from 0 to 4 points; individuals most opposed to nuclear power would receive a 0, those most in favor would receive a 4.[1] Thus we can order each individual from most to least in favor of nuclear power plants. We have an ordinal scale. What we cannot do, however, is to say that Mary Mosley, who received a score of 4, is twice as much in favor of nuclear power plants as Joe Lombra, who received a score of 2. Ordinal scales do not allow us to assume there are equal intervals between each point on our scale. We can say that Mosley is more in favor of nuclear power plants than Lombra, but we do not know how much more.

Interval and ratio level measures allow us to make exact determinations of the distances between two points; they have fixed and equal intervals. **Interval and ratio measures** generally are based on an agreed upon standard, such as weight, height, time, or money. Dollar cost is an interval level measure. We can say that something that costs $1 million is half as expensive as something that costs $2 million. Mortality rates, number of patients treated, age, crime rates, years of education, and income are all interval level measures. Such measures convey the most information because they allow us to classify, to order, and to array along a clearly delineated scale. Because they are precise numerical measures, the most powerful statistical techniques can be used to summarize and analyze them, as we shall see in Chapters 8 and 9. For the practical purposes of policy researchers, there is little difference between interval and ratio measures. Ratio scales have absolute and fixed zero points, such as occur in percentage or proportion measures like percent urban, percent female, crime rate per 1,000 population, and so forth. In policy research we use the same statistical techniques for ratio as for interval measures. In sum:

  Nominal: classifies only.

Ordinal: classifies and orders, "more than" or "less than."

Interval: classifies, orders, and assumes a fixed interval.

Ratio: classifies, orders, assumes fixed intervals, and has an absolute zero.

In the following chapters we will discuss the statistical techniques appropriate to each level of measurement.

EXERCISE

3-1 What level of measurement are the following variables most likely to be?

    a. Whether a city is located in Illinois or Ohio or Indiana.

---

[1]To simplify this discussion, all questions were worded so that an "agree" favors nuclear power. In actually constructing scales, however, you would want to have some items where a "disagree" is a pro-nuclear response. For example, "We should not build any more nuclear power plants until we solve the problems surrounding them."

b. Traffic fatalities.
c. Attitude toward health maintenance organizations.
d. School enrollment.

CRITERIA FOR MEASUREMENT

Validity

One important criterion for a good measure is that it be **valid**; that is, it should measure what it is supposed to measure. For example, in assessing the quality of some service, your measures should assess quality and not some other dimension, such as quantity. Or as another example, if you want to measure public reaction to a policy, be sure you are measuring public opinion rather than that of the press or political decision makers.

How do you know your measure is valid? While problems of validity (or lack thereof) are at issue in most scientific studies, whether physical science, biology, or social science, they are especially grave in the social sciences, the disciplines upon which policy research is largely based. Therefore you must give careful consideration to the validity of your measures. The problem for both the novice and the experienced policy researcher is, however, that there are no hard and fast rules for testing whether a measurement is valid. But there are some widely accepted methods for deriving evidence of validity, although technically speaking, each constitutes a separate form of validity.

Common sense is a key test. Does your measure, on its face, seem reasonable? This check is called **face validity**. Beyond an intuitive consideration of whether your measure makes sense, you might also consider whether the measure has been used before. If it has, and there is acceptance of that research by experts in the field and by users of the research, then this is some indication that others have accepted the measure as valid. Be sure, however, that the measure was used in other studies to measure the same concept you wish to measure.

Content validity means that the measure encompasses the totality of elements thought to be part of the concept you are attempting to measure. For example, a measure of success in hiring minorities as part of an affirmative action plan should encompass all relevant minorities, not just one or two. A measure of public attitudes toward postal service should include a wide range of such attitudes, and not just public attitudes about the cost of mailing first-class letters.

Another test of validity is **predictive validity**. If a graduate college's aptitude and skill tests are valid, they should be related to the academic success students have in graduate school. In fact, they are. Grade point averages compiled in graduate school, for example, could be the criteria by which to validate graduate college aptitude tests.

Construct validity is a fourth test for validity. Assume you are developing a scale to measure attitudes toward household energy conservation. If each item met the criterion of construct validity, each would be measuring the abstract concept "attitude toward energy conservation." One way to test the construct validity of each item would be to select characteristics known to be true of people with pro- and anti-energy conservation views. Perhaps from previous research, we can determine, for example, that older people are more likely to favor energy conservation. We would then test each individual item to see if it correlated with age. If not, we have a lack of construct validity: age is related to the general construct of energy conservation attitudes but not to an item purporting to measure these attitudes. Of course, in that situation, it could be that we have incorrectly identified age as being related to the general construct of energy conservation. This possibility must be weighed in determining whether the criteria of construct validity are met.

Reliability

A second key criterion for a good measure is reliability. A **reliable measure** is one that, if applied time after time, will yield the same results (assuming no change in the item being measured). For example, a reliable measure of crime will report the same incidence of crime in 2001 as in 2000 if indeed crime was the same in those two years. In fact most measures of crime are not reliable; changes in police administrations from year to year, variations in reporting across governmental units, and changing attitudes about whether or not to report crimes to the police all make the Uniform Crime Reports a rather unreliable measure of crime.

How can reliability be distinguished from validity? A simple example might help clarify these two concepts. Let's assume you have a bathroom scale that indicates a person is ten pounds heavier than he really is. The scale always indicates ten pounds heavier than the actual weight no matter how much the person gains or loses. This scale is reliable; it gives the same information time after time. You can have confidence that the scale always tells you that you weigh 10 pounds more than you actually do. The scale is not valid, however, because it does not tell what you really weigh. Thus a valid scale is always reliable, but a scale may be quite reliable without being valid.

Unreliability is a continuing problem in social science research. In survey research, this is often because researchers ask questions that are too vague, too complex, and not relevant to the respondents, or because the respondent does not understand a question. But sometimes even simple questions can yield a high degree of unreliability. Panel studies conducted before and after elections inevitably show a few people who changed sex in a few weeks. Racial designations are also subject to change. As another example, researchers twice questioned individuals on several personal characteristics over an interval of three months as part of a larger study of health risks.[2] Ten percent of the sample

---

[2] Jeffrey Sacks, W. M. Krushat, Jeffrey Newman, "Reliability of Health Hazard Appraisal," *American Journal of Public Health*, July 1980, pp. 730–32.

reported different heights at the two points in time, 20 percent changed their reports about their history of drinking and smoking, and 33 percent gave different responses as to their parents' ages. Some respondents even reported themselves as younger in the second interview than in the first! Perhaps we should be happy that the majority were consistent in these responses, but it is clear that reliability in such surveys is something about which to be concerned.

How do you decide if a measure is reliable? Several specific tests have been developed to test for reliability in a measure. One is called the **test-retest** **method**. A reliable measure gives the same findings when applied at different times, assuming no change in what is being measured. Therefore if you apply a measure of verbal ability, for example, to a group of children in March and then apply the same test in May, the results should be the same. Children who score low in March should continue to score low in May if the test is reliable. In a test-retest method, March scores are correlated with those in May.[3] If the scores are the same or similar (that is, if the correlation is high), then we can be pretty sure that the measure is reliable.

However, if the scores are not the same we cannot conclude that the measure is unreliable. Maybe real "learning" took place in the two-month interval. The learning may have been substantive learning: that is, between March and May the children were taught some skill needed to obtain a high score on the test. Or, people may remember specific test items, or they may simply be more skilled in taking that kind of test.

There is an inevitable dilemma here. The shorter the interval between the test and retest, the more likely there is some learning about how to take the test or even recall of the specific test items. The longer the interval between the test and retest, the more likely that there is real change in the dimension being measured.

A second method of checking reliability is the **split-half technique**, which avoids these problems. You administer a test or questionnaire to a group of subjects. Then you correlate the responses on one random half of the questionnaire with the responses on the other random half. For example, assume you have designed a ten-item questionnaire dealing with attitudes toward services at city parks. Is your set of items a reliable measure of these attitudes? Assume an individual can be scored 1 on each item where she gives a positive response about the parks, 0 where her views are negative. If you checked reliability with a split-half test, you would randomly divide the ten items into two groups of five, sum the answers in each half, and correlate the responses. Thus if your ten items were reliable, you would assume that people scoring 5 (5 would be the maximum positive score, 0 the least positive) on one half of the test would also score 4 or 5 on the other half. If people who score 4 or 5 on one half consistently score only 1 or 2 on the other half, you can assume that

---

[3] See Chapter 8 for a discussion of correlation. Just what is a "high correlation" is a subjective matter. The closer the correlation to 1.0, the more reliable the measure.

all of your items are not measuring the same things. So the ten-item scale is not reliable.

In sum, reliability is an important feature of measurement. Always attempt to check reliability before placing much confidence in your measures.

Comprehensibility

Comprehensibility is another important consideration in choosing measures in policy research. A policy researcher will usually be writing for readers who are not specialists in the field, perhaps legislators, bureaucrats, and members of the public. Therefore it is very important to choose measures that are understandable to the potential audience. Measures that are too esoteric, no matter how reliable and valid, will not be understood. You will have wasted a lot of time and money and gained little in knowledge of the policy.

Cost

No matter how precise a set of measurements are, if they call for expenditures beyond your budget, they are not practical. Cost is a real factor in trying to make decisions about which measures to use in a study. It is often wise to spend more to get a better measure if possible. If your measure is not reliable or valid, no matter how cheap it is to collect, you will not have achieved anything in the study. However, in most cases there are alternative measures that might be valid and reliable. For example, novice researchers often think it is necessary to take a public opinion poll (which is very expensive) when in fact the information they need might be found in prior surveys or in census data. Cost and the wise use of resources are important considerations for the policy researcher; there will usually be a trade-off between cost and other criteria. Maximizing reliability may mean increasing cost.

Completeness

Completeness is another characteristic of a good measure. Think back to the example of the nuclear power plant discussed above. A four-item scale gave much more information about an individual's attitudes toward nuclear power than did simply asking one question. This is true for most measures. Multiple indicators also tend to be more reliable than single indicators. Again suppose you are interested in residents' attitudes toward the city park systems. You could ask a rather general question: "Do you believe the city park system is of high quality or not?" However, this question, because it is pitched at such a general level, is likely to elicit answers that are neither very reliable nor very informative. People may not consider what they are answering or may consider only one aspect of the park service. For example, John Booth might say he believes the park to be of high quality because he is thinking of the playground equipment his child enjoys. Nancy Straka might say she does not believe the parks to be of high quality because she has been reading about two muggings that took place in one of the parks the day before. Different people will be thinking of different aspects of the park in answering a general question such as this. So it is preferable to try to ask about specific dimensions of the park service in which you are interested. This is also much more useful to those who will use your policy research because it will give them specific information about what is right and what is wrong. You could ask a series of questions about the parks, such as:

1. Do you usually find them clean or dirty?
2. Is the playground equipment adequate or not adequate?
3. Are they convenient to your home or not?
4. Do you feel safe in them or not?
5. Are there enough picnic facilities or not?

The answers you receive will give you a more complete understanding of public reactions to the city parks and are likely to be a more reliable measure of these attitudes than the single question. The more abstract the concept you are measuring, the more thought you must give to completeness. Of course, twenty questions would give you even more information but would be more expensive to collect. Again, maximizing one criterion of measurement may limit another.

EXERCISE

3-2 Think of two possible measures for each concept. Discuss each measure in terms of its potential validity, reliability, comprehensibility, cost, and completeness.

a. Citizen support for the current city government.
b. The incidence of chronic illness among those over sixty-five in your state.
c. Citizen satisfaction with garbage collection in your community.

CONSTRUCTING INDICES AND SCALES

AN EXAMPLE OF A SCALE

We have stressed that good measures are complete and that they adequately cover all important aspects of the concept being measured. Often, this cannot be done with a single measure, such as one question on a survey. In many circumstances, a researcher will want to obtain several measures and combine them in an index, or **scale**. We will use the term scale in this discussion, though some people prefer to use the term index for scales that are computed simply by adding together a number of items.

A scale can be constructed from two items to two hundred or anything in between. Scales can be constructed from items asked in public opinion surveys, or based on data found in public records, or gathered from personal observation. In survey research, an upper limit on scale size is posed by people's tolerance level in surveys. A person may be willing to answer six questions about his community's park facilities, but probably would balk at six dozen such questions. Scales constructed from survey responses generally tend to comprise from two to ten items, though occasionally they may be longer.

The simplest scale involves merely adding together several responses. Suppose you were interested in assessing the impact of a husband's sharing household duties on a couple's tendency to divorce. You might ask the husband how much time he spends doing household chores, but this might lead to substantial unreliability. To complement such a single measure, you might wish to construct a scale composed of something like the following:

Which of the following household chores do you regularly do (check all that apply):

_____ Washing up after meals.

_____ Preparing meals.

_____ Doing the laundry.

_____ Routine household cleaning.

_____ Shopping for groceries.

_____ Caring for the children.

One could simply add together the number of checks each person made and obtain a scale of household chores. The scores could range from zero to six. If one wanted a check on reliability, one could ask the same question of the wife of each man to see if she agreed with her husband's assessment.

Even though such a scale might be better than simply asking the husband if he helps with household chores, there are some problems. For one thing, perhaps all of these chores are not equal in magnitude. Having major responsibility for child care, for example, takes much more time than washing up after meals, even if the cook is exceptionally messy and the children well behaved. One way to refine the scale, then, would be to give each chore a weight based on some kind of estimate of the relative importance or time of each chore. Household cleaning, caring for the children, and preparing meals might receive weights of two, the others, one. In scoring, this scale could be worth a total of nine points.

Deciding on weights for the items is, however, a tricky business. The relative importance of these chores would not be agreed upon by all. Indeed, the relative importance and time spent in different chores would vary from household to household. Child care of an infant is certainly more time consuming (even if not more psychologically stressful) than that of a teenager. In some households, neither husband nor wife do some of the chores: cleaning ladies clean, teenagers wash up after meals, and so forth.

Another way to improve the likely reliability of the measure is to gain an assessment of the proportion of each chore the husband assumes. In many households, at least some of these tasks are shared to some extent. We might improve our scale by asking each respondent not just to check whether he does each task, but to estimate the proportion of the task he does.

We are interested in who performs each of the following household chores. Check the most appropriate response for each:

	I DO IT ALMOST ALWAYS	I USUALLY DO IT	I DO IT HALF OF THE TIME	I DO IT OCCASIONALLY	I NEVER DO IT
Washing up after meals	[ ]	[ ]	[ ]	[ ]	[ ]
Preparing meals	[ ]	[ ]	[ ]	[ ]	[ ]
Doing the laundry	[ ]	[ ]	[ ]	[ ]	[ ]
Routine house-hold cleaning	[ ]	[ ]	[ ]	[ ]	[ ]
Shopping for groceries	[ ]	[ ]	[ ]	[ ]	[ ]
Caring for the children	[ ]	[ ]	[ ]	[ ]	[ ]

A matrix of answers such as this would allow several different versions of a scale. You could add together only those where the husband responded that he did it almost always. Alternatively, you could add together those responses of "almost always" and "usually do it." Or you could decide on weights for the items; for example, give the husband 4 points for each "almost always," 3 for "usually do it," 2 for "about half," 1 for "occasionally," and 0 for "never." Each of these versions would allow you to compare husbands in their extent of responsibility for household chores. Note, however, that this is an ordinal, not interval, scale. We have no absolute rule about what numbers to assign each category. Instead of 0 to 4, we could equally well assign these categories numbers 1 through 5 or 0 through 1, using .25, .5 and .75 in between.

Even this simple example should alert you to the possible complexities of scale construction. How will you know if the scale is reliable when you finish? How do you choose among different possibilities for constructing the scale? We can answer these questions by describing the scale construction process.

CHOOSING ITEMS

The first step in constructing a scale is to choose the items. You must be concerned with face validity and content validity. Do all potential items relate to the concept you are trying to measure? Are all relevant aspects of the concept included in your scale? If you examine the scale items for measuring the concept of the husband's participation in household chores, you might find that important aspects of household chores are not included. For example, perhaps

Research in Practice 3A

In recent years, many elected officials have supported initiatives to "reinvent" government. These initiatives, similar to those found in some businesses and corporations, generally involve trying to make government more efficient and to provide better service to the public.

To convey the extent to which states have undergone reinvention, to allow comparisons among states, and to analyze the factors that promote state progress in this area, a group of three policy analysts constructed "reinvention" scales. The analysts used information from a mailed survey of heads of ninety-three types of agencies in all states. The survey included eleven items focusing on reinvention, including training programs to improve client or customer service, quality improvement (CQI or TQM) programs, benchmarking to measure program outcomes, strategic planning, reduction in levels of bureaucracy, and privatization.

For each of the eleven reinvention strategies, the analysts asked managers to rate their reinvention efforts on a Likert-type scale from 0 to 4, with 4 indicating full implementation of the change and 0 representing no change considered at all. The scores were then summed for all eleven strategies for each agency, resulting in a simple scale ranging from 0, if none of the reforms were considered, to 44, if all had been fully adopted. Then, within each state, the scores for agencies were averaged, so that each state could be rated on the same 0 to 44 scale.

The analysts displayed a comparison chart showing the progress of each state on reinvention initiatives (Florida and Oregon were at the top, Alabama and Rhode Island at the bottom). Then they used the agency reinvention scores as a dependent variable in a regression to identify factors explaining progress on reinvention. Among other findings, they discovered that agencies most likely to have undertaken the reforms were those most closely linked to gubernatorial influence, larger agencies, those in states where other agencies were also undergoing these reforms, and those with more conservative directors.

Summarizing the movement toward reform in one simple scale allowed them to explain and describe overall trends in a much more parsimonious fashion than examining each element of reform separately. Of course, they could also examine different types of reform in separate analyses by creating subscales from their overall scale.

SOURCE: Jeffrey Brudney, F. Ted Hebert, Deil S. Wright, "Reinventing Government in the American States: Measuring and Explaining Administrative Reform," *Public Administration Review* 59 (January/February, 1999): p. 19–29, 301.

you need to include such chores as "yard work," or "major household cleaning." If an important aspect is omitted, then the scale will lack content validity. The researchers constructing the reinventing government scale were concerned to choose only the items best measuring reinvention.

An essential strategy in scale construction is to inspect the work of others working in this same field. What kinds of chores do they normally include in assessing division of labor in the household? Or in measuring "reinvention?" Another strategy is to include an "other" category in a pretest. If you ask state leaders what other initiatives they took to reinvent state government, perhaps you will find one or more particular initiatives cited by several. Then you could include those frequently-mentioned items in the questionnaire.

ITEM INTERRELATIONSHIPS

A second step in scale construction is to look at interrelationships among the items. If all items are purporting to measure the same concept, they should be related to one another and to the overall scale. Scales should be unidimensional, that is, only measuring one thing. In the case of state governments, you would want to make sure that states that have initiatives to promote a service orientation among staff are also those engaging in total quality initiatives. If the states doing those two things are different, then those two actions are not part of a unidimensional "reinvention" concept.

If you are trying to differentiate husbands who share a large proportion of household chores from those who share in a smaller portion, those men scoring high on one item should tend to be those who score high on the others. Of course, there will be exceptions, but if consistently those men who say they shop regularly say they never do the washing up, and *vice versa*, then it may be that all of the items are not measuring the same thing. Perhaps we are measuring two or more dimensions of household chores.

To look at the interrelationships among the items, you will have to administer a version of your items to a small sample of potential respondents. Then examine the response patterns. In Chapters 6 and 8 you will learn some cross-tabular and correlational techniques to do this. If you find that one item does not have patterns consistent with the others (it has a very low correlation, we will say), then that item should be dropped. If two items have exactly the same response patterns or nearly so, then one of them should also be dropped, as it adds nothing to the scale. For example, suppose you had separate items for "washing up breakfast dishes" and "washing up dinner dishes." If all men who responded they washed up breakfast dishes also said they washed up dinner dishes, then one of the items should be dropped, or the items combined into "washing up dishes after meals."

You also need to compare each individual item to the total scale score. This is called item analysis. If individuals score high on one item, but low on the whole scale, then that item is not measuring the same thing as the other items, and should be dropped.

SCORING THE SCALE

A third step is to score each respondent on the scale. This step involves deciding on weights, if any, to assign various responses, then summing each respondent's responses. After that, you might cluster respondents in a few categories, such as high, medium, or low, or you might need to recode the scale in another form. In most scales, the extreme scale responses are few in number. For example, assume we gave the six-item scale above to 100 married men, and scored each item using the 0 to 4 metric. The maximum score would be 24 (6 items times 4 points each), and the minimum, 0. We might find that only three men scored over 20, while only two men scored under 6. If so, we might want to recode our scale so that the final version has respondents at every score. This might mean scoring as 0 all those who got below 6, then scoring those who initially received 6's as 1's, 7's as 2's, and so forth. At the other end of the scale, those who got 20 or more might be coded together at the new scale score of 15.

We will discuss recoding of scales further as we proceed to the statistical part of our text in Chapter 5. But for now, just remember that the initial score values are not etched in concrete, and may need to be regrouped for different statistical purposes.

Another problem in scoring the scale is to decide what to do with missing data. In most surveys, some respondents will not answer some of the questions. Suppose in the six-item survey above, one person did not answer each of the items. Unfortunately, there is no perfect nor agreed-upon way to handle missing data. Here are some possibilities:

1. Delete the individuals with missing data from the analysis. In that case, your sample of 100 would shrink to 94, assuming the non-respondent was different on each item. That strategy is fine when the proportion of cases with missing values is small, but suppose three men did not answer each of the items, and each non-respondent was a different person. Then you would lose 18 of your sample of 100, a serious matter. In that case, you probably would not throw the respondents out. You might consider several other possibilities.

2. Ignore the missing responses by assigning them a 0. *This should not be done.* You are treating missing responses the same as if they had responded "never" to that item.

3. Give each respondent who misses an item the average score on that item. Let's say the average score on the first item, "washing up after meals," was a 2, "do it half the time." Those individuals who had missing values on that item could be given a 2. This is frequently done, and you may want to do it. The problem with this strategy is that it does not take into account that particular missing individual's likely response. Perhaps this is an individual who has responded "4" to most other questions.

4. Another strategy is to assign an individual with a missing item his own average score on the items he has answered. If a particular husband has answered "4" on each of the items, but omits one item, a reasonable solution would be to assign him a 4 on the omitted one. This strategy also has problems. Perhaps the reason the item was omitted was because it was not a chore he did.

Most researchers would use strategies three or four above unless the proportion of cases with missing items is extremely small, in which instance they would follow strategy one of simply omitting the cases. However, strategy one, dropping the respondent, should usually be followed only when any particular individual has more items missing than complete. For example, individuals who responded only to one or two (or possibly three) of the items in the six-item scale should be excluded from the analysis. Assigning them scale scores on the basis of such limited information is clearly adding unreliability to the scale.

If you have too many missing values, something is wrong with your questionnaire. For example, perhaps some items are unclear, the questionnaire is too long or poorly laid out, or the questions are of little interest to your respondents.

VALIDATING THE SCALE

A final step in building a scale is to validate it. Researchers often ignore this part. Here you might assess how well your scale relates to other variables presumed to be related to it (construct validity). For example, suppose that other researchers on family chores found that younger husbands share more household tasks than older ones. You need to examine your scale to see if this is true in your sample. If you find that older husbands score higher on your scale, then you must consider whether your scale is valid. Perhaps it is. Maybe your sample is unique. Or maybe times have changed. But it might also be that there is something wrong with your scale.

Another way to examine your scale is to assess its reliability. Two ways are the split-half technique and the item analysis discussed earlier.

LIKERT SCALES

There are many different types of scales. One is the **Likert scale**. Likert scales are additive scales generally employed in attitude measurement. They are based on the idea that an individual's intensity of feeling toward something can be measured. Instead of asking individuals whether they agree or disagree with some statement, you assess them along a 5- or 7-point scale of agreement. Usually, individuals are asked whether they strongly agree, agree, are uncertain, disagree, or strongly disagree. The procedures for constructing and scoring Likert scales are identical to those we have just discussed for scales in general.

Figure 3-1 shows a Likert scale containing five items that illustrates the general format of these scales. They are scored by assigning points ranging (usually) from 1 to 5 to the response categories. In this example, the scale purports to measure sympathy toward pro-business development policies. That being the case, a scale developed from these items should have a high range indicating individuals who are especially favorable to pro-business development policies and a low range comprising people less sympathetic. Items one through four should be scored so that a "5" is assigned to the strongly agree response and a "1" to the strongly disagree. Item five, however, should be scored the opposite way, a "1" to the strongly agree response and a "5" to the strongly disagree, because it is worded so that someone who strongly favors pro-business development policies would strongly disagree.

As with any scale, after trying to validate a particular set of Likert scale items, you might discover that the scale is not unidimensional, the items are not related to one another, or that the scale does not seem to relate in the expected way to other variables. This illustration, for example, consists of items that proved to be not highly related to one another when tested on a sample of state legislators. When that happens, a researcher will often have to make the best of a bad situation by using only a subset of items, or even just one item.

EXERCISES

3-3 Look at research articles in the past several issues of *Public Administration Review, Policy Studies Journal, Evaluation Review,* or another policy-oriented journal. Find two examples of scales.

How well did the researcher document the construction and validation of the scale? What steps did he or she omit?

3-4 Construct items for a simple index designed to measure employee morale in your office or student morale in your class or program. How would you next proceed to score and validate the scale?

3-5 Construct a ten-item Likert scale to measure public attitudes toward unionization of public employees. Put the scale in proper Likert format.

DATA COLLECTION

As a public manager or policy analyst, you will have different lead times for collecting and organizing your data. Sometimes you will need to do a quick data collection project; in another instance you will have the time and resources to do a more thorough job. Whichever situation is the case, do not imagine that you must invent all the measures you need and collect all the

FIGURE 3–1 **Some Likert Scale Items**

Please express your agreement or disagreement with each of the following statements about policymaking.*

	STRONGLY AGREE	AGREE	NEUTRAL	DISAGREE	STRONGLY DISAGREE
1. Generally, I approve of unlimited development in this state; if business wants to invest in new enterprises, the state should go along.	[ ]	[ ]	[ ]	[ ]	[ ]
2. The federal income tax exemption of state and local taxes should be retained.	[ ]	[ ]	[ ]	[ ]	[ ]
3. The federal government should allow state and local governments to use industrial revenue bonds to finance whatever projects they choose.	[ ]	[ ]	[ ]	[ ]	[ ]
4. I believe we should generate new state revenue through user charges rather than through new taxes or tax increases.	[ ]	[ ]	[ ]	[ ]	[ ]
5. To generate new state revenue we should cut some of the tax breaks now given to businesses.	[ ]	[ ]	[ ]	[ ]	[ ]

*This scale was drawn from a questionnaire prepared by Margery Ambrosius, Kansas State University.

information single-handedly. In fact if you can utilize measures and data already used and verified by others and these measures are appropriate to your needs, then you are far ahead in your research. For example, if you are studying crime rates, you would probably want to consider using the Uniform Crime Reports (UCR) simply because they are the basis for much of what we know about crime. You may decide not to use them or to supplement them with other kinds of crime data, such as victim surveys. But knowing that the UCR exists will be valuable to you. Similarly, if you are studying unemployment, you would want to consider using the Labor Department and Census statistics on unemployment. If you are doing attitudinal research, you might find reports of attitude measures others have used by checking Buro's Handbook of Mental Measurement or the University of Michigan's handbooks cited in Research in Practice 3B. So look around at what others have done before you leap into a large data collection project yourself. In addition to library resources, there is an incredible amount of survey and census data available freely on the Internet. Research in Practice 3B provides you with some starting points for your data search.

Assume you are a member of a state health planning agency and you are asked by your supervisor to prepare a report on hospital bed occupancy in the state. You are to describe occupancy rates of various kinds of hospitals and to analyze differences based on the age structure of the population, number of hospital beds to county population, income levels, counties, and so forth. You have only a few weeks to do the project. How would you go about doing it? Where would you turn?

EXISTING DATA

All governments and large bureaucracies keep records. These records may go back over a long time. They may be published as census information, crime reports, statistics on school attendance, and so forth. Some government records are not intended to be published, such as records on clients kept by hospitals, schools, welfare agencies, and the like. Before you embark on an extensive and expensive data collection project, check to make sure that the information you need is not already tabulated and even published by someone else.

As a health planner, you will be aware that hospitals keep occupancy records. If you are lucky, your agency has already collected them. If so, obtaining the individual hospital records should be easy. If the agency has not already collected the information, then you can do so by writing each hospital. If your state has hundreds of hospitals and you have limited time, write only to those in counties of a certain size or larger or only to public or nonprofit ones. How far you can go in delimiting your task depends, of course, on the directives and objectives of the original request and how flexible it was. Your request to the hospitals should specify exactly what information you need, including the dates of the information wanted and any information necessary to interpret the information sent.

Your task also includes explaining occupancy rates in terms of community age structures and other relevant factors. Here you can turn to published data. The U.S. Census publishes all sorts of demographic, economic, employment, quality of life, and other information aggregated by census districts, communities, counties, SMSAs (standard metropolitan statistical areas), states, and other units. The Census also publishes extensive information on the governmental units themselves, that is, on city and county expenditures, employment, programs, and so forth. Much of that information is available on the web (start at the Census home page, http://www.census.gov).

Since you are doing a study based on the county unit, you can probably find most of the demographic information you need in the published (including web based) census records. CD-Roms containing the raw data are also available from the Bureau of the Census or from certain data repositories (such as the Inter-University Consortium for Political and Social Research at the University of Michigan). By obtaining these data, you can aggregate information in different ways than in the published data. Research in Practice 3B lists numerous sources of published data that should help in a wide variety of data collection efforts.

Agency files would probably be the best source of other health related information you might need (such as morbidity rates or proportions of residents in each county that have health insurance). Sometimes if you run up against a brick wall in locating information you think should exist, try consulting your local library. If you are located near a large research library, then the reference or other specialized personnel there should be a great source of help. Then, of course, there may be experts at a local college or university who might be willing to help. Usually public and some private universities have research institutes of business and economics and of govermnental affairs that collect and maintain data relevant to your state or locality.

In this example, you as a research analyst can rely mostly on already aggregated data collected by hospitals and by the Census Bureau. But sometimes your task will not be so simple. Assume you are a staff member of the auxiliary services department in a large public hospital. The hospital administration is interested in implementing a better series of workshops on infant care for new mothers who have delivered babies at your hospital. The workshop planners want more information about these mothers. In particular your supervisor wants you to collect information about the number of first-time mothers who have given birth in your hospital during the past year, as well as age and marital status of each. Further, you must find out what proportion of these mothers had a helper at home (other than a working spouse) to assist in caring for the baby during the first few days.

These are presumably simple questions, but answering them may not be as simple as it appears on first glance. The hospital, of course, like other bureaucracies, maintains records on each patient. But the data were collected for purposes other than the purposes of your research. Thus the information may be incomplete for your purposes. For example, it would likely reveal the mother's age, marital status, and whether she has other children, but it may not note whether there is another adult in the household to help with infant care.

The data may also be classified in a way difficult for you to use. For example, the hospital may keep records alphabetized by patient when you need records organized by year and categorized by hospital service (i.e., obstetrics).[4] However, most hospitals have computerized record systems that could allow you to search by the information you need. If so, you can reclassify the

---

[4] Similar problems are found when using records of other bureaucracies. The police department may keep arrest records by day, when you would like to have records by individual. Or the records may be incomplete for your purposes; police records may not contain information on crucial demographic variables that are necessary to control in your study, such as occupation, education and residential history.

Research in Practice 3B

USEFUL DATA SOURCES FOR POLICY ANALYSTS

The following are a sample of some important data sources of special use to policy analysts. We have included web sites as well as published material. The list is divided into general references, data sources for the U.S. national government, data sources for state-local governments, and data sources for other nations.

GENERAL REFERENCES

Facts on File. New York: Facts on File, Inc. Weekly compendium of important news events in the United States and the world. A biweekly cumulative index is published.

Institute for Social Research (ISR). *Measures of Political Attitudes*. Ann Arbor: University of Michigan, 1998. Excellent place to start looking if you are constructing attitude scales because it contains items used and tested by others.

Li, Tze-chung. *Social Science Reference Sources: A Practical Guide*. Westport, Conn.: Greenwood Press, 2000. A guide to basic reference works in the social sciences.

Public Affairs Information Service (PAIS). A quarterly index (by subject and author) to information in dozens of periodicals.

U.S. NATIONAL GOVERNMENT

Federal Web Locator, The Center for Information Policy and Law— Intended to be a one-stop shopping for federal government information on the World Wide Web. http://www.law.vill.edu/Fed-Agency/fedwebloc.html

FedStats—Provides links to over seventy federal agencies. The place to start when searching government for federal and international statistics. http://www.fedstats.gov

Fedworld—Access to thousands of U.S. government web sites, over one million government documents and other information. http://www.fedworld.gov

Government Information Sharing Project, Oregon State University—A great place to start with demographic information on U.S. counties, states and the nation along with statistics on education, economics and links to other government web sites. http://govinfo.kerr.orst.edu/

Findlaw—A clearinghouse for all types of legal information such as cases, codes, law reviews. http://findlaw.com

Library of Congress—Resource page for state and local governments, providing links to several key sources of information and data. http://lcweb.loc.gov/global/state/stategov.html

Public Agenda—Provides detailed information on public opinion and policy analysis. http://www.publicagenda.org

Catalog of U.S. Government Publications—Search and retrieval service that provides bibliographic records of U.S. government information resources. It can also be used to link the Federal online agencies or to look up material in the Federal Depository libraries. http://www.access.gpo.gov/su_docs/dpos/adpos400.html

Direct Search U.S. State and City Resources, George Washington University—Compilation of many specialized, searchable and interactive databases. http://gwis2.circ.gwu.edu/~gprice/state.htm

Social Indicators from the United Nations—Comparative data on a variety of social indicators. http://www.un.org/Depts/unsd/social/main.htm

University of Michigan Documents Center—Provides a clearinghouse of online data of all types of government statistics. An excellent site to start your search for any level of government. http://www.lib.umich.edu/libhome/Documents.center/stats.html

Thomas, U.S. Congress on the Internet—First stop in looking for data and information from Congress. http://thomas.loc.gov

U.S. Census Bureau Data—Source of demographics and statistics in a variety of subject areas, e.g., housing, for the nation, states and counties. http://www.census.gov

U.S. Congress—Provides official, searchable databases with origins in the U.S. Congress. http://www.access.gpo.gov/congress/index.html

White House—Access to virtual library and other important links to government information/data. http://whitehouse.gov

Congressional Staff Directory. Mount Vernon, Va. An annual listing of the names and addresses of Congressional staffers. http://csd.cq.com/

Congressional Quarterly Weekly Reports. Washington, D.C.: *Congressional Quarterly*. A guide to events in Washington with a special focus on Congress. Contains voting records of members of Congress as well as summaries of major legislative proposals and legislation passed. *Congressional Quarterly* also publishes an annual summary *(Congressional Quarterly Almanac)* and special reports. http://library.cq.com

Federal Regulatory Directory. Washington, D.C.: *Congressional Quarterly*. Annual profiles of regulatory agencies including key personnel, organizational structure, relevant authorizing legislation and congressional committees, information sources, data sources, and references.

General Social Survey. Annual survey of the American public covering a variety of social, political, and demographic issues. http://www.icpsr.umich.edu/gss/home.htm

Historical Statistics of the United States, Colonial Times to 1970. Washington, D.C.: U.S. Government Printing Office, published since

1910. A compilation of various U.S. economic and demographic statistics. See online United States Historical Census Data Browser—Data that describe the people and economy of the U.S. for each state and county from 1790–1970. http://fisher.lib.virginia.edu/census/

Inter University Consortium for Political and Social Research (ICPSR). A huge repository of survey research, census, and other data sources from all over the world. http://www.icpsr.umich.edu/

Monthly Catalog of United States Government Publications. Washington, D.C.: Superintendent branches of the U.S. government. An indispensable reference guide to finding U.S. documents.

National Journal. Washington, D.C. Weekly review of events in Washington with a focus on the administration and bureaucracy. Some free access at http://nationaljournal.com

Scammon, Richard, ed. *America Votes: A Handbook of Contemporary American Election Statistics.* Washington, D.C.: *Governmental Affairs Institute and Congressional Quarterly,* published since 1956. Data by state on presidential, senatorial, congressional, and gubernatorial elections since the 1940s.

Social Security Bulletin. Washington, D.C.: Department of Health and Human Services, Social Security Administration. A monthly compilation of a variety of statistics concerning social security, Supplemental Security Income (SSI), and Aid to Families with Dependent Children (recipients and dollars paid). Many of the statistics are categorized by state. http://www.ssa.gov/statistics/bulletin.html

Statistical Abstract of the United States. Washington, D.C.: U.S. Government Printing Office. Issued by the Bureau of the Census—provides important and useful information about U.S. population, economy, education, health, national defense, elections, energy, and other information collected by the government. http://www.census.gov/stab/www/

U.S. Bureau of Labor Statistics. Washington, D.C.: U.S. Government Printing Office. An annual publication but kept current by quarterly supplements. Deals with summary of earnings: (1) wages, (2) hours of labor, and (3) cost and standard of living statistics in the United States. The Bureau of Labor Statistics also publishes annually the *Occupational Outlook Handbook* which describes what workers do on the job; the training and education they need; earnings, working conditions, and expected job prospects for hundreds of occupations and thirty-five industries. http://stats.bls.gov/

Vital Statistics of the United States. Washington, D.C.: U.S. Government Printing Office, published annually since 1937. Volumes for 1937–44 issued by the U.S. Bureau of Census; 1945–58 by the National Office of Vital Statistics; 1959-62 by the National Vital Statistics

Division; 1963 to 1992 by the National Center for Health Statistics and the Division of Vital Statistics.

Volume I: Natality. Statistics on fertility and births.

Volume II(A): Mortality. Statistics on general mortality, infant mortality, fetal mortality, accident mortality, and life tables.

Volume II(B): Mortality. Mortality statistics for each state and county, urban, metropolitan, and nonmetropolitan counties, population size groups, and standard metropolitan areas.

Volume III: Marriage and divorce. Historical and contemporary statistics.

A web source to a wide variety of statistics on health is the National Center for Health Statistics, http://www.cdc.gov/nchswww/about/about.htm

Washington Information Directory. Washington, D.C.: *Congressional Quarterly,* annual.

Information on government and private agencies, policies, and personnel. Organized by subject. Indexed by subject and agency or organization.

STATE AND LOCAL GOVERNMENTS

Direct Search U.S. State and City Resources, George Washington University—Compilation of many specialized, searchable and interactive databases. http://gwis2.circ.gwu.edu/~gprice/state.htm

National Association of Counties—Some free access to valuable county data and other information. http://www.naco.org

"Blue Books" of the states. Each state issues an annual or biennial handbook often called "Blue Books." Though varying in content from state to state, they usually provide information on state officeholders, state agencies, state history, state election returns (sometimes including legislative races), and referenda. They usually include election results on constitutional amendments.

Book of the States. Chicago, Council of State Governments, annual. Information on activities of the state governments including elections, office holders, public policies, and finances. http://dhrinfo.hr.state.or.us/intranet/statesbk.htm

Census of Governments. Washington, D.C.: U.S. Bureau of the Census. By state and community. Information on finances and employment. Includes: city government finances, state government finances, finances of employee retirement systems of state and local governments.

Census of the Population. Washington, D.C.: U.S. Bureau of the Census. Organized by state and locality, this is the basic source of demographic information on the population. Useful breakdowns of all sorts of information by sex, race, age, and urban or rural residence. Some data aggregated for standard metropolitan statistical areas (SMSAs). http://www.census.gov

County and City Data Book. Washington, D.C.: U.S. Bureau of the Census, since 1949. Contains statistical information for each county in the United States, standard metropolitan statistical areas, and cities with populations of more than 25,000. The information includes demographics, such as age, race, educational distributions in the population, and other policy-relevant information including crime rates. http://fisher.lib.virginia.edu

Municipal Year Book. Washington, D.C.: International City Managers Association, annual. Provides information on local governments, individual and aggregated. Covers government employment and finance; features on specific policies change from year to year. Also contains list of reference sources.

The National Directory of State Agencies. Arlington, Va.: Information Resources Press, annual. Lists names of agencies and agency heads in each state, organized and indexed by functional responsibilities (i.e., welfare, children's services).

Quarterly Summary of State and Local Tax Revenue. Washington, D.C.: U.S. Census Bureau.

Social Security Bulletin. See listing under U.S. national.

Statistics of Income. Washington, D.C.: Internal Revenue Service, annual. http://www.irs.ustreas.gov/prod/tax-stats/index.html

SOURCES OF DATA ON OTHER NATIONS

Countries of the World and Their Leaders: Yearbook and Supplement, Detroit, Mich.: Gale Research, 1997. Heads of state and cabinet officials of the world's nations, location of U.S. embassies and consulates and the officials at each, and profiles of political, religious, and other characteristics of each nation.

Demographic Yearbook. New York: United Nations Publications, since 1948. Contains worldwide population data, by country. Even though it is one of the best sources, data are incomplete and sometimes dated.

information in a way that is suited to your purpose. If there is no computerized system, you would have to hand sort the records.

In trying to find this information, you will face another problem with individualized agency records: confidentiality. As a member of the staff, you will undoubtedly be allowed to see the records, but you may not be allowed to contact the patients to obtain the additional necessary information. The hospital

European Historical Statistics. Mitchell, B. R., ed. London: MacMillan, 1975. A compendium of longitudinal data on the nations of Europe.

Index to International Public Opinion, 1997–98. Survey Research Consultants International. Westport, Conn.: Greenwood Press, 1980. An annual series containing results of surveys taken in various nations around the world. Both cross-national and single nation studies of economic, political, and social issues are included. Indexed by subject and country.

Inter University Consortium for Political and Social Research (ICPSR). A huge repository of survey research, census, and other data sources from all over the world.
http://www.icpsr.umich.edu/

Political Handbook of the World. Banks, Arthur, ed. New York: McGraw-Hill. Annual survey of world politics. Chronology of major world events, information on the United Nations and demographic and political data for 165 nations.

Social Indicators from the United Nations—Comparative data on a variety of social indicators.
http://www.un.org/Depts/unsd/social/main.htm

Statistical Abstract of Latin America. Wilkie, James, ed. Los Angeles: UCLA, 1997. Social, economic, geographic, and political data on Latin America. Published twenty times since 1955.

Statistical Yearbook. New York: United Nations, since 1948. Provides data by country on population, income, education, occupation, fertility, etc.

Statistical Yearbook for Asia and the Pacific. New York: United Nations, 1998. Socioeconomic data on the countries of Asia and the Pacific.

United Nations Documents Index. New York: United Nations, annual. An indispensable reference in searching for U.N. publications.

Yearbook on International Communist Affairs. Stanford, Conn. Hoover Institution Press, annual. Presents current and historical information on Communist parties in ninety-four countries. Also includes biographies of prominent Communists.

may be very reluctant to let you contact patients for fear of violating their privacy and the confidentiality of the records. This may be an insuperable problem, but it may be that you can reach some agreement.

Researchers from outside the agency may have even more difficulty obtaining access. As we will discuss in Chapter 12, if you are given access, it is of utmost importance to keep confidential material confidential when you are using these or any similar kinds of records. To reveal confidential material is a grave breach of research ethics.

If the hospital will not allow you to call or write each patient to obtain the requisite information, you may have to collect this information on current patients. For example, you could make arrangements with the hospital admittance office to ask first-time mothers a question as to who, if anyone, will be helping them at home when they return. If you can collect data on all mothers giving birth in your hospital for a month or two (or whatever time you have), and they appear to be similar in age and marital status to those whose records you surveyed from the previous year, then you can reasonably and confidently assume that the information about their infant-care help is probably also similar.

This is an example where fairly simple and straightforward information is sought, but substantial research may be necessary to retrieve the information. Nevertheless, with the cooperation of your agency combined with some hard work and common sense, some relevant information can be obtained without a major research effort.

In general, public records are especially useful when you are doing a study requiring data over a long period of time. Governments keep accurate records about all sorts of things: traffic accidents, unemployment, motor vehicle licenses issued, usage of state parks and other kinds of public facilities, dog tags sold, patients admitted to hospitals, patients discharged from mental hospitals, crime rates, and so forth. Be careful, however, when using these kinds of longitudinal records that the definition of the problem has stayed the same, for example, what defines a crime? Also find out if reporting has improved or decreased substantially. Otherwise, comparability over time would be low (the instrumentation problem we discussed in Chapter 2). For example, the classification of poverty levels changes from time to time, so longitudinal studies using that variable would have to take these changes into account. Also be careful in comparing across different political jurisdictions. Both definitions and record-keeping practices vary from state to state and city to city (e.g., the definition of a felony differs from state to state). Classification practices at mental institutions, in transportation systems, and in most areas of public policy vary widely in different areas and institutions.

In-Depth Interviews

Sometimes the information you need will be available simply from talking to people. If you are trying to understand how a program works, its legislative history, how clients react to the program, or many other types of questions, you may find it useful to conduct in-depth interviews with participants and knowledgeable observers.

Many social scientists are uneasy with this sort of information, but it can yield valuable insights. It is often the only way you can collect the information you need in a short period of time. To improve the quality of information you glean in this sort of process:

1. Prepare yourself in advance by reading as much as you can about the program and questions you are interested in.
2. Try to talk with as many different kinds of people as possible—people with different institutional and political perspectives.
3. Respect the confidentiality of what is told to you; do not repeat to interviewee one what interviewee two told you; at least do not mention interviewee one by name or repeat her remarks so they can be identified.
4. Ask those you interview if there are any others they believe you should interview.
5. If appropriate, ask the person you are interviewing for copies of documents, correspondence, or reports that are mentioned in discussions with you.

This kind of interviewing, though not yielding systematic data amenable to statistical analysis, can be one of the most useful sources of information for the policy researcher. In using it as the basis for a report and recommendations, however, be sure that you have talked to a wide enough circle of people to have gotten as much of the true picture as possible and that you have documentary material to verify the important points where possible.

RATINGS OF CONDITIONS BY TRAINED OBSERVERS

Aside from obtaining individual or aggregate records, how else do you collect data? Taking measurements of conditions using trained observers has been a growing practice in both academic and evaluation research.[5]

For example, one of the functions of a public works department is to provide streets free of debris and unsafe conditions. Suppose as a manager in that department, you are to assess the relationship between the cleanliness and safety of the streets and the frequency of the street crews' maintenance efforts. One way both to operationalize and measure the dependent variables (i.e., cleanliness and safety) is to develop an assessment method whereby trained observers can categorize both the cleanliness and the safety of the streets. Trained observer ratings are also useful in terms of certain transportation characteristics, such as presence and condition of traffic control signs, street name signs, traffic hazards, and so forth. Trained observers could also be used in quantifying certain kinds of transactions as they

---

[5] Many of the ideas in this section are drawn from Harry P. Hatry et al., *How Effective Are Your Community Services?* Washington, D.C.: The Urban Institute, 1977 and 1992.

frequently have been in basic psychological and sociological research, i.e., small group experiments. The key to the success of using observer ratings as measurements in policy research is to train the observers carefully. In measuring conditions such as street cleanliness, it is useful to train observers using photographs that the observers can keep and refer to (i.e., this is a picture of what category A of street cleanliness looks like, this is category B, and so forth).

The idea is for observers to compare actual conditions to the various conditions identified with particular ratings or scores. The best discussion of the use of this type of information is in the Hatry et al. book listed at the end of this chapter.

Reliability is a potential problem in using trained observers. That is, can independent observers consistently arrive at the same ratings? Experience by those that have used this method has shown that carefully trained observers can give ratings with a high degree of reliability (i.e., that observers one and two will both rate a particular condition the same). Of course, it is important that the trained observers are not those with a high stake in the outcome (in the previous example, those responsible for cleaning the streets).

To ensure reliability, perform a test where two or more observers rate a large number of sites independently. The ratings of the observers should then be compared to ensure that they are in fact producing the same results. Correlating the independent judgments of raters or coders is called an interceder reliability check. Good reliability occurs when coders agree 85 to 95 percent of the time. Rarely will reliability be higher. Where the same results are not found, the characteristics of deviant sites should be examined in depth to find out why certain sites yield divergent results. If one or more raters deviate from the general pattern, further training is necessary for them. If results are still not satisfactory, then the coders should not be used or you should determine if training procedures are at fault.

Although the trained observer technique may be more expensive than using existing data, it expands the range of policy questions you are able to test and in many cases allows you to get more directly at the problem and at less cost than employing a survey of public attitudes. For example, instead of assessing how clean the public thinks the parks are, you can measure their cleanliness directly. Both assessments may be relevant, but in some cases public opinion data is a poor substitute for information on actual conditions.

FOCUS GROUPS

Focus groups are specially selected groups of individuals (8 to 12, for example) brought together to discuss a particular set of issues. For example, in political campaigns, candidates may bring together groups of citizens to discuss issues, campaigns, and the candidates. Focus groups are led by a trained facilitator, who is a neutral party in the discussions.

The results of focus groups are not a scientific sample of public opinion, and should not be portrayed as such. However, the results can help a researcher understand the broader context of the issue or the more complex feelings that underlie short answers to a survey questionnaire. For example, a focus group could provide insight into how a group of citizens view an issue, such as the impact a new highway project is likely to have on a community, or an organization, such as the functioning of a local United Way agency. The kind of information gleaned from a focus group session could help researchers understand the complexity and intensity of beliefs in ways not captured in closed-ended questions in surveys. However, if you are using focus groups as part of your information collecting procession, you need to be careful not to generalize. In other words, just because the people in your focus group feel that the local United Way is run ineffectively does not mean most of the public also feels that way. However, the kinds of criticisms made in a focus group could be a clue to the perceptions about the agency held by a broader public.

How do you set up a focus group? It is important to have a trained facilitator, someone who will be neutral in the discussion but active in getting all participants to speak. The facilitator should also be skilled in managing conflict and knowing when and how to get a conversation back on track if it wanders into irrelevant areas.

Participants can be solicited through newspaper ads, church bulletins, or in other ways if a community group is being organized. If you want individuals within a particular organization or agency, then you can use organizational communication channels. Because there is no need for randomization, elaborate processes are not necessary (for more on this see Bader and Rossi, 1998).

However, you need to give thought to the composition of your group. Do you want it relatively homogeneous or relatively mixed? For example, imagine you were conducting focus groups within your agency on attitudes about the effectiveness of the personnel system, preparatory to reworking the position classification and pay systems. In a large organization, you would probably want to conduct more than one focus group discussion. But do you want several relatively homogenous groups or several mixed groups? Should staff assistants be in the same groups as executives and managers, or separate ones? The advantage of separate ones is that within an organizational hierarchy, lower ranking employees might defer to higher ranking ones and their voices would not be heard. But by separating different groups of employees, perhaps important facets of the issue would not be brought up. In the latter case, however, well trained facilitators can put issues on the table for discussion.

If you are conducting focus groups around issues of performance of community service agencies, as another example, you would probably want to have separate groups with users of the service and providers of the service.

In sum, focus groups can be a useful tool in helping you understand the phenomenon you are studying. But they should never be used to assess public or employee attitudes in place of a well designed survey.

OPINION SURVEYS

Sometimes you need information on citizen satisfaction with public services. At other times you are interested in the rate of utilization of a particular service or why the eligible nonusers are not using the service. In these and other cases where you need to know citizen attitudes, an appropriate method to collect relevant data is a public opinion survey. Unfortunately a survey is the most costly of the methods we have discussed, so it should not be used unless it is clearly the best way to get the needed information.

Conducting a public opinion survey is a complicated operation, and you should check with an expert to make sure you are following sound procedures. Otherwise the results of your study will be meaningless. Good overviews of survey research are found in the Babbie book listed at the end of the chapter.

There are three major tasks in carrying out survey research: first, decide who and how many should be surveyed; second, determine how to carry out the survey; third, design a questionnaire incorporating appropriate measures of the variables you are dealing with. Let's take each step individually.

Who Is To Be Surveyed?

It is important to be clear about what your universe and units of analysis are. That is, whose opinions are you interested in? Is it the adult population of a particular community or state? Is it members of a particular ethnic group? Is it households in a county? Is it adults meeting some special criteria, i.e., those who have been ill in the past two years? Each of these constitute a universe. It is important to consider carefully what the most appropriate universe is for your particular research problem. If you want to assess food stamp utilization among those eligible, your universe would be those eligible for food stamps as measured by income and family size. If you want to assess community attitudes toward recreational facilities, your universe would be the entire population (probably over a certain age) in the community.

In most cases you will not be able to survey every member of your universe (i.e., all adults in Chicago). Therefore you must draw a sample. A sample is just a subset of the members of your universe; you use a sample to make judgments about the attitudes or behavior of your universe. Let's assume you are interested in the usage and satisfaction that the adult residents of Columbus, Ohio, have with their park system. Your universe, then, is all adult residents of Columbus, which you define as those eighteen or over. You decide to exclude those living in prisons, nursing homes, and student dormitories. You may have to make other decisions about whether to include specific classes of people. Obviously you cannot query every resident, so you must draw a sample. In Chapter 7 we will discuss the more technical details of determining sample size and type of sample to use.

Three Major Types of Surveys

There are three methods of conducting surveys, each with its particular advantages and drawbacks. First, you can use **mail questionnaires.** Mail questionnaires have the advantage of being cheap. With lots of hard work, one person can conduct a mail survey. This has the disadvantage of often yielding low response rates. That is, you may send out 1,000 questionnaires but only get 200 back. You cannot assume that the 200 who did respond are like the 800 who did not respond. So even though your initial procedures in selecting the sample were random, the final result would not necessarily reflect your population. Non-responders usually come from lower-income and less-educated groups, so there might be a definite class bias in the procedures.

However there are ways to get around low response rate. One can do follow-up mailings, ideally sending another questionnaire and a request to help with the survey. A telephone follow-up can also be effective. By using these techniques you can often increase an initial poor percent response rate to 60 percent by second and third mailings. Another way to increase response rate is to keep the questionnaire short and simple; this will encourage people to respond because it will take little time and be readily understandable. And, sometimes a letter from an official of a group is useful if you are sending questionnaires to group members. For example, if you are surveying members of Chambers of Commerce and can include a letter endorsing your survey from the national Chamber of Commerce president, that should give your study more weight and thus increase your return. Similarly, if you are a manager in a state agency and are surveying local agencies, you can expect a high response rate by virtue of your position.

A second type of survey, phone surveys, is increasingly used in survey research. The Census reports that 97 percent of all households have telephones. Phone surveys usually cost more than mail questionnaires because of interviewer time. Still, response rates are usually better. Random-digit dialing overcomes problems of unlisted phone numbers and people who have moved, changed numbers, and so forth. If you have competent interviewers, you can get more complete information than often comes back on mailed questionnaires. In mail questionnaires, people often skip questions, or give incomplete answers.

Many phone surveys today used computerized survey software that assists the interviewer with moving through the questionnaire. The computer randomly selects and dials a household telephone number. The video screen displays the introduction the interviewer is to give, and the first question. After the interviewer reads these, she types in the respondent's answer to the first question and, if a correct code is entered, the next question appears. If the interviewer has entered an out-of-range code, the computer will prompt her for a correction. An out-of-range code occurs when the interviewer enters a response that is not appropriate for the range of values that a variable is to take (for example, if the interviewer entered an age of 232, or if the digit 5 was entered in a "yes or no" question which was to be coded 1 or 2). The computer also checks responses so that if, for example, an interviewer entered a yes response to a question about whether the respondent is pregnant, the computer makes sure that the sex of the respondent had been coded as female and if not, alerts the interviewer. Once an acceptable response has been obtained, it is stored in the computer and the next question appears on the screen. The software also helps the interviewers sort through different options on the surveys (if one set of questions applies to married people and another to those divorced or single, for example).

This widely used technology has several advantages. It eliminates printing and duplicating questionnaires. It ensures that values are coded within the acceptable range for each item, thus increasing coding accuracy and reducing the amount of "cleaning" of the data that must be done before analyzing it. It makes it impossible for interviewers inadvertently to skip over a question on the survey or ask the wrong set of questions to a particular person. It also allows for analysis of partial samples; the researcher does not have to wait until the survey is complete to begin examining the data.

Telephone interviews are increasingly becoming the norm in survey research. Telephone interviewing yields about as representative a sample as face-to-face interviews, which is the third type of survey method. Face-to-face interviews are generally thought to get the best response rate, but because they are expensive, and because potential respondents are concerned about personal safety issues in letting strangers (the interviewers) into their homes, face-to-face surveys are rarely used today.

There is some debate as to whether you can get at sensitive information better through personal or telephone interviews. You can conduct longer interviews in person than on the telephone, although telephone interviews averaging forty-five minutes have been done without many interviewees terminating the interview before completion. Face-to-face interviews take longer to conduct (i.e., because of interviewer travel time) and do not allow for as close a supervision of interviewers as do phone interviews. But you still get more in-depth material in person and you can use visual aids to assist in asking complex questions. Further, if you are especially concerned with obtaining information for people who are less likely to have phones (low income people), face-to-face interviews seem best. For other situations, phone interviews are at least as adequate as in-person interviews and are considerably cheaper and easier to do.

EXERCISES

3-6 List two kinds of data that you might use to answer each of the following questions.

    a. Do poor parts of town have more poorly maintained streets than richer parts of town?

    b. Will raising the bus fare lower the number of bus riders?

    c. Will the neighborhood resource officer program in a large city reduce crime and increase citizen confidence in the police?

    d. Is the fire department doing a more effective job today than years ago?

e. Has the rape crisis line improved the situation of rape victims in the community?

f. Is the street maintenance program in the community effective?

3-7 In the exercises in Chapter 2, you were called upon to construct designs to assess (a) the effectiveness of your adult diversion program and (b) the effectiveness of a neonatal program. Now that you have the design, describe and discuss your measurement and data collection procedures for each case.

Questionnaire Construction

Constructing the questionnaire is a third task in doing a survey. Whole books have been written about this, but here we will discuss a few general points about questionnaire construction. Whatever the nature and content of your questionnaire, be sure your directions within the questionnaire are clear. This is crucial whether the survey is self-administered by the respondent (as in a mail questionnaire), or administered by the interviewer. Provide some introduction to the nature of the questionnaire. Mail surveys should have a brief cover letter introducing the survey and requesting the cooperation of the respondent. Interviewers doing phone and in-person interviews should be provided with a standard set of introductory remarks serving the same purpose.

Types of Responses

Each question or set of questions should have clear instructions as to how the respondent is to answer the question. Is the respondent to provide one answer only?

"From the list below, check the item indicating the primary reason you decided to relocate your factory in Emporia."

Or can the respondent provide more than one answer?

"Why did you relocate your factory in Emporia? Check as many reasons as apply."

Sometimes respondents will be asked to rank a series of items. This is not a very good form of question. It is often hard for respondents to make fine judgments involved in a ranking, so often you will get unreliable answers. If you use this type of question make sure to specify how many items the respondent is to rank and what codes are to be used in the ranking.

From the following list, rank the three most important reasons that you relocated your factory in Emporia. Place a "1" beside the most important reason, "2" beside the second most important, and "3" beside the third most important.

_____ Access to modern transportation systems.

_____ Quality of life in the community.

_____ Local tax rates.

_____ State tax policies

_____ Characteristics of the local workforce.

_____ State labor laws.

_____ Wage rates in community.

_____ Financial incentives offered by community if I would relocate.

A better format than ranking might be to ask the respondent to rate each of the alternatives in a way such as this:

Rank the importance of each of the following reasons for your decision to relocate in Emporia by checking whether each reason was "very important," "somewhat important," "not too important," or "not at all important."

	VERY IMPORTANT	SOMEWHAT IMPORTANT	NOT TOO IMPORTANT	NOT AT ALL IMPORTANT
Access to modern transportation systems	[ ]	[ ]	[ ]	[ ]
Quality of life in the community	[ ]	[ ]	[ ]	[ ]
Local tax rates	[ ]	[ ]	[ ]	[ ]
State tax policies	[ ]	[ ]	[ ]	[ ]
Characteristics of the local workforce	[ ]	[ ]	[ ]	[ ]
State labor laws	[ ]	[ ]	[ ]	[ ]
Wage rates in community	[ ]	[ ]	[ ]	[ ]
Financial incentives offered by community if I would relocate	[ ]	[ ]	[ ]	[ ]

LENGTH AND APPEARANCE OF QUESTIONNAIRE

In general, questionnaires should not be too long, though people are much more tolerant than one might suppose. With phone interviews, forty-five minutes is probably the limit, and shorter interviews are even more desirable. Most questionnaires designed for evaluation research can probably be relatively short. Typically, evaluation will involve only one or two issue areas.

In a mail survey or a non-computer aided telephone survey, it is important that the questionnaire look professional. Such an appearance will undoubtedly help stimulate cooperation in a mail questionnaire, and will probably help convince interviewers of your competence as a survey researcher in a phone or in-person survey. With desktop publishing software and a high quality printer and copier, it is not expensive to produce professional looking questionnaires.

It goes without saying that there should be no typographical errors on a questionnaire. Further, a professional looking questionnaire contains plenty of white space on each page. Questions should not be squeezed together to save space. It may seem like a good idea to cram questions together, because it makes the questionnaire look shorter, but it is really detrimental. Too many questions per page can be confusing to the respondent or the interviewer, who may overlook a question or be confused about the possible responses. Such a questionnaire also looks messy and unprofessional.

For computer assisted surveys, you need to check the flow of the questionnaire very carefully. Where there are different sets of questions for different types of individuals, make sure your different branches work correctly.

Content

In many policy surveys, you will want to ask the respondent about a series of personal demographic items: age, educational level, perhaps income, and so forth. These standard questions allow you to compare attitudes, information, or behavior among different population groups, and they often serve as your control variables. Personal questions of this nature, except where they are used to screen respondents, should be asked toward the middle or end of the questionnaire; they are not very interesting to the respondent and may arouse a defensive reaction if asked too early. However you may have to ask some of them early, such as how many people there are in the household, ages of family members, and so forth. But save income, education, and other status questions until the end. Put them all at the end in mail questionnaires.

In a questionnaire or interview schedule, you are interested in obtaining information about independent and dependent variables in order to test one or more hypotheses. If your approach is survey research, you probably are concerned with utilization of, and public attitudes about, a program or policy. Thus you will need to construct questions that deal with usage, satisfaction, or whatever other variables you are investigating. Generally, you will be measuring behavior, information, and attitudes in addition to demographic characteristics. Research in Practice 3C shows types of survey questions you will want to avoid because they give poor results.

Behavioral measures ask the respondent to recall whether he or she engaged in particular kinds of behavior in the past day, week, month, year, and so on. For example, in a study of citizen satisfaction with the park system, you would want to find out how many times the respondent has visited each park in the past month. Having this kind of information can allow you to see if satisfaction with the recreational services varies according to use. In asking for behavioral data, it is unwise to ask the respondent to recall too far back. Studies have shown that people's sense of when something occurred is not very good, even for important events like a marriage or birth of a child.

If your sample is large enough, you might ask about things they did the past month. If you are trying to get at information that is rare (i.e., being a

Research in Practice 3C

EXAMPLES OF BAD SURVEY QUESTIONS

There are some general rules in constructing questions for surveys. Here are some examples of bad survey questions and a brief explanation of why they are bad.

1. *Problem:* Respondents are unlikely to have the required information.

   Sample question: The courts should change their abortion rulings.

   Analysis and solution: This is a bad question because the respondents cannot be assumed to have the information required to answer the question. Few people keep up with Supreme Court rulings. Many respondents will not even know the general rulings, let alone anything specific that you are trying to find out. If you want to know where a respondent stands on abortion, a better solution is to ask questions as to whether the respondent approves of abortion under certain specific conditions that you name. One question could deal with abortion if the woman had been raped, another if the couple does not want another child, and so forth. If you are interested in attitudes toward the court, a more general question about whether the respondent has confidence in the court might be appropriate.

2. *Problem:* Negative wording.

   Sample question: The police should not increase their enforcement of the driving-while-intoxicated law.

   Analysis and solution: In general, questions that contain a negative lead to misunderstanding. You are asking the respondent to agree to a negative condition. You might ask the respondent to agree or disagree with the question in another form such as "The police enforce the drunk driving laws adequately in our state."

crime victim), then you may have to ask about a longer time period, but the information will be less reliable.

Information may be sought with either open-ended or closed-ended questions. Open-ended questions are those in which a set of possible responses are not read to the respondent; closed-ended questions are those in which a set of possible response questions are read to the respondent. An example of an open-ended question is: "What do you think of Lincoln's parks?" A closed-ended question is: "How do you rate the quality of Lincoln's parks: excellent, good, fair, poor, terrible?" Remember, in getting attitudinal measures, there may be many dimensions of satisfaction with parks (or anything else) to

3. *Problem:* Double meaning.

Sample question: The city should turn garbage collection over to a private agency and spend the savings from that on keeping the streets cleaner.

Analysis and solution: Here you are really asking two separate questions: Should the city turn garbage collection over to a private agency? Should more money be spent on street cleaning? The two aspects of the question may be unrelated in most respondents' minds. Perhaps they do want privatization of the garbage service, for reasons other than keeping the streets cleaner. Or perhaps they think more money should be spent on keeping the streets clean but do not believe in privatization of garbage collection. The conclusion: Do not ask two questions in one. Each question should ask about one, and only one, point.

4. *Problem:* Vague wording.

Sample question: When you were growing up, did you live on a farm or in the city?

Analysis and solution: This is a bad item because the phrase "when you were growing up" is too vague. Perhaps the respondent lived in a city until she was six and on a farm when she was sixteen. It is better to pinpoint a specific age, and ask about that. Then all respondents will be comparable.

5. *Problem:* Omitted possible responses.

Sample question: When you were sixteen, did you live on a farm or in the city?

Analysis and solution: This version eliminates the problems referred to above, but the choice "on a farm or in the city" is also vague and does not include all the possibilities. For example, perhaps some respondents lived in the suburbs or in small towns. A better version would be to list specific possibilities from which the respondent could choose: cities over 100,000, cities from 25,000 to 100,000, towns from 2,500 to 25,000, towns less than 2,500, and farms. This adds specificity and includes all possibilities.

consider. For example, in addition to general satisfaction, you might ask about satisfaction with equipment, safety, cleanliness, helpfulness and availability of staff, sanitary conditions, and other dimensions of satisfaction.

Sometimes you want to assess information. Have you ever heard of the crisis line? The women's shelter? The office assisting low income people with heating needs during the winter? The local government coordinating council? It is useful to assess information before attitudes. There is no point in trying to find out attitudes if people have no information on which to base the attitudes. Under those circumstances, the information given will probably not be very useful.

QUESTION FORMAT

The format of the questionnaire is important. Plenty of space should be left for answers. Ideally, a box should be included in front of each possible answer.

☐ Excellent
☐ Good
☐ Poor

When typing questionnaires, you can substitute square or curved brackets for the box by typing the left bracket, leaving a space, then typing the right bracket:

[   ] Excellent
[   ] Good
[   ] Poor

Although some people prefer to use square brackets as they better approximate a box, parentheses as brackets ( ) are all right too. Do not, however, try to type an actual box by using slashes and underscores:

/ ‾/ Excellent
/ ‾/ Good
/ ‾/ Poor

These not only take much longer to produce than simple bracketing, they look unprofessional and, when stacked on top of each other, messy. You should also avoid open blanks:

_____ Excellent
_____ Good
_____ Poor

Such blanks have a tendency to lead respondents to make larger than necessary check marks. This may make it difficult for you to figure out which response was intended. The same type of problem can arise if you ask respondents to circle the correct answer.

BRANCHING, OR CONTINGENCY, QUESTIONS

Some questions are to be answered only if the respondent answered a prior question in a certain way. These are called **contingency questions**. For example, to determine individual reactions to a particular program, you would want to first find out if a person had used the program. Those who had used it would be asked questions about it, those who had not should be routed to another part of the questionnaire.

In computer aided surveying, you program the computer to handle branching. In printed surveys, there are two ways to handle this type of branching. The first is by use of arrows:

Have any of your children attended a Head Start program in this community during the last five years?

   ┌─[ ] Yes
   │ [ ] No
   └──────→ How would you rate its quality:

                [ ] Excellent
                [ ] Good
      ┌─   [ ] Poor
      └──────────→ What didn't you like about the program:
                       [ ] Quality of instruction
                       [ ] Physical facilities
                       [ ] Competence of teachers
                       [ ] Too few instructors
                       [ ] Type of skills taught
                       [ ] Other (*list*) _____

This procedure works well if the arrow leads to only a few questions. However, if those who gave a particular response in the original contingency question are to answer a long series of questions, stretching over more than a page, the following format is better:

1. Have any of your children attended a Head Start program in this community during the past five years?
    [ ] Yes Please answer questions 2 through 10 and then continue with question 11.
    [ ] No Please skip to question 11.

Ordering Questions in a Questionnaire

In constructing a questionnaire, you need to think about the order of questions. The order will depend both on considerations of format and substance. In a typical survey, respondents are often asked to answer a variety of questions that use the same format (perhaps Likert items) or questions where respondents are asked to rank the importance of several conditions in their decision (for example, to relocate a factory). Such questions should be grouped together.

Grouping makes the respondent's work easier, saves time, and may make the responses more parallel; that is, an "agree" response to one item is likely to mean the same as an "agree" response in another item. When widely separated, the comparability may be lost.

On the other hand, a long series of items with similar formats may lead to what is called response set. This means that a subject might simply check "agree" to all the responses or "disagree" to all without considering their substance. This is especially likely to happen if the survey researcher words almost all the questions so that "agree" can only mean one attitude (satisfaction or dissatisfaction). For example, if we were measuring attitudes toward city parks, it would not be a good idea if all the items required an "agree" response if the person was satisfied with the parks:

	STRONGLY AGREE	AGREE	UNCERTAIN	STRONGLY DISAGREE	DISAGREE
City parks are clean	[ ]	[ ]	[ ]	[ ]	[ ]
City parks provide adequate children's playground equipment	[ ]	[ ]	[ ]	[ ]	[ ]
City parks are safe	[ ]	[ ]	[ ]	[ ]	[ ]
I enjoy the time I spend in the parks	[ ]	[ ]	[ ]	[ ]	[ ]

Instead, some agree responses should mean satisfaction, while some should indicate dissatisfaction. Similarly, some disagree responses should mean satisfaction, while others should denote dissatisfaction. This will not necessarily eliminate response set, but it encourages respondents to read or listen to the items more carefully. Further, those responding "agree" or "disagree" to all the items would fall at the middle of the scale and be less likely to bias your findings. The following are examples of items worded to reduce response set:

The city parks are clean.
City parks need more children's playground equipment.
City parks are unsafe.
I enjoy the time I spend in the parks.

Substance also determines the ordering of questions in a survey. Do not ask questions early in the questionnaire that might cause a bias in later questions. If you have asked respondents a number of questions concerning crime in America then later ask them to name America's most significant problems, the incidence of those who say "crime" will be greater than if the crime questions were saved until last. For this reason, general evaluative questions are usually asked early in the survey (What kind of job do you think the local schools are doing? What are the issues you think are important in this election campaign?). Sometimes there is no way around the problem of contamination, but the researcher should consider the order carefully.

Questions dealing with similar subject matter should be grouped together. The reason for this is that when respondents start a particular train of thought, asking several questions about that subject is less distracting than jumping from questions about crime to recreation to transportation, and back again. Sensitive questions should probably be asked in the middle of the questionnaire after an initial rapport is established but before interviewee fatigue sets in. But they should not be asked too early, so that if the respondent gets angry and decides to terminate the interview, most information will already have been gathered. Appropriate transitional lead-ins to different sections of the questionnaire are helpful. "Now I would like to ask you what you think of the schools of this community."

TAKING CARE IN WORDING

Another important aspect of questionnaire construction is to remember that extremely small changes in wording can cause shifts in responses. For example, a much greater proportion of the public will support more government spending to "help the needy" than to pay for "welfare." Wording of questions is especially important when assessing change over time. To get reliable before-and-after data you must word the question exactly the same. Sometimes that means that survey researchers involved in longitudinal studies will stick with an item they know is not very good. If they change the item, then they will lose comparability over time. For example, the national election studies done at the Center for Political Studies at the University of Michigan since the 1950s have asked respondents about their feelings of control over their government (a concept called political efficacy). They know that some of these items are not very good (for example, asking respondents to agree or disagree that "Voting is the only way that people like me have a say in government"), but they continue to ask that in order to continue their temporal series. Of course, new and better items are added each year, but the old items are retained for the sake of comparability. Consumers of policy research need to be especially wary of longitudinal survey data. A careless, not very knowledgeable, or dishonest researcher could find "changes" in public opinion about controversial events and policies simply because of slightly changed question wording.

Pretesting a Questionnaire

Never go into the field with a questionnaire until you have pretested it. By this we mean that you should ask a small group of people similar in characteristics (if possible) to your ultimate sample, to complete the questionnaire. If it is to be a written questionnaire, ask them to fill it out themselves; if it is to be a phone or in-person survey, administer it to them in that way. Inevitably, you will find that questions that mean a particular thing to you do not mean that to everyone else. You may also find problems with question format or the sequence of questions asked. Pretesting allows you to fix problems before wasting time and money administering the questionnaire to dozens or hundreds of people.

How big should a pretest be? There is no hard and fast rule, but you should generally sample at least ten people and probably no more than thirty. Research in Practice 3D discusses some points that policy researchers should keep in mind when doing citizen surveys.

Research in Practice 3D

PITFALLS FOR OFFICIALS USING CITIZEN SURVEYS

On the basis of their experience with citizen surveys, Webb and Hatry of the Urban Institute warn public officials about some pitfalls of relying too heavily on these surveys. They list several "bewares," some of which are summarized:

1. "Beware of opinion polls on complex issues about which citizens lack information." Examples: Asking citizens to rank or evaluate little-known public services or little-discussed issues.

2. "Beware of citizen responses reflecting short-run considerations to the neglect of long-term problems." Examples: Citizens will respond to short-term crises, such as a crime wave, major street closings, or economic problems. Officials must deal with these problems but must also take a long-term view.

3. "Beware of surveys that appear to interfere with elections." Webb and Hatry warn officials never to appear to try to be biasing an election or referendum by a single-issue survey too near to the time of the election.

4. "Beware of using surveys to hide from controversy and responsibility." Webb and Hatry warn that sometimes managers should not just "ride with the tide" but should exert leadership to change or modify opinions. They urge that surveys be designed to compare clientele groups so that differences in services to one or more groups can be highlighted even in the face of majority satisfaction.

5. "Beware of question wording—what is said or not said can be misleading." Examples: Small shifts in wording of question items or in alternative responses offered can change the types of responses given. Hatry and Webb suggest the use of experienced survey researchers to minimize this problem.

6. "Beware of nonrepresentative results if inadequate procedures are used." Example: If people do not respond because of inadequate sampling (use of out-of-date or biased listings, for example) or high refusal rate, then the results may be invalid. One should always compare demographic characteristics of the sample against the characteristics of the universe which the sample is to represent.

SOURCE: Kenneth Webb and Harry P. Hatry, *Obtaining Citizen Feedback: The Application of Citizen Surveys to Local Governments* (Washington, D.C.: The Urban Institute, 1973), pp. 33–39.

Research in Practice 3E

OBJECTIVES AND PRINCIPAL EFFECTIVENESS MEASURES FOR
SOLID WASTE COLLECTION

Suppose you are interested in evaluating the effectiveness of the solid
waste disposal services in your community. What kinds of measures of effectiveness could you use? The following list, compiled by Harry Hatry,
should stretch your thinking and give you clues for constructing measures
in other policy areas.

OBJECTIVE	QUALITY CHARACTERISTIC	SPECIFIC MEASURE	DATA COLLECTION SOURCE/PROCEDURE
Pleasing aesthetics	Street, alley, and neighborhood cleanliness	Percentage of: (a) Streets (b) Alleys, the appearance of which is rated as satisfactory (or as unsatisfactory)	Trained observer ratings
		Percentage of: (a) Households (b) Businesses rating their neighborhood cleanliness as satisfactory (or as unsatisfactory)	a. Citizen survey b. Business survey
	Offensive odors	Percentage of: (a) Households (b) Businesses reporting offensive odors from solid wastes	a. Citizen survey b. Business survey
	Objectionable noise incidents	Percentage of: (a) Households (b) Businesses reporting objectionable noise from solid waste collection operations	a. Citizen survey b. Business survey
Health and safety	Health hazards	Number and percentage of blocks with one or more health hazards	Trained observer ratings
	Fire hazards	Number and percentage of blocks with one or more fire hazards	Trained observer ratings

Research in Practice 3E *(continued)*

OBJECTIVE	QUALITY CHARACTERISTIC	SPECIFIC MEASURE	DATA COLLECTION SOURCE/PROCEDURE
	Fires involving uncollected waste	Number of fires involving uncollected waste	Fire department records
	Health hazards and unsightly appearance	Number of abandoned automobiles	Trained observer ratings
	Rodent hazard	Percentage of: (a) Households (b) Businesses reporting having seen rats on their blocks in the last year	a. Citizen survey b. Business survey
	Rodent bites	Number of rodent bites reported per 1,000 population	City or county health records
Minimum citizen inconvenience	Missed or late collections	Number and percent-collection routes not completed on schedule	Sanitation department records
		Percentage of: (a) Households (b) Businesses reporting missed collections	a. Citizen survey b. Business survey
	Spillage of trash and garbage during collections	Percentage of: (a) Households (b) Businesses reporting spillagae by collection crews	a. Citizen survey b. Business survey
	Damage to private property by collection crews	Percentage of: (a) Households (b) Businesses reporting damage to property by collection crews	a. Citizen survey b. Business survey
General citizen satisfaction	Citizen complaints	Number of verified citizen complaints by type per 1,000 households served	Sanitation department records

SOURCE: Harry P. Hatry et al., *How Effective Are Your Community Services?* Washington, D.C.: The Urban Institute, 1992, p. 8. Copyright 1992. The Urban Institute.

Research in Practice 3F

SUMMARY OF PRINCIPAL EFFECTIVENESS MEASURES FOR FIRE
PROTECTION SERVICE

Suppose you are interested in evaluating the effectiveness of fire protection services in your community. Think about what measures you might choose; then compare your ideas with the list below.

OBJECTIVE	QUALITY CHARACTERISTIC	SPECIFIC MEASURE	DATA COLLECTION SOURCE/PROCEDURE
Overall loss minimization	Civilian casualties	Number and rate of civilian injuries and deaths per 100,000 population	Data generally available today, though not always expressed as rates.[1]
	Firefighter casualties	Number of firefighter injuries and deaths per 100 employees	Casualty reports
	Property loss	Direct dollar loss from fire per $1,000 property served	Insurance company or fire department estimates
Suppression	Fire-fighting Effectiveness (dollar loss)	Average direct dollar loss per fire for fires not out on arrival, by size on arrival and type of occupancy	Necessary data (except size on arrival) generally available
	Fire-fighting Effectiveness— spread	Percentage of fires (not out on arrival of first fire unit) in which spread after arrival is limited to x square feet (or y percent or one step of the extent-of-flame scaled)[2] by size on arrival and type of occupancy	Spread after arrival is the difference between the extent of fire damage on arrival of first unit and at extinguishment as estimated by fire officer at scene. Note that this measure is not the overall extent of damage
	Fire-fighting Effectiveness- time	Time to control or confirm spread has stopped[3] by size on arrival and type of occupancy	Data should be recorded by fire officer at scene or taken from dispatcher records

Research in Practice 3F *(continued)*

OBJECTIVE	QUALITY CHARACTERISTIC	SPECIFIC MEASURE	DATA COLLECTION SOURCE/PROCEDURE
	Speed of providing service	Percentage of response times that are less (or more) than x minutes. Average response time by type of fire	Response time would be defined as "time elapsed from time fire is reported to the fire department to time of arrival of first unit at scene." This data is often available from fire department's dispatching centers[4]
	Rescue effectiveness	Number of "saves" versus number of casualties	Data collected by fire officers at the scene. Data should be reported separately by risk to victim and type of rescue action
Prevention	Reported fire incidence rate	Number of reported fires per 1,000 population total and by type of residential occupancy[5]	Data generally available
	Reported building fire incidence rate	Number of building fires per 1,000 occupancies by selected occupancy types (e.g., single-family dwellings, duplexes, apartments, mobile homes, small stores) and by fire size	Number of occupancies by type may be estimated from planning department data (for residences) or from prefire inspection records for commercial/industrial occupancies. Fire size estimated by fire officer at scene
	Reported plus unreported building fire incidence rate	Number of unreported plus building fires per 1,000 households (or businesses) by type of occupancy	Survey of a representative sample of citizens and fire incident reports. Reasons for underreporting should also be solicited

Research in Practice 3F *(continued)*

OBJECTIVE	QUALITY CHARACTERISTIC	SPECIFIC MEASURE	DATA COLLECTION SOURCE/PROCEDURE
	Prevention of fires	Percentage and rate of fires that are relatively preventable by inspection or education	Intended for internal fire department analysis based on judgments as to relatively preventability of various types of fires[6]
	Prefire inspection effectiveness	Rates of fires in inspected versus uninspected (or frequently inspected versus infrequently inspected)[7] occupancy and risk class	Data obtained by linking fire incident reports to fire inspection files (probably feasible manually in most jurisdictions under one million population)
	Apprehension effectiveness for fire-related crimes	Clearance and conviction rates for arson, incendiarism, false alarms, and code violations	Data obtained by linking fire incident and fire inspection data to police department arrest records on case dispositions
	Deterrence effectiveness for fire-related crimes	Number of (a) incendiary and suspicious origin fires per 1,000 population, (b) false alarms per 1,000 population.	Data generally available
	Detection-response effectiveness	Distribution of sizes of fires at arrival	Sizes are estimated by fire officer at scene
Overall	Citizen satisfaction	Percentage of population rating fire protection service as satisfactory	Survey of a representative sample of citizens. Data should be reported separately for persons with firsthand contact with fire department. Reasons for dissatisfaction also might be solicited.

Research in Practice 3F *(continued)*

OBJECTIVE	QUALITY CHARACTERISTIC	SPECIFIC MEASURE	DATA COLLECTION SOURCE/PROCEDURE
			Separate surveys might be used for businesses and households.

[1]Also take the workforce and visitor population into account, casualty rates per 1,000 average daily population, including residents, workers, and visitors, might also be considered.

[2]It may be useful to report the "Spread after arrival" in three parts: the spread in flame damage; the spread in total fire damage (including smoke and heat); and the spread in total damage from fire and fire fighting. Although data on the amount of damage from fire fighting for a particular fire are hard to evaluate without knowing a great deal about the fire, cumulative data on fire-fighting damage might give some clues to performance over time. Measures other than of flame damage have not been tested for reliability, however.

[3]Other useful versions of this measure are the mean and median times to control, also by size of fire and occupancy type.

[4]To be of most use, the data would also be collected so as to permit classification by the major components of response time; time from call to dispatch; time from dispatch to arrival; and time from arrival to putting water (or other extinguishing substances) on the fire.

[5]The term occupancy refers to a piece of property in terms of its use. For example, the following might be considered separate occupancy types: detached houses containing only one household, duplexes, apartments, sheds, drug stores, warehouses, and blocks of offices with a single owner.

There may be more than one occupancy in a particular building and some occupancies for example, phone booths, garbage dumps, and piers, are not buildings at all. Analysis of fire effectiveness data by occupancy type is useful because it compares experience among places with the same kinds of materials present and the same kinds of activities going on.

[6]For example, fires started by inflammables stored near ignition source, or in buildings with firecode violations relevant to the fire start, would be "highly preventable." Fires started by hidden equipment defects not common to that equipment would be relatively unpreventable. Fires might also be classified by the government action needed to aid in preventing, for example, the percentage of fires for which an inspection a week before the fire would have detected a hazard, or the percentage of fires in which building code change would have removed the cause.

[7]For categories in which almost all occupancies are inspected, as is usually the case for commercial occupancies, it may not be possible to clearly separate those frequently inspected from those not, within a given risk class. In that case, statistics on times since last inspection for fires and for buildings in general may be used to determine how much the likelihood of fire increases (if it does) as the time since last inspection increases. (If inspections are effective, there should probably be fewer fires in more recently inspected occupancies.)

SOURCE: Harry P. Hatry et al., *How Effective Are Your Community Services?* Washington, D.C.: The Urban Institute, 1977, pp. 57–60. Copyright 1977. The Urban Institute.

Summary

As a public manager or a policy analyst, you will not often be in the position of having to formally test hypotheses; rather you will have to produce simple data fairly quickly. Whether you are engaged in major research efforts or whether you are simply charged with the task of quickly collecting and analyzing some data about your own or other agencies, the problem of data collection is an important one. In thinking about your data collection task, remember the following points:

1. Usually more than one kind of data is appropriate in any project. If your first choice is too expensive or unobtainable, think about alternative sources. Research in Practice 3E and 3F provide some interesting insights into alternative measures of productivity of two widely varying types of public services, waste disposal and fire protection. These tables, drawn from Harry Hatry et al., *How Effective Are Your Community Services?* show a great deal of imagination and thought. Still, the variety of measures illustrated there can also be applied to almost any other type of public service.
2. Turn to existing data first. If it is not appropriate, collect the data yourself. Before launching such an effort, check to make sure that your agency or other agencies do not have the material you need or that it is not already in published form. This preliminary checking may save a lot of time in the long run.
3. Do surveys only when a survey is the most appropriate form of data and there are no other surveys that give you the information you need.
4. Don't be afraid to call on other experts for help in locating fugitive data.
5. Always respect the confidentiality of any individual records to which you are given access.

Exercise

3-8 Assume you are doing a survey of residents of your community concerning their satisfaction with the quality of local public schools. Construct a questionnaire of at least twenty items. Assume the questionnaire would be given in a telephone interview. Your questionnaire should include an appropriate introduction and transition sentences. Include at least one set of items for an index. Do not forget to ask demographic information you believe to be pertinent.

KEY TERMS

Nominal level of measurement
Ordinal level of measurement
Interval level of measurement
Ratio level of measurement
Validity
Face validity
Predictive validity
Content validity
Construct validity
Reliable measure
Test-retest method

Split-half technique
Scale
Likert scale
Mail questionnaires
Phone survey
Computer-assisted telephone interview
Contingency questions

FOR FURTHER HELP

Babbie, Earl. *Survey Research Methods,* Second Edition. Belmont, Calif.: Wadsworth, 1990. A good handbook for conducting survey research.

Bader, Genia and Catherine Rossi. *Focus Groups: A Step by Step Guide.* The Bader Group, 1998.

Converse, Jean and Stanley Presser. *Survey Questions: Handcrafting the Standardized Questionnaire.* Sage, 1987. An excellent source to consult if you are putting together a questionnaire.

Fowler, Floyd J., Jr. 1993. *Survey Research Methods.* Newbury Park, California: Sage Publications. An excellent handbook to guide you through the stages of survey research.

Hatry, Harry P., et al. *How Effective Are Your Community Services?* Washington, D.C.: The Urban Institute, 1992. Good source for discussion on where to get measures of community services.

Murphy, Jerome T. Getting the Facts: *A Fieldwork Guide for Evaluators and Policy Analysts.* Santa Monica, Calif.: Goodyear Publishing, 1980. A "how-to" book on conducting intensive interviews and doing other onsite research to conduct policy evaluation.

Nachmias, David, and Chava Nachmias. *Research Methods in the Social Sciences,* Fifth Edition. New York: St. Martin's Press, 1995.

4

Using the Computer in
Policy Research

Computers are invaluable tools for policy research. They can help you analyze data quickly and efficiently, aid in the management of fiscal and personnel records necessary to understand your organization, facilitate research through the use of the web, and speed the preparation and editing of research reports.

Today the computer is a ubiquitous tool in all public and private offices. The technological revolution offers increasing access to ever more powerful computing. Think about the evolution of the room-size computer of forty years ago to the five pound laptop computer of today! Any specific information about software we provide you in this text is likely to be outdated in a short time (and for this reason, this chapter does not focus on specific uses of specific software).

Despite the pervasiveness of computers, many novice researchers are often quite timid about using the computer for anything other than E-mail and web browsing. Some people are especially intimidated by using them for data analysis. Sometimes a new researcher will say "I should use the computer, but it's just as easy to do the data analysis with my hand calculator since I only have fifty cases." Our advice is that if an adequate computer is available, always plan your data collection procedures so that you can use it when you have even the simplest statistics to calculate. There are several reasons for this:

1. User-friendly statistical packages make it easy for the computer novice to do all sorts of data analysis on the computer. No knowledge of programming is necessary.
2. Even with only a few cases, the researcher rarely wants one frequency distribution or average value. Rather, the analyst will usually want to examine the data in many ways. To do so by hand means laboriously recalculating every statistic. For example, assume you are examining crime incidence data for fifty precincts in your city. You may initially think that all you want to do with the data is to examine the distribution of crime rates. After collecting the data, however, you decide that it would be useful to compare these crime rates to income levels in the

precinct, to the racial composition of each precinct, and to the type of housing stock predominating in each precinct. By the time you do even one of these comparisons, you would be better off having put the data on the computer.

3. Computer analyses are, on the whole, less subject to error than human calculation. You eliminate one source of error when you let the computer perform the calculations. Although you can certainly make mistakes entering the data, the computer doesn't make subtraction mistakes, misplace the decimal point, take the square root instead of squaring, or forget to divide by a constant. Of course there are plenty of sources of error in any data analysis no matter whether you use the computer or not, but at least you can eliminate one kind.

Using the computer is relatively simple, saves time, and eliminates some kinds of errors: all good reasons to try your hand. But throughout the process outlined below, consult with knowledgeable computer users at your installation. They can tell you about the programs available and help with the details necessary to give you access to the computer. It is also useful to consult with someone familiar with social science research. Some computer experts would be at a loss to assist with the data coding and formatting discussed below.

LEARNING THE JARGON

SOFTWARE AND HARDWARE

Before proceeding, some definitions are in order. You will hear discussions of computer "hardware" and "software." **Hardware** refers to the actual machines, the computers themselves. **Software** refers to the languages and systems used to program the computer. An IBM PC is a piece of hardware, the word processing program you use on it is an example of software.

TYPES OF COMPUTERS

You will also hear about desktops, laptops, and servers. **Desktops** and **laptops** are personal computers distinguished by their size and cost. Costing from a few hundred to several thousand dollars (and more for specialized, high capacity machines), both desktops and laptops have increasingly large capacities to store and process data. The average desktop has greater speed and capacity than the average laptop, but some laptops are considerably faster and more capacious than some desktops. Laptops generally weigh less than seven pounds and are more expensive than desktops.

Servers are computers, usually desktops, that are configured with extra large amounts of memory and speed so that they can serve as the hub for other computers connected to them through a network. The advantage of a network is that software, such as data analysis software, calendars, backup facilities, or any other application, can be shared by all users rather than needing to be purchased for each computer separately.

Desktop and laptop computers can be linked to a server permanently, through Ethernet cables similar to telephone lines but with higher speed and capacity, or temporarily over a standard telephone line through what is called a **modem**. Modems (which can be external or internal to the computer) allow those who are away from their offices the opportunity to connect to their office networks from anywhere in the nation, and increasingly from most places in the world. Wireless connections are beginning to be used but do not yet (as of 2000) compete in terms of speed, security and accuracy.

MEMORY, CAPACITY, AND SPEED

In discussing computers, you will hear phrases such as "the computer has 32M (megs) of memory." The "M" stands for megabyte. The term "memory" refers to the amount of information the computer can store internally at one time. This includes its own operating instructions as well as information that the user enters, such as a specific software program, a set of data, or a text of a paper. A 32M machine would allow thousands of pages of text and complex computer software.

A megabyte is somewhat more than 1 million bytes of memory. A byte, in turn, is the primary measure of capacity that you as a user need to be concerned with. One byte stores one piece of information, such as the number eight or the letter Z. A byte is actually composed of bits (which stand for binary digits), each bit containing either a 0 or a 1. The combination of bits within each byte represents the letter, number, or other character that the user enters.

The first personal computers had only 8 or 16 kilobytes of memory (a kilobyte is 1,024 bytes of memory). Now computers with sixty-four megabytes, and more, of memory are common.

Another aspect of capacity that you will hear about in shopping for or discussing computers is disk space. Hard disk space is simply the permanent storage system of your computer, storing not just the programs and data sources you are using at the moment, but all the software, data bases, and other files you have saved on your computer. Currently disk space is discussed in terms of gigabytes, with multiple "gig" disk drives being common. (A gigabyte is 1,000 times a megabyte, or about 1 billion bytes.) Many computers also have disk drives holding portable diskettes or CD-ROM drives. These drives allow you to back up files, or transfer files from one machine to another.

Another indicator of computer functioning that you should be familiar with is its processing speed, indicated by megahertz (MHz). The larger the number, the faster the processing of the computer. The standards are increasing rapidly, so what was considered "fast" a few years ago (200 MHz) is already antique compared to newer models with many times that speed.

OPERATING SYSTEMS

Put simply, the **operating system** is what allows the user to talk to the computer and the network. It enables the operator to access the disks, communicate with the network, provide instructions to the printer, use the computer's memory, and read from the monitor. The operating system generally contains a standard set of commands so that the user can easily perform routine operations such as access, modify, copy, and erase files and other essential tasks. In the early days of computers, each manufacturer had a unique operating system. Currently, there is considerable standardization, with IBM and its clones using one system, and Macintosh products using another system. Windows 2000 is an example of an operating system.

PLANNING FOR COMPUTER ANALYSIS

Consider the needs of efficient data analysis from the time you begin planning your research design and data collection procedures. Keeping these needs in mind as you design data collection forms can save you time later.

Let's assume you are a state government personnel department analyst undertaking a study of job classifications and salary as they relate to employee and minority status. You are interested in the relationship between an employee's gender and minority status and the employee's salary and job classification, controlling for training, experience, and years with the state civil service.

CODING

You have decided that your unit of analysis will be the individual; that is, you will collect data on each of the state's 5,000 employees. You then consider what information you want to collect for each employee and decide that eight variables will be sufficient for the needs of your study:

1. Gender.
2. Ethnic status.
3. Year joined the state's workforce.
4. Years of education.
5. Year started in current position.
6. Annual salary.
7. Job classification.
8. Birth year.

In addition, you want to be able to identify each worker with a unique identification number. This is important in case you want to verify data, update the files, or correct erroneous information. If you are using confidential information, such as the personnel study here, it might not be appropriate to code the person's name into the data file. There is no need for the name if a unique identification number has been assigned. Sometimes, however, a case name is useful, as when the units of analysis are cities, states, countries, or other identifiable but not confidential entities. In those cases, having the name can allow you to print out data associated with each city or county by name. Even in those cases, a unique identification number is useful.

How would you go about setting this up for the computer? A first step would be to develop codes for each category of each of the variables. In recording data for each individual employee, you would need a unique code for each relevant category of each variable. For example, for the variable "gender," you would decide on a code for males and females; perhaps you would code females as 1 and males as 0, or vice versa. Remember that for nominal-level data, the numeric values you assign need not be in any particular order. Here are a few other things to remember in developing codes:

1. It is generally better to use numeric than alphabetic codes for variables you will analyze. If you use alphabetic codes, you will have to recode them for statistical analysis. You cannot add or multiply an A and a C in the same way you can add or multiply a 1 and a 3. Thus, alphabetic codes will needlessly complicate things when you try to use them in statistical analysis because they ultimately must be translated into numbers. So use numeric codes to begin with, if possible.

2. Allow enough codes for the number of categories you have. That is, if you have fifty job classifications you deem relevant, have a numeric code from 1 to 50. As you code the data, you will probably find that you will need a few more codes (51 through 59, for example, for cases uncodable in the normal sequence). The Y2K problem was caused by programmers using only two codes for year, dropping the nineteen from numbers like 1953 or 1999. That made sense in the early days of computing because the storage was so limited, as we have described. Now there is no reason to try to save space in that way.

3. For each variable, assign one unique number to represent missing information. Usually the numbers assigned are 9, 99, or 999 depending on whether you have a one-, two-, or three-column code. In survey research, coders sometimes use three different missing codes: 7 or 97 where the respondent doesn't know; 8 or 98 where the question is inappropriate (i.e., asking an eighty-year-old woman how many more children she intends to have); and 9 or 99 for a refusal. In other kinds of research, one missing data code is usually adequate. It is usually not a good idea to assign a 0 as the missing data code because in some cases 0 can be a legitimate code (for example, as in a question asking for the number of children, previous marriages, or number of previous arrests).

After you decide on the codes, prepare a code book or code sheet so that those doing the coding will have precise guidelines as to how they are to assign values for each variable. Your code sheet might look like this:

Sample Code Book Page

Variable 1. Gender
1. Female.
2. Male.
9. Missing information.

Variable 2. Minority or ethnic status
1. Black.
2. White, non-Spanish-speaking, or surname.
3. Spanish-speaking, or surname.
4. Asian.
5. All others.

Variable 3. Years in state employment
Code from 0 up. Round to nearest year. If less than six months, code lower year; if more than six months, code higher year.
99. Missing information.

Variable 4. Educational achievement
1. Less than high school diploma.
2. High school diploma.
3. High school diploma plus technical training.
4. High school diploma plus some college.
5. College degree—bachelor's level.
6. Advanced college degree.
9. Missing information.

Variable 5. Years in current position
Round to nearest year from 0 up.
99. Missing information.

Variable 6. Salary
Code exact yearly salary. If an hourly employee, calculate yearly salary on basis of 2,080 hours per year.
99. Missing information.

Variable 7. Job classification
1. Administrator or official.
2. Professional.
3. Paraprofessional.
4. Technical.
5. Skilled crafts.
6. Protective service.
7. Maintenance workers.
8. Clerical workers.
9. Missing information.

Sample Code Book Page *(continued)*

Variable 8. Birth year
99. Missing information.

The code book should also indicate special instructions for coding. In the example above, there would also probably need to be special instructions for coding the eight job classification categories unless that classification came directly from the employee's file. Instructions about how to differentiate technical training from college might be important too.

Even though you are doing the coding yourself and think you can remember all the special decision rules you use, you should still write them down. Perhaps you will have an assistant assigned to help you. Or perhaps you will be interrupted in your coding task and have to return to it after a month or year's interval. You may even want to recheck some values long after you have finished coding and when you are near completion of the analysis. In any of these cases, written instructions are necessary to ensure consistency. Furthermore, any report of your findings should describe how you classified the data. It is much easier to copy this information from your code book than to try to remember what you did.

ENTERING THE DATA

There are three common ways of entering the data for use in a statistical package. One is to enter the data on a spreadsheet, such as Excel or Lotus Notes (see p. 97 for a discussion of spreadsheets). In doing so, each row would represent one employee. Each column represents one variable (gender, education, for example). Figure 4-1 shows how the first four rows of such a spreadsheet might look for a data set comprised of states as units of analysis and population characteristics as variables.

Before entering data on a spreadsheet, make sure that the statistical package you plan to use can read the spreadsheet program. In other words, if you develop an Excel spreadsheet, verify that your data analysis program reads Excel. In SPSSPC, (See Research in Practice 4A), if you click on "file," then "open," at the top of your screen, options include opening Excel, Lotus Notes, or dBase files. Once you open the data, you will have an opportunity to define the variables' names, missing values, and other information by clicking on "data," and then "define variables."

A second method of entry is one that is built into standard statistical packages. For example, in SPSS, one of the choices when you log in is "Type in data." If you choose that option, the program offers you an empty matrix into which you can type both variable names and the data itself. If you click on

FIGURE 4-1   State Populations by Ethnic and Racial Origin

ID	STATE	ASIAN	HISPANIC	AMERICAN INDIAN	AFRICAN AMERICAN
1	Alabama	28,000	43,000	1,500	1,132,000
2	Alaska	28,000	24,000	100,000	24,000
3	Arizona	98,000	963,000	256,000	169,000
4	Arkansas	19,000	49,000	14,000	408,000

SOURCE: Statistical Abstract of the United States 1999, Table 34.

"data" at the top of the matrix page, and then on "define variables," you will be prompted to provide information that allows the system to label the variable and the values, identify missing data codes and data formats, and align the numbers the way you want. Of course, you do need to follow the procedures we have outlined for developing codes for your variables.

Finally, if your data is from a telephone survey, it is likely that the data have been entered into a computer assisted data input (CADI) system as the questions were being asked (see chapter 3). If so, then the CADI system provides the data in a matrix or other machine readable form.

DATA STORAGE

You will give your data set a file name, just as for any file you have on your computer. It is very important to make at least one back up of this file. You will no doubt have made the original copy of your data on either your hard disk (your C drive, perhaps) or the network. You should make sure it is backed up, again, either on the network or on a drive different from the original.

ANALYZING YOUR DATA

So you have your data ready for analysis. Now you need to analyze it. Most computer installations have one or more social science statistical software packages.

CHOOSING A STATISTICAL PACKAGE

You may not have a choice of statistical packages. Many government agencies and universities support a standard set. Packages are not necessarily expensive to buy, but they do need personnel to maintain them and to serve as consultants for users. These packages, several of which are named in Research in Practice 4A, are designed to allow the user to do a variety of statistical routines from the very simple to the quite complex. The packages also facilitate data transformations, those changes that allow the user to easily recode variables in the data, declare some values missing, create new variables from combinations of old ones, and so forth.

If you have a choice about which package to use, you would want to examine the following criteria:

1. Does the package have the special features you might need? While all packages have basic frequencies, measures of association, and correlation programs, the packages do differ on the combinations of more sophisticated procedures they allow. Make sure the one you choose has what you need.

2. Is the system compatible with other software you have? For example, if you want to transfer information between spreadsheet and word processing programs, make sure the programs you buy will do that.

3. How good are the graphics? If it is important to you to produce nicely labeled tables and figures for reports, investigate the capabilities of each package in doing that.

4. If you are working with an existing data set, check that the package you choose is compatible with your data. In most cases this will not be a problem, but if your data have alphabetic characters, are "packed," have multiple punches, or are peculiar in some way, consider this in relation to each package.

5. How many variables and cases can the package handle? Does it meet your needs?

6. How do the hardware and operating system requirements mesh with your equipment? Cheap software is not cheap if you have to upgrade your entire system or buy a new one.

7. How easy is the system to use? Some systems are designed for quick learning but do not have the flexibility of more complex systems. Others require more of an initial learning investment, but have great flexibility. You need to consider your own needs. If you use the system only infrequently, and for relatively simple analysis tasks, then a software package that maximizes ease of learning makes sense. If you make heavy use of a system, and do complex tasks, then a more sophisticated system with greater flexibility, capacity, and comprehensiveness is more appropriate.

8. Does the package allow you to make data transformations easily, or do you have to perform the recoding operations yourself before accessing the package? Choose a package that allows you to input data in raw form, do needed data transformations, then run your procedures all in one operation. Some packages allow matrix manipulations while others do not, and this could be important to some people.

9. How does the software handle missing data? Some statistics packages make it very difficult to work with missing data; others present no

problems. If the data sets you are using have missing data (and most do), make sure the software can handle it.

10. How well is the system documented and how much user assistance is provided? Some packages have excellent manuals, on-line help, and a toll-free phone number where you can get assistance. Other systems have none of these. These are important considerations.

Early in your data collection project, consult with knowledgeable people at your computer site to see which packages are available and to make sure your data meet the requirements necessary for whatever software package you will use.

STATISTICAL PROCEDURES

After you have defined the data and done any data transformations you need, you will then need to identify what statistics you want to compute. In most packages the statistical routines have descriptive names, such as REGRESSION or CROSSTABS or FREQUENCIES. Associated with the statistical procedure

---

Research in Practice 4A

WIDELY USED STATISTICAL PACKAGES FOR THE PERSONAL COMPUTER

With the exception noted, these are currently used general statistical packages with options ranging from simple frequencies to complex multivariable procedures. Today's descriptions of these systems will soon be out of date, because these companies are continually upgrading their systems, adding new features and expanded capabilities. Thus, we list only a web page source of information. Check before you buy. Menu-driven systems are probably easier to get started on because all the options are displayed on a menu to which you return after each procedure. Command-driven systems are probably superior once you have learned the system; they are faster and you need fewer commands.

MINITAB (http://www.minitab.com/)

SAS (http://www.sas.com/)

SPSS (http://www.spss.com/)

STATA (http://www.stata.com)

SYSTAT (http://www.spss.com/software/science/systat/)

STATISTICA (http://www.statsoft.com/)

LIMDEP (http://www.limdep.com/index.htm) A general econometrics program for use with dependent variables of limited categories. Calculates linear and non-linear models.

command, you will be asked to provide information, such as what variables you want the statistics performed on, what is to be done with the missing values, and the statistics you want computed. For example, with a frequency distribution you might choose one, none, or all of several associated statistical measures of central tendency, dispersion, and range (see Chapter 5).

After the job runs, then what? You want to see if it ran correctly and what your results are. Your output will appear on the screen in some form. If it did not run, you can find your error, then erase the output without printing it. Or you can print the output, or save it to the disk.

EXERCISE

4-1 You are setting up a program to monitor the length of patient stays at the hospital where you are on the administrative staff. The hospital administration is concerned about excessive hospital stays as they contribute to increased costs. You decide to collect the following information:

Patient ID number from file.
Admitting doctor.
Ward or unit to which admitted.
Ward or unit from which discharged.
Age of patient.
Sex of patient.
Date of admission.
Date of discharge or death.
Living status of patient (i.e., lives alone or not).
Care-giving status of patient (i.e., responsible for care of minors or others on a day-to-day basis).
Employment status of patient.

Based on the information for the first twenty patients (listed on opposite page):

   a. Provide appropriate values for each variable and prepare a code book.
   b. Code the information for the twenty patients.
   c. Enter the data onto a spreadsheet and then into your statistical software system, or enter directly into the statistical software system.
   d. Process a job so that the frequencies on each variable are run (e.g., what percent are male, what percent are female).

SPREADSHEET ANALYSES

Researchers and managers often need to make extended series of calculations in what is termed a spreadsheet. By this, we mean something like the following display of Wildlife Protection Agency salaries. This type of data display is a matrix, that is, a group of numbers arranged in columns and rows. Changing

Patient Number	Doctor	Ward Admission	Ward Discharge	Age	Sex	Date Admitted	Date Discharged	Living Status	Employment Status	Caregiving Status
10359	Brown	Surgery	Same	59	M	10/8/01	10/18/01	Not alone	Yes	No
10360	Schroeder	Maternity	Same	35	F	10/8/01	10/11/01	Not alone	Yes	Yes
10361	Bledsoe	Maternity	Same	22	F	10/8/01	10/10/01	Not alone	No	Yes
10362	Lopez	Pediatrics	Same	6	M	10/8/01	10/12/01	Not alone	No	No
10363	Gruhl	General	Same	71	F	10/8/01	10/12/01	Alone	No	No
10364	Schroeder	Maternity	Same	18	F	10/8/01	10/11/01	Not alone	Yes	Yes
10365	Bracken	Intensive care	Pediatrics	8	F	10/8/01	10/20/01	Not alone	No	No
10366	Lopez	Pediatrics	Same	3	M	10/8/01	10/9/01	Not alone	No	No
10367	Winter	General	Surgery	62	M	10/8/01	10/15/01	Not alone	Yes	No
10368	Winter	Maternity	Same	38	F	10/8/01	10/10/01	Alone	Yes	Yes
10369	Davison	Surgery	Same	55	M	10/8/01	10/30/01	Not alone	No	No
10370	Schroeder	Maternity	Same	29	F	10/8/01	10/12/01	Not alone	No	Yes
10371	Grubel	Intensive care	General	80	F	10/8/01	10/25/01	Alone	No	No
10372	Grubel	General	Same	40	M	10/8/01	10/15/01	Alone	Yes	No
10373	Jones	Oncology	Same	53	F	10/8/01	10/14/01	Not alone	Yes	No
10374	Lopez	Pediatrics	Same	9	F	10/8/01	10/12/01	Not alone	No	No
10375	Washington	Oncology	Deceased	63	M	10/8/01	10/14/01	Not alone	Yes	No
10376	Maresh	Oncology	Same	30	F	10/8/01	10/25/01	Not alone	No	Yes
10377	Brown	Surgery	Deceased	77	F	10/8/01	10/10/01	Alone	No	No
10378	Schroeder	Maternity	Same	30	F	10/8/01	10/11/01	Not alone	Yes	Yes

a number in any of the columns or rows requires recalculation of several cells in the matrix. For example, if the proposed percent increase for J. Cougar was .035 instead of .03, that would affect his dollar increase, the total dollar increase, Cougar's projected salary, and the total projected salary. Before the age of computers, spreadsheet work required extensive calculation and recalculation. Of course, in this simple example, it is easy enough to do all calculations quickly with a hand calculator. But if your spreadsheet includes hundreds of rows or columns, help from a computer is extremely desirable.

Salaries of Employees of the Wildlife Protection Agency

NAME	2000 SALARY	PROJECTED % INCREASE	PROJECTED $ INCREASE	2001 SALARY
J. Cougar	$ 40,000	.03%	$1,200	$ 41,200
A. Lynx	22,500	.015	338	22,838
P. Bear	18,000	.05	900	18,900
Z. Hawk	32,500	.04	1,300	33,800
T. Fox	26,800	.06	1,608	28,408
Total	$139,800		$5,346	$145,146

Two of the most common spreadsheet programs are Lotus 1-2-3 and Excel. Spreadsheet programs contain a set of commands that allow the user to build a matrix, rearrange it, calculate sums, percentages, rates of return, and even regression coefficients (see Chapters 8 and 9).[1] Sort options allow the user to examine different subgroups and calculate subgroup statistics. Most have capabilities for creating graphs from the data. These programs (with the proper instructions from the user) automatically retotal columns, rows, or both when new entries are made, e.g., J. Cougar's salary changes.

In Lotus, for example, the program starts by presenting an empty matrix of pre-defined cells labeled A,B,C . . . ZZ on the columns and 1,2,3 . . . N on the rows. Each cell has a unique name composed of the row and column where it lies, A3, WZ99, and so forth. By moving the cursor from cell to cell, the user can enter information, such as the names and salary information. Entering a formula in a cell, such as directing that the contents of cell C5 be added to that of D5, directs the program to make that calculation and place the results in E5. If such a formula were entered in cell E5, and the value of C5 was three and D5 was eighty-seven, ninety would automatically appear in cell E5.

Pressing the slash (/) brings up a set of commands from which the user may choose, allowing one to change the size of cells, move rows or columns, add labels, sort the data (for example, an alphabetical list of employees could be

---

[1]Home pages supporting Excel are found at http://www.microsoft.com/office/excel/default.htm; supporting Lotus notes at www.lotus.com/home.nsf/welcome/123.

resorted by salary level or years of seniority), reformat data, print, copy cells, rows, and columns, draw graphics, and so forth. Copying a formula from one cell to an entire row or column directs the program to replicate the formula down the line or across the row. Copying the E5 formula (C5 + D5) to cell E6 directs the computer to add the contents of C6 and D6 and place the sum in E6. Once the formulas are entered, changing the contents of any cell involved in the formula (for example, cells C6 or D6) will cause the contents of other cells to change (in this case, cell E6 and any cells that use the sums in E6 in further computations).

This sort of program not only is useful for budget managers and fiscal policymakers, but it is also useful for policy analysts. For example, using a spreadsheet program with the kind of salary data shown above, coupled with spreadsheet information on each employee's race, sex, year of appointment, and job classification, analysts can sort and resort by individual and by job classification to examine salary levels among different classes of employees. Categories can be grouped and summary statistics obtained on various subgroups. Such information is useful in determining whether race or sex discrimination was occurring, to examine the relationship of seniority to pay, to compare wage rates for different job classifications, and for many other purposes.

Spreadsheet analysis can be useful for forecasting problems, too. (We will examine forecasting in Chapter 10.) Such analyses can be used to generate projections quickly and easily. In forecasting school enrollment in a community, for example, different estimates of population projections, birth rates, school retention rates, and other salient data for projecting school enrollment can be entered and projections on these different assumptions quickly calculated. Such sophisticated programming has a good deal of relevance to policymakers. For example, when discussions of federal aid bills or other federal spending programs occur, Congressional staffers test which kind of aid formula (for example, relative weights are allotted to population versus income need versus tax effort, and so on) results in the highest yield for their member's own district. Before the computer age, such calculations took considerable time and effort, and only a few alternative formulas were tested. Now, dozens of different aid formulas can be checked to find the one most advantageous to one's own district, state, or region. Members can enter into negotiations over the details of a bill being quite familiar with how these details affect their constituents' interests.

Spreadsheet programs are also useful for management of small data sets, such as client or student records. For example, the director of an MPA program could set up a file of MPA candidates, with each row holding data on one individual, and each column holding one variable (year admitted, amount of current financial aid, undergraduate institution, full or part-time status, progress on degree, and so forth). Spreadsheet options make it easy to sort files both on numeric data (year of admission to program, number of years of financial aid), and alphabetic information (last name, previous degree).

Spreadsheet programs are not the most efficient system for large data bases, however. For that, we need data base management systems described below.

Most widely used spreadsheet programs are now compatible with word processing, statistical analysis, and other software.

EXERCISE

4-2 Working with a Spreadsheet

COUNTY	2000 POPULATION	PROJECTION 1 - POPULATION INCREASE BY 2020 (PERCENT)	PROJECTION 2 - POPULATION INCREASE BY 2020 (PERCENT)	ESTIMATED PERSONS PER HOUSEHOLD BY 2020
Berger	180,000	1.1%	5.0%	1.6
Brinkerhoff	890,000	15.8	25.0	1.9
Cope	250,000	5.5	8.0	2.3
Maslowski	540,000	10.3	8.0	1.5
White	22,000	0.5	0.2	3.0

a. Set up this spreadsheet problem, using a spreadsheet package that your instructor directs.
b. Using the spreadsheet program, calculate the estimated population growth (in numbers of people) in each county under projections one and two.
c. Calculate the total population in each county under projections one and two, and the total state population (five counties) in 2000 and 2020 (each projection).
d. Using the estimated persons per household projected, estimate how many new housing units will be needed in 2020 in each county, and overall.
e. Print out your matrix, using an appropriate table title.

DATA BASE MANAGEMENT SYSTEMS

Data base management programs are another type of program of use to public managers. Examples include dBase or Microsoft Access.[2] Data base programs allow the user to file and sort data on individuals, agencies, or other units. That is, data management programs can be compared to a library card catalog. The totality of cards in the catalog is equivalent to one data base file. Each card is equivalent to one computer record. And the entries on the card (author, title, year and place of publication, call number) are equivalent to entries on each computer record.

---

[2]Home pages for Microsoft Access are located at http://www.microsoft.com/office/access/default.htm; dBase at http://www.dbase2000.com/

There are several advantages to a computer file for these types of records. In a library, the card catalog usually needs three copies of each card, so that the book can be filed by its author's name, its title, and its subject. If there are joint authors, more cards are needed to cross reference the authors. A library of 1 million books would need more than 3 million card entries. A computer file requires only one record per case (per book, in this instance). From this one record, the "cards" or records can be sorted by any entry on the cards, not only by author, title, or subject, but also by year published, place of publication, call number, or any other piece of information entered systematically on all the cards.

Sophisticated data base systems are relational. That is, they allow the file to be manipulated in ways that result in creation of new files by means of merging information from one file with information from another that has at least one common variable. Thus, in our library example, a file of user requests for new books, listed by author or title, could be cross-checked against existing holdings, so that user requests for books already held by the library could be flagged.

Data management systems are particularly useful for personnel records, inventory control, constituency or client records, as well as for libraries. In personnel systems, each employee is one record. On that record can be entered all sorts of data about the employee that traditionally is found in a file folder. Using the data base system, employee records can be sorted and analyzed by any bit of information on these records. Relational database systems can calculate simple statistics such as sums and averages, as well as sort and merge records and files. Most are compatible with certain word processing and spreadsheet programs, too.

EXERCISE

4-3 A data base management exercise: Here is a file of employees in the local animal control department. Using a data base program designated by your instructor:

a. Set up a file of employees.
b. Sort the rows by the employees' last names, and print a table showing each employee and that employee's race, sex, and salary.
c. Calculate the average salary of the employees.
d. Sort the files to order employees by hiring date. Print a table showing name, hiring date, salary, sex, and race.
e. Order employees by salary level within each sex. Print a table showing the same data as in (d), including (if possible) average salary for each sex.

Personnel Records (Wildhare, Minnesota Animal Control Department)

EMPLOYEE	DATE HIRED	SALARY	SEX	RACE/ ETHNICITY*
Marian Lombra	1/5/80	$60,000	F	W
Michael Filippelli	2/15/78	$55,000	M	W
Nancy Stolte	5/9/84	22,000	F	W
Eric Boosalis	1/7/86	32,000	M	W
Brian Paterno	8/26/76	35,000	M	W
Joan Lincoln	12/1/79	74,000	F	AA
Tillie Straka	8/8/85	28,000	F	W
Marcia Esteban	5/13/84	19,500	F	H
Andrew Marshall	6/15/84	63,000	M	W
Alan Johnson	3/2/80	26,000	M	W

*W = white, non-Hispanic. AA = African American. H = Hispanic.

COMPUTING COSTS

Computing requires an investment in hardware and software, and in most organizations, the cost of computer support, that is, for the people who plan, maintain, and upgrade technology systems, far exceeds hardware and software cost.

Focusing on hardware, it is difficult to estimate costs of computing equipment, since prices are constantly changing and new options are available continuously. For the last decade, however, it was safe to say that for $1,500 or less you could purchase a good Pentium based-system with capacious disk space and memory. Each year, the same dollars buy more capacity and speed (but then, of course, expectations about capacity and speed increase each year too).

Software costs are variable. Some software comes preloaded on new computers. Other, more specialized, software must be purchased separately.

In general, standardizing equipment and software will reduce support costs considerably. The more different hardware configurations you have in your organization, and the more types of software, the more you will have to invest in the people who keep the systems running.

SOME FINAL THOUGHTS

This chapter has only provided a brief peek at the potential applications of computers for use by public managers. There are hundreds of more specialized programs for purposes ranging from cost accounting to managing apartment buildings, from billing for legal services to organizing physical exams, from keeping church records to managing golf leagues. The main problems for a potential user are first to determine what jobs you need computer assistance for, and then to find out what is available and whether it meets your needs.

To determine what kind of software (and hardware) you need, make a list of the major things you want the program to do. You may not know everything, especially if you have never used a computer before, but at least you know some things about the task that the computer might help with. If you are buying a data management system, for example, you need to think about whether it should be compatible with a word processing system you already have. What kinds of reports will you need to generate with the system? How long? What kinds of sorting will you need to do? Will you need to generate address labels from the program? How many entries will you be making per record? Will you need to merge different files? Delete records from your file? Do you need to calculate statistics on your files? These are the kinds of questions that will get you started in making a decision about what kind of a system you need. Once you have a general idea of your needs, then you might search your library for issues of magazines designed for users of particular microcomputers. There are magazines for every user, novice or sophisticate. By browsing through them, you can find out what kind of software is available. Most contain regular reviews of software. After getting a general picture, talk to other users. See if you can try out their software. Visit dealers. Be sure to try a system before you buy it.

Of course, your new computer software will eventually make your data analysis, filing, or other tasks much easier. However, be prepared for some initial frustrations. Don't expect to learn the process in one day. It will take time to learn about your software and how your system operates. But the best way to learn is to try a job, find the errors, and try again. Your first try will probably not be successful; maybe your job will bomb several times. But your initial frustration should soon yield to a sense of satisfaction and to the knowledge that with computers, your data analytical capabilities have increased dramatically.

You will soon reach the point where you can do a wide variety of jobs using the computer. Even advanced statistics are easy to calculate. But without a knowledge of what these statistics mean, you may be generating meaningless information, or you may be interpreting your findings incorrectly or inappropriately. So in the next five chapters of this book, we will introduce you to a variety of the most commonly used statistics and show you what they mean, when they should be used, and how they should be interpreted.

Key Terms

Hardware

Software

Desktops

Laptops

Servers

Operating system

Modem

Hard disk

Memory

Spreadsheet software

Data base management program

For Further Help

In this area, books cited here today will be outdated tomorrow. For this reason, we offer only a few, general suggestions.

Go to your local bookstore and look under the computing section. You will find dozens of "how-to" books for the novice and for the sophisticate. These handbooks are generally grouped under the relevant application. So, for example, if you want help with Excel, you will find several useful Excel manuals. In another area, you will find how-to books for Windows, for web page designers, and for a myriad of other types of applications. A quick search through the books reveals the level of prior knowledge assumed. If you prefer browsing in online bookstores, such as Amazon.com or barnesandnoble.com, you can search under a particular topic with the same result. Here it is more difficult to judge the suitability of the book, though some of these web sites feature reviews by other users which can give you some sense of the book's usefulness.

There are some publishers that have published a whole series of books on various computer topics. For example, IDG Books publishes the *For Dummies* series, such as *Windows98 for Dummies*. As the title suggests, these books are designed for beginners. We have found them very helpful. McGraw Hill publishes a *Complete Reference* series, with entries on topics such as Excel and Access.

5

ANALYZING SINGLE VARIABLES: FREQUENCY DISTRIBUTIONS AND SUMMARY MEASURES

It is difficult to avoid statistics in today's world. Both the government and private sector generate volumes of data and information every day—the Dow Jones average, the Consumer Price Index, the unemployment rate, the crime rate, and much more. The public is constantly bombarded with reports, articles, and new stories where data or information are described and summarized in some fashion. Many others work with data in their jobs, organizing, describing, and summarizing information for clients, governing boards, committees, and the public. Those aspiring to a career in policy research as well as those who will become managers in public and private organizations need to know how to read and interpret data and how to organize and present it. The director of city libraries needs to know how many library books were loaned last year and be able to present the information to the city council. The state director of mental health needs to know how many patients were treated at the regional mental health centers and present it to the governor and state legislature. The local hospital administrator needs to know what proportion of hospital beds are occupied on an average day and be able to communicate it to the hospital board and relevant government agencies. The city attorney needs to know how many people were charged with felonies last year, how many were convicted, and share it with the mayor, council, law enforcement agencies, and a public concerned with its safety. In this chapter, the task is to show how data can be presented and summarized in a way that others can understand it. It identifies methods and procedures for analyzing a single variable.

Table 5-1 displays information on a single variable—in this case, response time in minutes of a local fire department to fire calls. The column headed number of calls is a **frequency distribution**. It contains the values of the variable response time and the frequency with which each value occurs. At the base of this column is 200, the total number of calls. The column headed percent of calls is a **percentage distribution**. It converts the frequency of each value to a percentage.[1] At the base of this column is 100% representing the total number of calls. Including the percentage distribution is another way to present information and may make it easier to understand the information. For example, one can note that the fire department responds to 80 percent of fire calls within ten minutes. The table also contains two measures of central tendency: the mean and the median. Measures of central tendency summarize the values in a distribution in a single coefficient, the "average." In addition to the mean and median, another measure of central tendency, not shown but discussed later, is the mode. Table 5-1 also contains the standard deviation, a measure of dispersion or spread, which indicates how values in the distribution are clustered around the mean and is very important in understanding bivariate and multivariate techniques treated in Chapters 9 and 10.

CONSTRUCTING AND PRESENTING FREQUENCY DISTRIBUTIONS

While constructing a frequency distribution by hand is something one is unlikely to do—virtually all software packages can accomplish the task with a click of the mouse—doing so is important for understanding what is involved. Continuing with the example in Table 5-1 and assuming the information is in fire department files, the files would be examined and the response for each call recorded on a worksheet like the following:

TABLE 5-1   Response Time of Fire Department, Beaver Falls, Oregon, 1999

RESPONSE TIME	NUMBER OF CALLS	PERCENT OF CALLS
Less than 5 minutes	50	25%
5 to 9.9 minutes	110	55
10 to 14.9 minutes	30	15
15 minutes or more	10	5
Totals	200	100%
Mean response time	= 8.3 minutes	
Median response time	= 6.2 minutes	
Standard deviation	= 3.0 minutes	

SOURCE: Computed from data collected by the Beaver Falls Fire Department.

---

[1]For example, to calculate the percent of calls in the less-then-5-minutes category, divide the number of calls responded to in less than five minutes (50) by the total number of calls (200) and multiply by 100, (50/200) * 100 = 25 percent.

Response Time	Number of Cases
Less than one minute	///// ///// ////
One to two minutes	///// //
Two to three minutes	///// /
Three to four minutes	////
.	
.	
Twenty-four to twenty-five minutes	/

Note that the worksheet contains more and smaller values, one to two, two to three, and so on, than those presented in Table 5-1. Because it is impossible to know at this stage how the information will be grouped or categorized when presented in a table, it is best to record the information as it appears in the files. One would not want to go through all the files recording information only to discover at the end that the categories or intervals to which each call or case was assigned were too broad or simply inadequate for conveying a clear picture of the speed at which the fire department responds. For example, if response time was recorded into fifteen minute intervals, all but five percent of the cases would fall into a single category. It is wise to think about the categories or intervals shortly after the recording task begins and make adjustments if need be to insure that the final presentation will contain the desired information.

The final task is to simply tally the number of calls in each category. For example, there were fourteen calls where the response time was less than one minute, seven where the response time was between one and two minutes, and so on. Once the tally is complete, one can decide whether or not to combine categories or values. If combining is desirable, consider the following:

1. Categories should be equal in size. In Table 5-1, except for the last, categories are equal, 0 to 4.9, 5.0 to 9.9, etc. In some instances, this may not be possible or desirable, when, for example, values are concentrated in one or two categories.
2. Beginning and ending categories can be open-ended. One might, for example, opt for a category 15 minutes or more, as in Table 5-1.
3. If there are "natural" divisions, these should be taken advantage of in establishing categories. Consider Tables 5-2 and 5-3.

Given the distribution in Table 5-2, natural divisions in the data occur between 4 and 6 and between 9 and 11. One might categorize these data as shown in Table 5-3.

In constructing a table displaying a frequency distribution, there are a few simple rules to insure information will be presented clearly.

1. Label the table. It must be clear to readers what information is being presented. Be as specific as possible. Identify the variable (response

TABLE 5-2   Number of Crisis Line Calls Per Day, Sun City, California—1999

NUMBER OF CALLS	NUMBER OF DAYS
0	0
1	0
2	1
3	1
4	10
5	2
6	1
7	10
8	20
9	15
10	3
11	25

TABLE 5-3   Number of Crisis Line Calls Per Day, Sun City, California—1999

NUMBER OF CALLS	NUMBER OF DAYS
0–4	12
5–9	48
10–11	28

time), time (1999), location (Beaver Falls), and other pertinent information.

2. Label both the columns and rows. In Table 5-1, both columns and rows are identified. The columns identify the number and percentage of calls. The rows identify response time in minutes. Column totals are included at the base of each.

3. Decide on if and how the data should be grouped or pooled for presentation. If pooling is desirable, the frequency distributions should contain as few categories or values as possible while still capturing and conveying variation in the data. One should also consider the target audience. For example, if data are to be presented to the public, they need not be cut as finely and precisely as they would need to be for a team seeking to improve the response time of the fire department.

4. Display both frequencies and percentages. This is desirable unless the distributions of a number of variables are included in the table and space and layout become an issue. Percentages standardize the information and make comparisons easier. For example, one might want to compare the distribution of response times in 1999 with those

in 1997 and 1998. The total number in the distribution, often designated N, is always included.

Research in Practice 5A

FREQUENCY AND PERCENTAGE DISTRIBUTIONS

Frequency and percentage distributions are not hard to find. Government reports are typically loaded with tables displaying each. Both can also be found in published research. The following is an example. The human resource officers in the nation's counties and cities over 100,000 population were surveyed regarding whether or not workplace violence was a problem in their city or county government and whether or not the local government had programs to deal with it. The survey probed the source of violence, whether for example it was coming from clients, coworkers, strangers, former employees, inmates and prisoners, employee relatives, or terrorists, who or what in the local government—administrators, employees, labor or community groups—was most responsible for developing programs to deal with workplace violence and the types of programs. For local governments without programs, the study probed the reasons why. Responses to this question, as well as others, were presented as frequency and percentage distributions similar to those in Table 5-A.

TABLE 5-A   Reasons For Not Having a Workplace Violence Policy

REASON	% GIVING THE REASON
Workplace violence is not a problem	54.0
Existing personnel rules and regulation are adequate	46.9
Exposure to workplace violence is too low to worry about	21.1
Nobody has ever suggested a workplace violence policy is needed	15.0
Cost of implementation is too high in light of projected benefits	3.6
Organized labor has opposed such a policy	.5
Other reasons	31.1

Note that Table 5-A is not a single percentage distribution. Multiple responses were acceptable. For example, 54 percent mentioned that "workplace violence was not a problem," while 46 percent did not mention this.

SOURCE: Lloyd Nigro and William L. Waugh, Jr., "Workplace Violence Politics of U.S. Local Governments, "*Public Administration Quarterly* (Fall, 1998): 349–363.

5. Include summary statistics. It is desirable to include summary measures, such as the mean and standard deviation, discussed later.
6. Identify the source of the data. The source where the information can be found is identified immediately following the table.

Research in Practice 5A illustrates how frequency and percentage distributions are employed in research.

EXERCISES

5-1 The planning director in the agency where you are employed wants to know the average daily patient loads at 24 public mental health clinics for the year 1999 in the state. The relevant data are identified below. Generate a table which provides the information the director needs.

Clinic	Average Number of Patients	Clinic	Average Number of Patients	Clinic	Average Number of Patients
1	55	9	159	17	101
2	300	10	60	18	136
3	210	11	163	19	222
4	150	12	189	20	93
5	155	13	301	21	382
6	347	14	215	22	273
7	210	15	260	23	173
8	182	16	112	24	122

5-2 A citizens' committee on which you serve has responsibility for operating a personal crisis line. To ensure that enough volunteers are on duty to answer the phone, it is necessary to know at what time and on which days calls are made. From the data below, collected over a six-month period, construct two frequency distributions, one showing the distribution of calls by day, the other by time of day.

Time	Sunday	Monday	Tuesday	Wednesday	Thursday	Friday	Saturday
12–4 A.M.	42	51	100	42	21	36	77
4–8 A.M	55	36	61	29	19	42	52
8–12 A.M.	100	72	121	49	45	55	89
12–4 P.M.	259	65	96	77	100	71	152
4–8 P.M.	203	99	132	113	123	111	141
8–12 P.M.	230	200	177	156	176	166	301

5-3 Prepare a frequency distribution on years of median education in either: (a) counties in your state or (b) the 50 states. Use the census data references identified in Chapter 3.

GRAPHS AND CHARTS

Sometimes it is desirable to present information in a graph or chart. Both will generally provide a more attractive and easily understood display than a table. Some people, particularly those uncomfortable with figures, may prefer a graph or chart to a table. Charts and graphs are often preferred when the target audience is the public. A former student, now a planner in a police department, reported that her supervisor would not allow her to display information except in a graph or chart.

BAR GRAPHS

Figures 5-1 and 5-2 are bar graphs. **Bar graphs** are particularly useful in drawing attention to comparisons among frequency or percentage distributions. Figure 5-1 compares the average salary of men and women at various academic ranks at Excalibur University and reveals that men earn more than women at the professor and associate professor levels but earn less at the assistant professor level. Figure 5-1 can be used to make comparisons among the ranks too, but if this is the desired comparison, a presentation such as Figure 5-2 might be more revealing. Figure 5-2 shows that those at the higher ranks, men and women, earn more than those at lower ranks. Thus, it is important in constructing bar graphs

FIGURE 5-1   **Mean Salaries of Professors at Excalibur University by Sex and Rank, 1997–1998**

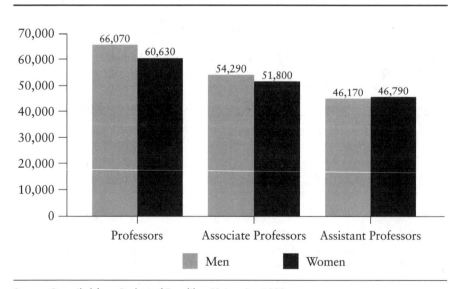

Source: Compiled from Budget of Excalibur University, 1999.

Figure 5-2   Mean Salaries of Professors at Excalibur University by Rank and Sex, 1997–1998

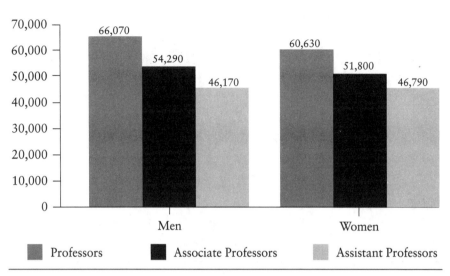

Source: Compiled from Budget of Excalibur University, 1999.

to be clear regarding which comparison is to be highlighted. As with tables, graphs and charts need to be titled and labeled.

Line Graphs

Line graphs are also used to display the distribution of a single variable. Consider the data in Table 5-2, the number of calls per day to a crisis line. These data can be graphed as in Figure 5-3 with the number of calls reflected on the horizontal or X axis, the number of days on the vertical or Y axis. Data points, the number of calls to the crisis line paired with the number of days on which a particular number of calls were made, can then be plotted on the graph. For example, five calls occurred on ten days. Thus, one moves along the X axis five spaces and up ten on the Y axis and plots a point. Note that no days had no calls so there is nothing to plot at the zero point on both axes.

After plotting each point, the points can be connected with a line. The line provides a good visual representation of the fluctuations in calls per day in a way quite different from the frequency distribution in Table 5-2.

A line graph is also useful for charting information over time. For example, Figure 5-4 shows the fluctuating levels of outpatient and residential mental health populations in a state. A dramatic decline is visible in patients served in residential facilities, while an equally dramatic upsurge is visible in patients served in outpatient clinics. Also shown is a gradual increase in the total mental health patient population.

FIGURE 5-3   **Number of Crisis Line Calls Per Day, Sun City, California—1999**

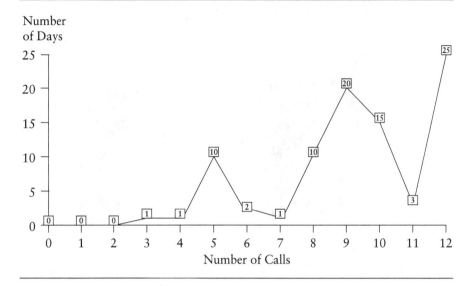

Figure 5-4 illustrates some additional guidelines for constructing graphs and charts.

1. When time is a variable, choose an appropriate interval. In Figure 5-4, a ten-year interval is used. The same data could have been plotted using a one- or five-year interval. In some instances, a monthly or weekly interval might be appropriate. Choose an interval that minimizes the number of data points but at the same time captures the pattern of variation in the data.

2. The intervals on the X and Y axes should be equal. For example, in Figure 5-4 the interval on the Y axis, patients, is displayed in increments of 5000, on the X axis, years, in increments of ten years. On occasion, one might encounter a graph where the Y axis is broken. This means a different length of interval above and below the break. This technique might be useful in displaying data extending over a wide range. For example, if the total number of mental health patients in Figure 5-4 numbered in the millions, and one wanted to show this in the same graphic display with those treated in outpatient clinics which numbered only in the thousands, the Y axis could be broken with the intervals below the break measuring in the thousands and the intervals above the break measuring in millions. As a rule of thumb, this kind of display should probably be avoided, but if used, it is important to convey to readers exactly what is going on.

3. Excluding the situation identified in 2 above, if more than one line is plotted, each line should be plotted using the same scale. For example, Figure 5-4 plots the total number of mental health patients, the number

FIGURE 5-4   Use of Mental Health Facilities, State of Michigan, 1940–1990

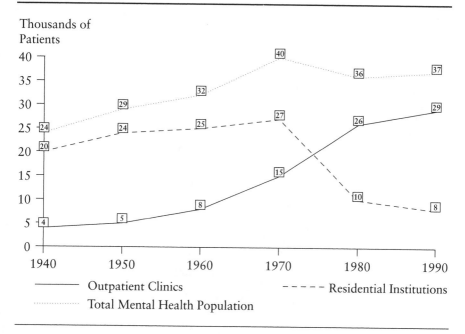

Thousands of Patients

Outpatient Clinics ————   Residential Institutions – – – – –
Total Mental Health Population ....

treated in residential institutions, and the number treated in outpatient clinics. It would be unclear, for example, to report number of outpatients in the 100s and residential patients in the 1,000s.

4. The X and Y axes must be clearly labeled. In Figure 5-4, time is reflected on the X axis and number of patients on the Y.

STEM-AND-LEAF

Another way to display distributions graphically is with a **stem-and-leaf chart** shown in Table 5-4. The variable is median family income in each of the 50 states. The first two digits of income are arrayed on the left side of a line called the stem. The next digit is written to the right of the stem. For example, one state has a median income of $49,800. This is reflected in the table by 49 on the left side and 8 to the right. Five states had median incomes between $39,000 to $40,000. Thirty-nine is entered to the left of the line, five digits to the right. The zeros indicate that two states have median incomes of $39,000, the three that one has a median income of $39,300, and the two sevens that two states have median incomes of $39,700. The values to the right are written in ascending order: The stem-and-leaf displays each value in the distribution and at the same time conveys the shape of the distribution as a whole.

A variant of the stem-and-leaf is presented in Table 5-5. State abbreviations are used to identify states that fall within particular income ranges. We

TABLE 5-4   Median Family Income by State, 1998 ($00)

51	
50	06
49	8
48	
47	49
46	55
45	
44	29
43	13
42	3
41	348
40	2689
39	00377
38	69
37	003
36	22467
35	678
34	09
33	247
32	
31	557
30	3
29	1
28	
27	6
26	7

lose information regarding a specific dollar amount but gain information regarding the specific states in each condition.

PIE CHARTS

Pie charts are often used to display budgetary information. As the name implies, they are shaped like a pie with each wedge representing a portion of the total. They are useful in displaying proportions and percentages as in Figure 5-5.

A pie chart does not provide anything beyond what is revealed in a table. It is simply another way of presenting information. Pie charts are useful when the target audience is the general public who may be less likely to focus on or grasp the point of a tabular presentation.

Virtually all the major word processing, spread sheet, and statistical packages can generate basic graphs and charts. These are menu driven so anyone

TABLE 5–5   Median Family Income by State, 1998 ($000)

51					
50	Al	Md			
49	NJ				
48					
47	Ms	Wa			
46	Co	Cn			
45					
44	NH	Ut			
43	Va	Il			
42	Ma				
41	Mn	De	Ws		
40	Ca	Ha	RI	Mu	
39	Ne	In	Vt	Or	Pa
38	Oh	Ga			
37	NY	Az	Ia		
36	Kn	Id	Ne	Ab	Ky
35	Wy	NC	Tx	Me	
34	Fl	Tn			
33	Ok	SC	SD		
32					
31	La	Mi	NM		
30	ND				
29	Ms				
28					
27	Ak				
26	WV				

can give presentations a very professional look and illustrate the point of a presentation in a way most readers can grasp and understand. Care, however, should be exercised to avoid going overboard. Just because a feature is available does not mean one should use it.[2] Avoid extraneous material and clashing colors. Three dimensional charts should be used only with data that have three dimensions. Even grid lines such as in some of our examples are not always necessary. In other words, simpler is usually better even though it is sometimes hard to resist the temptation to employ the fancy graphics that can be produced with today's software.

---

[2] See various books by Edward Tufte, including *The Visual Display of Quantitative Information,* Graphics Press, *1983; and Visual Explanations,* Graphics Press, 1997.

FIGURE 5-5   **Source of Local Revenue, Prairie City, Illinois, 1998**

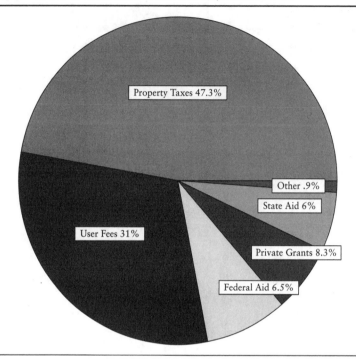

EXERCISES

5-4 Graph or chart each of the following, making sure that each is correctly labeled and titled:

a. Percent poverty in Bevo City, Colorado from 1990 to 1999 among whites, African Americans, and Latinos:

	WHITE	AFRICAN AMERICAN	LATINO
1990	7	17	25
1991	6	18	26
1992	8	17	27
1993	7	15	25
1994	6	16	24
1995	4	16	23
1996	4	12	24
1997	3	11	26
1998	3	10	28
1999	2	9	26

b. City expenditures in Dizzy City, Florida, 1998. Streets and highways, 20 percent; Other public works, 5 percent; Libraries, 10 percent; Parks, 15 percent; Health and welfare, 5 percent; General administration, 5 percent; Police, 25 percent; Fire, 15 percent.

c. Average daily detained population in Crimoville, Missouri, 1998. City jail: 75 African Americans, 200 whites; juvenile detention facilities: 300 African Americans, 250 whites; involuntary detoxification center: 10 African Americans, 15 whites.

5-5 Using census data sources identified in Chapter 3, prepare a frequency distribution and a stem-and-leaf chart for (a) median income in your state's counties or (b) the proportion of African Americans in each state.

MEASURES OF CENTRAL TENDENCY

Usually an analyst will want to provide a summary of the distribution along with a tabular or graphic presentation of a frequency or percentage distribution. This can be done with measures of **central tendency,** also referred to as "averages," that include the mean, median, and mode.

The **mean** is probably the best known and most commonly used measure of central tendency. The mean is what people usually have in mind when they use the term "average." It is calculated by adding the values in a distribution and dividing by the total number of values. This is reflected in the following formula:

$$\overline{X} = \frac{\Sigma x}{N}$$

where

$\overline{X}$ = Mean of the x values

x = The individual x values in the distribution

N = The number of x values

Σ = The summation sign indicating the individual x values are to be summed

Consider the following simple example. What is the mean of 4, 5, 6, 7, and 8? To calculate it, add the numbers (4 + 5 + 6 + 7 + 8), the total of which is 30. This value is represented by Σx in the formula. The next step is to divide by N (5), the total number of values. The mean $\overline{X}$ equals 30/5, or 6. Another example is based on the information that follows.

PATIENT	DAYS IN HOSPITAL	PATIENT	DAYS IN HOSPITAL
1	5	13	2
2	3	14	4
3	10	15	25
4	1	16	150

Research in Practice 5B

FREQUENCY DISTRIBUTIONS AND SIMPLE GRAPHS

A university-based research team was asked to collaborate with a community group formed to combat a neighborhood health and aesthetic problem: the large and increasing amount of dog feces on sidewalks and lawns. The team used a time series design. The "treatment" consisted of approaching dog owners who were walking their dogs on a Saturday. The owners were informed about a city ordinance requiring owners to carry a receptacle to clean up after their dogs. If the owner did not have such a receptacle, they were provided with a bag or newspaper. Owners who took the bag or newspaper or who already had one were thanked for their cooperation; those who did not were simply told that the volunteers were trying to increase awareness of the ordinance. Additionally, flyers were handed out urging owners to pick up after their dogs.

Was this one-day intervention successful? To answer this question, the researchers measured the number and weight of dog droppings on several streets every day for nine mornings prior to the intervention. Following the intervention similar measurements were taken on six days.

Findings indicated the intervention had a moderate short-term effect in limiting the amount of dog waste found on the street, although after a couple of days, the amount began increasing again. The results are shown graphically in Figure 5-B.

PATIENT	DAYS IN HOSPITAL	PATIENT	DAYS IN HOSPITAL
5	2	17	3
6	3	18	3
7	4	19	5
8	3	20	4
9	5	21	8
10	100	22	7
11	5	23	10
12	3	24	15

What is the mean number of patient days in the hospital? Summing the columns headed days in the hospital and dividing by 24, one finds the mean equal to 15.8 (380/24).

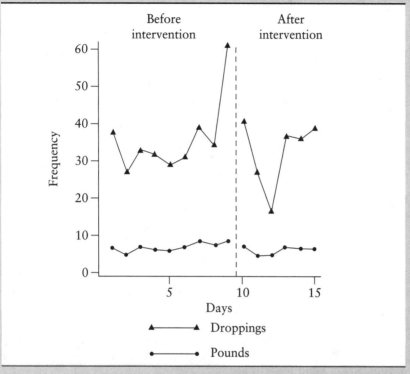

FIGURE 5-B   Daily Rates of Droppings and Pounds Before and After Intervention

SOURCE: Leonard A. Iason, Kathleen McCoy, David Blanco, and Edwin S. Zolik, "Decreasing Dog Litter," Evaluation Review, June 1980, pp. 355-69.

Based on the mean, should one conclude that most patients stayed 16 days or that about as many patients stayed 16 days and over as stayed less than 16 days? These questions point to the limitations of the mean as a summary measure. No patients stayed 16 days and only a few were close to 16. Most patients stayed less than 16 days; only a few stayed more. Thus in addition to the mean, the median is often reported in summarizing a distribution.

The **median** represents the middle value in a distribution ordered in ascending or descending order or the value that divides an ordered distribution in half such that one half of the values fall below this value and one half fall above it. To compute the median, one firsts orders a set of values, then locates the middle value. The median of the set of numbers (7, 5, 3, 6, 9) is 6. Ordering the numbers (3, 5, 6, 7, 9) finds 6 in the middle. In an even set of numbers, the median will not be an actual value in the distribution, but the mean of the two middle values. For example, the median of the following set (2, 5, 8, 11, 13, 20, 25, 30) is 12, the mean of 11 and 13. So the median in this instance identifies a value but not one that is actually part of the set of values in a distribution.

What is the median value from the information on length of hospital stays in the table? First, one needs to order the information and then locate the middle value.

1 2 2 3 3 3 3 3 3 4 4 4 5 5 5 5 7 8 10 10 15 25 100 150

The middle values are four and five, the 12th and 13th value in the distribution. The middle value or median is the mean of four and five or 4.5. The median, 4.5, indicates that one-half of the patients stayed less than this, one half stayed longer.

Notice that the mean, 15.8, and the median, 4.5, are quite different. The mean, much more sensitive to extreme values than the median, is pulled in the direction of those who had very lengthy hospital stays, the patients who stayed 100 and 150 days. Also notice that the median would not change if the patient who stayed 100 days had only stayed 5 and the one who stayed 150 days had only stayed 10. The mean, however, would be 6. The mean takes into consideration the actual scores in a distribution, the median does not.

A report on the duration of hospital stays would not want to ignore that some patients had very long stays, but it would also want to convey information on the typical length of stay. Because the mean and median convey different information, it is advisable to report both.

Often the mean and occasionally the median are expressed in units that do not make sense. For example, one might read that the mean family size is 3.3 persons or communities over 10,000 average 5.2 swimming pools. While families cannot have fractional persons or communities fractional swimming pools, such figures do permit comparisons among distributions. For example, one could compare the mean number of automobiles owned per person in one state with the number in another.

The **mode**, still another measure of central tendency, identifies the typical or most frequently occurring value. In the set of numbers (500, 511, 600, 600, 600, 850, 910, 910, 1,000), the mode is 600.

Refer back to the length of patient stays. The mode is three; more patients (six) stayed three days than any other single length of time. Thus, three is the modal length of hospital stay.

By knowing the mean, median, and mode, one can provide a fairly complete picture of a frequency distribution. For example, with respect to patient stays, one can point out that the mean stay of 15.8 days reflects the fact that a few patients had very long stays; the median of 4.5 indicates that half the patients stayed 4.5 or less days and half stayed 4.5 or more; while the mode shows that more patients stayed three days than any other length of time.

In practice, the mean and median are used more frequently than the mode. As noted earlier, the mean is particularly important in the calculation of other important statistics. The median is desirable when extreme scores are likely to distort the mean and make it less useful in providing summary information. For example, the Census Bureau provides the median income for communities rather than mean in order to avoid the distorting presence of a few wealthy persons in a community. Whether one uses the mean, median, or mode also depends on the level of measurement. If one is summarizing nominal data, only the mode will be meaningful, while any of the three can be used with interval data.

EXERCISES

5-6 Assume that you are a program analyst for a remedial education program, writing a report on the reading levels of some children after they have taken a six-month intensive reading program. Below are the scores on a reading test (possible range 0 to 100) of 30 children. Calculate the mean, median, and mode and write a paragraph interpreting them (i.e., explaining to a naive reader what the differences are between them).

Hypothetical reading scores for 30 children:

90	15	75	20	75	75	15	75	90	75
65	85	20	95	70	80	60	15	85	70
10	90	75	5	65	10	50	80	45	65

5-7 Utilizing the data sources identified in Chapter 3, locate data on fire and police expenditures for U.S. cities over 50,000 population. Calculate the mean and median expenditure level for either police or fire protection in Illinois and Colorado. Compare and interpret the findings. Illustrate the distribution of values, choosing an appropriate chart or graph.

5-8 Calculate the mean, median, and mode of the data you collected in Exercise 5-5.

COMPUTING A MEAN AND MEDIAN FROM GROUPED DATA

If one is confronted with a distribution of grouped data, that is, a distribution where frequencies are reported for a range of values, one can also compute a mean and median. In calculating a mean for grouped data, the midpoint of each interval is multiplied by the frequency of the interval. These numbers are summed and the result divided by the total frequency. Assume the following distribution for number of employees in 25 agencies of Bureau City, Pennsylvania.

NUMBER OF EMPLOYEES	AGENCIES	×	MIDPOINT OF INTERVAL	=	MIDPOINT × NUMBER OF AGENCIES
1–25	5		13		65
26–50	3		38		114
51–75	7		63		441
74–100	6		88		528
101–125	4		113		452
Total	$\Sigma = 25$				$\Sigma = 1,600$

The midpoint of each interval is shown. The product of each frequency and midpoint is also shown. The mean of the distribution equals 1,600/25 (25 agencies), or 64.

To calculate the median of the distribution, first determine the interval in which the median is located. In the above case, the median is located in 51-75. Of the 25 agencies, the middle case or 13th agency, falls here. If we assume, as we must if we are to calculate the median, that the seven agencies in this interval are spread evenly throughout, the median equals 50 (the ending value of the previous interval), plus 5/7 of the interval distance between 51 and 75 or 5/7 of 25, which is 17.9. The median is 50 plus 17.9, or 67.9.

One should never compute the mean or median for grouped data if the raw data are available. Means and medians calculated in this way can only be considered estimates.

EXERCISE

5-9 Calculate the mean and median for the reading scores from Exercise 5-6 grouped into the intervals below. Compare the grouped mean and median with the mean and median from Exercise 5-6.

READING SCORES	FREQUENCY
1–25	8
26–50	2
51–75	12
76–100	8

MEASURES OF DISPERSION

Two sets of values may have identical means yet have very different distributions. Consider the data in Table 5-6. The mean patient load per day in each clinic is identical. Overall "productivity" is identical. Yet, it is obvious that the distribution of the workload is not the same. In E-Z Care Clinic, the patient load is unequally distributed, with doctors D and E doing five times the work of doctors A and B. In Welrun Clinic, patients are equally distributed among the doctors. Neither the mean, median nor mode reveal this difference. This difference is reflected in **measures of dispersion** or spread which summarize the degree of variation in a set of values.

TABLE 5-6   Patient Load per Day by Doctor in Two Clincis, Health City, Texas—1990-1995

E-Z CARE CLINIC		WELRUN CLINIC	
Doctor	Patients	Doctor	Patients
A	10	F	28
B	20	G	29
C	30	H	30
D	40	I	31
E	50	J	32
	$\overline{X} = 30$		$\overline{X} = 30$

The Range

One simple measure of dispersion is the **range**. The range is simply the largest value less the smallest value in a distribution. If the range is narrow, values are close together. If the range is large, they are far apart. The range for E-Z Clinic is 40, for Welrun Clinic, 4. Patient loads in E- Z are spread out; in Welrun, they are clustered together. Because the range only considers the lowest and highest values in a distribution, it excludes much information. For example, the following two sets of numbers have the same range, but very different distributions.

A 10 30 30 30 30 30 30 50
B 20 20 20 20 20 20 60 60

Most of the values in A are equal to the mean (30), with 10 and 50 the lowest and highest values. In B, the mean is 30, but the values are all equal to the lowest and highest values, with none equal to or near the mean.

Average Deviation

It is often necessary to go beyond the range and look at each value in a distribution in relationship to a central value. One measure of dispersion that does this is the **average deviation**. It examines each value in relationship to the mean. One can compute the average deviation by doing the following:

1. Calculate the mean ($\overline{X}$). Note that the median, while less often used, can be employed in the computation of the average deviation also.
2. Subtract the mean from each value ($X - \overline{X}$).
3. Take the absolute value $|X - \overline{X}|$. The absolute value disregards the sign. That is, the absolute value of -10 is 10. The absolute value of $-.5$ is .5. The symbol for the absolute value of 10 is $|10|$.
4. Sum these values $\Sigma|X - \overline{X}|$.
5. Divide the sum by the total number of cases $\Sigma|X - \overline{X}|/N$.

The average deviation for E-Z Care Clinic is computed below.

Computation of the Average Deviation for E-Z Care Clinic:

Doctor	X	$(X - \overline{X})$	$|X - \overline{X}|$
A	10	-20	20
B	20	-10	10
C	30	0	0
D	40	10	10
E	50	20	20
	$\overline{X} = 30$	$\Sigma = 0$	$\Sigma = 60$
	$N = 5$		

$$\text{Average deviation} = \frac{\Sigma|X - \overline{X}|}{N} = \frac{60}{5} = 12$$

An average deviation of 12 means that the typical patient load deviates from the mean patient load by 12. Notice that the $\Sigma(X - \overline{X})$ is 0. Thus, it is necessary to compute the absolute value of each deviation. Similarly, the average deviation for Welrun Clinic can be calculated.

Computation of the Average Deviation for Welrun Clinic:

DOCTOR	X	$(X - \overline{X})$	$|X - \overline{X}|$
A	28	−2	2
B	29	−1	1
C	30	0	0
D	31	1	1
E	32	2	2
	$\overline{X} = 30$	$\Sigma = 0$	$\Sigma = 6$
	$N = 5$		

$$\text{Average deviation} = \frac{\Sigma|X - \overline{X}|}{N} = \frac{6}{5} = 1.2$$

Here, the average deviation of patient loads is 1.2, one-tenth the average deviation of 12 in E-Z Care Clinic.

STANDARD DEVIATION

As simple as the average deviation is to compute, it is not widely used. The most frequently used measure of dispersion is the **standard deviation**. The steps in calculating the standard deviation are identical to the average deviation except that instead of the absolute value of $(X - \overline{X})$, this value is squared. Then, after summing and dividing by N, one takes the positive square root in order to express the measure in the original unit of measurement, that is, in the case of E-Z and Welrun, patients per doctor rather than patients squared per doctor. The formula for standard deviation is:

$$S = \sqrt{\frac{\Sigma(X - \overline{X})^2}{N}}$$

The steps for computing the standard deviation are as follows:

1. Calculate the mean $\overline{X}$
2. Subtract the mean from each value $(X - \overline{X})$
3. Square these values $(X - \overline{X})^2$
4. Sum the total $\Sigma(X - \overline{X})^2$
5. Divide the sum by the total number of cases $\dfrac{\Sigma(X - \overline{X})^2}{N}$

6. Take the positive square root $\sqrt{\dfrac{\Sigma(X - \bar{X})^2}{N}}$

The standard deviations for E-Z Care and Welrun are calculated below.

Computation of the Standard Deviation for E-Z Care Clinic:

DOCTOR	X	$(X - \bar{X})$	$(X - \bar{X})^2$
A	10	−20	400
B	20	−10	100
C	30	0	0
D	40	10	100
E	50	20	400
	$\bar{X} = 30$	$\Sigma = 0$	$\Sigma = 1,000$

$$\text{Standard deviation } (S) = \sqrt{\frac{1,000}{5}} = \sqrt{200} = 14.14$$

Computation of the Standard Deviation for Welrun Clinic:

DOCTOR	X	$(X - \bar{X})$	$(X - \bar{X})^2$
A	28	−2	4
B	29	−1	1
C	30	0	0
D	31	1	1
E	32	2	4
	$\bar{X} = 30$	$\Sigma = 0$	$\Sigma = 10$

$$\text{Standard deviation } (S) = \sqrt{\frac{10}{2}} = \sqrt{2} = 1.41$$

In reporting the results of this analysis, one would say that in E-Z Care Clinic, the mean patient load per doctor is 30 patients per day with a standard deviation of 14.1. While in Welrun Clinic, the mean patient load is 30, but the standard deviation 1.4. As with the range and average deviation, the smaller standard deviation in Welrun indicates there is less spread or dispersion among patient loads. The size of the standard deviation of a distribution is meaningful only in relation to the mean of the distribution. For example, a standard deviation of 14 would be considered small if the mean was 1,000. If, on the other hand, the mean was 10, a standard deviation of 14 would be quite large. The larger the standard deviation in relationship to the mean, the more dispersed the values of a distribution.

FIGURE 5-6   **Distribution of Students' Test Scores on Verbal Ability**

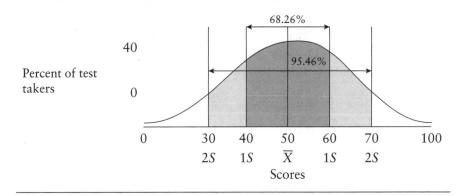

VARIANCE

Another measure of dispersion, associated with the mean and closely related to the standard deviation, is the **variance.** The variance is simply the square of the standard deviation. Thus, the variance is calculated in the process of deriving the standard deviation.

$$\text{Variance} = S^2 = \frac{\Sigma(X\text{-}\overline{X})^2}{N}$$

INTERPRETING THE STANDARD DEVIATION AND THE NORMAL CURVE

In order to illustrate the procedures involved in calculating the standard deviation and other measures of dispersion, the previous examples involved a small number of cases (five doctors, 25 patients, etc.). The research projects one is likely to become involved with will rarely involve so few. More typically, these will deal with hundreds or perhaps thousands of values. In some instances, the distribution of these values will look like the familiar bell-shaped or **normal curve.** Consider scores on a test of verbal ability administered to several thousand students in a school district. One can anticipate that a small number will receive very high scores. Likewise, a small number will get very low scores. Most, however, will get scores in the middle and the distribution would look like Figure 5-6 and constitute what is called a **normal distribution.**

A normal distribution has an equal number of values above and below the mean, with a high percentage of values clustered near the mean and relatively few in the tails or at the extremes of the distribution. If the distribution is normal, 68 percent of the values will fall within one standard deviation of the mean, and 95 percent within two standard deviations of the mean. In figure 5-6, 68 percent of the students would have scores between 40 and 60 (50 +/- 10);

95 percent have scores been 30 and 70 [50 +/− (2 x 10)]. Almost all the students would score within 20 points of the mean. The shaded portion in the figure represents the area within one standard deviation, the lined portion within two standard deviations. Ninety-nine percent of the scores would fall within three standard deviations of the mean.

If one found that the patient load per day of doctors working in a clinic distributed normally with a mean of 30 and a standard deviation of 5, this would mean that 68 percent of the doctors saw between 25 and 35 patients per day and that 95 percent saw between 20 and 40 per day. Over 99 percent saw between 15 and 45 per day.

These properties of the normal distribution not only allow one to know the shape of a distribution and how values are distributed around the mean, it allows the drawing of inferences when the research results one observes may have been produced by variations in the data owing to chance or random fluctuations. Statistical inference is the topic of discussion in Chapter 7.

HINGE, MIDSPREAD, AND PERCENTILE

While the average and standard deviation involve spread about a mean value, the **hinge** and **midspread** are measures of dispersion associated with the median. Recall that the median is simply the middle number in a distribution of values ordered from lowest to highest.

21 45 52 91 103 136 149 163 174 189 218

In the above series, 136 is the median. The lower hinge is the number below which one-fourth of the values lie and above which three-fourths lie; the upper hinge is that number above which one-fourth of the values lie and below which three-fourths lie (one-fourth of the values is called a "**quartile**"). In the above series, the lower hinge is 52, the upper is 174. The distance between the lower and upper hinge is called the midspread, or the **interquartile range**. The midspread in this example is 174 − 52, or 122. The midspread is the range within which half the values fall. Note that the lower and upper hinge and midspread are not affected by extreme values. The value 218 could be 2,180 or 21,800, and the hinge and midspread would remain the same.

Percentile is another measure one is likely to encounter. One percentile is 1/100 of a distribution. A given percentile indicates the proportion of values falling below that number. To say, for example, that a student's score is in the 90th percentile indicates that 90 percent of the scores are below it.

EXERCISE

5-10 Using the data collected in either Exercise 5-3 or 5-5, calculate (a) the mean, standard deviation, and variance, and (b) the median, lower and upper hinges, and midspread. In doing (a), you will probably want to use a computer to calculate the variance, (b) can be done easily by hand. Write a paragraph summarizing the findings. What is the interval one standard deviation around the mean? How does it compare with the midspread? In standard deviation units, what is the range of the midspread?

COMPUTING THE VARIANCE AND STANDARD DEVIATION FROM GROUPED DATA

As with the mean and median, it is also possible to compute the standard deviation and variance with grouped data. One begins by calculating the grouped mean. The midpoint of each interval is then subtracted from the mean and this difference squared. Each squared value is multiplied by the frequency of the interval and the results summed. Division of this total by the total number of cases or N yields the variance, the square root of which is the standard deviation. Follow these calculations below, using data from the section on computing a mean and median from grouped data. Recall that the mean of the distribution was 64.

NUMBER OF EMPLOYEES	AGENCIES	MIDPOINT OF INTERVAL	MIDPOINT MINUS THE MEAN	(MIDPOINT − MEAN)²	AGENCIES × (MIDPOINT − MEAN)²
1-25	5	13	−51	2,601	13,005
26-50	3	38	−26	676	2,028
51-75	7	63	− 1	1	7
76-100	6	88	24	576	3,456
101-125	4	113	49	2,401	9,604
					28,100

$$\text{Variance} = \frac{28,100}{25} = 1,124$$

$$\text{Standard Deviation} = \sqrt{1,124} = 33.5$$

STANDARD SCORE (Z SCORES)

Occasionally, it is desirable to compare scores in two or more distributions that have different means and standard deviations. For example, one might be interested in comparing test scores on different tests administered by different school districts. Assume one test has a mean score of 100 and a standard deviation of 10, while the other has a mean score of 750 and a standard deviation of 100. How does a score of 75 on the first test compare with a score of 600 on the second? A way to compare these distributions is to convert them to standard, or Z scores. The conversion is available as part of most standard statistical software. The formula for converting scores is:

$$Z = \frac{X - \overline{X}}{S}$$

where

Z = the standard, or Z score

X = the score to be converted

 = the mean of the distribution

S = the standard deviation of the distribution

Thus, a Z score is simply the difference between a score and mean of all scores divided by the standard deviation. The distribution of Z scores will have a mean of zero and a standard deviation of one. If one assumes a distribution with a mean of 10 and standard deviation of 5, the Z score for the mean equals zero.

$$Z = \frac{10 - 10}{5} = \frac{0}{5} = 0$$

Likewise, calculating a Z score for the mean plus the standard deviation equals one.

$$Z = \frac{15 - 10}{5} = \frac{5}{5} = 1$$

Continuing with the example above, if one wishes to compare a score of 75 on one test with a score of 600 on the second, one does the following:

$$Z = \frac{75 - 100}{5} = \frac{-25}{10} = -.25$$

$$Z = \frac{600 - 750}{100} = \frac{-150}{100} = -1.5$$

In the first instance, the test score is 2.5 standard deviations below the mean, while the second score is only 1.5 standard deviations below. On the first test the score is lower compared to the mean of the group than the score on the second.

Z scores are also useful in determining what proportion of a distribution lies between two scores. If the mean of a normal distribution is 450 and standard deviation 120, the Z transformation can be used to find what proportion of scores lie between two scores. For example, to determine what proportion of scores fall between 450 and 350, convert 350 to a Z score.

$$Z = \frac{450 - 350}{120} = \frac{100}{120} = .83$$

One can then turn to a normal table (Appendix B) and locate Z = .83. The number is .2967. This is the proportion of scores that falls between 0, the mean of a normal distribution, and a Z of .83. Thus, nearly 30 percent (.2967 x 100) of the scores fall between 450 and 350. To find the proportion of scores between 550 and 450, one does the same thing, except $Z = -.83$. Because the normal curve is symmetrical, that is, has an equal number of values or scores above and below the mean, the same proportion of scores falls between 450 and 550. Thus, to find the proportion of scores between 350 and 550, one simply has to multiply .2967 by 2.

EXERCISES

5-11

50	70
30	60
20	80
30	40
40	30

a. Assume that you are a research analyst in the city streets department putting together a report on pothole repair. The data above have been collected and represent the number of potholes repaired each day for the past 10 days. Compute the mean, median, range, average deviation, standard deviation, and variance. Write a brief paragraph summarizing what your computations show.

b. Instead of being based on 10 days, assume the mean and standard deviation are based on 1,000 days and that the distribution is normal. Calculate the following:

(1) The interval one standard deviation around the mean;
(2) The interval two standard deviations around the mean;
(3) The proportion of values in the intervals specified in (1) and (2).

5-12 The Health Department of Broken Branch, Idaho, kept records of employee absences over 10 years. Based on a sample of 100 employees, the department found that the mean number of absences per employee for medical reasons was 4.4 days per year, with a standard deviation of 1.2. Assuming a normal distribution: (a) what is the Z score for 3 days absent? 5 days absent; (b) what proportion of employees have between 4.4 and 5 days absence? What proportion between 3 and 4.4 days absence?

5-13 Assume the state of Minnesota gives a paramedical certification test with a mean score of 70 and a standard deviation of 10. The state of Wisconsin gives a test with a mean score of 150 and a standard deviation of 30. Compare a score of 82 on the Minnesota test with a score of 185 on the Wisconsin test. If a passing score in Minnesota is .5 standard deviations above the mean, what is the score?

OTHER DISTRIBUTIONS

One cannot assume a normal distribution even with large numbers of values. For example, some distributions are U shaped, with most values at the extremes and relatively few clustered around the mean. Figure 5-7 is such a dis-

FIGURE 5-7   A "U" Shaped Distribution of Student Scores

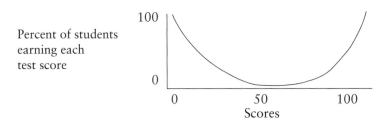

FIGURE 5-8   A Flat Distribution of Student Scores

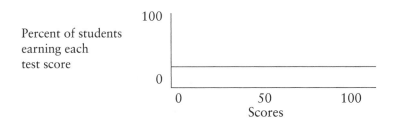

FIGURE 5-9   Skewed Distribution of Student Scores

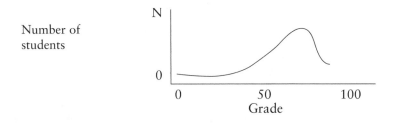

tribution. It indicates that most students either did very poorly or very well. Very few scored in the middle of the distribution. In this distribution the standard deviation is large in relationship to the mean.

Another distribution is flat: the values are distributed evenly over the range of possible scores, as in Figure 5-8. Here, the same number of students are found at each score from 0 to 100.

Another distribution is found in Figure 5-9. This looks very much like a grade distribution for a high school or college examination. Few values are below 60, while most are between 75 and 85. This distribution is **skewed** in the direction of higher values. That is, there are more values at the higher than lower end of the distribution. The scores are clustered at one end rather than in the middle.

Seldom will a distribution be normal, and thus one cannot assume 68 percent of the cases will fall within one standard deviation of the mean. But the normal distribution can be used to draw inferences where random variations might be a factor. Chapter 7 will discuss the normal distribution and its role in statistical inference.

KEY TERMS

Frequency distribution	Average deviation
Percentage distribution	Standard deviation
Bar graphs	Variance
Line graphs	Normal curve
Stem-and-leaf chart	Normal distribution
Pie chart	Hinge
Central tendency	Midspread
Mean	Quartile
Median	Interquartile range
Mode	Percentile
Measures of dispersion	Z scores
Range	Skewed

FOR FURTHER HELP

Hagle, Timothy. *Basic Math for Social Scientists: Concepts* and *Basic Math for Social Scientists: Problems and Solutions*. Sage Publishing, 1995.

Hartwig, Frederick, with Brian E. Dearing. *Exploratory Data Analysis*. Beverly Hills, Calif.: Sage University Papers, 1979. Good coverage of less frequently discussed terms and techniques, such as stem-and-leaf chart, hinge, and midspread, and some fairly simple data analytic techniques that are not covered in this text.

Tukey, J. W. *Exploratory Data Analysis*. Reading, Mass.: Addison-Wesley Publishing, 1977. Coverage of simple and complex techniques of exploratory data analysis.

Weisberg, Herbert. *Central Tendency and Variability*. Beverly Hills, Calif.: Sage University Papers, 1992.

6

ANALYZING THE RELATIONSHIP BETWEEN
VARIABLES: PERCENTAGE TABLES AND
MEASURES OF ASSOCIATION

Managers and analysts want to do more than describe a variable; they will want to show how one variable affects another. For example, the personnel director of a large government agency may be concerned that the women employees seem to be promoted more slowly then men. Or maybe a police department's community relations officer suspects that African American citizens are more hostile toward the police than white citizens. A newspaper story may have quoted African American community leaders commenting that local police officers are prejudiced toward the African American community. A public health official may suspect that a dumpsite is responsible for widespread illness in the neighborhoods close by.

Examining the link between such variables is a necessary step in fashioning solutions to deal with these kinds of problems. If men are promoted faster than women are, personnel policies can be modified to insure that qualified women are part of the promotion pool. If African Americans are more hostile to police than are whites, police officers can be trained to build support and trust in the minority community. If illness is more likely to occur in neighborhoods bordering a dumpsite compared to those farther away, the site can be cleaned up or citizens relocated. Each of these potential links raises an implicit research question that can be stated as a question or hypothesis as noted in Chapter 2. One might ask, for example, are men promoted faster than women or are African Americans more hostile to the police than whites? The same questions can be formulated as hypotheses: men are promoted faster than women and African Americans are more hostile to the police than whites.

How does one answer such questions or test such hypotheses? The answer is by examining the relationship between two variables. One way to do this is by constructing a table, called a **contingency or cross-classification table**, where the values of one variable are cross-classified with values of another. To understand how this is done, recall the discussion of frequency distributions in Chapter 5. A frequency distribution displays the values of one variable and the frequency with which each value occurs. One might, for example, encounter the following frequency distribution regarding promotions in an agency of city government.

Table 6-1 shows that among the employees in Parks and Recreation in 1999, twenty-two were promoted during their first year of employment, twenty-six their second year, twenty-nine their third year, and eight their fourth year. N equals the total number of employees. These numbers can be converted, and often are, to percentages and yield the following percentage distribution.

This table shows that 26 percent of the workforce was promoted their first year of employment, 31 percent their second and so on. These numbers are obtained as described in Chapter 5 by dividing each frequency by the total in the distribution (eighty-five) and multiplying by 100. For example, 26 percent equals 22 divided by 85 multiplied by 100. Although there is only one distribution in Table 6-2, the use of percentages rather than frequencies facilitates comparisons among distributions and makes it easier to draw conclusions from them.

Suppose a complaint has been filed by an employee in Parks and Recreation alleging that men are promoted more quickly than women are. The charge calls for a comparison of how quickly men and women are promoted. It is necessary to compare the distribution of men with the distribution of women. Another way to say this is that one must cross-classify year of promotion with gender. Table 6-3 does this.

TABLE 6-1   Year of Promotion, Parks and Recreation Department, Falls City, Ohio—1999

YEAR OF PROMOTION	
First year of employment	22
Second year of employment	26
Third year of employment	29
Fourth year of employment	8
N	85

TABLE 6-2   Year of Promotion, Parks and Recreation Department, Falls City, Ohio—1999

YEAR OF PROMOTION	
First year of employment	26%
Second year of employment	31%
Third year of employment	34%
Fourth year of employment	9%
Total	100%
(N)	(85)

TABLE 6-3 Year of Promotion by Gender, Parks and Recreation Department, Falls City, Ohio—1999

	MEN	WOMEN	TOTAL
First year of employment	14	8	22
Second year of employment	12	14	26
Third year of employment	7	22	29
Fourth year of employment	4	4	8
N	37	48	85

TABLE 6-4 Year of Promotion by Gender, Parks and Recreation Department, Falls City, Ohio—1999

YEAR OF PROMOTION	MEN	WOMEN	TOTAL
First year of employment	38%	17%	26%
Second year of employment	32	29	31
Third year of employment	19	46	34
Fourth year of employment	11	8	9
Total	100%	100%	100%
(N)	(37)	(48)	(85)

Based on Table 6-3, is the complaint justified? Because there are fewer men than women, it is difficult to draw a conclusion based on frequencies. It would be easier to draw a conclusion if the number of men and women were equal. As they are not, it is necessary to transform or scale the frequency distribution so that numbers are based on the same standard. This is done by converting the frequency distributions to percentage distributions, in effect imposing the same scale on the frequency distributions for men and women and facilitating comparisons between them. This is done in Table 6-4.

A quick glance at the columns headed men and women reveals that men are promoted earlier in their careers than women. Whereas 38 percent of the men are promoted their first year, only 17 percent of the women are. Thirty-two percent of the men are promoted their second year, compared to 29 percent of the women. Note that the column at the right is the percentage distribution for year of promotion for men and women combined shown earlier in Table 6-2. This distribution is referred to as the marginal distribution for year of promotion.

CONTINGENCY TABLE ANALYSIS

DETERMINING THE INDEPENDENT VARIABLE

In assessing the relationship between two variables like those shown in Table 6-4, an analyst looks for differences between or among categories of the independent variable. Recall from Chapter 2 that the independent variable is hypothesized to influence or act upon the dependent variable. In Table 6-4, the independent variable is gender. The dependent variable is year of promotion. Thus, in assessing the relationship between gender and promotion, compare men to women.

When you are the analyst, the independent variable will be readily apparent. You, after all, will formulate the hypothesis and should have a clear idea as to which is the independent (the "cause") and which is the dependent (the "effect") variable. If this is not clear, it means that you have not thought about the research question carefully enough. When reviewing someone else's work, you also should be able to discern which is the independent variable by examining the hypothesis or research question. On occasion, however, you may be puzzled about which is the independent variable.

When this happens, use common sense. Consider Table 6-4. Promotion could not influence gender, so gender must be the independent variable. Assuming or establishing a temporal sequence between the variables may also help in determining which is the independent and which is the dependent variable. Again, with respect to Table 6-4, it is clear that gender occurred before promotion.

In some situations, however, there are no clues. Consider, for example, the relationship between the number who are mugged over a period of time and the number of police officers employed by cities of a certain size. Which is the independent variable? Common sense might suggest that it is the number of police officers that influences the number of muggings; more police officers would, one hopes, lead to fewer muggings. However, cities with large numbers of muggings may be pressed into employing more officers, so that more muggings produce more police officers. In such cases, sorting out which is the independent and which is the dependent variable may be impossible, especially in non-experimental research.

CONSTRUCTING A TABLE

While one will rarely ever generate a contingency table by hand, it is useful in understanding the mechanics of table construction to do so. As with calculating a frequency distribution, keep a running tabulation of the data. In the example here, begin with two columns, one labeled men, one women, and four rows, one for each year of promotion. For each employee, one would initially determine gender, then the year in which the person was promoted. Finally, make a check in the appropriate column and row, also called a cell, as illustrated below.

	MEN	WOMEN
First year of employment	JHT JHT IIII	JHT III
Second year of employment	JHT JHT II	JHT JHT IIII
Third year of employment	JHT II	JHT JHT JHT JHT II
Fourth year of employment	IIII	IIII

After having worked through all the data, the check marks can be converted to a frequency distribution and this would, of course, look exactly like the information in Table 6-3. This information can in turn be converted to a contingency table much like Table 6-4. It is a simple task to generate this information with a personal computer and standard software package. Thus, no one need go through this process.

However, it will still be necessary to construct a table containing the information. There are rules for doing so. Tables are numbered and labeled. The label should identify the variables displayed in the table. The independent variable is identified at the top of the table with its values clearly labeled. The dependent variable is located at the side with its values clearly labeled. Only the percentages are normally included. The marginal frequency for the independent variable is included at the base of the table as in Table 6-4, with column frequencies enclosed in parentheses. By including this information, the cell frequencies can be calculated if desired. The column labeled "total" would normally not be included.

Note that percentages in Table 6-4 are computed on the basis of column frequencies, that is, within categories or values of the independent variable. The percentages add to 100 within their specific columns. You might think that this is the obvious thing to do because the point of the task is to compare men with women. We want to know how the percent of women promoted in their first year compares to the percent of men promoted their first year, and so on. Thus we need to standardize the distributions based on the number of men and women. A rule of thumb is that percentages are always computed on the basis of totals within values of the independent variable, in this case gender. The influence of the independent variable is assessed by comparing across such values, in this case, for example, determining that only 17 percent of the women compared to 38 percent of men are promoted in their first year.

Deciding which way to calculate the percentages in a table is sometimes confusing because statistical software will compute multiple sets of percentages. For example, one commonly used package generates percentages based on column totals, row totals, and the total number in the table. If you are confronted with several sets of percentages, first locate the independent variable and then select the set that adds to 100 percent within values of the independent variable.

To avoid confusion and allow the reader at a glance to know which way percentages have been calculated, 100 percent should be included at the base of the column, assuming that the independent variable is located at the top of the table, as in Table 6-4. The column totals may vary from 99 to 101 percent due to rounding. This is often noted in a footnote located immediately below the table. If decimals are included, one place is sufficient for most analyses.

Sometimes tables exclude some of the information in Table 6-4. For larger tables and those that deal with more than one independent or dependent variable, information may be excluded for reasons of space or aesthetics. A rule of thumb with respect to leaving out information is to omit only that which can be derived from what is included. If, for example, the dependent variable is dichotomous, it is perfectly acceptable to include only one value, inasmuch as readers can derive missing information for themselves. That is, if the table shows the percent who responded "yes" to a dichotomous item, it is easy to calculate the percent who said "no," and thus redundant to show that in a table. The important thing is for readers to be able to easily understand what the table is trying to show.

It should be obvious at this point how to interpret Table 6-4. One compares men with women and finds that men get promoted earlier in their employment career than women.

In interpreting contingency tables, there is the temptation to focus on single values of the independent variable and report, for example, that 38 percent of the men are promoted their first year, 32 percent their second year, 19 their third, and 11 their fourth, then report the percentages for the other values. This kind of summary obscures the comparison between men and women. A more revealing presentation would point out that 38 percent of the men are promoted their first year compared to 17 percent of the women, 32 percent of men their second year compared to 29 percent for women, and so forth. (See Research in Practice 6A for another example of contingency table analysis.)

With larger tables, those with more than two values of the independent and dependent variable, interpretation becomes more difficult, but the procedure is the same. One still looks for differences across values of the independent variable. Table 6-5 is a two by four table (two rows and four columns). Comparing across the independent variable, one observes that productivity is related to promotion. The more productive employees get promoted faster than the less productive. A higher percentage of the most productive (level 1) employees get promoted the first year than the next most productive (level 2) and a higher percentage of level 2 employees get promoted the first year than level 3 and so on.

In general, the larger the table, the more difficult the task of interpretation. Thus, it is advisable to limit table size to something manageable for both you and the reader. While table size is less of a problem when the goal is simply description, as in statistical documents such as census reports, when the task is assessing the relationship between variables, smaller is better. Three or four values for the dependent variable and six or seven for the independent variable are probably the outside limits for ease of presentation and interpretation. Variables extending beyond these limits can perhaps be treated as interval scales of measurement and modes of analysis other than a contingency table used (see Chapter 9), or values of variables may be collapsed.

Often, interval level variables such as income and education are collapsed to three or four categories encompassing a range of values. The collapsed categories need to make sense. For example, education might be collapsed into zero through eight years, nine through twelve years, and thirteen or more years. These points represent meaningful divisions: elementary school, high school, and college. Categories also need to consider the frequency distribution

Research in Practice 6A

CONTINGENCY TABLE ANALYSIS

Who are the homeless? Identifying their characteristics may help in ameliorating the extent of homelessness by identifying possible solutions to the problem. In this research project, the authors were particularly interested in the characteristics of the Hispanic (Latino) homeless population in one community.

The researchers surveyed homeless people in Lincoln, Nebraska, an urban area located in a predominantly rural, agricultural state. Due to the various, rather obvious difficulties in employing random sampling of the homeless population, they used a nonrandom sampling strategy to locate 133 respondents in homeless shelters. They asked questions about race, education, marital status, age, employment status, and migration patterns.

The researchers discovered that while Hispanics make up only 2 percent of the population of Lincoln, they were 21 percent of the sample. They did not discuss the extent to which this discrepancy could be due to the sampling strategy used, a distinct possibility in this instance.

The researchers used contingency tables to analyze the data, with ethnicity (Hispanic and non-Hispanic) the primary independent variable of interest. They discovered that, compared to those who were not Latino, the Hispanic respondents were much younger, less educated, more likely to be married, and less likely to be employed.

A contingency table that examined race in relation to migration patterns provided the most striking results. Almost all of the Hispanic respondents were born outside the United States. Thus, it is not surprising that Latino respondents were newer to Lincoln, with 86 percent having been in Lincoln for less than a year, compared to only 45 percent of non-Hispanic respondents. The Hispanic homeless had come to Lincoln primarily because of work, or the desire for work. Over two-thirds of Hispanic respondents, compared to only 37 percent of others, listed work as their reason for being in Lincoln.

The authors concluded that the homeless composition in Nebraska is different than found elsewhere. Examining Hispanic homeless men and women, they point out that most are new to the state and come to Nebraska seeking employment. This is likely the result of the demand for migrant and temporary labor in agriculture and in meat processing. Consequently, the authors suggested that rural, agricultural states develop programs that address the particular concerns of these low-income workers such as temporary housing, job assistance, and transportation.

SOURCE: Sharon Lord Gaber and Rodrigo Cantarero, "Hispanic Migrant Laborer Homelessness in Nebraska: Examining Agricultural Restructuring as One Path to Homelessness," *MARS: Social Thought and Research* (1997): 55–72.

TABLE 6-5   Year of Promotion by Productivity, Parks and Recreation Department, Falls City, Ohio—1999

	Level of Productivity			
YEAR OF PROMOTION	1	2	3	4
First Year	75%	66%	61%	45%
After First Year	25	34	39	55
	100%	100%	100%	100%
	(8)	(29)	(26)	(22)

of the variable being measured. The above breakdown would not be appropriate if only a few persons had thirteen or more years of education. In this case, one might consider zero through eight, nine through eleven, and twelve or more. The analyst also should maintain reasonably large frequencies within the cells of contingency tables. Avoid collapsing in ways that reduce some cells to zero or so few observations (cases or units) that make it impossible to draw any meaningful conclusion. In general, the number of categories as well as cutoff points should reflect a concern to preserve as much information as possible while at the same time reducing information to a manageable level, both in terms of analysis and presentation.

EXERCISES

6-1 The supervisor of a state welfare office believes new computer software can add to the productivity of caseworkers under her direction. The software is made available on a trial basis to some caseworkers. After six weeks, the following information is available for analysis:

CASE WORKER	SOFTWARE	EDUCATION	EXPERIENCE	JOB SATISFACTION	PRODUCTIVITY
1	Yes	MA	1	Low	20
2	Yes	BA	5	High	35
3	Yes	MA	2	Low	40
4	Yes	MA	5	High	38
5	Yes	MA	6	High	18
6	Yes	BA	7	High	42
7	Yes	SC	10	High	35
8	Yes	SC	10	High	31
9	No	BA	4	High	33
10	No	BA	5	High	36
11	No	BA	9	Low	23
12	No	MA	8	High	32

CASE WORKER	SOFTWARE	EDUCATION	EXPERIENCE	JOB SATISFACTION	PRODUCTIVITY
13	No	SC	15	High	38
14	No	BA	5	Low	23
15	No	BA	4	Low	36
16	No	MA	11	High	25
17	No	SC	3	Low	24
18	No	BA	4	Low	32
19	No	SC	10	High	35
20	No	MA	13	High	32

Variables: Software: Yes, No; Education: SC = Some College, BA = Bachelors, MA = Masters; Experience: Years on the job; Job satisfaction: Positive feeling toward the job; Productivity: Average number of clients served per week over the past six months.

a. Calculate and properly label a contingency table showing the relationship between use of the new software and productivity. Which is the independent and dependent variable?

b. Describe the relationship between use of the new software and productivity.

6-2 State officials are concerned with the efficacy of managed care versus fee for service delivery of health care to Medicaid clients. During the past six months, 310 of 1,880 patients treated through managed care were later admitted to a hospital for treatment of illness. Of the 860 treated through fee for service, 430 were later admitted to a hospital. Construct a contingency table based on this information, and interpret the results.

6-3 Of twenty-seven senior diner centers in Topeka, Kansas, twelve average fifty or more participants per week, ten from twenty-six to forty-nine, and five less than twenty-six. The director of the program suspects that participation is related to the proximity of the centers to city bus lines. Construct a contingency table based on the following information, and evaluate the director's suspicion.

AVERAGE NUMBER OF PARTICIPANTS	ON A BUS LINE	ONE QUARTER MILE	ONE HALF MILE
1–25	0	1	4
26–49	2	6	2
50 or more	8	3	1

6-4 A police department has isolated a number of high-accident intersections, and the chief wants to know if his decision to station officers at several of these sites during rush hour the past six months has reduced traffic accidents. What can you tell him from the following information?

	Number of Accidents	
	LOW	HIGH
Officer	13	14
No Officer	3	9

6-5 The program director in a state department of education is preparing a report concerning variations in median education levels across counties in her state. She speculates that low levels of formal education are associated with low median incomes. You are assigned to prepare documentation dealing with this point. Using the appropriate census data profiled in Chapter 3, find median income on a county-by-county basis in your state or in Illinois if your state has only a few counties. Find median years of education for the same units and prepare a three by three table showing the relationship between education and income. Considering education the independent variable, calculate the correct percentages, and write a paragraph interpreting the findings.

6-6 Using information in Exercise 6-1, determine if productivity is linked to education, experience, or job satisfaction. Calculate and properly label contingency tables to display these relationships.

The Concept and Measurement of Association

In assessing the relationship between two variables, we are interested in the degree or strength of **association** between them. While this information is reflected in a contingency table, measures of association capture it in a single coefficient. **Measures of association** do not take the place of contingency tables but supplement them. They are useful summary measures, just as the mean is a summary measure for a frequency distribution.

One can begin to understand the concept of association by considering the extremes, **zero** or **no association,** on the one hand, and **perfect association** on the other. What would one have to observe in a table to conclude that there is *no* association between two variables? What would one have to observe to conclude that there is *perfect* association between two variables?

Think for a moment about the first example. Recall Table 6-4. If there were no relationship between gender and promotion, there would be no differences across values of the independent variable. Table 6-6A indicates zero association between ethnicity and promotion. Each value of the independent variable (in this example African Americans and Hispanics) has exactly the same percentage distributions for the dependent variable. Twenty-seven percent of African Americans were promoted their first year. Similarly, 27 percent of Hispanics were promoted their first year. Zero association can also be thought of as no differences between the **expected and observed frequencies** in the cells of a table. In Table 6-6B, twenty-three employees, or 27 percent of both African Americans and Hispanics were promoted their first year on the job. If there were no differences between African Americans and Hispanics, we would expect 27 percent of each group to be promoted their first year. The frequency represented by 27 percent of each group is the expected frequency for the respective cells. Since there are forty-eight Hispanics, the expected frequency for Hispanics promoted the first year is thirteen (27/100 multiplied by 48). As there are thirty-seven African Americans, the expected frequency for African Americans promoted the first year is ten (27/100 multiplied by 37). The expected frequency for the remaining cells are thirty-five (73/100 multiplied by

48) and twenty-seven (73/100 multiplied by 37). If the observed cell frequencies, those that are generated from the research, match the expected cell frequencies, there is zero association between the variables, or another way of saying the same thing, there is no relationship between them.

TABLE 6-6   Zero Association

A. (No differences across values of the independent variable)

YEAR OF PROMOTION	AFRICAN AMERICANS	HISPANICS
First year of employment	27%	27%
After first year	73	73
	100%	100%
	(37)	(48)

B. (Expected frequencies for 6-6 A)

YEAR OF PROMOTION	AFRICAN AMERICANS	HISPANICS	TOTALS	PERCENT
First year of employment	10	13	23	27%
After first year	27	35	62	73%
	37	48	85	100%

Another way to calculate expected cell frequencies is to multiply the row frequency by the column frequency for each cell and divide by the total number in the table. For example, to compute the expected cell frequency for African Americans promoted their first year, multiply 23 (the row total) by 37 (the column total) and divide by 85. The result is 10, as shown in Table 6-6B, the expected frequency for African Americans promoted during their first year of employment.

Table 6-7 calculates the expected frequencies for the information contained in Table 6-4. It also shows the observed frequencies, which can be calculated from Table 6-4 or taken directly from Table 6-3. Comparing the two, men are promoted somewhat faster than women. Whereas the expected frequency for men being promoted their first year is 9.6, the actual number promoted is 14. While the expected number of women being promoted their first year is 12.5, the actual number is 8. While there are few or no differences for second and fourth year promotions, fewer men than expected are promoted their third year, while more women than expected are promoted their third year. The differences reveal that gender is related to promotion and that the association between the two variables is greater than zero.

One should now be comfortable with the idea that expected cell frequencies in a table are what one would expect based on the percentage distribution

TABLE 6-7   Calculating Expected Frequencies

YEAR OF PROMOTION	PERCENTAGE DISTRIBUTION FOR MEN AND WOMEN COMBINED	EXPECTED FREQUENCY FOR MEN	OBSERVED FREQUENCY FOR MEN	EXPECTED FREQUENCY FOR WOMEN	OBSERVED FREQUENCY FOR WOMEN
1	26%	$.26 \times 37 = 9.6$	14	$.26 \times 48 = 12.5$	8
2	31	$.31 \times 37 = 11.5$	12	$.31 \times 48 = 14.9$	14
3	34	$.34 \times 37 = 12.6$	7	$.34 \times 48 = 16.3$	22
4	9	$.09 \times 37 = 3.3$	4	$.09 \times 48 = 4.3$	4
	100%	37.0	37	48.0	48

of the dependent variable, and if what one observes matches expectations, there is zero association between the variables, and to the extent that the two depart, the association between the variables increases to a maximum upper limit or what is called **perfect association.**

Perfect association is easiest to illustrate with a 2 × 2 table. If zero association reflects no differences across values of the independent variable as in Table 6-6A, perfect association reflects maximum differences across values of the independent variable. In a 2 × 2 table, this occurs when all observations fall in the diagonally opposite cells of the table as shown in Table 6-8A and B. Not only do each of these patterns reflect maximum differences across values of the independent variable, they allow for perfect prediction of values on the dependent variable. In the case of A, if one is a man, promotion comes the first year of employment. For women, promotion comes after the first year. In the case of B, just the opposite is true.

TABLE 6-8   Perfect Association

A.

YEAR OF PROMOTION	MEN	WOMEN
First year of employment	100%	0%
After first year	0	100
	100%	100%
	(37)	(48)

B.

YEAR OF PROMOTION	MEN	WOMEN
First year of employment	0%	100%
After first year	100	0
	100%	100%
	(37)	(48)

Measures of association are simple ratios; they reflect difference across values of the independent variable divided by the maximum possible difference. Consider Table 6-8. If one observed the pattern in either A or B, the difference across values of the independent variable would be 100 percent (the percentage of men promoted their first year minus the percentage of women promoted their first year). The maximum possible difference would also be 100 percent. Treating the percentage difference as a measure of association would yield in this instance a value of one.

$$\frac{\text{Differences Across Independent Variable}}{\text{Maximum Possible Difference}} = \frac{100\%}{100\%} = 1$$

If there were no differences across values of the independent variable as in Table 6-6A, the percentage difference is zero. Dividing by 100 percent (the maximum possible difference), yields a value of zero. Some measures of association, like the one above based on percentage difference, range from zero, denoting zero association, to one, denoting perfect association. Others range from minus one to plus one and are employed when the independent and dependent variables reflect values that range from low to high rather than nominal values such as Protestant, Catholic, and Jew that have no ordered metric. Minus one denotes perfect negative association and plus one perfect positive association. Zero still denotes zero association.

Such measures are said to be **directional,** that is, they reflect the direction of the relationship or association. Perfect positive association denotes that high values of one variable are matched with high values of another; perfect negative denotes that high values of one variable are matched with low values of another. Both are illustrated in Table 6-9. Perfect positive reflects higher levels of education paired with higher salaries. Perfect negative shows higher levels of education paired with lower salaries. The first instance would yield a value of plus one, the second, minus one. Values in between zero and one and minus one and plus one reflect different degrees or magnitudes of association.

Assuming that a relationship or association exists between two variables, directional measures of association will reflect this only if the pattern of relationship approximates a straight line or what is referred to as a **linear** pattern. Linear relationships do not change direction across values of the independent variable. Table 6-10A is a linear pattern. Although short of perfect where all the observations would fall in the diagonal cells, the relationship approximates a straight line. Most of the low values on one variable are paired with low values on the other, most middle values are paired with middle values, most high values paired with high values. Nor does the pattern of relationship change direction across values of the independent variable. Table 6-10B, on the other hand, is not linear. While most low values on one variable are paired with low on another, most middle values are paired with high values and most high values with low values. If a line was drawn to describe this pattern, it would fall and than rise, what is called a **curvilinear pattern.**

TABLE 6-9   Perfect Positive and Perfect Negative Association

Perfect Positive Association

	Education	
	LESS THAN 12 YEARS	MORE THAN 12 YEARS
Income		
$25,000 or more	0%	100%
less than $25,000	100	0
	100%	100%
	(37)	(48)

Perfect Negative Association

	LESS THAN 12 YEARS	MORE THAN 12 YEARS
Income		
$25,000 or more	100%	0%
Less than $25,000	0	100
	100%	100%
	(37)	(48)

TABLE 6-10

A. *Linear Pattern*

	Low	MIDDLE	HIGH
High	10%	10%	80%
Middle	10	80	10
Low	80	10	10
	100%	100%	100%

B. *Non-Linear Pattern*

	Low	MEDIUM	HIGH
High	10%	80%	10%
Middle	10	10	10
Low	80	10	80
	100%	100%	100%

A directional measure of association describing B above would yield a value close to zero, indicating no relationship between the variables when, in fact, there is a relationship. The relationship is just not linear. Thus, it is advisable to know whether a relationship approximates the linear pattern before selecting a measure of association to summarize it. If the pattern is linear, a directional measure of association is appropriate. If not, a non-directional measure is preferred. Because of the potential to select a measure inappropriate to the particular pattern one wishes to describe, it is always wise to inspect the contingency table along with generating a measure of association. Most software that generates contingency tables also provides an option for generating a host of measures of associations. Thus, it is a simple task to generate both.

Another important characteristic of measures of association is symmetry. **Symmetrical** measures yield the same value regardless of which variable is considered independent. **Asymmetrical** measures, on the other hand, yield different values depending on which variable is considered independent. Some measures have both a symmetrical and asymmetrical form. If a measure is asymmetrical, you will obtain different values depending on which variable you identify as the independent variable. Most software identifies in some fashion whether or not a particular measure is symmetrical or asymmetrical.

SOME FREQUENTLY USED MEASURES OF ASSOCIATION

CHI-SQUARE BASED MEASURES

Chi-square, symbolized χ^2, is not a measure of association but a number of measures are based on it. It compares observations with expected frequencies using the formula:

$$\chi^2 = \sum \frac{(\text{Observed} - \text{Expected})^2}{\text{Expected}}$$

In calculating chi-square, the expected frequency in each cell of a table is subtracted from the observed frequency for the cell and squared. This quantity is then divided by the expected frequency for the particular cell. These quantities are then summed over all the cells. Chi-square equals zero when two variables are unrelated but has an upper limit greater than one. The family of chi-square based measures adjusts for this in various ways, insuring a range from zero to one.

Cramer's V takes the square root of chi-square and divides by the product of the number of observations (cases) and one less than either the number of rows or columns, whichever is smaller.

$$V = \sqrt{\frac{\chi^2}{N(M - 1)}}$$

where M equals the lesser of either the number of rows or columns.

TABLE 6-11   Landfill Use and Gate Fees

	Gate Fee			
	YES	No	TOTALS	PERCENT
Landfill Use				
High	18	14	32	47%
Low	8	28	36	53%
Totals	26	42	68	100%

TABLE 6-12   Calculating Chi-Square

	OBSERVED FREQUENCY	EXPECTED FREQUENCY	OBSERVED − EXPECTED	$\dfrac{(\text{OBSERVED} - \text{EXPECTED})^2}{\text{EXPECTED}}$
High landfill use, gate fee	18	$.47 \times 26 = 12$	6	3.0
High landfill use, no gate fee	14	$.47 \times 42 = 20$	−6	1.8
Low landfill use, gate fee	8	$.53 \times 26 = 14$	−6	2.6
Low landfill use, no gate fee	28	$.53 \times 42 = 22$	6	1.6
				Total = 9

$$\chi^2 = \sum \frac{(\text{Observed} - \text{Expected})^2}{\text{Expected}} = 9$$

To illustrate, assume the information in Table 6-11.

We are interested in whether the implementation of a gate fee controlling citizen access to landfills in various cities reduces citizen use. Preliminary to calculating V, we need to determine the expected frequencies from Table 6-11 and chi-square. Recall that the expected frequencies for each cell are based on the percentage distribution of the dependent variable. The number of high landfill-use cities, 32, is 47 percent of the total number of cities; the number of low landfill-use cities, 36, is 53 percent of the total. Calculation of the expected frequencies along with chi-square is shown in Table 6-12.

Once chi-square is computed, it is a simple matter to generate V.

$$V = \sqrt{\frac{\chi^2}{N(r \text{ or } c - 1)}} = \sqrt{\frac{9}{68(2 - 1)}} = .36$$

Measures of association based on chi-square are asymmetrical, nonlinear, and nondirectional. They are typically employed with variables that simply classify objects into categories—nominal levels of measurement—where there is no implied order among the categories. The principle advantage of the chi-square measures[1] is that they can be applied in any analysis situation. One need not make assumptions. Moreover, chi-square has a known probability distribution, as we will discuss in Chapter 7. This distribution can be used to assess the likelihood that a particular value for V might have occurred by chance, suggesting a relationship between two variables when in fact there is none.

A weakness of the chi-square measures is that it is the difficulty of interpreting values greater than zero and less than one. Zero, of course, means absolutely no association between variables, and one means perfect association, but intermediate values have no precise interpretation. To be sure, a V of .20 is less than one of .40, but beyond this, these values have no concrete interpretation in terms of accounting for or explaining the dependent variable. Because of this, V is less preferred than Lambda and several rank-order measures of association.

LAMBDA

Like the chi-square measures, **lambda** (λ) is typically employed with nominal level variables. It compares the number of errors involved in predicting the dependent variable without knowing the distribution of the independent variable with the number of errors when the distribution of the independent variable is known. A lambda of .40, for example, means that by knowing the value of the independent variable, we can reduce the number of errors in predicting the dependent variable by 40 percent. This **proportional reduction in error (PRE)** interpretation makes lambda an appealing alternative to V.

Assume that 580 respondents from a statewide survey of 1,000 favored property tax relief for farmers. Employing the best prediction rule (one that minimizes errors in prediction) and knowing only the overall distribution of responses, one's prediction would be that all favored relief. Such a prediction would be correct 580 times but incorrect 420. Using this rule, one would make 420 errors in prediction. If, however, the breakdown in Table 6-13 existed, employing the same prediction rule and knowing the type of community in which a respondent lived, we would commit 165 errors for respondents living in large cities, 135 for those living in suburbs, and 30 for those living in small towns and on farms (a total of 330 errors).

Knowing where a person lives, one can reduce errors in prediction by 90, 420 without this information and 330 with, a 21 percent reduction. The computation formula is:

---

[1]In addition to V, other measures include the contingency coefficient C, Phi ϕ, and Tschruprow's T.

TABLE 6-13   **Property Tax Relief by Place of Residence**

	LARGE CITY	SUBURBS	SMALL TOWNS AND FARMS	TOTAL
Opposes Relief	165	135	120	420
Favors Relief	385	165	30	580
	550	300	150	1,000

$$\frac{\begin{matrix}\text{(The sum of the cells with the}\\\text{largest number of observations}\\\text{within values of the dependent}\\\text{variable)}\end{matrix} - \begin{matrix}\text{(The largest cell frequency}\\\text{of the dependent variable)}\end{matrix}}{\text{(Number of observations)} - \begin{matrix}\text{(The largest cell frequency}\\\text{of the dependent variable)}\end{matrix}}$$

One can insert the values from Table 6-13 and compute the value of lambda.

$$\frac{(385 + 165 + 120) - 580}{1,000 - 580} = \frac{90}{420} = .21$$

Lambda is a more conservative measure of association than V in that its value will be lower. V equals .34 for the information in Table 6-13. Lambda's PRE interpretation may make it more desirable than V, however, its reliance on modal categories means some information is ignored, a concern especially with larger tables with several values for the dependent variable. Furthermore, lambda cannot be used if the modal category is the same for each value of the independent variable. Note that if the mode for small towns and farms in Table 6-13 was 120 favoring relief, the sum of the cells with the largest number of observations within values of the independent variable would equal the largest cell frequency of the dependent variable and the numerator in the formula for lambda would equal zero.

RANK-ORDER MEASURES OF ASSOCIATION

Rank-order measures of association require at least an ordinal level of measurement. Those treated here are based on the analysis of pairs. For example, if one is comparing the use of food stamps to median income for the eighty-two counties in Mississippi, each county can be paired with every other county, with the number of possible pairs equal to $N (N-1)/2$, where N equals eighty-two, or the number of observations in the analysis. If, in examining each pair of counties, one finds that the order on the independent variable (median income) is the same on the dependent variable (use of food stamps), these measures yield a

Research in Practice 6B

CHI-SQUARE MEASURE OF ASSOCIATION

Public as well as private firms face important decisions about technology. For example, governments must decide whether to use a central computing system (mainframe, minicomputer, multi-user microcomputer) or personal computers (PCs). Once having chosen a system, it is difficult, expensive, and time consuming to reverse course. Consequently, managers must carefully weigh the evidence in deciding which computing system to adopt.

To develop a better base of evidence regarding such decisions, two researchers examined satisfaction with PCs and mainframe systems in local governments in over 2,500 U.S. cities. The researchers wanted to test the common perception that PC computing is more flexible, more capable of adapting to technological innovation, and less trouble free than mainframe computing. Using 1993 data collected by the International City Management Association (ICMA), the authors employed Cramer's V to test the differences between cities using PCs and those using centralized computing systems.

In this study, the type of computing system was the independent variable. Dependent variables included a set of questions measuring how readily the city adopted technological innovations in computing, such as portable computers, CD-ROMs, scanners, e-mail, graphic information systems, and fax boards. Somewhat of a surprise, the study found that those using central systems were more likely to report the adoption of these innovations, often by margins of two or three to one. For example, 38 percent of the central systems used portable computers compared to only 19 percent of the PC-only environments. The relationships measured by V ranged from .12 to .22.

In a second part of the analysis, the study examined perceived problems with computer systems, ranging from difficulties with training to equipment performance and reliability. Here the research found that fewer problems were reported with PC-systems, but the differences were quite small, reflecting margins of less than two to one. V values ranged from .03 to .11, with one as high as .19.

The study concludes that PCs have been overrated relative to central computing systems. Based on perceptions of users, PCs are less likely to lead to the adoption of computing innovations and only slightly more likely to be free of problems associated with training and performance.

SOURCE: Donald Norris and Kenneth Kraemer, "Mainframe and PC Computing in American Cities: Myths and Realities," *Public Administration Review* (November/December, 1996): 568–575.

TABLE 6-14 **Food Stamp Use and Income**

		Income	
		Low	High
Food Stamp Use	Low	A	B
	High	C	D

value of plus one, perfect positive association. If the order on the independent variable is the exact opposite of the dependent variable, they yield a value of minus one, perfect negative association. Zero denotes zero association and that the ordering of pairs is random, or that the order on the independent variable bears no relationship at all to the order on the dependent variable.

In any given instance, some pairs will be ordered the same on both variables, while other pairs will be reversed on both variables. For example, Jefferson Davis County in Mississippi maybe ranked higher than Tallahatchie County in median income and also higher in food stamp use, and higher than Noxubee County in median income but lower in food stamp use. **Concordant pair** is the term for those pairs where ordering is the same. **Discordant pair** is the term for those where the order is reversed. All of the measures reviewed here compare the number of concordant with discordant pairs.

One can gain a clearer and better understanding of rank-order measures of association with an illustration. Consider a situation where there are just four observations: A, B, C, and D. Think of them as counties and assume interest is in the relationship between income and food stamp use measured as a simple ordinal classification, high and low as shown in Table 6-14.

With four observations, one can discern the number of concordant and discordant pairs quite easily as well as those that are neither. These, of course, are pairs that have the same value on either the independent or dependent variable or both; that is, they are tied on one or both variables.

PAIRS	DESCRIPTION
AD	Concordant. A is lower than D on income and lower in use of food stamps.
CB	Discordant. C is lower than B on income and higher in use of food stamps.
AB	Neither concordant nor discordant. A is lower than B on income and tied with B on use of food stamps.
AC	Neither concordant nor discordant. A is lower than C on use of food stamps and tied with C on income.
BD	Neither concordant nor discordant. B is lower than D on use of food stamps and tied with B on income.
CD	Neither concordant nor discordant. C is lower than D on income and tied with D on use of food stamps.

Of the six possible pairs, one is concordant, AD, and one discordant, CB. A is lower than D on both variables; C is higher than B on one variable and lower on the other. The remaining pairs are neither concordant nor discordant. They are tied on one of the variables.

In order to determine whether pairs are concordant, discordant or tied, do the following:

1. First, order the variables such that the independent variable at the top of the table ranges low to high from left to right and the dependent variable at the side ranges from high to low from the top down.
2. Concordant pairs are then determined by multiplying the frequency of each cell by the sum of the cells higher and to the right.
3. Discordant pairs are determined by multiplying the frequency of each cell by the sum of the cells lower and to the right.
4. Pairs tied to the dependent variable are determined by multiplying the frequency of each cell by the sum of the cells directly to the right.
5. Pairs tied to the independent variable are determined by multiplying the frequency of each cell by the sum of the cells directly below.
6. Pairs tied to both the dependent and independent variable are determined by multiplying the frequency of each cell by one less than the cell frequency and dividing by two.

These rules can be used to determine pairs that are concordant, discordant, and tied in Table 6-15.

Starting at the left, concordant pairs are determined by multiplying 14 by the sum of the cells higher and to the right. There is only one; 14×7 equals 98 concordant pairs. Discordant pairs are determined by multiplying 40 by the

TABLE 6-15   Calculating pairs

	Income		
	Low	High	Totals
Food Stamp Use			
High	40	7	47
Low	14	21	35
Totals	54	27	82

Concordant = $14 \times 7 = 98$

Discordant = $40 \times 21 = 840$

Tied on use of food stamps $(14 \times 21 = 294) + (40 \times 7 = 280) = 574$

Tied on income $(14 \times 40 = 560) + (21 \times 7 = 147) = 707$

Tied on both $(14 \times 13/2 = 91) + (21 \times 20/2 = 210) + (40 \times 39/2 = 780) + (7 \times 6/2 = 21) = 1{,}102$

sum of the cells lower and to the right. Again, there is one; 40×21 equals 840. Total pairs equals 3,321. The information can be used to calculate several measures of association.

GAMMA

Gamma (γ) subtracts the number of concordant from discordant pairs and divides by the total of concordant and discordant pairs. When the number of concordant pairs outnumber discordant pairs, gamma is positive; when discordant outnumber concordant, gamma is negative.

$$\text{Gamma} = \frac{C - D}{C + D}$$

Inserting information from Table 6-15,

$$\text{Gamma} = \frac{98 - 840}{98 + 840} = \frac{-742}{938} = -.79$$

Gamma is a symmetrical measure with a PRE interpretation. With respect to the above, one can say that for those pairs on which there are no ties, errors in predicting the rank-order of pairs on one variable can be reduced by 79 percent using the inverse rank-order of pairs on the other variable as a prediction rule. Gamma, as well as all the rank-order measures of association, is a directional measure incapable of accurately summarizing nonlinear associations. Because gamma fails to consider pairs that are tied, where the number of ties is large, either tau$_b$ or Somer's d may be preferred. Like gamma, **tau$_b$** compares concordant with discordant pairs, but, its larger denominator, which considers pairs tied on both the dependent and independent variable, insures that it will always be smaller. Taking information from Table 6-15 and using the formula below, tau$_b$ equals:

$$\text{Tau}_b = \frac{\text{Concordant} - \text{Discordant}}{\sqrt{\begin{array}{l}(\text{Concordant} + \text{Discordant} + \text{Ties on dependent variable}) \times \\ (\text{Concordant} + \text{Discordant} + \text{Ties on independent variable})\end{array}}}$$

$$\text{Tau}_b \frac{-742}{\sqrt{(98 + 840 + 574) \times (98 + 840 + 707)}} = \frac{-742}{1,577} = -.47$$

A peculiarity of tau$_b$ is that it can only achieve a value of plus or minus one for square tables (those where the number of rows equals the number of columns). For non-square tables, a variation Tau$_c$ is available.

SOMER'S d

Another measure of this type is Somer's d. It makes adjustment for ties only on the dependent variable. It is calculated using the following formula:

$$\text{Somer's d} = \frac{\text{Concordant} - \text{Discordant}}{\text{Concordant} + \text{Discordant} + \text{Ties on dependent variable}}$$

Again taking information from Table 6-15,

$$\text{Somer's d} = \frac{98 - 840}{1512} = -.49$$

Because Somer's d only makes adjustment for ties on the dependent variable, it is an asymmetrical measure of association.

CHOOSING A MEASURE OF ASSOCIATION

One need not always include a measure of association in presenting a contingency table, but it is particularly helpful when a table is large, say greater than 3×3, and interpretation is likely to be difficult. Measures of association might also stand alone, that is, without a tabular presentation, especially if the alternative is a large number of tables that are likely to bore the reader and cause loss of interest. In such instances, information can be presented as in Table 6-16, and contingency tables, if necessary, included in an appendix.

We have mentioned some issues to consider when choosing a measure of association. Level of measurement is another consideration.

1. With nominal level variables, that is, those whose values do not represent an ordered metric, one of the chi-square measures or lambda should be used, as illustrated in Table 6-16 for region.
2. The rank-order measures require at least an ordinal level of measurement. Where the number of ties is large, either tau_b, tau_c or Somer's d is preferred to gamma. Tau_c or Somer's d is the choice when the number of columns and rows are not equal.
3. With interval variables, Pearson's correlation coefficient, discussed in Chapter 8, is often used. Pearson's correlation coefficient is sometimes used with ordinal variables if the number of values is five or larger by

TABLE 6-16   **Quality of State Highway System and Selected State Characteristics**

STATE CHARACTERISTIC	TAU$_c$
State Median Income (Measured as low, medium, high)	.15
Number of Cities over 500,000	−.23
Region of the Country (North, South, East, West)	.62*
State highway commissioner independent of governor (0 = no, 1 = yes)	−.04
Proportion of highway funds from federal government	.31

* Measure of association is lambda.

simply treating the ordered values as if they were measured as one, two, three, etc. Doing so often leads to results quite similar to the rank-order measures, and Pearson's measure has a simple and easily understood interpretation. Moreover, it is likely to be more familiar to other researchers, managers and practitioners, news people, and even the public at large.

EXERCISES

6-7 Compute Cramer's *V* for Exercise 6-2.

6-8 Compute gamma, tau_b, and Somer's d for Exercise 6-3.

6-9 Compute V, gamma, and tau_b for Exercise 6-4.

CONTROLLING FOR THE EFFECT OF ONE OR MORE VARIABLES

The purpose of most research is to isolate variables that explain or account for a particular dependent variable. While it is difficult to speak in terms of cause, we attempt to isolate those variables that can be considered causes of the dependent variable. For example, to assess whether or not a program keeps alcoholics from drinking, it is important to establish that it is indeed the program that is responsible and not other factors. To establish a "cause and effect" link such as this, several conditions must be satisfied. First, the dependent and independent variable must be related to each other. We must show, for example, that those who participate in the program are more likely to quit drinking than those who do not. Second, the independent variable must precede the dependent variable in time. We must show that those who ceased drinking did so after participating in the program. Third, the relationship between the dependent and independent variable must not be the result of a third variable that is related to both the dependent and independent variable. For example, alcoholics might quit drinking as well as enroll in a program because of family pressure. Concluding that the program was responsible without first controlling for the influence of family pressure might lead to a spurious or false conclusion. Fourth, the hypothesized link between the dependent and independent variable needs to make sense. There needs to be a reasonably strong argument for believing that the independent variable affects the dependent variable. One simply does not test for a relationship between two variables without first believing that one exists, a belief grounded in reason and logic.

As seen in Chapter 2, these conditions are present in experimental research. Randomization guarantees that changes observed in the dependent variable are produced by the independent variable. In non-experimental research, adjusting for the influence of control variables does this. **Control variables** were introduced in Chapter 2. To establish a "cause and effect" link, we need to eliminate the possibility that the relationship between two variables is the result of a control variable related to both. Of course, one cannot adjust for every potential control, and thus a definitive conclusion regarding the causal significance of an independent variable is impossible. However, with the adjustment for each additional control, confidence grows that a relationship is causal in nature. A method, known as the **elaboration model,** for adjusting for control variables in contingency table analysis involves dividing the objects or units being studied into subclasses of a control variable and examining the relationship between the independent and dependent variable within each subclass. If the relationship remains unchanged within subclasses, one can tentatively conclude that the relationship is genuine, not the product of some other variable. Evidence for causality is increased. If, however, the relationship between the independent and dependent variable disappears, it is clear that there is no relationship between the two, apart from that produced by the control, and that the variables are not causally related.

Table 6-4 presents information on the relationship between year of promotion and gender, and shows that men are promoted earlier in their careers than women. Table 6-5 shows that the more productive employees are promoted faster than the less productive. To establish a cause and effect link between promotion and gender, the influence of the control variable, productivity, needs to be considered. Men may be more productive than women, and it may be this that is responsible for early promotion. In examining the relationship between gender and promotion for each level of productivity, if the original relationship is unchanged, evidence for a causal link between the two increases. Many of the questions of interest to administrators and managers do not involve experimental research, but rather data gathered in surveys of some kind. Thus, although the elaboration model falls far short of an experimental design, it improves what would otherwise be a very weak design for drawing conclusions regarding cause and effect. While the discussion only deals with the possibility of a single control variable, any number of different controls can be examined individually or in combination. The only limitation is small cell sizes, leaving some cells empty or with so few cases that it is impossible to draw reliable conclusions.

Building on the procedure outlined earlier, in controlling for a variable one simply adds it as part of the tabulation involving the dependent and independent variable. Recall the mechanics of generating Table 6-4. There were two columns, one for men and one for women, and four rows, one for each year of promotion. To these can be added the control variable, productivity, as shown on page 160.

GENDER	YEAR OF PROMOTION	HIGH PRODUCTIVITY
Men	One year	卌 |||
	After one year	卌 卌 ||||
Women	One year	卌 |||
	After one year	卌 卌 卌 |||
		LOW PRODUCTIVITY
Men	One year	卌
	After one year	卌 卌	
Women	One year	||
	After one year	卌 卌 卌 卌

As before, the tabulation can be converted to percentage distributions and presented in a table as in Table 6-17.

Table 6-17 is an elaboration of Table 6-4. There are still eighty-five employees, thirty-seven of whom are men and forty-eight women. Now, however, both men and women are divided based on their productivity. As before, the table is clearly labeled, and percentages are computed on the basis of column totals or within values of the independent variable. Interpretations are based on comparisons across values of the independent variable. If productivity rather than gender is contributing to promotion, one would expect men and women at the same level of productivity to be promoted at the same rate. The percentages would be the same. This, however, is not the case. Regardless of productivity, men are still promoted earlier than women are. This is especially true among the less productive workers. Productivity is important in promotion. The more productive employees regardless of sex are promoted earlier than the less productive, but productivity does not diminish the relationship between gender and promotion. Controlling for productivity, men are still promoted more quickly than women are.

The introduction of a control variable may reduce the strength of a relationship or eliminate it altogether. When this occurs, two possibilities exist for the causal sequence among the variables. The control variable may be antecedent to both the independent and dependent variable, that is, precede both

TABLE 6-17   Year of Promotion by Gender and Productivity, Parks and Recreation Department, Falls City, Ohio—1999

	High Productivity		Low Productivity	
YEAR OF PROMOTION	MEN	WOMEN	MEN	WOMEN
First year	36%	31%	27%	9%
After first year	64	69	73	91
	100%	100%	100%	100%
	(22)	(26)	(15)	(22)

FIGURE 6-1   Antecedent and Intervening Control Variables

A. Control is antecedent

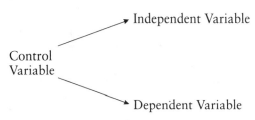

B. Control is intervening

Independent Variable ⟶ Control Variable ⟶ Dependent Variable

as shown in Figure 6-1A. This is an example of **spurious correlation** discussed in Chapter 2. The control variable may also intervene, that is, follow the independent variable but precede the dependent variable, as shown in B.

As the relationship between the independent and dependent variable is reduced or eliminated in both, the two situations can only be distinguished by logic and reasoning. Consider Table 6-18. Is the pattern more likely to be spurious, where the control variable precedes both the independent and dependent variable (A above)? Or is the pattern an example of an intervening variable (B above)?

One might answer this by asking whether productivity could cause gender and promotion. Clearly, productivity cannot influence gender. Thus, gender influences productivity, which in turn influences promotion. Therefore, productivity intervenes between gender and promotion.

If controlling for education eliminated the relationship between productivity and promotion, is it reasonable to assume that education is antecedent to both or that it intervenes? The first assumption seems more plausible, and thus, the relationship between productivity and promotion is spurious.

TABLE 6-18   Year of Promotion by Gender and Productivity, Parks and Recreation Department, Falls City, Ohio—1999

| | *High Productivity* | | *Low Productivity* | |
YEAR OF PROMOTION	MEN	WOMEN	MEN	WOMEN
First year	32%	35%	13%	14%
After first year	68	65	87	86
	100%	100%	100%	100%
	(22)	(26)	(15)	(22)

Research in Practice 6C

THE ELABORATION MODEL AND THE USE OF CONTROLS

Although violent crime decreased during the 1990s, it has increased significantly since the 1960s. While there is a great deal of research on the causes of violent crime, there is little research on the victims of violent crime. Using data from the National Crime Survey, researchers were interested in victims who "fight back," whether or not they use weapons, if so what type, and under what conditions. Of 1,213 victims who fought their assailant, 2.3 percent fought back with a gun, 8.2 percent with a weapon other than a gun, and the remainder (89.4 percent) without a weapon. Table 6C-1 shows that victims were more likely to use a weapon if their assailant used a gun. Whereas 16.1 percent used a weapon to defend themselves when their assailant used a gun, only 7.9 percent used a weapon when their assailant did not use one. The strength of relationship, measured by gamma, is .39; p stands for probability and is discussed in Chapter 7. As the use of a weapon in self-defense is related to the gender of the victim, researchers controlled for gender.

TABLE 6C-1   Type of Victim Defense by Whether or Not Assailant Used a Gun

| | Assailant Used A Gun | |
TYPE OF VICTIM DEFENSE	No	YES
Gun	1.2%	4.5%
Other weapon	6.7	11.6
No weapon	92.1	83.8
	100.0%	100.0%
	(821)	(392)

gamma = .39 p = <.05

Adding control variables can lead to six outcomes: replication, explanation, interpretation, specification, suppression, and distortion.

Replication refers to a relationship that is unchanged with the introduction of a control variable. Relationships within subclasses of the control variable are identical to the original relationship. If, in Research in Practice 6C, both men and women were more likely to defend themselves with weapons when the perpetrator used a gun, that would be an example of replication.

Explanation occurs when the relationships among subclasses of the control are eliminated. For example, in the same instance, if neither men nor women were more likely to use a weapon if the perpetrator used a gun, we would say

Table 6C-2 reveals that male victims were more likely to use a weapon in self-defense when their assailant used a gun then they were when their assailant did not use one. Nearly 20 percent of men resorted to a weapon when confronted with an armed assailant, while only 5.7 percent responded in this way when their assailant was unarmed. The relationship, measured by gamma is .58, stronger than the relationship reported in 6C-1. In contrast, female victims are as likely or somewhat less likely to defend themselves with a weapon when their assailant is armed than when their assailant is unarmed. Measured by gamma, the relationship is −.15. In short, men are more likely to respond with some type of weapon if their assailant has one. Controlling for gender of the victim specifies the relationship.

Table 6C-2   Type of Victim Defense by Whether or Not Assailant Used a Gun Controlling for Gender of Victim

Type of Victim Defense	Victim is Man Perpetrator Used Gun		Victim is Woman Perpetrator Used Gun	
	Yes	No	Yes	No
Gun	5.5%	1.0%	1.1%	1.5%
Other weapon	12.8	4.7	7.5	9.9
No weapon	81.7	94.4	92.4	88.6
	100.0%	100.0%	100.0%	100.0%
	gamma = .58 $p = <.05$		gamma = −.15 $p = n.s.$	

Source: Chris Marshall and Vincent Webb, "A portrait of crime victims who fight back," *Journal of Interpersonal Violence* (March 1994): 45–74.

that gender explained the initial relationship between the victim using a weapon and the perpetrator using one. We have "explained away" the initial relationship. A good example of such a spurious relationship is the association between the number of storks and the number of births in some areas of Northern Europe. The relationship is spurious because the variable degree of urbanization explains both birth rates and the presence of storks. Urbanization is antecedent to both storks and high birth rates. Thus, the stork-baby relationship is spurious.

Interpretation describes relationships among subclasses that are eliminated or reduced, and where it is reasonable to assume that the control variable intervenes between the independent and dependent variable.

Specification refers to situations where relationships within subclasses differ from each other. If there are two subclasses, the relationship may be eliminated in one but reflect the original relationship in the other. One might say that the analysis has specified the conditions under which the original relationship holds. This is the case in Research in Practice 6C. Another example is in Table 6-18, where the difference between men and women in promotion was much larger at low levels of productivity than at higher levels.

Little or no relationship may exist between two variables, but the introduction of a control variable magnifies the relationships or causes them to change direction. These have been labeled the **suppressor** and **distorter** patterns, respectively.

These labels and the patterns they represent may not be particularly significant beyond sensitizing researchers to the need for controls. If complex social and political problems are to be fully understood, controls are a must. Without them, an analysis is incomplete. Further, each pattern has different consequences for analysis. If the introduction of a control proves irrelevant to a relationship, one is likely drop it from further consideration. If the introduction of a control shows a relationship to be spurious, the interest in the independent variable is likely to wane. If the control intervenes, it is likely that both the control and independent variable will remain a focus of attention.

While elaboration is a way to enhance the quality of research, seldom does it permit controlling for more than two or three variables at a time unless the number of observations or cases in the analysis is quite large. In addition to a proliferation of sub-tables, which make interpretation difficult, cell frequencies diminish rapidly. Some judgment is therefore required in selecting controls. Chapter 2 discusses some obvious categories of control variables including demographic, political, and economic factors. When selecting control variables, there is no substitute for a thorough knowledge of the subject. This kind of information will suggest which controls are most promising. Where the analysis calls for the simultaneous control of several variables, other analytical techniques, such as those discussed in Chapters 8 and 9, may be required.

EXERCISES

6-10 If one controlled for the effect of severity of health problems in Exercise 6-2 and found the following, how would it alter one's interpretation? Among those with severe problems, 88 out of 110 treated in HMOs required re-hospitalization, 350 of 520 treated as fee for service patients required re-hospitalization. Among those with less severe health problems, 260 of 1,770 treated in HMOs required re-hospitalization, while 42 of 340 treated as fee for service patients required re-hospitalization.

6-11

a. There seems to be a relationship between training dealing with diversity and civil rights on the part of police officers and the number of civil rights violations committed by officers. Controlling for the race of police officer, reveals the following:

	Diversity and Civil Rights Training	
CIVIL RIGHTS VIOLATIONS	YES	NO
No	74%	83%
Yes	26	17
	100%	100%

	African American Officers Training		White Officers Training	
CIVIL RIGHTS VIOLATIONS	No	YES	No	YES
No	89	91	68	71
Yes	11	9	32	29
	100%	100%	100%	100%

What is the impact of training? What is the impact of race?

b. Does the relationship, in (a) suggest a spurious or an intervening pattern?

6-12 A researcher is trying to isolate the causes of the high rate of teenage pregnancies. He finds that there is a strong relationship between race and teenage pregnancies, with African American teenagers likely to have more children than white teenagers. Is it reasonable to assume some intervening factors are at work here? What might these be? Using the material suggested in Chapter 3, collect and analyze data by state on teen pregnancies, race, and at least one potentially intervening variable. What conclusions can be drawn from the analysis?

KEY TERMS

Contingency table
Association
Measures of association
Zero association
Perfect association
Expected frequency
Directional measure of association
Linear relationships
Curvilinear pattern
Symmetrical measure of association
Asymmetrical measure of association
Chi-square (χ^2)
Cramer's V
Lambda (λ)
Proportional reduction in error (PRE)
Concordant pair

Discordant pair
Gamma
Tau_b
Somer's d
Control variables
Elaboration model
Spurious correlation
Intervening pattern
Curvilinear relationship
Replication
Explanation
Interpretation
Specification
Suppression
Distortion

FOR FURTHER HELP

Blalock, Hubert M., Jr. *Causal Inference in Nonexperimental Research*. Chapel Hill: University of North Carolina Press, 1964. An intermediate level treatment dealing with the logic of drawing cause-and-effect conclusions in nonexperimental research.

Davis, James A. *The Logic of Causal Order*. Beverly Hills, Calif.: Sage University Paper Series on Quantitative Applications in the Social Sciences, 1986. A review of such concepts as causal order, spuriousness, and the elaboration model.

Norusis, Marija J. *SPSS 8.0 Guide to Data Analysis*. Englewood Cliffs, NJ: Prentice Hall, 1998. Though most helpful to those using SPSS, this guide provides a good discussion of several measures of association, even if you are not using it, including chi-square-based measures, lambda, gamma, tau_b, tau_c and Somer's d. In addition to explaining the measures and how to interpret them, the guide shows how to set up the analysis on SPSS.

Rosenberg, Morris. *The Logic of Survey Analysis*. New York: Basic Books, 1968. Excellent, classic discussion of contingency table analysis.

Siegel, Sidney and N. John Castellan Jr. *Nonparametric Statistics for the Behavioral Sciences*. New York: McGraw-Hill, 1988. This second edition of a classic text still provides one of the most exhaustive treatments of measures of association — those treated in this chapter and many others.

7

Hypothesis Testing and Statistical Significance

From a study of 100 of your state's new employees, suppose you have determined that newly hired female managers with MPA degrees and no experience are paid an average of $30,000 and new male managers with the same degrees and experience are paid $32,000. Is this $2,000 difference large enough to indicate systematic discrimination? Suppose you are a consultant for a lawyer defending an African American defendant in a criminal case and you discover that, although the community is 50 percent black, no blacks are sitting on the jury trying the defendant. Does this indicate discrimination or just luck (or bad luck) of the draw? Suppose you are a program evaluator assessing the impact of a new counseling program for juvenile offenders. You find that 25 percent of those juvenile offenders participating in the program committed another crime within a year, while 40 percent not participating committed another crime. Is this difference large enough to say the program is working?

Each of these examples illustrates the need for going further than just describing a relationship. In each case you want to know if the outcome you have discovered reflects a real difference or whether it is simply because you are only looking at a small number of people at a particular point in time. Tests of statistical significance can help you deal with these kinds of questions. The concept of statistical significance is one of the most difficult you will encounter in this book, but it is well worth your time to examine it carefully and to understand it.

The Concept of Statistical Significance

As a policy analyst or a public manager dealing with such analyses, you will use statistical analysis to describe and explain variation in some property of a set of things (units of analysis). The units may be individuals, groups, institutions, or political subdivisions such as cities, counties, and states. Usually, for reasons of cost, time, and other considerations, it is not possible to examine all the units of interest, such as every citizen or every city. We then have the task of judging whether or not what we observe for the objects we investigated accurately reflects the objects we did not investigate. The problem involves deriving inferences about a population (all of the objects) from a sample (a subset of the objects) and relies on the branch of statistics called inferential statistics. In our three examples above, the policy analyst is concerned with:

1. Whether the salary differences in the sample of 100 new managerial employees actually reflect the salary patterns for all new managers.
2. Whether the all-white jury represents a phenomenon that could readily happen by chance or whether some deliberate discrimination was involved.
3. Whether the recidivism rate of the participants in a new program was really different from the old program or whether a 15 percent difference was mostly due to the fact that so few people had gone through the new program.

Thus, in each case, we want to know if the properties of the sample (the salaries of the 100 new employees, the race of the jurors, the recidivism rate of two groups of offenders studied) are accurate reflections of the properties of the population (all new managerial employees, all citizens of the community eligible to serve on juries, all juvenile offenders). No technique can answer these questions with 100 percent certainty, but tests of statistical significance can allow you to estimate the likelihood that the size of differences found between groups is due to chance.

A precise definition of statistical significance will be presented later after we have discussed several matters essential to an understanding of exactly what statistical significance is. In order to understand statistical significance, you first need to grasp the idea of sampling. Following the discussion of sampling, we will learn about statistical significance through an understanding of statistical inference and hypothesis testing. We will then discuss several useful tests of statistical significance. And finally, we consider some issues in significance testing.

SAMPLING AND SAMPLING PROCEDURES

TYPES OF PROBABILITY SAMPLES

Random Samples

There are a number of ways to draw a sample. However only a certain class, **probability samples**, allows you to judge how well sample results reflect the population. In a probability sample, every object or unit of population has a known probability of appearing in the sample. One kind of probability sample is a **simple random sample.** If you were to draw a simple random sample of 200 university students on a campus by drawing from a student roster of 20,000 names, every student would have a 1/100 chance of appearing in the sample. A simple random sample would require drawing students' names out of a hat, or the functional equivalent of assigning each student a number and choosing numbers through a table of random numbers such as the one in Appendix A. See Research in Practice 7A.

A variation of a simple random sample is a systematic sample. Using this kind of sampling procedure, you would pick a student randomly from the first 100 names on the list. You would then count down 100 names from that name and incorporate the next person into your sample. A count through another 100 names would yield another member of your sample, and so forth. Systematic sampling is usually easier than random sampling.

In deciding what fraction of names to choose in either the random or systematic method, you rely on the number of students needed in the sample (determinants of sample size will be discussed in the next section). In this case assume a sample of 500 students was needed from a student population of 20,000. Then divide the population by the desired sample size (20,000/500 = 40) to obtain the **sampling interval** (40). One divided by the sampling interval is called the **sampling fraction** (1/40), so you would pick 1/40 of the students to arrive at a sample of 500.

EXERCISES

7-1 Using the random numbers table (Appendix A) draw a sample of thirty names from the first four pages of listings in your phone directory (or other list as assigned by your instructor). Describe your procedures in enough detail so that the instructor can replicate them.

7-2 Using the same list, draw a systematic sample of thirty names. What is the sampling interval? The sampling fraction? Describe your procedures in enough detail so that the instructor can replicate them.

Stratified Samples

A **stratified sample** is another kind of probability sample. Here the population is divided into strata or classes, and a random sample is drawn from each. It has the advantage of reducing sampling error (to be discussed later in the chapter) for the stratification variable.

A stratum may be sampled in proportion to its numbers in the population (proportionate stratified sampling) or may be sampled above or below its proportion in the population (disproportionate stratified sampling). The latter technique is usually employed when you want to obtain an adequately sized sample of a group that is only a small proportion of the population from which you are sampling.

For example, in the case of sampling university students, assume you wanted to compare the opinions and university experiences of African

Research in Practice 7A

USING A TABLE OF RANDOM NUMBERS

A table of random numbers is presented in Appendix A. The table has columns of numbers in blocks of five. The order of all the numbers in a random number table, taken singly or in groups of two, three, four, or more, is random. How do you go about using this table to create a sample?

Assume you want to select a sample of 100 out of a population of 1,500 (each element of the population is one town or city). Take the following steps:

1. Number each city in the population, from 1 to 1,500.
2. Since there are 1,500 units in your population, you will need to use four digit numbers in creating your sample. If you chose only three-digit numbers from the table, you would not allow those cities numbered 1,000 to 1,500 any chance to enter the sample. Choosing five-digit numbers would work, but it would waste a lot of time since all numbers from 10,000 to 99,999 would have no corresponding member of your population.
3. Decide where you will start in the table. You could decide to simply close your eyes and put your finger down on a set of numbers and start there, or you could (without looking at the table) decide to start on a particular row and column (say row 7, column 5).
4. Decide whether you will move from the starting point across the table, up or down the columns, or diagonally. Then you have to decide if you will go to the left or to the right, up or down. It does not matter, but you should decide before starting the procedure. Let's arbitrarily decide to move down the columns, finishing each column and going to the top of the next column to the left.

American students and white students. You decide you need to interview at least 200 students of each race. However assume that only 1,000 of the 20,000 students are African American. If you apply the same sampling fraction to the whole list of students, only 400/20,000 (or 1/50) of 1,000, or about 20, of your final sample will be African American while 1/50 of 19,000, or about 380, will be white. You will fall 180 short of having 200 black students. There are two solutions to this shortage. One is to increase your total sample size to 4,000, which would mean a sampling fraction of 1/5 (4,000/20,000); this would yield a sample of 200 blacks and 3,800 whites, far more whites than are necessary for your study. Increasing the sample size to 4,000 also increases the cost dramatically. A second alternative is to use different sampling fractions for black and white students, a stratified sample. If you desired 200 black students in your

5. Decide how you will create the four-digit numbers. Since the numbers are in five-digit blocks, it is easiest either to choose the first four numbers of each block, or the last four numbers. You could, of course, choose the last two numbers of one block and the first two of the next, but there is no value in additional complication (sometimes in statistics complexity is necessary, but this is not one of those times). Let's say you decide to take the first four digits.

6. Now that you have made the decision where to start, how to move, and what digits to choose, the rest is mechanical. Turn to row 7, column 5 (as you decided in step 3). The number is 35,303. The first four digits of that number are 3,530. Since your population only goes to 1,500, that number can be ignored. So you move down one number (following your decision in step 4) and find that again the number is outside your universe. You go down the column one by one until you come to a set of numbers that is in your universe. That number is 13,746 in column 5, row 13. Taking the first four digits, 1,374, you pick that element from your population, the city that you have numbered 1,374. You then proceed down the column. The next usable number you will find is 1,286 so you select city number 1,286. After reaching the bottom of the column, you go to the top of the next column to the left as you decided in step 4. You find two more usable numbers in the first five numbers of that column (1,358 and 0930). You then continue in the same manner until you have found a total of 100 numbers between 1 and 1,500 and have chosen the city that corresponds to each number. You then have your simple random sample of units.

SOURCE: Donald Norris and Kenneth Kraemer, "Mainframe and PC Computing in American Cities: Myths and Realities," *Public Administration Review* (November/December, 1996): 568–575.

sample and there were 1,000 African Americans on campus, your sampling interval would be 5 (1,000/200), and your sampling fraction 1/5. If you wanted an equal sample of 200 whites, you would need a sampling fraction of 1/95 for white students (19,000/200 = 95). This would yield a total sample of about 200 African Americans and about 200 whites (assuming no persons of other races were among the 20,000 students).

Practically speaking, how would you go about this stratification? If you were fortunate, the university would provide you with a list of students with a race category indicated. Then it would be a simple matter to choose every fifth African American student and every ninety-fifth white student. But it is unlikely the university would release racial information on students. Perhaps a minority affairs office on campus would have an inclusive list of African

American students (but beware, their list might be incomplete and only include students who have made contact with the office, for example).

If solutions like these do not work, then you would need more elaborate procedures. Probably the simplest alternative would be to sample every fifth name, which would then give you a list including approximately 200 black students and 3,800 white students. Then in the actual interview setting, all African Americans, but only about 1/19 of the whites, would be asked to complete the interviews. This type of screening is possible when the interviews are face to face. But if the interviews were to be mail questionnaires, then you would simply have to request all 4,000 to return them, and the sample would no longer be stratified. You would simply have a random sample of 200 African American students and 3,800 white students.

In a phone interview, you can screen by asking about race at the beginning of the interview and then terminating the interviews of 18 out of 19 whites. The accuracy of the racial information given early in a telephone interview might be somewhat suspect, however. For another example of stratified sampling, see Research in Practice 7B.

Assuming you surmounted technical difficulties and were able to obtain a stratified sample based on a sampling interval of 5 for blacks and 95 for whites, in your analysis you will need to weigh the sample to approximate the original population proportions. If you want to make inferences about the entire student population, you cannot report the aggregate statistics for 200 African Americans and 200 whites because black students are over-represented in proportion to their fraction of the student body. You will need to adjust the scores you report to reflect this. Let's assume you wanted to report on the mean hours per week spent studying. You find black students reported studying 35 hours per week, white students 25. What was the average number of hours per week spent by the entire sample? If you neglect to adjust your scores, you would find the following:

$$(35 \times 200 + 25 \times 200) = 12{,}000 = \text{Total number of hours studied}$$
by members of the sample
$$12{,}000/400 = 30 = \text{Mean hours studied}$$

But you could not project this figure back to the entire student body since you have over-represented African Americans in the sample. Thus:

$$\overline{X} = W_{AA}\overline{X}_{AA} + W_{w}\overline{X}_{w}$$

where

$\overline{X}$ = Estimated population mean

$\overline{X}_{AA}$ = Mean of African American sample

$\overline{X}_{w}$ = Mean of white sample

Research in Practice 7B

STRATIFIED SAMPLING

Whether or not household crowding affects human health and behavior is a question with important public policy implications. One study which has attempted to assess the impact of household crowding used a stratified sample to obtain data on individual health, aggression, family relations, and other indexes of behavior.

The researcher wished to obtain about an equal number of households subjected to crowded conditions (operationalized as more than one person per room) and those not subjected to crowding. Because in North American cities there are few areas where half of the household units are crowded, he decided to stratify his sample. He chose 13 census tracts in Toronto, Ontario; from 12 to 28 percent of the households in each tract averaged more than one person per room. Every household was screened, and those with intact families with one or more children were chosen. These households were then divided into two groups based on the number of people per room in the household. To obtain a final sample of about 600 households from among the crowded group, every household was included in the sample. But from among the noncrowded households, only every fourth one was included. These different sampling fractions yielded a final sample of 48 percent crowded households and 52 percent noncrowded. Thus the researchers were able to make comparisons of households of different levels of crowdedness based on substantial numbers of both uncrowded and crowded households. Based on this sample, he found that crowding had minimal effects on health and behavior of adults, slightly more effect on children.

SOURCE: Alan Booth, *Urban Crowding and Its Consequences* (New York: Praeger Publishers, 1976).

W_{AA} = Weight given to African American mean =

$$\frac{\text{Number of African Americans in student body}}{\text{Total student body}}$$

W_W = Weight given to white mean =

$$\frac{\text{Number of whites in student body}}{\text{Total student body}}$$

Inserting the group means into the formula we have:

$$\bar{X} = \left(\frac{1,000}{20,000}\right)(35) + \left(\frac{19,000}{20,000}\right)(25)$$
$$= 1.75 + 23.75$$
$$= 25.5$$

In this instance the adjusted mean, 25.5, was somewhat less than the mean calculated without adjustment, 30; if the over sampling of black students was greater or the black-white differences were larger, then the differences between the unadjusted and adjusted means would be even larger. If you are using a computer to analyze the data, you would create a "weight" variable. Most software packages allow you to do this easily. In this case African American respondents would be weighted by .1, and white respondents would be weighted by 1.9. This is because black students are currently half (.5) of the sample. In their population proportion, they are only .05. So to determine the weight for African Americans:

$$.5 W_{AA} = .05$$

$$W_{AA} = .1$$

Similarly, for whites:

$$.5 W_W = .95 \text{ (white population proportion)}$$

$$W_W = .95/.5 = 1.9$$

In our first example, the weight variable would then be .1 for blacks and 1.9 for whites.

In another example, if women comprised 60 percent of the sample population and 75 percent of the total population, the weighting formula would be:

$$.60 W_W = .75$$

$$W_W = 1.25$$

Cluster Samples

A third type of probability sample is a **cluster sample.** If a sample of 1,000 residents is necessary to do a study of satisfaction with the system of city parks in a community and there are 100,000 households in the community, a sample will include every 100th household in the sample. Figures on the number of households can be obtained from the Census and current figures from local power companies. It would be possible to work your way through the city, calling on every 100th household, but this would not be very efficient. A more efficient way would be to identify every city block, pick 1/100 of these at random, and call on every household on the selected blocks. By employing this clustering technique, interviewer time is concentrated on fewer blocks, saving time and money, and every block (and thus every household) has an equal chance of being included in the sample.

Clustering techniques can also be used with voter registration lists, city directories, or other lists. If a cluster sample is drawn with a sampling fraction of 1/100, one could choose every 1,000th name and then draw 10 names before proceeding to the name 990 names away.

Make sure, however, that the list is appropriate to the study. A voting list would be appropriate only if the intended population is all registered voters. City directories tend to be outdated and not inclusive, you should find other alternatives, if possible.

You must also make sure that the number of clusters is large enough to avoid homogeneity in the sample. For example, if you used a list of registered voters organized by precinct and sampled 100 names within each of 10 precincts, you might have induced a homogeneity into the sample by focusing on only a few precincts. If there were 100 precincts in the community, you might do better by sampling 40 people from each of 25 precincts. In that way you would ensure that you have a greater distribution (and greater heterogeneity) of respondents from all parts of town rather than having a more homogeneous sample clustered in only a few parts of town.

The Survey Research Center (SRC) of the University of Michigan is a highly respected survey unit that conducts a variety of national surveys, including a national election study every two years. Their cluster sampling plan to obtain a national sample of respondents to be interviewed in person is shown in Figure 7-1 (more commonly these days, however, interviews are conducted by telephone).

1. The geographical area of the United States is divided into units called **primary sampling units (PSUs)**. These are generally metropolitan areas, groups of counties, or a single county. From all PSUs, several dozen are selected to be included in the sample through a stratified random procedure. Stratification is necessary to have a diversity of areas according to population density and region.
2. Within each PSU further subdivisions are made. These divisions are again done according to strata, whereby larger towns within the PSU comprise one strata, smaller towns another strata, and rural areas a third. From within each strata, sample places are selected randomly to be included in the study.
3. Each chosen **sample place** is further divided into chunks. These chunks might be a city block in a large city, or much larger areas defined by rural roads or county lines in smaller ones. After all sample places have been divided into **chunks**, some chunks are randomly selected for inclusion in the sample.
4. An SRC interviewer visits each sample chunk. Every dwelling unit is identified and listed. The lists are sent to SRC headquarters. From these lists smaller parts of the chunks, called segments, are randomly chosen from each chunk. These segments generally have four to twelve dwelling units.
5. In the last step, interviewers will interview in about four dwelling units per segment chosen. When the segment has more than four such units, interviewers are directed toward particular ones so that the random process is carried out through the last stage.

Figure 7-1 **Survey Research Center Sampling Method**

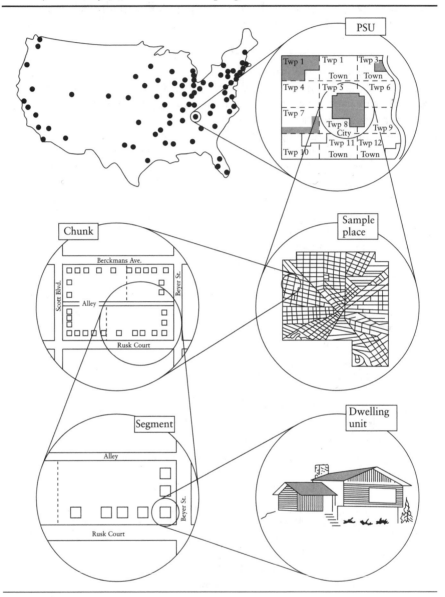

Source: The Survey Research Center, *Interviewers Manual,* Ann Arbor: Institute for Social Research, University of Michigan, © 1969, chap. 8.

This clustering technique is a time consuming, expensive process, but less so than if you tried to draw a national sample without clustering and thus had one respondent in each of more than 1,000 neighborhoods around the nation.

A much less expensive alternative is **random digit dialing,** which involves a similar though simpler multistage process. Given the very large costs of face-to-face personal interviewing, telephone sampling is becoming more and more common and has replaced in-person surveys except for a few special purposes. Most surveying done by policy researchers is done through telephone interviewing.

The procedure for sampling by random digit dialing is as follows. From the geographical area to be sampled (for example, a city, state, or nation), obtain a list from the telephone company of the telephone prefixes (i.e., the first three digits of your seven-digit telephone number), called a central office code (COC). Then randomly sample from that list. Within each COC selected, you will dial a series of four digits selected from a random number table or generated by computer. So, if one central office code is 864 and a random number chosen is 5347, the number 864-5347 will be dialed. There are 10,000 numbers attached to each COC (864-0000 to 864-9999). It is usually necessary to sample more numbers than the anticipated sample size because telephone numbers generated in this way are often unassigned or not working. In fact an SRC telephone interviewing project found that only about 22 percent of numbers dialed were working household phones; others were business phones, and a great many were unassigned (Groves and Kahn, 1979). The procedure, if done correctly, will yield a random sample of households with telephones. The number of COCs chosen and calls made for each will depend on the desired sample size.

Because this procedure yields so many nonworking household numbers, a refinement has been introduced.

1. The sample of COCs is drawn (if a large area is being surveyed, you would also sample from area codes).
2. Within each COC a random, four-digit number is chosen. This number is called a "primary" or "seed" number. Assume within COC 864 that 5347 is the primary number.
3. The number 864-5347 is then dialed; if it is not a working household number, then the next random set of digits within 864 is dialed. If 864-5347 is a working household number, then additional numbers within the 100 number range 864-5300 to 864-5399 (these 100 numbers are called a cluster) are dialed. These are called "secondary" numbers, and the number of secondary calls made would depend on the desired sample size. Let's say six secondary numbers are dialed.
4. If any of the six secondary numbers are nonworking, then another number within the same 100 series is dialed. Ultimately six working secondary numbers would be reached.
5. When that is accomplished, other primary numbers would be tried, and the process continues.

The advantages of this procedure are great. It eliminates clusters with no working household numbers. This is an advantage because many COCs have few numbers assigned. Perhaps in the COC 864, only 864-0000 to 864-1999

Research in Practice 7C

SAMPLING USING RANDOM DIGIT DIALING

Sampling adolescents is challenging. Often researchers resort to surveying students in their schools. However, school-based surveys exclude graduates, dropouts, absentees, and those in alternative schooling. Further, parental consent for participation in surveys is sometimes required by school districts. All of these factors can bias the results.

Because of these concerns, many researchers prefer to sample adolescents through random digit dialing. To assess the possible biases of random digit dialing in comparison to school-based surveys, one researcher used both types of sampling procedures on one adolescent population in northern California. Both surveys measured adolescent drinking, a particularly difficult behavior to assess.

The telephone survey was conducted in collaboration with an ongoing adult survey. Random digit dialing techniques were used to sample the adult population. From that sample, adolescents were asked to participate if parental consent was obtained. Over 600 adolescents agreed to participate, which amounted to a 59 percent response rate. In the school-based survey, in which the sample was also randomly selected, the response rate was 47 percent with nearly 675 participants.

The results of the study illustrate how the different procedures yield somewhat different samples. The sample drawn from random digit dialing

have ever been assigned. Complete random dialing within the range 864-2000 to 864-9999 would never yield a valid household. But once a valid number is found (say 864-1529), then the next six calls (secondary numbers) within the range 864-1500 to 864-1599 will have a high probability of yielding usable numbers. The fewer the numbers assigned within a COC, the more efficient this design. By using this design, incorporating nine numbers within each cluster in a nationwide study, the proportion of calls that yielded valid household numbers increased from 21.6 percent to 65.8 percent, and the number of nonworking numbers dialed was reduced from 53.3 to 20.8 percent (Groves and Kahn, 1979, 334). The dramatic reduction in time spent dialing nonworking numbers results in a substantial cost reduction for the survey. The larger the numbers used within each cluster (the secondary numbers), the greater the efficiency and cost savings. For an example of the random digit dialing procedure, see Research in Practice 7C.

In any probability sampling procedure, we would also need a mechanism to select someone at random to be interviewed from each household. This is necessary so that, for example, you do not interview a young adult female in every household.

had a larger representation of whites and a smaller number of Asian Americans. The sample from the random digit dialing survey had a higher average social-economic status. The random digit dialing survey respondents were slightly older than those from the school-based survey, presumably because random digit dialing did not necessarily exclude graduates, who would be older.

One of the presumed advantages of random digit dialing is that it would include dropouts. However, less than 1 percent of the respondents reported having dropped out of school, a much lower figure than expected.

Differences were also reported in drinking habits, the dependent variables of interest. The sample drawn from random digit dialing reported less drinking and fewer instances of driving while under the influence of alcohol. It may be that the greater anonymity of in-school surveys leads to more honest reporting of these behaviors, though this is speculation.

In short, the author concluded that random digit dialing should be used with caution in sampling difficult populations. While random digit dialing remedied some of the sampling problems with school-based surveys, such as by including graduates, it has its own problems, which potentially bias the results. Unfortunately, there is no one sampling procedure that is best for all situations.

SOURCE: Joel W. Grube, "Monitoring Youth Behavior in Response to Structural Changes: Alternative Approaches to Measuring Adolescent Drinking" *Evaluation Review* (April, 1997): 231-245.

Random digit dialing has become more complicated with new electronic technology. Cell phone users are probably less likely to respond than others. The growing number of cell phones also means that some households are over represented. Answering machines pose problems for survey researchers too. Individuals are probably less likely to return calls to surveyors than they are to respond spontaneously to a survey researcher on the phone. The development of what is known as "voice over IP" that will bring about a merger of voice and data transmissions through the Internet will no doubt further complicate the problems of sampling through random digit dialing.

NONPROBABILITY SAMPLES

A policy researcher might decide to sample users of a public park over a week's period to assess attitudes about park maintenance. This is one example of a **nonprobability** sample. Nonprobability samples do not allow you to judge how well a sample represents the population. This method of sampling is usually chosen for its convenience or the ready availability of subjects. Nonprobability samples can be useful if you recognize their limitations. A famous example of the failure to recognize the limitations of a nonprobability sample was the 1936 presidential poll of the *Literary Digest*. The *Digest* sampled 10 million voters, almost 25 percent, and concluded that Alfred Landon, a Republican, would receive 60 percent of the vote, Franklin D. Roosevelt, the Democrat, only 40 percent. We know, of course, that Roosevelt won in a landslide, receiving 62 percent. The major difficulty with the poll was that the sample was drawn from telephone directories and automobile registration lists. In those days only 40 percent of Americans had telephones and 55 percent owned cars. So the *Literary Digest* was sampling the upper strata of the population, those more likely to be Republicans.

Interviewing the first 100 clients to appear at a human service agency on a particular day would be a nonprobability sample of agency clients. The sample may provide an accurate reflection of all the agency's clients, but there is no way to judge this. For example, maybe clients that come in the morning are less likely to be employed, more likely to have children, are more energetic, or have some other distinguishing trait. With only a little more time and work, the researcher could sample 100 clients over a week's time to avoid whatever bias might occur from choosing clients that come in on one particular morning. Even sampling over a week would be a faulty procedure if the researcher were trying to determine such things as frequency of visits to the agency's office or reasons for not using agency services. If you were trying to assess attitudes or behavior of nonusers or infrequent users as well as regular users of the service, the surveyor must sample from those not appearing in the office within a given week as well as those who do. This, of course, would be difficult if the agency would not provide access to client records. One way to try to determine the behavior or attitudes of infrequent users would be to look at those infrequent users who happened to come into this office the week you were sampling. You might not have very many of them, however, which would argue for a longer sampling period and a bigger sample.

If on the other hand, the researcher was trying to measure average waiting time in the agency's office, a sample of users would be quite appropriate. In that case you would want to make sure that hourly, weekly, or seasonal variation in waiting periods was adequately taken into consideration. The likelihood of really bad results from nonprobability sampling methods depends on how carefully the researcher considers the questions he or she is trying to answer and the appropriateness of the sample to those questions.

One variation of nonprobability sampling is **quota sampling**, where interviewers are instructed to interview so many African Americans, so many females, so many with incomes less than $15,000, and so forth, all of which presumably match the percentages of these groups in the larger population. This type of sampling is rarely used in policy research. Although tempting to use, quota sampling is an undesirable way of drawing a sample. It gives great latitude to interviewers, some of whom will consciously or unconsciously choose people to interview who look friendly or choose households that look clean and pleasant. It is also undesirable because sampling on the basis of a few characteristics may ignore many factors important to the problem being studied. Modern, random digit dialing techniques yield much better results than quota sampling, so that reduction of costs is no longer an excuse to use quota sampling. For another example of nonprobability sampling, see Research in Practice 7D.

Other kinds of nonprobability samples also should not be used in policy research. Polls found at Internet sites and radio or television announcements inviting people to phone in their opinions on a particular issue are not likely to accurately reflect any particular population but those who enjoy calling in or sending in their opinions.

Sample Size

How big should a sample be? In general, assuming randomness, the larger the sample, the more accurately it will reflect the characteristics of the population from which it was drawn. The advantage of a probability sample is that it is possible to calculate the likely extent of the deviation of sample characteristics from population characteristics. **Sampling error** is the term used to refer to the difference between the results obtained from the sample and the results obtained if the entire population had been interviewed (recall that the term "population" has a specific meaning. It is the universe of cases from which the sample is drawn, for example, all clients of one program, or all community residents of nineteen and over, or all statewide residents with hearing impairments).

It is the absolute size of the sample rather than the ratio of sample size to population size that most affects the sampling error. At first this seems surprising and somewhat counterintuitive, but we will explore why.

In choosing a sample size, first determine how much error you can tolerate. For example, commercial pollsters predicting a close election race can tolerate very little error. They want their sample to reflect population characteristics as closely as possible so that if 52 percent of their sample chooses Senator Sludge, they can be sure that 52 percent of the voters will choose her too. Of course no sampling technique or size can guarantee exact results. But compare the desires of the election predictor with the needs of a policy analyst who wishes to determine the use that rural residents of a county might make of a mobile lending library. The analyst is concerned with approximate percentages, not specific amounts. He might be content with an error rate of 5, 7, or even 10 percent, knowing that 60 percent plus or minus 7 percent would use the library. The exact percentages would not matter too much. So a desirable sample size is a function of the error that can be tolerated in projecting sample results back to the population.

How does sampling error relate to sample size? Let's explore a simple example. Assume we were interested in the income levels of the parents of children participating in a free breakfast program. For simplicity's sake let's assume we have a population of ten children with their parents' incomes as

Research in Practice 7D

NONPROBABILITY SAMPLING

Sometimes probability sampling is difficult to use when the target population is rare or widely dispersed among a larger population. Examples are users of special government services, people with specific kinds of handicaps, or members of ethnic minorities in areas where they are a small proportion of the population.

One study attempted to sample Mexican Americans in Omaha, Nebraska; this group comprised only 8,000 of a community of nearly 400,000, or about 2 percent. Only three census tracts had a Mexican American population of 10 percent or more. A probability sample would thus require a huge number of households to be screened to yield even a small Mexican American sample. For example, to obtain a sample of 200 Mexican Americans, in a pure probability sample more than 10,000 households would have to be screened, clearly an expensive and time consuming operation.

Instead, a method of sampling by referral, sometimes called "snowball sampling" was used. When one member of the target population is found, he or she is asked to name other members of the target group, who are then interviewed and asked to supply additional names, and so forth. Normally this procedure is not effective because it tends to under sample isolated members of the community who are likely to be lower in education, social class, and income than those members of the community with more extensive social ties. Likewise it would tend to underrepresent deviants, those whose views or behavior may be unpopular. However, these problems can be minimized if the sample is large (so that many acquaintanceship networks are found and interviewed) and if there is some comparison group against which the researcher can check his or

follows: $3,000, $4,000, $5,000, $6,000, $7,000, $8,000, $9,000, $10,000, $11,000, and $12,000. The mean income of the parents is then $7,500 (denoted as μ). Suppose we are trying to estimate this income by drawing a sample of two. Given this procedure, we might estimate that the parent's mean income was as low as $3,500 if we only sampled the first two cases or as high as $11,500 if we sampled the last two.

In Figure 7-2, we plotted the means from each sample of two. In all, forty-five different samples of two could be drawn from these ten numbers (i.e., $3,000 + $4,000 is one sample, $3,000 + $5,000 a second, $3,000 + $6,000 a third, and so on). We can see that of the forty-five samples, a few showed means far from the true population mean, but most were closer to the mean. If larger samples were drawn, the clustering could be even closer to the her results. In this case the researchers selected five census tracts from among twenty with 2 percent or more Mexican Americans. The total Mexican American population in these tracts was slightly over 1,200, living in an estimated 290 households.

Within each tract interviewers screened every household until a Mexican American household was found. When one was found, the interviewers then screened the remainder of the block. At each interview with Mexican Americans, surveyors obtained information about other Mexican Americans living within the five tracts (a map was shown to the respondent), and those individuals named were then interviewed. By screening the entire block where at least one Mexican American household was found, it was possible to obtain a more representative sample of Mexican Americans than if only those households identified by others were included.

This procedure allowed the researchers to locate 226 Mexican American households of the 290 in the tracts sampled. The interviewers had to screen almost 2,700 households to find the 226 Mexican American households, but that represented a decided improvement over the 10,000 that would have had to be screened using a probability sample. By comparing those persons interviewed as a result of the referral procedure with those located and interviewed via the block screening method, the researchers were able to determine that those found through referral were slightly higher in income but that there were no other significant differences in demographic characteristics or attitudes. In this case, therefore, it appeared that the nonprobability sampling method worked well as a practical alternative to a more expensive probability method.

SOURCE: Susan Welch, "Sampling by Referral in a Dispersed Population," *Public Opinion Quarterly*, Summer 1975, pp. 237-55.

population mean. For example, no mean of a sample of five could be less than $5,000 (3,000 + 4,000 + 5,000 + 6,000 + 7,000/5) or more than $10,000.

The distribution portrayed in Figure 7-2 is called the **sampling distribution of the mean.** It consists of all possible samples of size N (in this case two) that can be drawn from the population. The mean of the sampling distribution of the mean is equal to the population mean. With a large sample the sampling distribution of the mean approximates a normal distribution.[1] We know from

---

[1] A general theorem, called the central limit theorem, states that if random samples of size N are drawn from any population having a mean μ and a variance σ^2, then as N becomes large, the sampling distribution of sample means approaches normality, with mean μ and variance $\dfrac{\sigma^2}{N}$.

FIGURE 7-2   Sample Means (sample size = 2)

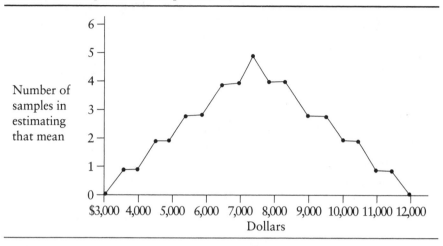

Chapter 5 that in a normal curve, 68.26 percent of the cases are within 1 standard deviation of the mean and 95.46 percent are within 2 (Figure 7-3). And statisticians have also calculated that 90 percent of sample means lie within 1.64 standard deviations of the mean, 95 percent within 1.96, and 99 percent within 2.58. This means that if we were to sample from a population 100 times, the sample means of 99 samples of the 100 would lie within 2.58 standard deviations of the population mean, while the sample means of 90 samples of the 100 would be within 1.64 standard deviations. The standard deviation of a sampling distribution of the mean is sometimes called a **standard error of the mean.**

The ranges—95 percent, 90 percent, 99 percent—are called **confidence levels.** In deciding how large a sample to draw, the researcher chooses a confidence level. If you need a very high degree of certainty that the sample findings are correct, say reflect the population 99 times of 100, then you choose a confidence level of .99. If you do not need such a high degree of certainty, you can choose a confidence level of .95. Rarely would surveyors use lower confidence levels than .95.

To calculate the error range in a sample, you need to know the confidence level and the population standard deviation (σ). Since in most cases when we are sampling we will not know the population standard deviation, we must substitute the estimated standard deviation of the population

$$\left(\frac{\sigma}{\sqrt{N}}\right).$$

Suppose we drew a sample of 100 cases and found a sample mean income of $7,000 and sample standard deviation (s) of 2,000. We can calculate the error range of that estimate of $7,000. Assume we had chosen a confidence level of .95, which we know is 1.96 standard deviations from the mean. We then multiply

FIGURE 7-3   **Normal Distribution**

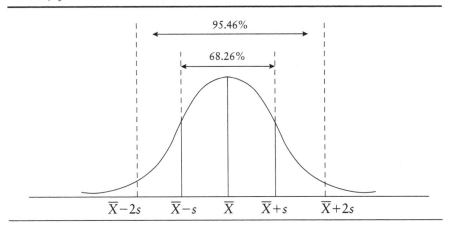

$\dfrac{2,000}{\sqrt{100-1}}$ by 1.96 and get \$394 $\left(1.96 \times \dfrac{s}{\sqrt{N-1}}\right).$[2] This indicates that our estimate of a mean salary of \$7,000 is accurate within \$394, 95 times out of 100. In other words if we drew 100 samples, the mean income would be between \$6,606 and \$7,394 95 times out of 100 (7,000 ± 394). This range is called a **confidence interval**. Note that if we had chosen a more stringent confidence level, .99, then the confidence interval would be greater $\left(2.58 \times \dfrac{2,000}{\sqrt{100-1}} = 519\right),$ so that the researcher can be 99 percent confident that the population mean would be within \$6,481 to \$7,519.

How does this relate to sample size? As the sample size increases, the standard error of the mean decreases. Notice that if our example had been based on 1,000 cases instead of 100, the confidence interval at .95 would be \$7,000 ± \$124 rather than \$7,000 ± \$394. *Increasing the sample size decreases the error range at each confidence level.* This phenomenon can be visualized by referring back to our original table of samples of size 2 drawn from a population of 10. Compare the distribution there with samples of size 6 and 8 (Figure 7-4).

We can see that the standard error becomes much smaller as the sampling sizes get larger; as the samples get larger, the sample means are much more clustered around the population mean. In fact the standard error is reduced in

[2]Because we are using sample statistics, we use $N - 1$ in the denominator rather than N.

Figure 7-4   **Distribution of Sample Means (Sample Sizes of 6 and 8)**

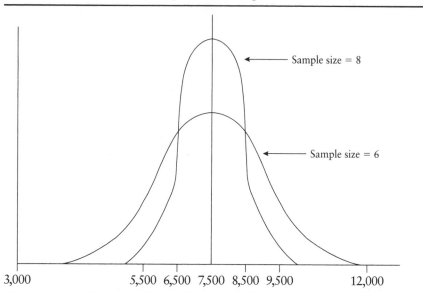

proportion to the square root of the sampling size. Thus as samples get larger, standard errors get smaller, and sampling error ranges also get smaller.

Fortunately you do not have to go through the calculations for sample size estimates in order to determine your sample size, because others have done it for you. Table 7-1 indicates the sample sizes needed for various levels of error and two different confidence levels. Again you can see that as the error decreases the sample size increases (e.g., a 2 to 1 percent error reduction requires a fourfold increase in sample size from 2,401 to 9,604). Rarely do researchers achieve a 1 or 2 percent error level because of the large sample size necessary. They usually settle for 3 percent or more.

The error ranges in Table 7-1 are valid for large populations. Table 7-2 illustrates the variation in sample size required as the population size varies. As you can see, once the population size reaches 20,000 or so, the sample sizes required do not differ much. For example, when the population being sampled is 50,000, the surveyor needs a sample of 381 to have a confidence level of .05; when the population is 500 million, only three more (384) are required for that same confidence level. And even when the population is only 10,000, the sample size required is almost as large as when millions are in the population. Thus sample size depends on the population size only when the population is small.

In reporting your findings based on samples, always indicate the sampling error and confidence level in a statement such as:

> Ninety-five percent of the time, the results from a poll such as this should differ by no more than 3 percent, in either direction, from what would have been obtained by interviewing all adults in the United States.

TABLE 7-1   **Sample Sizes**

	% TOLERATED	CONFIDENCE LEVELS
Error	95 in 100	99 in 100
1	9,604	16,587
2	2,401	4,147
3	1,067	1,843
4	600	1,037
5	384	663
6	267	461
7	196	339

SOURCE: Charles Backstrum and Gerald Hursh-Cesar, *Survey Research* (New York: John Wiley & Sons, 1981), p. 75.

The previous statement is based on a 95 percent confidence level and a 3 percent sampling error. Check the next newspaper story you see reporting a poll to see whether the polling organization reported these statistics. Reputable groups do. For policy research, a 95 percent confidence level is usually quite adequate.

There are a few other factors to consider in estimating sample size. Remember that you must always draw a larger sample than what is planned for in sampling human populations because some people will not be located, will never be home, or will refuse to be interviewed. These conditions are likely to hold for at least one-third of those questioned in a general population survey. And refusal rates are increasing. If you assume a one-third refusal rate in drawing your original sample, you would need to adjust it by the following formula in order to obtain the requisite number to meet sampling error requirements:

Desired final sample size + 1/3 total sample = Total sample

If the desired final sample size is 1,000, substitute in the equation ($1,000 + 1/3T = T$) and determine that you need an initial sample of 1,500 ($1,000 = 2/3T$, $3,000 = 2T$, $1,500 = T$). You should check with other survey groups in the area you will be sampling to ascertain the usual refusal rate.

Calculating the number of phones to be dialed or households to be surveyed also must include the fact that a certain proportion of telephone numbers are not assigned, are assigned to commercial establishments or other non-residences, or to children.

The sample size calculations presented here are based on simple random samples. Cluster sampling yields a somewhat higher error rate at each sample size. And if you are planning to focus on subgroups within your sample, remember that the sampling error as calculated refers to the sample as a whole. Sampling error within subgroups of the sample will be higher. If you have 100

Table 7-2   95 Percent Confidence Level

Size of Population	Sample size for reliability of				
	±1 percent	±2 percent	±3 percent	±4 percent	±5 percent
1,000	M*	M*	M*	375	278
2,000	M*	M*	696	462	322
3,000	M*	1,334	787	500	341
4,000	M*	1,500	842	522	350
5,000	M*	1,622	879	536	357
10,000	4,899	1,936	964	566	370
20,000	6,489	2,144	1,013	583	377
50,000	8,057	2,291	1,045	593	381
100,000	8,763	2,345	1,056	597	383
500,000 and more	9,423	2,390	1,065	600	384

*In these cases more than 50 percent of the population is required in the sample.

Source: Adapted from and extended from tables in H. R Hill, J. L. Roth, and H. Arkin, *Sampling in Auditing* (New York: The Ronald Press, 1962). Copyright 1962 by John Wiley & Sons. Reprinted by permission of John Wiley & Sons. Percent in population assumed to be 50 percent (see page 188).

Latinos in a sample of 500 and they are a random sample of Latinos in your population, then if you are making inferences about Latinos, the sampling error will be calculated on the basis of a sample size of 100, not on the basis of your entire sample size. Finally, our estimates of sampling error by sample size are conservative ones based on a nearly even distribution within your sample. The more lopsided the distribution becomes on a particular item, the less the sampling error. That is, questions on which the sample respondents are evenly divided (50 percent to 50 percent) will have a larger sampling error than questions on which an overwhelming majority of the respondents agree (90 percent to 10 percent, for example).

Calculating sampling error is straightforward in a random sample. Assume you have a sample of 400 divided by 75 percent and 25 percent on the question "Do you favor federally funded health insurance for all children?" Assume a .99 confidence level (where 99 percent of the population lies within 2.58 standard deviations of the mean [see a Z score table in appendix]). The confidence interval, or sampling error, then is:

$$2.58 \times \sqrt{\frac{(.75)(.25)}{400 - 1}}$$
$$= 2.58 \times \sqrt{.0004699}$$
$$= 2.58 \times .02168$$
$$= .056$$

Thus the 75 percent could be interpreted as .75 ± .056 or about 69 to 81 percent.

Calculation of error in stratified or cluster samples is more complex than this and is dealt with in technical works on sampling. Generally, sampling error is slightly less in stratified samples.

EXERCISES

7-3 Calculate sampling error for the following samples drawn from a population of 1 million. Assume a 50-50 response rate.

SAMPLE SIZE	CONFIDENCE LEVEL
a. 600	.99
b. 6,000	.99
c. 6,000	.95

7-4 Calculate the necessary sample size under the following conditions, assuming a population size of 100,000:

DESIRED SAMPLING ERROR	CONFIDENCE LEVEL	RESPONSE DISTRIBUTION
a. 3%	.95	90-10
b. 1.5%	.99	50-50
c. 3%	.95	50-50

7-5 You are planning a telephone survey of citizens of your community to assess their satisfaction with the tree planting programs in their neighborhood. You decide that a 5 percent sampling error rate is satisfactory and that a .95 confidence level is appropriate. Other survey firms in your area report that 80 percent of the numbers contacted in telephone surveys are not appropriate (i.e., business phones) or terminate in refusals.

a. What is your desired final sample size to achieve the error rate and confidence level you selected;

b. How many should be drawn in your initial sampling to obtain your desired sample size?

c. In reporting your results, what would you say about the error rate and confidence level?

7-6 You are a research analyst for a community action program. You discover that Latino residents of a low income area are not taking advantage of a subsidized home weatherization program to the same extent as are Anglos. You decide to survey Anglo and Latino residents of the neighborhood to determine more precisely rates of utilization and reasons for nonutilization. You decide you can tolerate a 7 percent sampling error rate for each group (i.e., 7 percent for an Anglo sample, 7 percent for a Latino sample). The area is about 25 percent Latino and 75 percent Anglo.

a. What kind of sample would you draw and why?

b. What is your desired total sample size? What is the size of each group's sample?

c. Assume there are 5,000 Latinos and 15,000 Anglos in the neighborhood. What is the sampling interval and sampling fraction for each sample?

d. Assume that the expected refusal rate for Latinos is 40 percent and for Anglos 25 percent. What is the initial size sample you will draw for each group?

e. Assume you found that 15 percent of the Latino and 25 percent of the Anglo sample used the weatherization program. Overall, what proportion of the population used the program? (Clue: weigh the samples.)

f. In your final sample of 205 Latinos, the mean number of years of education completed was 10.5 with a standard deviation of 3.2. Estimate the confidence interval at .95 confidence level. In other words, what are the likely population values for level of education?

Statistical Inference and Hypothesis Testing

Statistical Inference

The importance of probability samples is that they allow us to assess the accuracy of the sample compared to the population. Why is this so important? Remember that a good research design is one that eliminates plausible alternative explanations (i.e., alternatives to the effect of the independent variable) for any effect on the dependent variable. Chance is one alternative explanation. Samples will vary from their population by chance alone, as we have seen. Procedures for establishing statistical significance are a way to define the likelihood of chance as an explanation when randomness can be assumed in a sample (such as when units have been selected at random). Recall one of the examples at the beginning of the chapter, the situation where no African Americans had served on juries. Looking at that situation in more detail will help to understand statistical significance:

In a community that is 50 percent African American, what is the likelihood that no blacks will serve on any one jury? We will make the following assumptions.

1. That choosing each juror is an independent event; that is, the choice of Joe Hibbing as a juror has no influence on whether Sarah Bledsoe is chosen, and vice versa.
2. The jury comprises twelve people.
3. All citizens of the community are either black or white.

Given a set of independent events (i.e., each juror selection) and that each event has only two outcomes (black or white), we can determine the probability for any outcome, using a formula for the binomial distribution.[3] According to that

---

$^3 P_0 = C_0^{12} \, p^0 \, q^{12 - 0}$

where

p = probability of an African American being chosen if choice unbiased, i.e., 1/2

$q = (1 - p)$ or the probability of a white being chosen, i.e., 1/2

$C_0^{12} = \dfrac{12!}{0! \, (12 - 0)!}$

This is the probability of 0 African Americans chosen in 12 choices. The 12! means 12 factorial, or $12 \times 11 \times 10 \times 9 \times 8 \times 7 \times 6 \times 5 \times 4 \times 3 \times 2 \times 1$.

formula, the probability of 0 African Americans and 12 whites being on a jury is .0002.

Using the same formula, we could work out the probabilities of having each combination of black citizens and white citizens on a particular jury (Table 7-3). This is a probability distribution.

Thus the laws of probability tell us that in only two times out of 10,000 (.0002) would a jury be all white (or all black) if random selection were used to pick twelve jurors from a population pool that was 50 percent African American. We can also see that even in this evenly divided population, a jury of exactly half white citizens and half black citizens will only occur about 22.6 percent of the time, so that over three-fourths of the times we would expect juries to have more of one race than the other.

Some possible outcomes seem very likely to occur by chance, such as when seven or eight whites or seven or eight African Americans appear on a jury. But where do you draw the line in deciding that jury selection is biased or unbiased? Would a jury of nine whites and three African Americans indicate bias? Or ten whites and two blacks? Or does bias not seem to occur until we have a jury with only one African American or none at all?

FORMULATING A HYPOTHESIS

We begin by stating a hypothesis:

> The jury selection is unbiased, and the jury of twelve whites happened only by chance.

This is called a **null hypothesis** because it specifies that any patterns found are due to chance. The null hypothesis is usually one that the researcher wants to reject. If we reject the null hypothesis, declare it to be false, we accept the

TABLE 7-3   **Probabilities of Racial Combinations**

12 African Americans—0 whites	.0002
11 African Americans—1 white	.0029
10 African Americans—2 whites	.0161
9 African Americans—3 whites	.0537
8 African Americans—4 whites	.1208
7 African Americans—5 whites	.1934
6 African Americans—6 whites	.2256
5 African Americans—7 whites	.1934
4 African Americans—8 whites	.1208
3 African Americans—9 whites	.0537
2 African Americans—10 whites	.0161
1 African American—11 whites	.0029
0 African Americans—12 whites	.0002

alternative or research hypothesis, which in the above example is that the selection is biased in favor of whites.

The null hypothesis is, in a sense, the "strawman." It hypothesizes "no difference" or "no effect." As another example, if we believe that women in state employment earn less than men and we wish to test the hypothesis by drawing a random sample, the null hypothesis would be that women and men earn the same. If, following the test, we reject the null hypothesis, the research hypothesis is accepted. That is, if we conclude that the null hypothesis "the jury selection is unbiased" is false, then we accept an alternative hypothesis that it is biased.

Choosing the Statistical Test and Deriving the Sampling Distribution

In this case we are going to test our hypothesis about jury selection by using the probabilities associated with the various distributions of jurors by race found in Table 7-3. Suppose, however, that we wanted to determine the probabilities of selecting only 100 African Americans in a group of 2,000 juries. We would have a much bigger calculating job. Fortunately, statisticians have worked out the sampling distributions (probability distributions) for many different types of tests. In our example we are using the binomial distribution, but other tests are based on the normal curve, chi square, and others. We will review several of these tests in the next section.

Specifying a Significance Level and Critical Region

The **level of statistical significance** refers to the probability of rejecting the null hypothesis when it is true (this is also called a **type I error** or alpha error). In other words, the level of significance refers to the probability that we will reject the conclusion that the jury selection is unbiased when in fact it is unbiased. We make the selection of the significance level before computing the probabilities. We need to select a level of probability that we think is reasonable; if this outcome or one of lower probability occurs, the null hypothesis is rejected. In policy research, significance levels generally range from .10 to .001, with .05, .01, and .001 most common. If we select a level of significance at .01, only outcomes that have a probability equal to or less than this will allow us to reject the null hypothesis. By reducing the level of significance, we can reduce the prospect of rejecting the null hypothesis when we should accept it.

If you are an attorney for a African American defendant accused of a capital crime, you would want to choose a rather high significance level in testing the hypothesis about jury selection. Since your client's life may be at stake, you would rather the judge erroneously decide the juror selection process was biased, even if it were not, than to decide the selection process was not biased when it was. So, you might select .10 as the significance level. This could mean that you would reject the null hypothesis of an unbiased jury selection when the probabilities of getting a particular number of black jurors fell below 10 percent.

The attorney for the prosecution would argue (if he or she knew anything about statistics) that the significance level should be smaller, say, at .001. Selecting a small significance level means you reduce the likelihood of rejecting the null hypothesis when it is true; that is, reduce the likelihood of finding the jury selection biased when it is not. But you increase the likelihood of accepting the null hypothesis when it is in fact false (a **type II error**, or beta error) or finding that the jury selection is unbiased when it really is biased.

So, the attorney for the defendant would prefer a type I error; the attorney for the prosecution, a type II error. Table 7-4 illustrates these choices.

Another instance where a type II error is preferred includes such phenomena as testing new drugs. Let's say our hypothesis is:

The drug is not safe.

If we accept this hypothesis when in fact the drug is safe, we have committed a type II error and perhaps prevented some people from benefiting from the drug. However if we reject the hypothesis and find the drug to be safe when it is not, we have committed a type I error and perhaps caused illness or fatalities due to the dangerous drug (Table 7-5). As you can see in both these

TABLE 7-4   **Null Hypothesis: Jury Selection Is Racially Unbiased**

	IF TRUE	IF FALSE
Decision to accept null hypothesis	Correct decision: Jury is unbiased	Decision error: Type II
Decision to reject null hypothesis	Decision error: Type I	Correct decision: Jury is biased

TABLE 7-5   **Null Hypothesis: Drug Is Not Safe**

	IF TRUE	IF FALSE
Decision to accept null hypothesis	Correct decision: Drug is not safe	Decision error: Type II
Decision to reject null hypothesis	Decision error: Type I	Correct decision: Drug is safe

illustrations, the choice of significance levels in many instances is far from an academic question; it can have important implications for society.

If we divide our possible outcomes of the jury selection into those that allow us to accept our null hypothesis at a given level of significance and those that do not, the latter outcomes are denoted by the term **critical region.** The critical region is also called the region of rejection. *Outcomes falling here mean the null hypothesis is rejected.*

Making the Decision to Accept or Reject the Null Hypothesis

Assume that we chose a significance level of .10 for our test of whether the jury selection is unbiased. Figure 7-5 illustrates the probabilities of each combination of blacks and whites on the jury. If we are to reject the null hypothesis when outcomes occur the combined total of which is less than .1, we will reject the null hypothesis when the jury is composed of 12 whites and 0 African Americans, 11 whites and 1 African American, 10 whites and 2 African Americans, and 9 whites and 3 African Americans. The combined probability of 3 or fewer blacks on the 12 member jury is .0731 (.0539 + .0161 + .0029 + .0002), within our critical region set at .10. Notice that if the critical region had been set at .05, we would accept the null hypothesis of an unbiased jury when there were 9 whites and 3 blacks, but not if there were 10 or more whites. And if we had set the critical region very small, .001, we would only have rejected the null hypothesis if there were no African Americans on the jury at all.

The example of the jury selection bias is an example of hypothesis testing using what is called a **one-tailed test.** Our critical region is only on one side (one tail) of our distribution (look again at Figure 7-5). This is because we were only interested in testing whether African Americans were discriminated against in the selection procedure. If we were interested in whether the jury was racially biased, with either white or black citizens over-represented, we would choose a two-tailed test. Here we have a critical region at each tail. If the significance level is .10, then we reject outcomes lying in the less than .05 probability region at each end. See Figure 7-6.

Thus we would declare the jury racially unrepresentative if either race had 10 or more members on the jury. If we had set our significance level at .01, we would only reject outcomes falling within .005 percent at each tail or those where juries were eleven or twelve of one race.

When the direction of the outcome is predicted (we predict that African Americans are being discriminated against), it is appropriate to use a one-tailed test as we did originally. A two-tailed test should only be used when the direction of the relationship is uncertain.

FIGURE 7-5   **Accepting or Rejecting the Null Hypothesis**

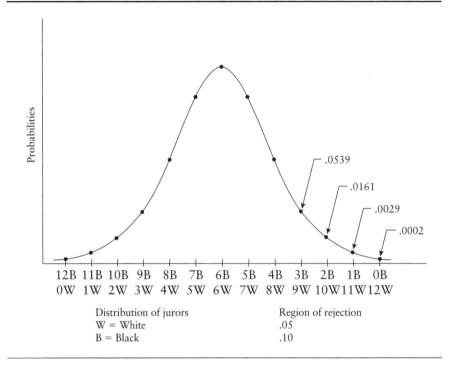

Distribution of jurors   Region of rejection
W = White   .05
B = Black   .10

SUMMARY

To summarize our procedures in hypothesis testing:

1. State the null hypothesis.
2. Choose a statistical test and derive the sampling distribution.
3. Specify a significance level and define the critical region.
4. Decide whether to accept or reject the null hypothesis.

EXERCISES

7-7 Using the example of the 12-member jury we have been discussing, state a null hypothesis. Would you use a one- or two-tailed test? Why? Is the null hypothesis true under the following conditions? Show with a schematic diagram.

a. 10 white jurors, 2 black, .10 level of significance
b. 11 white jurors, 1 black, .05 level of significance
c. 11 white jurors, 1 black, .001 level of significance

FIGURE 7-6   Two-tailed Test at .10 Significance Level

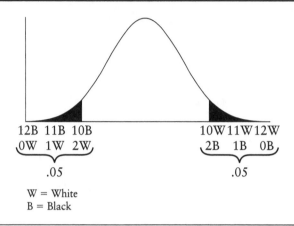

12B 11B 10B   10W 11W 12W
⟨0W 1W 2W⟩   ⟨2B   1B   0B⟩
     .05   .05

W = White
B = Black

7-8 Here is a problem analogous to the example just discussed. Some states now have juries of less than 12 persons. Suppose you were a researcher working for an ACLU attorney representing a Hispanic defendant living in a community where 50 percent of the eligible juror pool was Hispanic. If the jury contained no Hispanics and the probabilities for juries of various combinations of Anglos and Hispanics are as follows, show how you would test the hypothesis that the selection procedure was biased against Hispanics. What conclusions do you arrive at, and how do you arrive at them?

PROBABILITIES

0 Hispanics—6 Anglos   .016
1 Hispanic—5 Anglos   .094
2 Hispanics—4 Anglos   .234
3 Hispanics—3 Anglos   .312
4 Hispanics—2 Anglos   .234
5 Hispanics—1 Anglo   .094
6 Hispanics—0 Anglos   .016

SOME USEFUL STATISTICAL TESTS

TESTS INVOLVING SINGLE VARIABLES

Z Scores and the Normal Distribution

Usually when we are concerned with whether a sample reflects the population from which it is drawn, we are not dealing with a sample as small as in our previous examples. Nor would we always be dealing with a simple twofold category of responses, such as black or white. Frequently we would be comparing means and proportions. So we need to rely on sampling distributions that others have calculated.

Suppose we have drawn a random sample of Indiana high school seniors. We find that seniors of better-than-average intelligence are over-represented in the sample. We can make use of the normal distribution discussed in Chapter 5 to evaluate the null hypothesis, in this case, that the sample is random, and that these differences are due to chance fluctuations. Recall again from Chapter 5 that a normal distribution is reflected in the familiar, symmetrical, bell-shaped curve where 68.26 percent of the cases lie within 1 standard deviation from the mean and 95.46 percent within 2. Use of the normal distribution does not assume that the characteristics of a population (intelligence among high school seniors as measured by aptitude tests) are normally distributed. We can use the normal distribution however, because of the **central limit theorem**. That theorem tells us that regardless of the shape of the population, the sampling distribution of sample means will approach a normal distribution as the sample size increases. That distribution will also have a mean equal to the population mean and a variance equal to the population variance divided by the sample size. This is the same theorem referred to in footnote 1 when we discussed sampling distributions.

If statewide testing of all Indiana seniors indicates an average score of 600 ($\mu = 600$) and a standard deviation of 120 (σ) and our sample of 100 shows a mean score of $\overline{X} = 620$, can we conclude that the more intelligent students are over-represented in the sample and reject the null hypothesis of random sampling? We want to measure the distance between the sample mean and population mean (the mean of the sampling distribution) in terms of standard deviation units. Recall that in Chapter 5, we standardized scores in terms of standard deviation units. A similar version of the Z score is:

$$Z = \frac{\overline{X} - \mu}{\sigma / \sqrt{N}}$$

Here $\overline{X}$ is the mean of the sample, μ is the mean of the population, and σ is the standard deviation of the population.[4] The sample standard deviation can be used if the population standard deviation is unknown and the sample size is large. What is large? If the sample is over fifty, most would agree that you can be reasonably certain that the central limit theorem is applicable. If it is less than thirty, most would agree that N is too small. The range from thirty to fifty is somewhat ambiguous.

---

[4]Remember that the sampling distribution of sample means will have a variance equal to the population variance σ^2 as divided by the sample size N, or $\frac{\sigma^2}{N}$. If that is the variance, the standard deviation (called standard error) equals $\frac{\sigma}{\sqrt{N}}$.

We can insert the values from the above problem and compute Z.

$$Z = \frac{620 - 600}{120 / \sqrt{100}}$$

$$= \frac{20}{120 / 10}$$

$$= \frac{20}{12}$$

$$= 1.67$$

The sample mean is 1.67 standard deviations from the population mean. Is this sufficient to conclude that better-than-average seniors are over-represented? Before deciding, we must decide whether to use a one- or two-tailed test. Remember that two-tailed tests are employed when it is unclear in which direction the sample result will deviate from the population or when the deviation can be in either direction. One-tailed tests are used when the direction of deviation is clear or when the deviation can be in only one direction. Of course this would be decided before this point, but it is here that the decision becomes relevant. In our example the direction of deviation is known. We knew that the sample mean was larger than the population mean, so a one-tailed test is appropriate. See Figure 7-7. If we set the significance level at .05,

FIGURE 7-7   One-tailed Test at .05 Significance Level

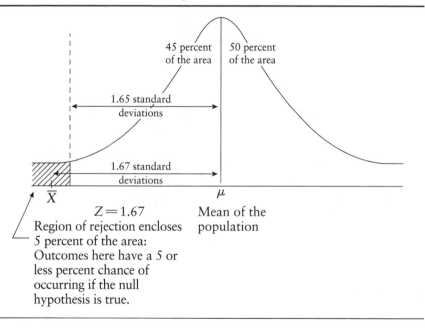

we would need to obtain a Z of at least 1.65 in order for us to reject the null hypothesis. We know that information by consulting a table of "areas under the normal curve," such as in Appendix B. (Or if, as is likely, we were doing this problem with the computer, it would provide us with an assessment of the significance level. In that case, be sure you know if the computer is giving you the significance level for a one-tailed or two-tailed test.)

The number 1.65 comes from the "areas under the normal curve" table and is the Z value which includes 95 percent (one-tailed test) of the cases or, if you prefer, 95 percent of the area under the normal curve. Therefore a Z of 1.67 falls inside the critical region, that is, it is an outcome that has less than a 5 percent chance of occurring if the null hypothesis is true. *Having set the significance level at .05, we reject the null hypothesis.* So we conclude that intelligent students are systematically over-represented in our sample.

We can perform a similar test with proportions. Consider the problem of whether motor vehicle inspection is operating efficiently in a county. Assume there is a statewide inspection standard for counties that at least 90 percent of all licensed vehicles must be inspected. If we draw a random sample of fifty licensed vehicles in a county and find only 85 percent have been inspected, can we conclude inspection enforcement is below standard? Relying on the central limit theorem, again we can use the normal distribution. The formula here is:

$$Z = \frac{P_S - P_\mu}{\sqrt{P_\mu Q_\mu / N}}$$

Where

$$P_S = \text{Sample population}$$
$$P_\mu = \text{Population proportion}$$
$$Q_\mu = \text{1 minus the population proportion}$$
$$N = \text{Sample size}$$

We can insert the above values and perform the calculations:

$$Z = \frac{.85 - .90}{\sqrt{(.90)(.10)/50}}$$

$$= \frac{-.05}{.0424}$$

$$= -1.18$$

At the .05 level of significance (Z = 1.65), we would accept the null hypothesis and conclude that inspection enforcement is not significantly different from the standard. If, however, only 83 percent had been inspected, we would reject the null hypothesis. (Why?)

t TESTS

Usually one will not know the population variance (if we did we would probably know other things about the population and would not have needed a sample). In the absence of such information, we can use a test and sampling distribution known as the **Student's *t* distribution.**[5] This procedure allows you to substitute the sample standard deviation, which would be known, for the population standard deviation, which is often unknown. To use the *t* distribution, you need to assume that the sample is drawn from a population that is normal. The formula for the *t* statistic is similar to that for Z and, with large samples, Z and *t* will yield similar results:

$$t = \frac{\overline{X} - \mu}{s / \sqrt{N - 1}}$$

Again $\overline{X}$ is the sample mean and μ the population mean; s is the standard deviation of the sample (its computational formula was discussed in Chapter 5). The difference between the formula for *t* and Z is that for *t* we have substituted the sample for the population standard deviation in the denominator, and it is divided by the square root of the sample size minus 1. Unlike the Z test, the *t* test can be used with very small samples, assuming the population is normal. The *t* distribution varies with the sample size. In the *t* tables, this is indicated by what is called "degrees of freedom."

   Degrees of freedom is a concept used in many statistical tests. A definition of degrees of freedom is "the number of quantities that are unknown minus the number of equations linking these unknowns."[6] An example will clarify this. Suppose you had two variables (x and y) where values were unknown. You could, if you wish, assign any value to x and any value to y. You would have two free choices or two degrees of freedom. But suppose you know that $x + y$ = 30. Then you would only have 1 degree of freedom because once you assign a value to x, the value of y is determined (i.e., if x equals 11, y has to equal 19). Similarly, if you had three unknowns, x, y, and z, you would have 3 degrees of freedom. But if you knew that $x + y + z = 50$, then you have reduced your degrees of freedom by 1, since now knowing any two values would determine the third (i.e., if $x = 10$ and $z = 35$, then $y = 5$). And if you have two predictive equations such that you know $x + y + z = 50$ and $x + y = 20$, then you are left with only 1 degree of freedom, since if you assign values to any one variable, you automatically know the values of the others (if $x = 13$, for example, then since $x + y = 20$, y must equal 7. If $x = 13$ and $y = 7$, z must equal 30 since $x + y + z = 50$).

---

[5]The test was derived by W. S. Gossett, writing under the name of Student, hence Student's *t*.
[6]Hubert M.Blalock, *Social Statistics* (New York: McGraw Hill, 1979), p. 205.

We can calculate t for the problem involving a difference in test scores between a sample and the population of graduating seniors. Recall that the sample mean was 620, the population mean 600. Thus the difference was 20 points. If we assume a sample standard deviation of 125, we get:

$$t = \frac{20}{125\sqrt{100-1}}$$

$$= \frac{20}{12.6}$$

$$= 1.59$$

You can see that the difference between Z and t is not very large; but t is below the value necessary to reject the null hypothesis at the .05 level (approximately 1.63 for a one-tailed test) with 99 degrees of freedom. In a t test, degrees of freedom equal $N - 1$.

In the table of t values in Appendix B you will see degrees of freedom down the left-hand column. While there is no value for 99, we see that for 120 degrees of freedom, the t value is 1.658. Since the computed t is less than this, we accept the null hypothesis.

We can also derive a t for 99 degrees of freedom by interpolation. First we divide the difference between 1.671 (60 degrees of freedom at the .05 level) and 1.658 (120 degrees of freedom) by 60 (120 − 60) in order to calculate the decreasing t value needed for each increase of 1 degree of freedom. This equals .0002. We then multiply .0002 by 39 (since 99 degrees of freedom is 39 more than 60) to obtain .008. We can then subtract this from 1.671 and get 1.663, the approximate t for 99 degrees of freedom. Fortunately the computer will calculate this exactly.

You can also see that the closer the sample standard deviation is to the population standard deviation, the less will be the difference between Z and t. For larger samples the standard deviations are likely to be very close; therefore we can substitute the sample standard deviation for the population standard deviation and evaluate the null hypothesis by reference to the normal table.

EXERCISES

7-9 Calculate a Z score when:

Sample mean	Population Mean	Standard Deviation of the Population
a. 8	10	3
b. 100	125	20

In each case, would the difference be significant at the .05 level?

Now, assume that the standard deviation of the population is the standard deviation of the sample. Calculate *t*. In each case, would the difference be significant at the .05 level?

7-10 Specify for each problem: (1) the null hypothesis; (2) the appropriate statistical test and why it is appropriate; (3) the significance level; (4) whether a one- or two-tailed test is appropriate and why; and (5) the decision on the null hypothesis.

a. A random sample of 300 state employees shows a mean salary of $16,500. If the mean salary for all state employees is $24,000 and the standard deviation is $3,000, can we assume the sample is unrepresentative of the population?
b. A random sample of seventy-five police vehicles in a large city reveals 40 percent should be withdrawn for maintenance. The chief feels this is high. Previous records on every vehicle indicate only 6 percent require maintenance. What can you tell the chief about the likelihood of the sample if his information is correct?
c. A random sample of twenty-five farms in a state reveals the average size to be 1,800 acres with a standard deviation of 500. If we know the average size to be 2,500 acres statewide, can we conclude the sample is unrepresentative?

TESTS INVOLVING TWO OR MORE GROUPS

Difference of Mean Tests

Recall one of the examples with which we started this chapter. We wanted to determine if the $2,000 difference between a sample of newly hired female MPAs and male MPAs reflects a real salary discrepancy in the population of all newly hired MPAs. This is a typical kind of problem for a policy researcher in that most of the time hypothesis testing will involve more than a single variable. We will be interested in making comparisons among several groups on some dependent variable and asking if the difference is sufficiently large to conclude that a difference exists in the population. These comparisons may involve data gathered through random sampling or generated from units assigned randomly to different experimental conditions.

A useful test involves comparing the mean values of two groups, a **difference of means test**. If the sample is large, we can make use of the central limit theorem and the normal distribution. Like the sampling distribution of the mean, the sampling distribution of the difference between means approximates a normal distribution. The formula is

$$Z = \frac{\overline{X}_1 - \overline{X}_2}{\sqrt{\dfrac{\sigma_1^2}{N_1} + \dfrac{\sigma_2^2}{N_2}}}$$

$\overline{X}_1$ and $\overline{X}_2$ = Group means
σ_1 and σ_2 = Group standard deviations in the population
N_1 and N_2 = Group sizes

We are measuring the difference between the means in terms of standard deviation or standard error units. With large samples, the sample standard deviation can be substituted for the population standard deviation. For smaller samples the following formula which uses the t distribution can be employed.[7]

$$t = \frac{\overline{X}_1 - \overline{X}_2}{\sqrt{\dfrac{S_1{}^2}{N_1 - 1} + \dfrac{S_2{}^2}{N_2 - 1}}}$$

Assume that 50 male MPAs and 50 females were sampled randomly. With 50 in each sample, we use the normal distribution and Z test (if we had 25 or 30 in each sample and we could assume a normal distribution, we would use the t test). We choose a significance level of .05, and because we know the direction of the difference and are concerned about salary discrimination against women, we choose a one-tailed test. Since we do not know the population standard deviations, we will substitute the sample standard deviations into the formula.

X_F = 30,000 (mean salary for females)
X_M = 32,000 (mean salary for males)
S_F = 2,000 (standard deviation of salaries for females)
S_M = 3,000 (standard deviation of salaries for males)
N_F = 50 (number of females sampled)
N_M = 50 (number of males sampled)

Substituting in the formula:

$$Z = \frac{32,000 - 30,000}{\sqrt{\dfrac{3,000^2}{50} + \dfrac{2,000^2}{50}}} = \frac{2,000}{\sqrt{180,000 + 80,000}} = \frac{2,000}{509.90} = 3.92$$

Consulting the areas under the normal curve table in the appendix, we see a Z of 3.92 is higher than the highest value in the table, thus it corresponds to a value greater than .4993. Since the total area equals 1 and the area to the right of the mean equals .5, subtracting .4992 from .5 leaves .0008. This is well within the critical region, 05. Thus, the value 3.92 also falls within the critical region and the null hypothesis is rejected. The differences in salaries between men and women employees were not likely to occur by chance. See Figure 7-8.

---

[7]This formula assumes that the population standard deviations for both groups are different. If they are the same, the pooled estimate of the standard deviation of the sampling distribution can be computed. The formula for t becomes somewhat more complicated.

$$t = \frac{\overline{X}_1 - \overline{X}_2}{\sqrt{\dfrac{N_1 S_1{}^2 + N_2 S_2{}^2}{N_1 + N_2 - 2}} \sqrt{\dfrac{N_1 + N_2}{N_1 N_2}}}$$

FIGURE 7-8   Normal Curve

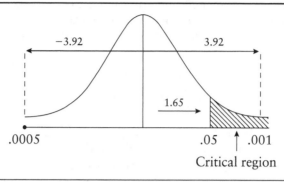

If our Z value had been negative, we would use the same table and the same values (i.e., -3.92 also corresponds to a value higher than .4993). The only difference would be that a negative value means the left-hand tail rather than the right-hand tail of the normal curve. In either case we reject the null hypothesis of no difference in salary.

Consider another example that makes use of the t test. A state is considering whether to increase admission fees to parks. Of 24 parks, 11 are randomly chosen to have a $1 increase in admission fees, and 13 are allowed to keep the same admission as before. Before the increased admission fee is levied in the 11 parks, the mean attendance at the two sets of parks is the same. In the three months following the raising of fees, the mean number of persons visiting parks with the higher fee is 3,500 and without the higher fee is 3,590. Can we conclude that there is a difference in use between parks charging the higher and lower fees?

	Higher fee	Lower fee
Mean	$\overline{X}_1 = 3,500$	$\overline{X}_2 = 3,590$
Standard deviation	$S_1 = 1,000$	$S_2 = 1,200$
Number in sample	$N_1 = 11$	$N_2 = 13$

Because the sample size is small and we assume a normal distribution in attendance in the population of parks, t is the appropriate test.

$$t = \frac{3,500 - 3,590}{\sqrt{\dfrac{1,000^2}{11 - 1} + \dfrac{1,200^2}{13 - 1}}} = \frac{-90}{\sqrt{100,000 + 120,000}} = \frac{-90}{469.04} = -.192$$

Again we assume we had set the significance level at .05. We now consult the t distribution table. In order to use it we need to know the degrees of freedom. We can estimate degrees of freedom: $N_1 + N_2 - 2$ or $11 + 13 - 2 = 22$.

Research in Practice 7E

Using the *t* Test to Assess Significant Differences

Although abortion is a very controversial issue, there is relatively little research on the impact of state regulations on abortion rates. Two evaluators used a before-and-after-only design with comparisons to examine the impact of state policies requiring parental consent or notification before a minor can have an abortion.

The evaluators decided to compare abortion rates in states with and without parental consent laws before and after the laws were imposed. Parental consent or notification laws apply only to girls under eighteen. They do not apply to women eighteen or older. Thus, they also contrasted abortion rates for girls under eighteen, to whom the policies applied, and women eighteen and nineteen, to whom they would not. The evaluators did not examine older women, presumably to confine the comparison as narrowly as possible to teen-aged women.

The authors chose 1980 and 1990 as their comparison points. Parental consent laws were not permitted in 1980, before the Supreme Court allowed them to be enforced, but were permitted by 1990. In states with parental consent laws, the abortion rate for both minors and older teenagers decreased between 1980 and 1990. The decrease was significant and similar in both age groups. The authors used a *t* test to measure significance, and found it to be 3.69 for the minor group and 2.26 for the older group. This suggested to the evaluators that it was something other than the parental consent laws that caused the decrease. In looking at the states without parental consent laws, abortions among younger teens decreased, but not significantly ($t = 1.45$), and among older teens decreased significantly ($t = 2.88$).

The complexity of the design allowed the researchers to go beyond the simple finding that abortions decreased significantly among minors in states with parental consent laws to show that this decrease extended to women not affected by the law. In a further refinement, the authors used other techniques to look at abortion rates in the context of other factors causing abortions. Page 240 in Chapter 9 provides a further discussion of this evaluation.

Source: Anita Prichard and Sharon Kay Parsons, "The Effects of State Abortion Policies on States' Abortion Rates," *State and Local Government Review* 31 (Winter, 1999): 43–52.

At 22 degrees of freedom, a *t* value of .19 is much smaller than the 1.717 value necessary to be significant at .05. Thus we can conclude that the differing park attendance is not significant and that the fees have had little impact on attendance. See Research in Practice 7E.

Exercise

7-11 Specify for each problem: (1) the null hypothesis, (2) the appropriate statistical test and why it is appropriate, (3) the significance level, (4) whether a one- or two-tailed test is appropriate and why, and (5) the decision on the null hypothesis.

a. A community survey of 1,000 indicates that the mean number of annual visits to the library among those sixty-five and older is eight; for those under sixty-five, it is six. If the sample standard deviations for each group and the size of the groups are respectively 1.5 and 2 and 200 and 800, is there a real difference between the two groups?

b. A comparison of drought and non-drought counties revealed a difference in mean gross farm income between the two of $175,000 and $250,000, respectively. If the fifteen counties were selected at random, is the difference significant enough to conclude that the drought significantly decreased farm income?

	Drought	Nondrought
$\overline{X}$	$175,000	$250,000
s	$ 45,000	$ 50,000
N	5	10

Chi-Square Test

Another test of statistical significance is chi-square (χ^2). We are already familiar with chi-square from our discussion of measures of association in Chapter 6. Recall that it compares expected with observed frequencies. The sampling distribution of χ^2 values is presented in Appendix C. A given value of chi square can be compared with the values in the table to determine the probability of its occurrence. Chi-square tests should only be used with large samples.

Where chi-square is employed in assessing the relationship between two variables, the null hypothesis is that no relationship exists between two variables in the population. When the observed and expected frequencies are the same, chi-square equals zero. The greater the difference between the observed and expected, the larger is χ^2. Once we have computed chi-squares we consult the chi-square table or note the probability of the computed chi-square generated by the computer.

In Chapter 6, the chi-square value associated with the following table was 9.

		Legal spending limits in city	
		Yes	No
Personnel turnover among city employees	High	Observed: 18 Expected: 12	Observed: 14 Expected: 20
	Low	Observed: 8 Expected: 14	Observed: 28 Expected: 22

$$\chi^2 = \frac{(\text{Observed} - \text{Expected})^2}{\text{Expected}} = \frac{(18 - 12)^2}{12} + \frac{(14 - 20)^2}{20}$$

$$+ \frac{(8 - 14)^2}{14} + \frac{(28 - 22)^2}{22}$$

$$= 3 + 1.8 + 2.6 + 1.6$$

$$= 9$$

Like t, chi-square varies with the degrees of freedom. Here, however, degrees of freedom are defined by the number of rows and columns in the table, $df = (\text{rows} - 1)(\text{columns} - 1)$. For a 2×2 table, there is one degree of freedom ($df = (2 - 1)(2 - 1)$). The table illustrating the distribution of χ^2 (see Appendix C), indicates that the chi-square value associated with one degree of freedom at the .05 level is 3.8. Since 9 is larger than 3.8, we can therefore reject the null hypothesis and conclude that the presence of spending limits is related to turnover in the population. For another example of the chi-square test, see Research in Practice 7F.

Exercise

Problem 6-2 on page 143 of Chapter 6 involves data generated through random procedures. Specify what would constitute the null hypothesis in each instance and evaluate the hypotheses with a chi square test.

Nonparametric Tests

There are other tests, so-called nonparametric tests, which do not require the assumption of a normal distribution in the population. You may sometimes encounter them in research reports: the Mann Whitney test, the Wilcoxon test, the Kolmogorov Smirnov test, the Wald Wolfowitz runs test are some that are used with interval level data; the Kruskal Wallis test and the Friedman two-way analysis of variance are two used with ordinal data. While they may sound like a page from a New York telephone directory, these tests can be useful. However they are little used in policy research, and we doubt that very many of you will use them extensively. We simply alert you to their existence and note that if you need to find out more about them, Blalock (1979) and Siegal and Castellan (1988) have good descriptions of their assumptions, computations, and uses.

These tests do not require assumptions of normality, but they are not used frequently in policy research, partly because researchers are more familiar with parametric techniques. Moreover, for some kinds of problems, good nonparametric alternatives do not exist, so that researchers are not in the habit of exploring alternatives to the standard parametric tests. Then too,

Research in Practice 7F

USE OF THE CHI-SQUARE TEST

Administrators at colleges and universities are very concerned about the impact of alcohol on the behavior and well being of their students. Every year, these administrators develop and offer a variety of health education programs focusing on the risks and dangers of excessive alcohol consumption. An important focus of this concern is the link between being intoxicated and engaging in risky sexual behavior.

In order to develop programs that are seen as relevant and appropriate, health educators need to know which kinds of students are most likely to drink and get involved in such behavior. Two researchers attempted to shed light on this question by assessing whether gender and membership in sororities or fraternities made a difference in whether or not individuals linked drinking and drug use to sexual intercourse (this is considered a risky behavior because those under the influence of drugs and alcohol are less likely to take precautions to protect against pregnancy and sexually transmitted diseases, and are more likely to be the victims or perpetrators of rape).

The researchers, focusing on one midwestern university, surveyed over 700 students at floor meetings in the residence halls and house meetings in fraternities and sororities. The chi-square test of statistical significance was used to compare different categories of students, since both the independent and dependent variables were measured categorically.

The researchers found that among both men and women, those living in fraternities and sororities, and those who were members of fraternities or sororities were more likely to use alcohol or drugs prior to sexual intercourse. However, the chi-square indication of difference between men and women (5.32) was not large enough to be statistically significant according to the .01 standard the authors set (the probability was .021). Differences between members of fraternities and sororities and those living in residence halls were significant, however (a chi square of 8.80 with a significance level of .003, indicating only three chances in 1,000 that a difference of this size does not reflect a real difference in the population).

Overall, the research showed that the sample engaged in a significant amount of sexual activity coupled with a high frequency of risky behaviors (failing to use a condom, having multiple partners, and using alcohol or drugs before sex). Members of fraternities and sororities were more likely to engage in these risky behaviors than others. Knowing this should help health advocates design better programs to reduce the incidence of these behaviors.

SOURCE: Mark K. Dinger and Nancy Parsons, "Sexual Activity Among College Students Living in Residence Halls and Fraternity or Sorority Housing," *Journal of Health Education* (July/August, 1999):242–246.

nonparametric tests are less powerful than parametric ones; that is, they have a lower probability of rejecting the null hypothesis when it is false. And in most cases researchers do not know whether the population is or is not normal so they will choose the more powerful technique. Finally, in many cases, the parametric and nonparametric tests will yield similar results.

THE *F* TEST

Here we will only mention the *F* test, one of the most used tests of significance. It will be treated in detail in Chapter 9 when regression is discussed.

SOME ISSUES RELATED TO THE USE OF STATISTICAL TESTS

Before concluding this chapter, we offer some general comments on the use and interpretation of statistical tests. First, when should statistical tests be employed? They are appropriate where data are generated by a probability sampling procedure from some well-defined population. Tests serve as a check on whether variation in sample results is sufficient to conclude that it was produced by something other than sampling variability or random allocation.

You may, however, be familiar with research where tests of significance are employed where the data base is the population or where data have been generated by nonprobability sampling. Used in this way, tests deal with other sources of variation, such as measurement error or some undefined random process; i.e., variation produced by other than random sampling. If, for example, you are trying to explain why cities with at-large elections have fewer minority council members than cities with district elections, before suggesting an explanation based on segregated housing patterns, you would want to try to make sure the differences in minority representation were not just random variation produced by dividing cities into two groups. Therefore you might use tests of significance even though all cities of a certain size, rather than a sample, were analyzed. So when your purpose is trying to explain a relationship, in addition to describing it, statistical tests are appropriate.

Second what do statistical tests tell us? The answer to this question may be not much. To be able to reject the null hypothesis that there is no relationship between two variables in some population does not communicate a great deal. The relationship may be quite small, significant in a statistical sense but not in any substantive way. In short, to establish statistical significance may not mean very much. It is usually more revealing to know the strength of a relationship. Remember too that achieving a statistically significant result is a function of sample size. Thus very small relationships or differences between groups can be statistically significant if based on a large sample. Increasing the sample size can usually ensure a statistically significant outcome. We also need to remember that some relationships will reach a particular level of significance by chance. For example, if we performed 100 difference of means tests, we would expect five of them to meet the criteria of the .05 or smaller. So don't get overly excited about weak relationships even if they are statistically significant. Statistical tests are only a supplement to substantive findings.

KEY TERMS

Probability sample	Sampling distribution of the mean
Simple random sample	Standard error of the mean
Systematic sample	Confidence levels
Sampling interval	Confidence interval
Sampling fraction	Null hypothesis
Stratified sample	Level of statistical significance
Cluster sample	Type I error
Primary sampling units (PSUs)	Type II error
Sample places	Critical region
Chunks	One-tailed test
Random digit dialing	Central limit theorem
Nonprobability sample	Student's *t* distribution
Quota sampling	Degrees of freedom
Sampling error	Difference of means test

FOR FURTHER HELP

On Sampling

Babbie, Earl. *Survey Research Methods*. 2nd edition. Wadsworth, 1990. A good introduction to survey research.

Couper, Mick, Reginald Baker, Jelke Bethleham, Cynthia Clark, Jean Martin, William Nicholls II, and James O'Reilly. *Computer Assisted Survey Information Collection*. New York: John Wiley, 1998. A fairly technical and very thorough review of various computer assisted survey collection techniques, including CATI.

Groves, Robert M., and Robert L. Kahn. *Surveys By Telephone*. New York: Academic Press, 1979. An excellent overview of random digit dialing.

Hatry, Harry, John Marcotte, Thesese Van Houten, and Carol Weiss. *Customer Surveys for Agency Managers*. Washington DC: Urban Institute Press, 1997. A very practical, hands-on guide to how to do various kinds of surveys one might use to assess usage of and attitudes about public services.

Kish, Leslie. *Survey Sampling*. New York: John Wiley & Sons, 1967. For those who wish to find out more about the mathematical underpinnings of sampling theory.

Sudman, Seymour. *Applied Sampling*. New York: Academic Press, 1978. Another good and practical discussion.

On Significance Tests

Blalock, Hubert M. *Social Statistics*. New York: McGraw Hill, 1979. A fine intermediate level treatment of hypothesis testing and statistical significance as well as topics in applied social statistics. See especially Chapters 8 through 12.

Henkel, R. *Tests of Significance*. Beverly Hills, Calif.: Sage Publications, 1976. A good introductory treatment.

Siegal, Sidney and John Jr. Castellan. *Nonparametric Statistics for the Behavioral Sciences*. New York: McGrawHill, 1988. The second edition of a classic text is still the best comprehensive handbook for nonparametric techniques.

8

ANALYZING THE RELATIONSHIP BETWEEN VARIABLES: REGRESSION ANALYSIS

Chapter 6 described how to analyze the relationship between variables using percentage tables and measures of association. Such techniques are useful and appropriate when variables are measured as unordered categories (Catholic, Protestant, and Jewish) or ordered but broad general classifications (low, medium, and high). If variables are measured with a precise metric such as dollars, years, or time, a technique called regression analysis is preferred.

Assume that the task is to examine the relationship between the number of friends who are drug users and the number of opportunities to use drugs over the past six months among a group of persons who have completed a drug rehabilitation program. Since both variables represent a numbered metric and the values on each are likely to be unique and vary over a wide range, a contingency table would be difficult, if not impossible, to interpret. One could collapse the values of each variable into a smaller set of categories, but this needlessly sacrifices information. While sometimes one might do this despite the loss of information, the preferred technique is regression analysis and this chapter demonstrates why.

Assume the following information for five individuals who completed a drug rehabilitation program in the past year:

Person 1—Two friends who use drugs; twelve opportunities to use drugs

Person 2—Four friends who use drugs; twenty-four opportunities to use drugs

Person 3—Six friends who use drugs; thirty-six opportunities to use drugs

Person 4—Eight friends who use drugs; forty-eight opportunities to use drugs

Person 5—Ten friends who use drugs; sixty opportunities to use drugs

The first set of values, friends who use drugs, is the independent variable; the second set, opportunities to use drugs, is the dependent variable. In regression analysis, we typically denote the dependent variable as Y, the independent variable as X. The hypothesis, of course, is that persons with more friends who use drugs have more opportunities to use drugs. One can plot these values on the

FIGURE 8-1   **Relationship of Opportunities To Use Drugs and Friends Who Use Drugs**

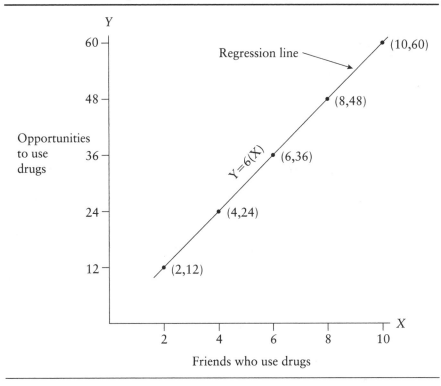

axes labeled X and Y in Figure 8-1. Such figures are called **scatter diagrams (scattergrams) or scatter plots.** The dependent variable is represented on the Y axis; the independent variable on the X axis.

A plot of the values yields a straight line (a **regression line**) that passes through each pair of values. A straight line, or linear relationship as noted in Chapter 6, is only one of a number of possible relationships, including no relationship at all. As in contingency table analysis, the independent variable is hypothesized to influence or act upon the dependent variable. Another useful way of stating this is that variation in the independent variable accounts for or explains variation in the dependent variable. This is an important concept in understanding regression analysis.

From Figure 8-1 it is clear that variation in the number of friends who use drugs (X) is related to the number of opportunities to use drugs (Y). Aside from being a pattern pleasing to policy researchers and analysts, the relationship is one of a class of relationships referred to as functional, where Y is a perfect function of X. The relationship can be specified in terms of the mathematical rule: $Y = 6X$ (on average, one has six times as many opportunities to use drugs as one has drug-using friends). Not only does the rule specify the relationship between friends who use drugs and opportunities to use drugs, it can be used to predict the number of opportunities from the number of friends. For example, if an individual has six friends who use drugs, the predicted number of opportunities to use drugs is 36 ($6 \times 6 = 36$). The rule can even be used to predict beyond the range of available data. With twelve friends who use drugs, the prediction is seventy-two opportunities, although one needs to be mindful that the rule might not work the same way when projecting to data values that do not exist. One might, for example, expect that opportunities for drug use to level off at some point regardless of the number of friends who use drugs.

For the policy researcher, director of a public agency, or elected public official who seeks to understand how the world operates and affect it in a positive way, this kind of information is invaluable. Continuing with the above example, if one wishes to minimize the opportunities to use drugs by former drug users, the friendship structure of the individual has to be manipulated in some way. In a word, people need to be separated from their current friendship cadre or at least a part of it; then the number of opportunities to use drugs will decline. The value of regression is that one can derive a reasonably precise estimate of what the impact of changing the friendship network is likely to be.

THE LOGIC OF REGRESSION

Regression analysis is simply an extension of the exercise undertaken in Figure 8-1. An important difference, however, is that the dependent variable will never be perfectly related to X. In other words, it will not be possible to predict the dependent variable without some degree of error. The error reflects the impact of other variables on the dependent variable. For example, if an individual has six friends who use drugs, but reported only twenty opportunities to use drugs, the prediction employing the above rule would be sixteen opportunities too low. Where the independent variable equals six, the prediction for the dependent variable is thirty-six. In addition to friends who use drugs, the number of opportunities to use drugs can be influenced by the frequency of interaction with friends who use them, the setting in which interaction occurs, or any number of other variables. Of course, the smaller the error, the better one can predict the dependent variable. As policy researchers and program analysts trying to understand complex social phenomena, such as drug use and how to deal with it, the goal is to come as close as possible to the pattern displayed in Figure 8-1.

Consider another example. Assume the task is to study the relationship between unemployment among teens (the independent variable) and the number of teenage drug arrests (the dependent variable) in the 100 most populated cities in the United States. In each city, we can record the percentage of teenage unemployment and the number of teenage drug arrests during a fixed length of

FIGURE 8-2   Hypothetical Relationship between Teenage Drug Arrests and Teenage
Unemployment

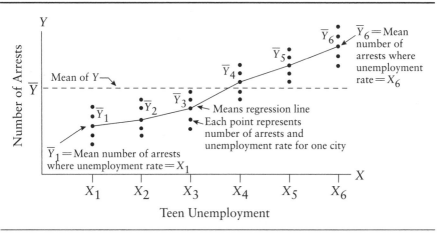

Teen Unemployment

time, for example, the past year.[1] For each percentage point of unemployment, ranging from zero to some higher value, there is a distribution of arrests. In other words, not all the cities with the same percentage of unemployment have the same number of arrests, so one cannot predict drug arrests from unemployment without error. The pattern of plotted values might look something like Figure 8-2.

Asked to predict the number of arrests for any city, the best guess, in the absence of other information, would be the mean rate for all cities, designated $\overline{Y}$ on the vertical axis in Figure 8-2. In addition to the Y mean for all cities, there is a Y mean for each X value or percentage of teen unemployment, designated $\overline{Y}_1, \overline{Y}_2, \ldots \overline{Y}_6$. Connecting these means yields a regression line that can be described by a mathematical rule as the relationship in Figure 8-1. Normally, as in Figure 8-2, the regression line improves the accuracy of prediction above that achieved by the Y mean alone. In other words, a city's number of teenage arrests can be predicted more accurately on the basis of its percentage of teenage unemployment rate than on the basis of the number of teenage arrests for all cities. Pairs of values or data points come closer to the regression line than they do the overall or grand mean of Y. The distance between the points and regression line is less than the distance between the points and mean of Y. It is possible in this example to predict a city's number of arrests from the percentage of unemployment. It is not possible to do so without error. There is some variation in number of arrests for each percentage of unemployment.

If the average value for the number of arrests for each percentage of unemployment were the same, then the two variables would be unrelated. The

---

[1] To insure comparability among the cities with respect to teenage population, it is desirable to measure the number of arrests per 100s of the teenage population.

FIGURE 8-3   A Pattern of No Relationship

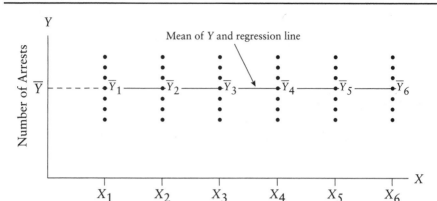

Teen Unemployment

pattern of points would look like Figure 8-3. Knowledge of unemployment would not help in predicting the number of arrests. The overall mean of the number of arrests in the cities and the line produced by the means of the number of arrests for each percentage of unemployment would be the same. On the other hand, should all cities fall on the line connecting the means, arrests would be, as in Figure 8-1, a perfect function of unemployment. In other words, there would be no spread of values or points around the Y means and knowledge of unemployment would allow one to predict drug arrests without error.

In everything but hypothetical examples, there will always be error. Because of this, variation in the dependent variable can be thought of as reflecting two components: variation accounted for by the independent variable or **explained variation** and variation unaccounted for by the independent variable or **unexplained variation**. These components are illustrated in Figure 8-4. Variation among cities in the number of arrests is partially dependent on variation in unemployment (this is "explained" variation), but variation in number of arrests is not completely accounted for by unemployment (this is "unexplained" and means some of the variation in number of arrests is attributable to other differences among the cities than teenage unemployment). To the extent that explained variation is maximized and unexplained variation minimized, one can understand a little better how the world operates and make better predictions relevant to policymaking to deal with it.

In the example, a causal relationship is assumed, i.e., that changes in unemployment produce changes in the number of teenage drug arrests. Of course, as noted in Chapter 6, number of arrests and unemployment may co-vary without being causally related. The relationship could be spurious.

FIGURE 8-4   Explained and Unexplained Variation

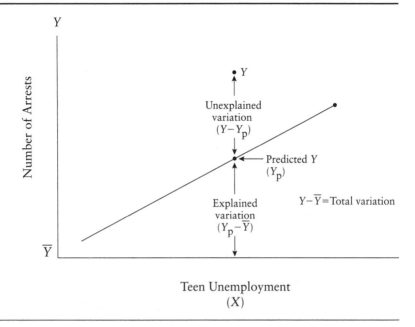

Part of the task of the policy researcher is to determine if a relationship is causal or not.

LINEAR REGRESSION

In **linear regression** the concern is whether the pattern among pairs of values on two variables can be described by a straight line. The mathematical formula for a straight line is $Y = a + bX$. As before, Y represents the dependent variable, X the independent variable. The values a and b are constant terms, so-called because they do not vary, and define the nature of the relationship between X and Y. The a, or **Y intercept**, is the value of Y when X equals zero. From the previous example, it represents the predicted number of arrests when unemployment equals zero (see Figure 8-5). The b, or **regression coefficient**, defines the slope of the line and is the change in Y associated with a one-unit change in X (i.e., the change in Y between X_3 and X_4 in Figure 8-5). It would represent, for example, the amount of change in the number of teenage arrests associated with a one percent change in unemployment. The greater the slope, the greater the influence of X on Y and the more change in Y associated with a change in X.

The regression coefficient is typically more important than the intercept from the perspective of the policy researcher, inasmuch as it defines the

FIGURE 8-5   **The Intercept and Regression Coefficient**

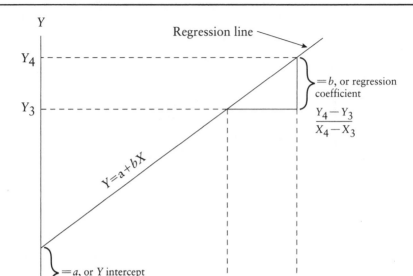

influence of the independent variable on the dependent variable. For example, if it is known that each percentage point increase in unemployment increases the number of drug arrests by a specific amount, the information can be used in developing programs to deal with teenage drug abuse in anticipation that drug arrests will decline. Not only is it known that employment will reduce drug arrests, but there is some idea of just how much of a decline to expect.

Before turning to procedures for deriving values for a and b, one needs to look again at the linear formula, $Y = a + bX$. To reflect the fact that values or data points are spread about the regression line owing to the influence of factors other than X on Y, an **error term** is added and the formula becomes $Y = a + bX + e$. This error, also called the residual, reflects the component of unexplained variation discussed earlier. The magnitude of the error term reflects the goodness of fit of the linear regression, that is, the closeness of the values or points to the regression line. The smaller the error term, the closer the points are to the line and the better the fit. The relationship can be considered linear and described by a straight line. The error term becomes particularly important in deriving values for a and b and may provide some insight into factors other than X that may be influencing Y. Inspecting cases that deviate significantly from the line may suggest what these factors are. For example, should one city have substantially fewer arrests in spite of high unemployment, one might wish to learn more about this city in anticipation of finding a condition or set of conditions that work to lower teenage drug arrests even when unemployment is high.

DERIVING VALUES FOR *a* AND *b* IN LINEAR REGRESSION

Linear regression presumes that the relationship between two variables can be described by a straight line. In order to establish where this line falls, one needs to derive values for *a* and *b*. One approach is to simply draw a line by inspecting the scatter of points and guessing where the line should be. The intercept would, of course, be where the line crossed the Y axis, and the regression coefficient would be the distance traversed on the Y axis for a single unit of X. While this approach may provide a reasonable estimate, there are more precise ways of deriving the line which eliminate the subjective assessment of the analyst. The **least squares** criterion is the approach typically employed in policy research. Least squares establishes the unique line that minimizes the square of the distances between each point and the regression line. Only one line satisfies this criterion. The least squares line can be derived using the following formulas:

$$b = \frac{\Sigma(X_i - \overline{X})(Y_i - \overline{Y})}{\Sigma(X_i - \overline{X})^2}$$

$$a = \overline{Y} - b\overline{X}$$

where

X_i = values of the independent variable
$\overline{X}$ = mean of the independent variable
Y_i = values of the dependent variable
$\overline{Y}$ = mean of the dependent variable

The X's and the Y's in each formula are, of course, known; they are the values of the independent and dependent variable for each case. If one is computing *a* and *b* by hand, *b* is generally computed first, then *a*. Of course, with computers, we can avoid the tedium of having to make the computations.

In calculating *b* with the above formula, the **joint variation** or **covariation** of X and Y is compared to the total variation in X. The covariation is the extent to which two variables change together or co-vary. To calculate the covariation, start with one X, Y pair. For example, in Table 8-1, Set A, where $X = 1$, $Y = 1$, $\overline{X} = 3$, $\overline{Y} = 3$, subtract the mean of X from its value and you get -2 $(1 - 3 = -2)$. Similarly, subtract the mean of Y from Y to get -2 $(1 - 3 = -2)$. Now multiply $(X - \overline{X})$ by $(Y - \overline{Y})$ to get 4 $(-2 \times -2 = 4)$.

TABLE 8-1   Computing Covariances

SET A: LARGE POSITIVE RELATIONSHIP BETWEEN X AND Y

X	Y	$(X - \overline{X})$	$(X - \overline{Y})$	$(X - \overline{X})(X - \overline{Y})$
1	1	-2	-2	4
2	2	-1	-1	1
3	3	0	0	0
4	4	1	1	1
5	5	2	2	4
$\overline{X} = 3$	$\overline{Y} = 3$			$\Sigma(X - \overline{X})(Y - \overline{Y}) = 10$

SET B: LARGE NEGATIVE RELATIONSHIP BETWEEN X AND Y

X	Y	$(X - \overline{X})$	$(X - \overline{Y})$	$(X - \overline{X})(X - \overline{Y})$
1	5	-2	-2	4
2	4	-1	1	-1
3	3	0	0	0
4	2	1	-1	-1
5	1	2	-2	-4
$\overline{X} = 3$	$\overline{Y} = 3$			$\Sigma(X - \overline{X})(Y - \overline{Y}) = -10$

SET C: LITTLE RELATIONSHIP BETWEEN X AND Y

X	Y	$(X - \overline{X})$	$(X - \overline{Y})$	$(X - \overline{X})(X - \overline{Y})$
1	3	-2	0	0
2	4	-1	1	-1
3	1	0	-2	0
4	5	1	2	2
5	2	2	-1	-2
$\overline{X} = 3$	$\overline{Y} = 3$			$\Sigma(X - \overline{X})(Y - \overline{Y}) = -1$

If this is done for each pair of X and Y values and these are added together, the total is 10 (see Table 8-1). When large deviations of X from the mean of X are paired with large deviations of Y from the mean of Y, as in Table 8-1, Sets A and B, the covariation will be large and b will be large, indicating X and Y are related. The relationship will be positive if positive deviations on X are paired with positive deviations on Y and negative deviations on X paired with negative deviations on Y (Set A). It will be negative if positive deviations on one variable are paired with negative deviations on the other (Set B). If X and Y are unrelated, large deviations on X will be paired with small deviations on Y and large deviations on Y with small deviations on X (Set C). In the latter instance, the summation of the product of X and Y deviations will approach zero, and b will be zero or close to zero. Notice the illustrations of each set of relationships in Figure 8-6 . Whereas Sets A and B yield sharply angled lines, Set C is nearly horizontal.

The quantity $\Sigma(X - \overline{X})^2$ is the variation of X. Note that this quantity is similar to the variance discussed in Chapter 5 except that it is not divided by N.

FIGURE 8-6   **Illustrations of Table 8-1 Relationships**

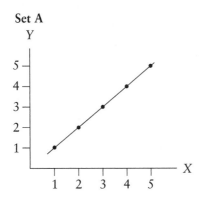

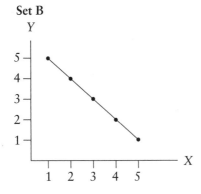

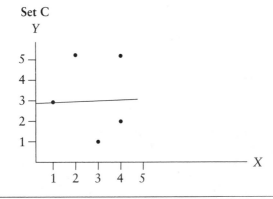

LINEAR REGRESSION: AN EXAMPLE

To illustrate the technique further, consider again the regression of teenage drug arrests on teenage unemployment. Assume that the analysis has generated the information in Table 8-2 for ten cities.[2] From the information, a and b can be calculated and the least squares regression line plotted. The values for X and Y represent each city's values for teenage unemployment and teenage arrests; $(X - \overline{X})$ and $(Y - \overline{Y})$ each city's value on each variable minus the mean for all cities on the variable, and $(X - \overline{X})^2$ the square of each city's value on X minus the mean for all cities on X. Summed over all cities, the product of $(X - \overline{X})$ and $(Y - \overline{Y})$ is the covariation of X and Y. $(X - \overline{X})^2$ is the variation in X. Both are needed, as noted above, in calculating b.

The first step in linear regression is to examine the **scattergram** or **scatter plot** to ensure that the relationship between arrests and unemployment is linear or approximates a straight line. If so, a and b can be computed and the least squares regression line plotted.[3] If not, pairs of values will have to be transformed to approximate a straight line, or a technique other than linear regression employed (see Chapter 9).

TABLE 8-2   Calculating a and b

CITIES	(X) PERCENT UNEMPLOYMENT	(Y) NUMBER OF ARREsts (00s)	$(X - \overline{X})$	$(Y - \overline{Y})$	$(X - \overline{X})^2$	$(X - \overline{X})$ $(Y - \overline{Y})$
1	7	100	−8	−370	64	2,960
2	11	400	−4	−70	16	280
3	11	300	−4	−170	16	680
4	12	400	−3	−70	9	210
5	13	500	−2	30	4	−60
6	15	600	0	130	0	0
7	17	500	2	30	4	60
8	18	700	3	230	9	690
9	21	600	6	130	36	780
10	25	600	10	130	100	1,300
	$\Sigma = 150$	$\Sigma = 4{,}700$	$\Sigma = 0$	$\Sigma = 0$	$\Sigma = 258$	$\Sigma = 6{,}900$

$\overline{X} = 15$; $\overline{Y} = 470$

---

[2] The illustration here deviates from the standard regression problem in that values of the independent variable are distributed randomly rather than fixed. This is of little consequence if one makes certain assumptions regarding the error variation or error term. These assumptions are discussed in Chapter 9.

[3] Of course, a computer program will compute a and b whether or not the relationship is linear. If, however, the relationship is not linear, the coefficients will be meaningless and might lead one to the wrong conclusions about the nature of the relationship between two variables.

FIGURE 8-7   **Number of Arrests by Unemployment**

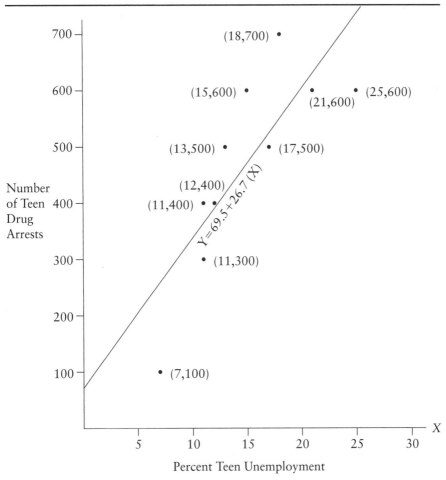

In this example, the scatter plot (Figure 8-7) reveals that linear regression is appropriate. Thus, b can be calculated and accurately describe the nature of the relationship.

$$b = \frac{\Sigma(Y - \overline{Y})(X - \overline{X})}{\Sigma(X - \overline{X})^2} = \frac{6,900}{258} = 26.7$$

The value of b is expressed in units of the dependent variable and can be interpreted, in this example, as the amount of change in the number of teenage drug arrests associated with a single unit change in the percentage of teenage unemployment. In other words, for every one percentage point increase in unemployment, the number of arrests increases by 26.7, a valuable piece of information for those interested in reducing teenage arrests.

With the computation of b, it is a simple matter to derive a.

$$a = \overline{X} - b(\overline{X}) = 470 - (26.7)15 = 470\text{–}400.5 = 69.5$$

Inserting the appropriate values, a equals 69.5. Thus, when teen unemployment equals zero, the number of teens arrested on drug charges is 69.5. It remains to derive another point to plot the regression line. Any point will do. If unemployment equals 10, $Y = 69.5 + 26.7(10)$ or 336.5. Connecting the intercept with the point $Y = 336.5$, $X = 10$ yields the regression line $Y = 69.5 + 26.7 (X)$. The calculations can be checked by deriving another Y value and the regression line should pass through each.

EXERCISES

8-1

a. Assume that you are interested in whether an increase in the percentage of patients in a state served by health maintenance organizations reduces the average cost per individual for medical care. The data are below:

STATE	PERCENT OF PATIENTS SERVED BY HMOs	AVERAGE MEDICAL COST PER INDIVIDUAL
S_1	1%	$ 500
S_2	8	700
S_3	3	1,000
S_4	6	200
S_5	4	300
S_6	2	600
S_7	1	600
S_8	1	700
S_9	10	400
S_{10}	5	300

b. Based on the information below, address the issue of whether or not expenditures per pupil are related to the average performance of pupils on a standardized basic skills examination.

SCHOOL DISTRICT	EXPENDITURE PER PUPIL	AVERAGE PERFORMANCE
D_1	70	160
D_2	150	190
D_3	220	180
D_4	170	200
D_5	90	150
D_6	100	160
D_7	120	160
D_8	150	160
D_9	110	150
D_{10}	190	170

Research in Practice 8A

REGRESSION ANALYSIS

Benchmarking important indicators of productivity is increasing in government, private industry, higher education, and elsewhere. In 1994, the International City Managers Association launched a major effort to streamline data collection and sharing of government performance measures. They focused on performance in police services, fire services, neighborhood services, and support services.

The data collectors worked to define precisely what kinds of data would produce the best measures of service performance. For example, to measure the effectiveness of police services, they decided to collect data on crimes per population, response time to top priority calls, traffic accidents per population, and several other measures. In the neighborhood services category, one of their measures was library circulation per capita.

The data evaluators recognized that a variety of factors in addition to the competence of the service providers themselves affect performance. For example, crime rates depend not only on the efficiency and quality of police forces, but also the income levels of the community and neighborhood being evaluated. Library circulation depends not just on the availability and ease of access to books, but the propensity of the population to read them.

The evaluators used regression to take into account other factors contributing to performance. For example, to evaluate library service, they regressed per capita book circulation in each community on median household income, to take into account the fact that households with more income generally use library services more. They found that income explained about 45 percent of library circulation, and that for every $1,000 of average household income, the book circulation increased by .6 per person. A constant of -9.1 indicated that there will be very little circulation at all until the mean income of the neighborhood or city reaches at least $9,000.[4]

Knowing this important contextual factor enables those making inter-city comparisons to compare more fairly city performance in this area by taking into account relative incomes of city populations. Similar adjustments are also made in other performance measures.

SOURCE: Mary Kopczynski and Michael Lombardo, "Comparative Performance Measurement: Insights and Lessons Learned from a Consortium Effort," *Public Administration Review* 59 (March/April, 1999): 124–134.

---

[4] Technically it means that the circulation is negative, but this is obviously impossible.

For both (a) and (b):

(1) Which is the dependent and independent variable?
(2) Prepare a scatter plot.
(3) Estimate the regression line.
(4) Calculate (a) and (b).
(5) Show the regression equation.
(6) Plot the regression line.

Is there a relationship in the above data? Is it linear? How do you know? What is the influence of the independent on the dependent variable? Write a paragraph summarizing the results of this analysis for an educated lay audience. What policy recommendation might you make based on your analysis?

GOODNESS OF FIT

After deriving the regression line, one wants to evaluate how well it summarizes or fits the data. As noted earlier, a regression line that passes through or near the plotted points summarizes or fits the data better than one where the points fall some distance from the line. The distance between the points and the line is error variation, referred to earlier. The smaller the error variation, the better the fit. One measure of fit is **Pearson's** product-moment correlation, or as it is more commonly referred to, the correlation coefficient, symbolized by *r*. It is a measure of association or strength of relationship and reflects the spread of points around the regression line. If the spread of points is random, as in Figure 8-3, *r* will approach zero. This means, of course, that the dependent variable is unrelated to the independent variable. In Figure 8-3, the number of teenage arrests is shown to be unrelated to teenage unemployment. If the spread is minimal, as in Figure 8-8, *r* will approach its upper limit of +1 in the case of a positive association (A in Figure 8-8) or its lower limit of −1 in the case of a negative relationship (B in Figure 8-8). In both cases it means that the dependent variable is strongly related to the independent variable; changes in the independent variable are associated with changes in the dependent variable. If all the data points fall on the line (in other words, there is no error variation) *r* will equal +1 (Figure 8-1). The formula for *r* (there are somewhat simpler computational formulas) is:

$$\frac{\Sigma(X_i - \overline{X})(Y_i - \overline{Y})}{\sqrt{\Sigma(X_i - \overline{X})^2 \Sigma(Y_i - \overline{Y})^2}}$$

Compare this formula with the one for the regression coefficient *b*. As with *b*, the numerator is the covariation, or joint variation of X and Y. Thus, there is a correspondence between *r* and *b*. When $\Sigma(X_i - \overline{X})(Y_i - \overline{Y})$ equals zero, both *r* and *b* will equal zero. Like *b*, *r* will be high if large deviations of Y scores from the Y mean are paired with large deviations of X scores from the

X mean, and low if large deviations on one variable are paired with low deviations on the other (see Table 8-1). Unlike b, however, r is symmetrical. Its value is the same, regardless of which variable is defined as independent, i.e., $r_{xy} = r_{yx}$. This is because the denominator for r is the product of the standard deviations of both X and Y (see Chapter 5), while the denominator in the formula for b contains only values of the independent variable X.

The interpretation of r, particularly for values other than 0 and 1, is more readily grasped in terms of the measure r^2, or what is technically referred to as the **coefficient of determination**. If you return to the idea that variation in the dependent variable reflects two components, variation accounted for by the independent variable (or explained variation) and variation unaccounted for (or unexplained variation), r^2 equals the ratio of explained variation to total variation, or

FIGURE 8-8   **A. Near Perfect Positive Association, r Approaching + 1**

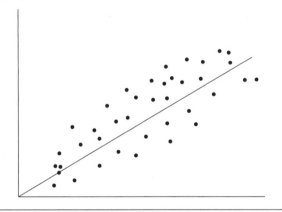

B. Near Perfect Negative Association, r Approaching − 1

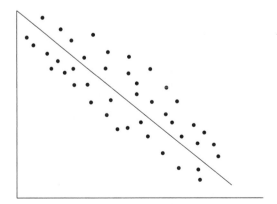

$$\frac{\Sigma(Y_p - \overline{Y})^2}{\Sigma(Y_i - \overline{Y})^2}$$

where

$\overline{Y}$ = the mean of Y
Y_p = the Y score predicted on the basis of the regression line
Y_i = the actual Y score

In Figure 8-9 note that the actual data point Y_i when, in this illustration, X equals 2. The distance between it and the value predicted on the basis of the regression line Y_p can be considered the unexplained part, referred to as a "residual." It is readily apparent that this distance is a portion of the total distance between the point Y_i and the mean of Y or $\overline{Y}$. The quantity Y_p can be considered the explained part. The sum $(Y_i - Y_p) + (Y_p - \overline{Y})$ represents the total variation in Y, $(Y_i - \overline{Y})$ at $X = 2$. Squaring the quantity $(Y_i - \overline{Y})$ and summing over all the Y's is, of course, the total variation in Y; squaring $(Y_p - \overline{Y})$ and summing over all the Y's is the variation accounted for or explained by X.

The value r^2 can be interpreted as the percent of variation in Y explained or accounted for by X. It also has a proportional reduction in error interpretation, which means that compared to prediction on the basis of the Y mean, prediction on the basis of X reduces prediction errors by r^2 percent. An r^2 equal to .50 means, for example, that 50 percent of the variation in Y, the dependent variable, can be explained by variation in X, the independent variable, or that errors in predicting Y can be reduced by 50 percent. Because r^2 is the square of the correlation coefficient, large values of r are necessary to produce moderate values of r^2. For example, it takes a correlation of .71 to produce an r^2 of .50. An r of .30 yields an r^2 of only .09; a correlation of .50, an r^2 of .25. To

FIGURE 8-9   **Explained and Unexplained Variance**

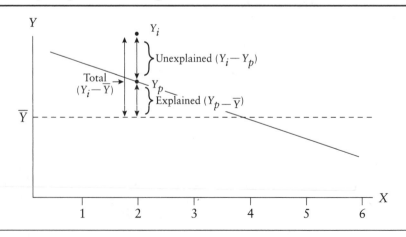

Research in Practice 8B

Correlation

Most graduate and professional programs have more applicants than they can accept. How do they decide among many seemingly qualified students? Obviously they want to use criteria that will predict success in the program. What kinds of indicators predict success?

In this study researchers analyzed the relationship of several pre-admission indicators to actual performance within a social work graduate program. Their sample included 235 students admitted to the program within a three-year period. Pre-admission information measured demographics, such as age and gender, academic preparation, such as grade averages and quality of undergraduate programs, and work experience. Performance was measured by grade point average for the first and second year within the graduate program.

Among statistical analyses they used, they examined the correlations between pre-admission selection criteria and actual performance for the entire sample. Interpreting r, they found that the final-year undergraduate GPA had a strong and statistically significant correlation with academic performance for both the first year of graduate school ($r = .423$, $p = .000$) and the second year ($r = .438$, $p = .002$). Age and previous work experience were not significantly correlated with performance. Interestingly, and contrary to other findings in the literature, the quality of undergraduate programs had a fairly strong and negative correlation with performance ($r = -.282$, $p = .024$).

The authors conclude that graduate programs should continue to use undergraduate GPA as a critical evaluative tool. They also warn that older students, or those who have worked within the field of social work, might be at a greater risk for poor performance. Thus, schools should work to meet the unique demands of non-traditional students. However, the findings are limited in that the number in the sample is fairly small and that the sample only includes one graduate program.

Source: William Pelech, Carol A. Stalker, Cheryl Regehr and Marilyn Jacobs, "Making the Grade: The Quest for Validity in Admission Decisions," Journal of Social Work Education (Spring/Summer 1999): 215–227.

compute r and r^2 for the data in Table 8-2, in addition to the information in the table, only $\Sigma(Y_i - \overline{Y})^2$, which equals 28,100, is needed. (Note: to arrive at this value, square $(Y_i - \overline{X})$ and sum over all Y's.) Thus the value r for the data in Table 8-2 equals $6,900/\sqrt{(258)(281,000)}$ or .81; r^2 equals the square of .81 or .66. Therefore teenage unemployment explains 66 percent of the variation in the number of teenage drug arrests.

Another measure of fit, although less familiar and less utilized, is the **standard error of estimate, se**. Like r, it is a measure of the spread of points about the regression line. It reflects the difference between predicted values (i.e., scores predicted on the basis of the regression line) and actual values, the quantity $(Y_i - Y_p)$ in Figure 8-9. Squared and summed over all the Y's, $(Y_i - Y_p)^2$ equals the unexplained or error variation, variation unaccounted for by X. Divided by N, it is the error variance.[5] The square root of this quantity is the standard error of estimate. The standard error of the estimate is simply the standard deviation of the points from the regression line. When the standard deviation—the standard error of the estimate—is small, the points are closer to the regression line than when it is larger.

$$se = \sqrt{\frac{\Sigma(Y_i - Y_p)^2}{N}}$$

The smaller the error variation, i.e., the closer the actual Y scores are to the regression line, the smaller is the standard error of estimate. Should all scores fall on the line, se equals zero. Thus when r equals 1, se equals 0. The upper limit of se equals the standard deviation of Y. In this case r equals zero. The regression line would be parallel to the X axis, and the predicted score for any particular Y would be the mean of Y. The value Y_p in the above formula would equal the mean of Y, and se the standard deviation of Y. Using the data from Table 8-2, procedures for calculating se are as follows:

TABLE 8-3   Calculating the Standard Error of Estimate

X	Y	STEP 1 $Y = 69.5 + 26.7(x)$	STEP 2 $(Y_i - Y_p)$	STEP 3 $(Y_i - Y_p)^2$
7	100	256.4	−156.4	24,461
11	400	363.2	36.8	1,354
11	300	363.2	−63.2	3,994
12	400	389.9	10.1	102
13	500	416.6	83.4	6,956
15	600	470	130	16,900
17	500	523.4	−23.4	548
18	700	550.1	149.9	22,470
21	600	630.2	−30.2	912
25	600	737	−137	18,769

Step 4. $\Sigma \dfrac{(Y_i - Y_p)^2}{N} = \dfrac{96,466}{10} = 9,647$

Step 5. $\sqrt{9,647} = 98.2$

---

[5] Or if the data are a sample of some population, divide by $N - 2$.

1. Derive a predicted value of Y for each X using the regression equation.
2. Subtract each Y score from the predicted value of Y.
3. Square the difference.
4. Sum and divide by N[6].
5. Calculate the square root.

A small standard error of estimate means a relatively good fit, i.e., a strong linear relationship. However, se also has an interpretation in terms of the normal curve. If the distribution of Y values for each X are assumed to be normal with equal variances, 68 percent of the actual values will fall within $\pm$ 1 standard error (95 percent within $\pm$ 2 standard errors) of the regression line. In the above example, 68 percent of the cities lie within a range of $\pm$ 98.2 arrests (se is expressed in units of the dependent variable) of the regression line.

EXERCISES

8-2 Calculate r, r^2, and the standard error for the data in Exercise 8-1 (a).

8-3 Calculate r, r^2, and the standard error for the data in Exercise 8-1 (b).

8-4 A correlation matrix among four items measuring citizen's respect for police showed the following:

ITEMS	A	B	C	D
A	—	.60	.40	.10
B	—	—	.50	.05
C	—	—	—	.15
D	—	—	—	—

a. What's the average inter-item correlation?
b. What is the alpha value?
c. How much would alpha improve if you deleted item D from the scale?

8-5 For each state, collect data on the number of physicians per 100,000 population, the rate of infant mortality, and the overall mortality rate (consult a recent Statistical Abstract). Using the regression software package your instructor directs, compute a regression with infant mortality as the dependent variable and the number of physicians the independent variable. Compute a similar regression with the overall mortality rate as the dependent variable. What is the b coefficient, the a coefficient (intercept), the standard error, the r^2 and the r for each? Write a sentence or two summarizing the impact of the number of physicians on mortality rates. Does the number of physicians affect infant mortality or overall mortality more?

---

[6]Again for a sample of some population, divide by $N - 2$.

Research in Practice 8C

CORRELATION AND ITS USE IN ASSESSING MEASUREMENT RELIABILITY

Chapter 3 discussed measurement reliability. Recall that a reliable measure is one that gives consistent results in repeated measurement applications. For example, if one were to measure students evaluations of an instructor the twelfth week of the semester and again the fifteenth week, one would expect each student's evaluation to be the same, assuming, of course, students did not change their evaluation.

No measure is perfectly reliable. But if the measure is somewhat reliable, one would expect those students who rated the instructor high during the twelfth week to give high ratings during the fifteenth week. Likewise, those who rated the instructor low the twelfth week would be expected to give low marks the fifteenth week. The more consistent the results given by repeated measurements, the higher the reliability of a measure.

There are several different methods for assessing reliability. Some of these were discussed in Chapter 3. All are based on the assumption that the correlation among different measures of the same thing (e.g., several survey questions purporting to measure an individuals attitude toward a new seatbelt law) is a measure of reliability. The higher the correlation, the more reliable the measures are considered to be.

One measure of reliability examines the internal consistency, measured by the correlation coefficient, of a number of items comprising a scale. The measure, **alpha (a)** is based on the assumption that items measuring the same thing will be highly correlated. The formula for alpha is:

$$a = N\bar{r}/[1 + \bar{r}(N - 1)]$$

where

N = The number of items in the scale

$\bar{r}$ = The mean inter-item correlation

THE ASSUMPTIONS OF REGRESSION

As with most statistical techniques, least squares linear regression requires the analyst to make certain assumptions. One of these involves the nature of the relationship between the dependent and independent variables. Linear regression assumes that the relationship between the two approximates a straight line. An examination of the scattergram will demonstrate if this assumption is correct. Variables generating nonlinear patterns can be transformed to satisfy this assumption or nonlinear regression can be used (Chapter 9).

Regression analysis also assumes an interval level of measurement. This assumption is often violated in social and policy research where measurement of a number of theoretically interesting variables is ordinal. While use of regression

The **inter-item correlation** is the correlation between each item, and the mean inter-item correlation, the mean of these correlations. For example, if the correlations among three items are as follows, the mean inter-item correlation is .30, (.40 + .30 + .20)/3 = .30.

	A	B	C
A (Seatbelts save lives)	—	.40	.30
B (Seatbelts are uncomfortable)	—	—	.20
C (Police should enforce seatbelt laws)	—	—	—

If the inter-item correlations average 1, alpha will equal 1, indicating perfect reliability. If the inter-item correlations average zero, alpha will equal zero. If the number of items and average inter-item correlation increase, alpha increases. Below is a table for various combinations of items and mean inter-item correlations. As a rule of thumb, alphas equal to or greater than .70 are desirable.

Values of Alpha for Various Combinations of Items and Average Inter-item Correlation

NUMBER OF ITEMS	Mean inter-item correlation					
	.0	.2	.4	.6	.8	1.0
2	.000	.333	.572	.750	.889	1.000
4	.000	.500	.727	.857	.941	1.000
6	.000	.600	.800	.900	.960	1.000
8	.000	.666	.842	.924	.970	1.000
10	.000	.714	.870	.938	.976	1.000

with ordinal measures is anathema to the statistical purist, most social scientists and policy researchers seem to be willing to sacrifice purity for the precision and power of the regression technique. Non-purists can take some comfort in research indicating that pinning numbers on ordinal categories and using regression results in very little distortion. However, with ordinal measures, the regression coefficient b is not, strictly speaking, interpretable. Here the standardized regression coefficient, or beta, discussed in Chapter 9, is more appropriate. For those who wish to adhere to the measurement assumption, it may be possible to create composite measures, scale or factor scores, based on a number of ordinal items. It is also possible to treat ordinal as well as nominal measures as a series of 0-1 dummy variables, a technique also discussed in Chapter 9.

SOME ISSUES IN THE USE OF REGRESSION AND CORRELATION

While correlation and regression are aspects of the same least squares technique, a distinction is sometimes made between problems appropriate to regression and problems appropriate to correlation. The discussion of regression began with the standard regression problem. It assumed a normally distributed dependent variable for fixed values of an independent variable. Rarely in policy analysis does this occur. More typically, both dependent and independent variables are random distributions, and discerning a causal direction is sometimes problematic. Given this, is it preferable to simply establish correlation rather than opt for regression where causal direction is assumed?

We believe that regression analysis offers more than correlation. Regression at least encourages the analyst to consider more carefully the causal direction between the variables, and this, of course, is desirable. A healthy degree of skepticism is always warranted regarding research findings, particularly when they have consequences for the public, but this should not deter one from understanding the connections between variables and consequently the social realities that underlie them. Clearly, a public policy advocate is on firmer ground in pointing to a regression analysis supporting the assumption of a causal direction than to one that simply establishes correlation. Regression also suggests that other factors may be important by directing attention to cases that vary widely from expectations. One can ask why particular cases or sets of cases vary and probe the factors that may explain this variation.

It should be clear at this point that regression is of considerable value to policy researchers and analysts, agency directors, and even elected officials. This will become even more evident in Chapter 9. Rarely is a policy analyst concerned with the influence of a single independent variable, because hardly ever is an important social phenomenon the consequence of only one factor. The focus will generally be two or more independent variables. Thus, in such instances, we use multiple regression, the topic of Chapter 9.

KEY TERMS

Scattergrams	Least squares
Regression line	Covariation
Explained variation	Pearson's correlation coefficient r
Unexplained variation	r^2(coefficient of determination)
Linear regression	Standard error of estimate (se)
Intercept	Alpha
Regression coefficient	Inter-item correlation
Error term	

FOR FURTHER HELP

Achen, Christopher H. "Interpreting and Using Regression." *Sage University Paper Series on Quantitative Applications in the Social Sciences.* Beverly Hills and London: Sage Publications, 1982. A discussion of the interplay between social science theory and regression analysis.

Fox, John. *Applied Regression Analysis, Linear Models, and Related Methods.* Thousand Oaks, California: Sage Publications, 1997. A more advanced treatment than presented here. Chapters 2 and 3 focus on simple regression.

Lewis-Beck, Michael S. "Applied Regression." *Sage University Paper Series on Quantitative Applications in the Social Sciences.* Beverly Hills and London: Sage Publications, 1980. A good introduction to regression.

9

ANALYZING THE RELATIONSHIP BETWEEN MORE THAN TWO VARIABLES: MULTIPLE REGRESSION

Chapter 8 described simple regression and related correlation techniques. The discussion focused on two-variable analysis, the effect of a single independent variable on a dependent variable. However, **multiple regression analysis** is even more useful because you can assess the influence of several independent variables simultaneously.[1] A researcher can evaluate the influence of a single independent variable controlling for the influence of other independent variables and measure the influence of the independent variables combined.

Multiple regression, like the elaboration process discussed in Chapter 6, enables the researcher to reduce the possibility that a relationship between a dependent and independent variable results from the relationship of both to some third or control variable. Whereas the elaboration process involving contingency tables is limited to one or two controls, multiple regression can accommodate a dozen or more. In this respect, multiple regression allows the researcher to approach the control of an experimental research design.

MULTIPLE REGRESSION

Multiple regression is an extension of simple regression. The multiple regression equation with two independent variables is $Y = a + b_1 X_1 + b_2 X_2 + e$ where X_1 and X_2 are independent variables. Of course additional variables can be included: $Y = a + b_1 X_1 + b_2 X_2 + ... + b_k X_k + e$ where k is equal to the total

---

[1]Sometimes analysts will distinguish between control variables and independent variables, but the distinction in multiple regression analysis is somewhat artificial. Usually the two terms are used when there are one or more independent variables of greatest interest, called independent variables and other variables—control variables—that are simply being controlled so that alternative sources of change in the dependent variable can be assessed. A multiple regression may explore the influence of several independent variables, several independent variables and control variables, and a single independent and several control variables. The status of a variable is determined by the particular research problem or hypothesis. For simplicity, the discussion in this chapter will refer to all the variables on the right side of the equals sign in the regression equation as independent variables.

number of independent variables in the equation. The number of independent variables will be a function of the research problem. Variables are not simply added for the sake of more, but because they bear on the research problem in some way.

As with simple regression, the Y intercept is the predicted value of Y when X_1 and X_2 are zero. However, unlike simple regression, there are at least two regression coefficients, b_1 and b_2. They have an interpretation identical to simple regression, except they are **partial measures**, which means that b_1 represents the influence of X_1 controlling for X_2, and b_2 represents the influence of X_2 controlling for X_1. Thus, b_1 is the amount of change produced in Y by a unit change in X_1 controlling for X_2, and b_2 is the amount of change produced in Y by a unit change in X_2 controlling for X_1.

The mechanics of controlling for a variable in regression analysis are not the same as in contingency table analysis, although the logic and interpretation are the same. In regression analysis, one makes a mathematical adjustment rather than sorts cases based on values of the control variables. Thus, the number of controls in multiple regression is not limited by diminishing cell frequencies or problems of interpretation associated with a proliferation of sub-tables. Indeed, multiple regression can accommodate a large number of controls, limited only by the number of cases in the analysis.[2]

We can illustrate the use of multiple regression by continuing with the example from Chapter 8. There, the number of teen drug arrests was regressed on teen unemployment. Cities were the unit of analysis. Let us add the variables measuring percentage of single-parent families and community population size to the regression. The equation would be:

$$\begin{aligned}
Y \text{ (Number of teen arrests)} = {}& a + b_1 X_1 \text{ (Percent teen unemployment)} \\
& + b_2 X_2 \text{ (Percent single-parent families)} \\
& + b_3 X_3 \text{ (Population)} + e
\end{aligned}$$

with b_1 indicating the influence of teen unemployment controlling for single-parent families and population, b_2 the influence of single-parent families controlling for teen unemployment and population, and b_3 the influence of population size, controlling for teen unemployment and single-parent families.

---

[2]There is no fixed rule regarding an upper limit on the number of independent variables in multiple regression analysis aside from the fact that the number of variables must be smaller than the number of cases. However, as the number of variables approaches the number of cases in an analysis, degrees of freedom are sacrificed and the predictive power of the equation will increase simply by virtue of the additional variables. Where the number of variables equals the number of cases, predictive power is maximized and explained variation 100 percent. With a large number of cases, the number of variables is of little concern. But with smaller data sets, such as the fifty states, or the number of counties within a state, the number of variables can become a concern. Of course, the goal is to have as parsimonious an explanation for variability in the dependent variable as possible; that is, we want to explain as much variation in the dependent variable as possible with the fewest independent variables.

Assume that the following resulted from the addition of the above variables to the regression:

$$Y = 15.6 + 25.6 \text{ (unemployment rate)}$$
$$+ 6.3(\text{Percent single-parent families})$$
$$+ -.000006(\text{Population}) + e$$

The regression coefficient for percent unemployment in this equation is reduced from 26.7, in the case where single-parent families and population are not included, to 25.6. This means that controlling for the percent of single-parent families and population reduces the influence of teen unemployment and that both unemployment and number of arrests are related to either single-parent families or population or both. To predict a city's number of arrests, multiply each b value by the city's value on the particular variable and along with the intercept add them together. A city with ten percent unemployment, twelve percent single-parent families, and 250,000 population would have the following predicted number of teen arrests:

$$Y = 15.6 + 25.6 \ (10) + 6.3(12) -.000006(250,000) = 346$$

As with simple regression, we evaluate goodness of fit by the degree of correlation between the independent variables and the dependent variable, referred to as the **multiple correlation coefficient or multiple R**. The square of the multiple correlation, **multiple R^2**, is the proportion of variation explained in the dependent variable by all of the independent variables. We can also assess fit by the standard error of estimate. Recall smaller is better. In simple regression, R^2 reflects the spread of points around the regression line. In multiple regression, the focus is no longer a line, but an n-dimensional plane reflecting the number of independent variables in the equation.

The intercept, the partial regression coefficients, multiple R, and multiple R^2 are standard output from all statistical software packages. Another useful statistic, part of most software packages, is the **standardized partial regression coefficient (beta)**. Beta, a transformation of the regression coefficient b, is particularly useful if the independent variables are measured in different measurement units. For example, one variable may be measured in dollars, another in years, and another in percentages. Beta is used to compare the relative impact of each independent variable on the dependent variable. It is derived by multiplying the regression coefficient b for a particular independent variable by the ratio of the standard deviation of the variable to the standard deviation of the dependent variable.[3]

$$B_1(\text{Standardized}) - b_1 \ (\text{Unstandardized}) \frac{\text{Standard deviation of independent variable}}{\text{Standard deviation of dependent variable}}$$

---

[3]Beta can also be calculated by transforming the dependent variable and independent variables to Z scores as described in Chapter 5 and generating the regression equation using the Z scores.

The standardized coefficients are interpreted as the amount of change in Y measured in standard deviation units produced by a unit change in X measured in standard deviation units controlling for all other variables. In effect, the transformation imposes the same measurement unit on each variable, and thus allows the coefficients to be compared with each other. In a regression with a single independent variable, the standardized regression coefficient is equal to Pearson's correlation coefficient r. Converting the partial regression coefficients in the regression equation reported on page 238 to betas generates the following equation:

$$Y = .78X_1 + .08X_2 + -.13X_3 + e$$

This equation shows that teen unemployment is more important than either single-parent families or population in predicting the number of teen arrests. The beta for teen unemployment is seven times greater than the beta for population and ten times greater than the beta for single-parent families.

So in assessing the relative impact of variables, beta is preferred to b. However, beta is not appropriate in comparing independent variables derived from regressions where data are drawn from different samples. For example, if you are interested in comparing the effects of teen unemployment on the number of arrests in cities over 500,000 with those less than 500,000, then the regression coefficient b is the appropriate statistic. Because beta reflects the influence of an independent variable as well as the variation of both the independent and dependent variables which are likely to vary from sample to sample, betas generated from different samples are also likely to vary. So while the value of b can be equal in two samples, indicating that the impact of an independent variable is the same in each, the value of beta may be different because the standard deviations of the independent and dependent variables in each equation are different. Relying on beta in such instances would misrepresent the relationship between the two variables. Research in Practice 9A and 9B provide illustrations of multiple regression.

Although it is not a part of regression analysis, **partial correlation** is another statistic worth noting here. Although a number of measures of association have partial measures, the term partial correlation coefficient refers to the partial for Pearson's correlation coefficient. The term partial, as noted earlier, suggests that the coefficient represents the association between two variables controlling for the influence of one or more others. The partial correlation coefficient squared is equal to the proportion of shared variation between two variables, controlling for one or more others. Although partial r can have a causal interpretation, it is less useful in this regard than the partial regression coefficient and is used less often.[4]

---

[4]The formula for partial correlation between x and y controlling for z is:

$$\frac{r_{xy} - r_{xz} r_{yz}}{\sqrt{1 - r_{xz}^2} \sqrt{1 - r_{yz}^2}}$$

Research in Practice 9A

MULTIPLE REGRESSION

In recent years, the Supreme Court has given states more discretion to regulate abortion. Many states have adopted policies designed to reduce the number of abortions provided. Two evaluators decided to examine the impact of some of these regulations on the number of abortions provided in the states.

The analysts assumed that the number of abortions in any state is dependent not just on state policy, but social and demographic conditions in the state. For example, abortions are more common in urban than rural areas, among low income and non white women, and those with fewer years of education. So it is important to take into account these factors when examining the impact of state policies. Moreover, the evaluators speculated that state legislative activity designed to reduce abortion will have an effect, even if the courts declare proposed policies unconstitutional (as they have for several attempts to outlaw abortion). The authors reasoned that such attempts reflect a negative climate toward abortion, and when publicized, deter women from pursuing this option.

In order to take into account these factors, the evaluators used multiple regression. They regressed the abortion rate per 1,000 women (the total number of abortions in the state in a year divided by the number of women in the state, multiplied by 1,000) on a variable measuring whether or not the state required parental consent or notification before a minor had an abortion, another variable indicating whether the state permitted Medicaid funding for abortions, a set of measures of state socio-economic conditions mentioned above, and two measures capturing state legislative anti-abortion activity.

In looking at the relationship between teen arrests and teen unemployment, we need to control for a third variable (single-parent families). To understand the concept of partial correlation and partial regression used in such an analysis, it is helpful to think in terms of two regressions, one where teen arrests is regressed on single-parent families and one where teen unemployment is regressed on single-parent families. The residual variation, that is, unexplained variation, from each regression represents what is left after any shared variation with single-parent families is eliminated or taken into account. Thus, partial r represents shared variation between teen arrests and teen unemployment after any shared variation of either variable with single-parent families has been removed. Partial b is the amount of change in teen arrests produced by a one percent change in teen unemployment after the amount of change produced by single-parent families has been removed. If partial r and partial b are reduced to zero with the addition of a control variable, this is evidence of

This process allowed the evaluators to see if policies had an impact beyond the demographic and social conditions that seem to promote or deter abortion. Overall, their model predicted abortion rates fairly well, with an R^2 of .68. They found that parental consent policies had no deterrent effect on abortions. Though states with parental consent laws had 1.86 fewer abortions per thousand than other states, controlling for other factors, the standard error was 2.25, much larger than the effect. Thus, the coefficient was not significant, and even its direction was questionable. Medicaid funding had a nearly significant positive effect. The major predictor of abortion rate, though, was the extent to which the state is urbanized. Urban states have a higher rate than less urban states, other things being equal

The authors then tested whether the presence of parental consent laws led women to go out of state to have abortions, using the same set of control variables as above. Their model fit considerably less well, with R^2 of only .25. Nonetheless, they found that these laws did not affect the out of state abortion rate. Again, however, the urban nature of the state was the primary predictor. Rural states tended to have more women leave the state for abortions, again reflecting the greater availability of abortion services in cities.

These findings will certainly not deter states from enacting abortion regulations, but they do shed light on the gap between policy objectives and policy impact in one controversial area.

SOURCE: Anita Prichard and Sharon Kay Parsons, "The Effects of State Abortion Policies on States' Abortion Rates," *State and Local Government Review* 31 (Winter, 1999): 43–52. See also Research in Practice 7E, p. 205.

spurious correlation, similar to the situation in contingency analysis when the relationship between two variables is eliminated with the addition of a control (that is, when the relationship is zero within sub-tables generated for each value of a control variable). Partial correlation can incorporate any number of controls, although different software packages may have limits.

As with means, proportions, and other statistics, the data being analyzed in regression analysis may be a sample of some population (with the goal of drawing inferences from the sample to the population). For example, one may be interested in drawing inferences by testing the null hypothesis that b equals zero, that is, that the independent variable has no predictive power with respect to the dependent variable. If the sample is large, this can be done with the t test. The formula for t in this regard is

$$t = \frac{b}{b_{se}}$$

Research in Practice 9B

MULTIPLE REGRESSION

Small rural communities throughout the Great Plains are dying. One of the key indicators of this slow death is the disappearance of business enterprises in rural towns. The shuttered windows on Main Street businesses are indicators of a town that has lost its viability. But what causes a decrease in business? Four researchers sought to answer that question using regression analysis as a technique.

Using counties as their unit of analysis, the authors accumulated data on all 438 nonmetropolitan Great Plains counties. They conducted four separate analyses, one for each decade beginning with 1950–1959. Their dependent variable was the percent change in retail and wholesale employment in the county. To predict that change, they included independent variables of population size at the beginning of the decade, the percent employed in retail and wholesale business at the beginning of the decade, the percent change in the number of retail and wholesale establishments, and the percent population change during the decade. Regression analysis allowed the authors to look at several possible predictors simultaneously.

They summarized their findings for each decade in the manner presented below.

INDEPENDENT VARIABLES	% CHANGE IN RETAIL AND WHOLESALE SECTOR EMPLOYMENT 1950-1960
Percent population change	.977***
Population size at the beginning of the decade	.0003*
Percent employed in retail or wholesale at the beginning of the decade	1.429***
Percent change in retail and wholesale establishments	.103

where b is the unstandardized partial regression coefficient and b_{se} is the standard error of b.[5] If the magnitude of b is large compared to its standard

---

[5]The standard error of b, like the standard error of the mean, is a measure of the standard deviation of a theoretical distribution (sampling distribution) of b values derived mathematically assuming an infinite number of samples of the same size.

Constant   38.56***

$F =$ 152.03***

Adjusted $R^2 =$ .586

$(N = 438)$

Note: (*p<.05, **p<.01, ***p<.001)

Coefficients are unstandardized regression coefficients

As we have illustrated for one decade, the model was fairly robust, although the adjusted R^2 was much larger for 1950-1960 and 1980-90 than for the intervening two decades. As the findings above indicate, population change has a strong positive effect on retail and wholesale business change. When a town's population decreases, so does employment in retail and wholesale businesses. In the 1950s, for example, for every change of 1 percent in the population, retail and wholesale employment changed in the same direction by .977 percent. During the 1950s, these findings also show that the larger the population size and the greater proportion of people employed in retail and wholesale enterprises at the beginning of the decade, the greater the decrease in that employment. In the 1950s, the percent change in the number of retail and wholesale establishments was unrelated to growth in employment.

Controlling for other factors, the authors demonstrate that population change was the most consistently related to retail and wholesale employment change across all time periods. In each case, it was statistically significant at a .05 level of significance.

The authors presented most of their key data in their article. We would recommend showing either the t values or the standard errors in addition to asterisks noting significance. This gives the reader more useful information. It is usually not necessary to carry the decimals to three places, though there is nothing wrong with that either (though it can add to the clutter in large tables).

SOURCE: Donald J. Adamachak, Leonard E. Bloomquist, Kent Bausman, and Rashida Qureshi, "Consequences of Population Change for Retail/Wholesale Sector Employment in the Nonmetropolitan Great Plains: 1950-1996," *Rural Sociology* (Nov/Dec, 1999): 92–112.

error, t will be large and statistically significant. If b is twice the standard error, t will equal two or more and mean that the probability of getting a b value of this size is .05 or less for the sample, if indeed the b for the population is zero. So with a t value of two or more, the null hypothesis that b equals zero is rejected and one infers that b is greater than zero in the population.

The *F* **ratio**, based on a comparison of explained variation, called regression sums of squares $\Sigma(Y_p - \overline{Y})^2$, and unexplained variation, called error sums of squares $\Sigma(Y_p - \overline{Y})^2$, is used to evaluate the significance of the overall regression. Dividing each quantity by the appropriate degrees of freedom (the number of variables minus one and the sample size minus the number of variables) yields mean square regression and mean square error: The *F* ratio or *F* is equal to:

$$\frac{\text{Mean square regression}}{\text{Mean square error}}$$

As with *t*, the null hypothesis, in this case that the regression equation is equal to zero (that is, that $b_1 = b_2 = b_k = 0$), is rejected at the .05 level of probability. Both *t* and *F* are produced by standard computer statistical software.

Table 9-1 summarizes the statistics related to a standard multiple regression analysis. Table 9-2 is a multiple regression output generated from SPSS 9.0 for Windows. The output is the basis for the regression equation on page 2. The first box identifies the variables included in the regression analysis along with user supplied labels for each variable. The output also identifies the procedure followed in entering variables into the regression analysis. Model 1 refers to the first regression equation produced with this particular set of commands. If the commands had specified a second regression, for example, with population removed, this would have been identified as Model 2.

The variables entered in the regression are identified with user defined labels that in this particular package are limited to eight characters. The labels are only for the analyst's convenience; they have no intrinsic measuring for the program. *Unemployed* refers to the percentage of teen unemployment, *single* to the percentage of single-parent families, and *pop* to population. The label *arrests* is used to identify the dependent variable, number of teen arrests.

"Enter" under method indicates that all the variables were added to the equation at the same time rather than in some sequence, such as step-wise (that procedure enters the variables in a particular order allowing each one in turn to explain all the variation it can in the dependent variable before entering the next). Step-wise regression, as it is called, is useful for observing the amount of variation explained by a variable after controlling for several others. For example, if one wanted to assess the importance of job training on income, variables reflecting personal characteristics and employment history might be entered first. Job training would then be available to explain remaining variation. The strategy provides a conservative estimate of the influence of job training on income and is reflected in the increase in *R* square. "Variables Removed" indicates that variables can be entered sequentially as well as removed in sequence, individually or in blocs.

The second box again identifies Model 1, *R*, *R* square, adjusted *R* square, and the standard error of estimate. *R* square of .682 indicates that the three variables do reasonably well in explaining the dependent variable. Adjusted *R* square is useful when the data are a sample of some population; it is a more accurate measure of reported fit of the sample regression to an estimate of the

Table 9-1   **Statistics from Multiple Regression**

Statistic	Interpretation
1. Intercept (a)	The value of the dependent variable when the independent variables are zero.
2. Partial regression coefficient (b)	The change produced in the dependent variable by a unit change in the independent variable, controlling for the other variables in the equation. Units are the same as the dependent variable. When measured without a meaningful metric, b is not easily interpretable.
3. Multiple R	The correlation between the dependent variable and all the independent variables in the regression equation. With a single independent variable, multiple R equals Pearson's r and the standardized regression coefficient.
4. Multiple R^2	The proportion of variance explained in the dependent variable by all of the independent variables in the regression equation.
5. Standard error of estimate	A measure of the difference between predicted and actual values on the dependent variable. The larger the standard error, the less accurately the regression can predict values of the dependent variable.
6. Partial standardized regression (beta)	The change produced in the dependent variable by a unit change in the independent variable when both are measured in standard deviation units. Betas in the same equation can be used to assess the relative influence of the independent variables even if their units of measurement differ.
7. Standard error of b	The standard deviation of b values from a theoretical distribution derived mathematically and necessary for statistical tests and estimation. A regression coefficient must be twice the size of its standard error to reject the null hypothesis ($b = 0$) at the .05 level.
8. Partial correlation	The correlation between two variables controlling for one or more others. Its square is equal to the proportion of explained variation controlling for other variables.
9. The t test	The statistical test of the null hypothesis that $b = 0$.
10. The F test	The statistical test of the regression equation that $b_1 = b_2 = b_k = 0$ or that the regression equation predicts values of the dependent variable better than the mean of the dependent variable.

population regression. With large samples, the adjustment will be less than with smaller samples. "Predictors" is another term for independent variables; "constant" refers to the intercept of a term.

Box three is an analysis of variance (ANOVA) table needed for the F test and assessing the significance of the regression equation. "Sig." is short for

Table 9-2   Sample Output for Multiple Regression

Variables Entered/Removed[b]

Model	Variables Entered	Variables Removed	Method
1	Unemployed Single Pop[a]		Enter

a. All requested variables entered.
b. Dependent Variable: Arrests

Model	R	R Square	Adjusted R Square	Std Error of the Estimate
1	.826[a]	.682	.523	122.0714

a. Predictors (Constant), Unemployed, Single, Pop

Anova[b]

Model	Sum of Squares	df	Mean Square	F	Sig.
1 Regression	191591.48	3	63863.828	4.286	.061
Residual	89408.515	6	14901.419		
Total	281000.00	9			

a. Predictors (Constant), Unemployed, Single, Pop
b. Dependent Variable: Arrests

Coefficients[a]

Model	Unstandardized Coefficients		Standardized Coefficients		
	B	Std Error	Beta	t	Sig.
1 (Constant)	15.634	254.103	.776	.062	.95
Unemployed	25.624	7.846	.352	3.26	3
Single	6.275	17.848	−.126	6	.01
Family	−6.48E-06	.000			7
				.352	73
				—	7
				−.541	.60
					8

a. Dependent Variable: Arrests

significance and indicates that the regression equation is significant at the .06 level of probability.

The final box reports the regression coefficients. The independent variables are identified along with the Y intercept labeled "constant" in this output. The regression coefficients (B's) and their standard errors are identified. As noted earlier, beta or the standardized coefficients show that teen unemployment is clearly the most important of the three independent variables. The t values confirm this by revealing that only unemployment is significant at the .05 level. Indeed, calculation of the exact probability shows unemployment significant at the .017 level.

EXERCISES

9-1 A research analyst in the state department of health is interested in the potential consequences of overbuilding hospital facilities. She has data from fifty metropolitan areas in the United States and information on the number of available hospital beds and the length of patient stays. She regresses the length of patient stay on the number of beds, the percentage of the population over sixty-five, the percentage covered by private insurance, the percentage covered by health maintenance organizations, and median income level for each community. The results of her analysis are as follows:

Multiple regression output

Dependent variable:	Mean length of hospital stay per patient (in days).
Independent variables:	Percentage over 65.
	Percentage covered by private health insurance.
	Percentage covered by a health maintenance organization (HMO).
	Median income level.
	Number of hospital beds per 1,000 population.
Multiple R	= .721
Multiple R Square	= .520
Standard Error of Estimate	= 1.5

INDEPENDENT VARIABLES	b	BETA	STANDARD ERROR OF b	t
Percent over 65*	.50	.36	.21	2.38
Percent covered private insurance	.23	.21	.15	1.53
Percent covered HMO	−.15	−.25	.07	−2.14
Median income**	.01	.10	.52	0.01
Number of hospital beds per 1,000 population	2.0	.42	.63	3.17

*Assume percentages are coded without decimals; i.e., 33 percent is coded as 33.

**Assume dollars are coded in hundreds; i.e., a median income of $8,000 is coded as 80.

a. Which variable has the most impact on patient stays?
b. Which variables have statistically significant (at .05) effects on patient stays?
c. What is the explained variation?

d. What is the effect on patient stays of increasing hospital beds by one per 1,000 population?

Write a paragraph summarizing the above findings. (Remember that the main purpose of the analysis is to investigate the influence of available hospital beds on patient stays.)

9-2 The analyst in 9-1 also examined the impact of number of hospital beds on the average daily cost of hospital care. Using the same sample but controlling for a cost of living index for the city instead of the percentage over 65, she found the following:

Multiple regression output

Dependent variable:	Average daily cost of hospital care.
Independent variables:	Cost of living index.
	Percentage covered by private health insurance.
	Percentage covered by a health maintenance organization (HMO).
	Median income level.
	Number of hospital beds per 1,000 population.
Multiple R	= .432
Multiple R Square	= .187
Standard Error of Estimate	= 19.81

Independent variables	b	Beta	Standard Error of b	t
Percent covered private insurance	.25	.21	.12	2.08
Percent covered HMO	−.05	−.10	.19	−0.26
Median income*	1.51	.18	1.03	1.47
Cost of living index**	2.59	.43	.95	2.73
Number of hospital beds per 1,000 population	1.24	.29	.43	2.88

*Assume dollars are coded in hundreds; i.e., a median income of $8,000 is coded as 80.

**Average cost of living in each metro area divided by the average cost of living in the United States times 100. The index is less than 100 where the cost of living is less than average, 100 where it is average, and more than 100 when it is greater than average.

Write a paragraph summarizing the findings of this analysis.

9-3 The analyst in 9-1 also examined the data on hospital beds and hospital costs for small counties. A regression analysis of 100 counties with less than 50,000 population reveals the following:

Multiple regression output

Dependent variable:	Mean length of hospital stay per patient (in days).
Independent variables:	Percentage over 65.
	Percentage covered by private health insurance.
	Percentage covered by a health maintenance organization (HMO).
	Median income level.

Number of hospital beds per 1,000 population.

Multiple R	= .862
Multiple R Square	= .743
Standard Error of Estimate	= .56

INDEPENDENT VARIABLES	b	BETA	STANDARD ERROR OF b	t
Percent over 65*	.62	.39	.19	3.26
Percent covered private insurance	.51	.40	.18	2.83
Percent covered HMO	−.02	−.05	.10	−.20
Median income**	.05	.08	.63	.08
Number of hospital beds per 1,000 population	1.55	.45	.52	2.98

*Assume percentages are coded without decimals; i.e., 33 percent is coded as 33.

**Assume dollars are coded in hundreds; i.e., a median income of $8,000 is coded as 80.

a. Do the number of hospital beds have more effect in larger or smaller communities? Which variables are significant in small communities but not in large ones?

b. Write a paragraph summarizing the findings for small communities. Compare them with findings from metropolitan areas.

THE LIMITS OF MULTIPLE REGRESSION

Multiple regression is a powerful analytical technique, but it is not without its limitations. Be aware of these limitations before forging ahead.

We introduced two assumptions of regression analysis in Chapter 8. These were that the relationship between the dependent and independent variable approximate a straight line, and that each can be measured with a meaningful, usually interval level metric. When these assumptions are met, the researcher can use the regression technique to assess how values of one variable relate to values of another. Nothing else is required. If, however, one wishes to estimate population characteristics from sample information, which is often the case, certain additional assumptions must be satisfied. Violations undermine the regression technique and can lead to faulty and erroneous conclusions.

The assumptions that bear on drawing inferences with regression are:

1. That the error terms[6] have a mean of zero.
2. That the error terms are distributed normally.

---

[6]The regression equation is written as if there is a single error term, $Y = a + bX + e$, but there is an error term with each observation (see discussion in Chapter 8) and it is the error term associated with each observation that is the focus here.

3. That the error terms are uncorrelated with values of the independent variables.
4. That the error terms are uncorrelated with each other.
5. That the variation in the error terms is constant over all values of the independent variable(s).
6. That the dependent and independent variables are measured without error.
7. That no independent variable is perfectly correlated with any other independent variable.

When the task is drawing inferences, it is helpful to think of two regressions. First, there is what might be called the "true" regression that reflects the relationships among the variables in the population. Seldom, if ever, will the researcher know what this regression looks like. The second is one based on the sample. The true regression can be estimated using the regression based on the sample, and can be done so accurately if the above assumptions are true.

Assumptions 1 through 5 involve the error term or terms, which reflect residual variation or variation in the dependent variable unaccounted for by the independent variables.

Assumption 1 bears on the intercept. If the mean value of the error terms is greater or less than zero, the estimate of the population intercept will be off by the degree to which the mean is greater or less than zero. If one is uninterested in predicting from the regression equation, getting an error free estimate of the intercept may not be not particularly important. It is generally the b values which are of more interest to the policy researcher.

Assumption 2 relates to the t test and test of the null hypothesis. To use t to evaluate the regression coefficient, the error terms for each X value of the independent variable should look like a normal distribution. If not, the sampling distribution of b, which is used to derive an estimate of the standard error of b, will not match the t distribution, and thus, the t test will not be a valid test of the null hypothesis. Remember that a b twice the size of its standard error generates a t sufficient to reject the null hypothesis. However, violating this assumption poses a threat to the analysis only when the sample is small (see Chapter 7). With large samples, the central limit theorem specifies that the sampling distribution of b will be normally distributed. Thus, the t test can be used with large samples even though the error terms are not normally distributed.

The remaining assumptions influence the ability to estimate the regression coefficient accurately and are not so easy to discount. When values of the independent variables are correlated with the error terms (assumption 3), it means that the wrong variables have been included in the regression. Either one or more variables have been included that are unrelated to the dependent variable or one or more that are related have been left out. In both cases, the researcher has misspecified the regression equation. This is called a **specification error**. In the former case, where the analyst adds variables unrelated to the dependent variable, the analysis itself will show if a variable should or should not be included. But, consider the situation where an important variable has been left out. Assume that a regression is specified as $Y = a + bX_1 + e$, but a better specification is $Y = a + b_1X_1 + b_2X_2 + e$. Because X_2 is left out, the variation it explains is incorporated into the error term. Explained variance is reduced. Moreover, if X_1 is related to X_2, part of the variation being explained by X_2 will be reflected in the coefficient for X_1. The regression estimate for X_1 will be higher than it should be. The higher the correlation between X_1 and X_2 the greater is the distortion. To improve the fit of the regression and get an accurate estimate of X_1, X_2 must be included in the equation.

While specifying the appropriate equation will always be somewhat problematic, it helps to know the subject. Regression or any other statistical technique is not a fishing expedition where the researcher throws everything into the mix. Knowledge of the subject can direct the researcher to variables that work and decrease the likelihood of misspecification.

Assumption 4 is most likely violated when one is analyzing a time series, that is, the same units at different points in time. For example, one might be interested in factors that explain variation in college enrollment among minority students over the past ten years in the nation's largest public universities. The unexplained variation in enrollment at any particular time is likely to be influenced by the same unknown factors that influence it at every other point in time, and thus, the error variation at one point will be correlated with the error variation at another point. This situation and how to deal with it are discussed in Chapter 10.

Assumption 5 requires that variation in the error terms is constant over the range of the independent variables. Unequal variation is rare but does occur. Correlated error terms, or **autocorrelation** as it is also called, and unequal variation, or **heteroscedasticity** as it is called, lead to a distorted estimate of the standard error of b. If the distortion underestimates the standard error, b may appear statistically significant when it is not. If overestimated, b may appear statistically insignificant when it is not. Neither autocorrelation nor heteroscedasticity, however, influence the estimate of b. Correlated error terms can be detected by the Durbin-Watson procedure discussed in Chapter 10. Unequal variation can be checked by regressing the error variation on each independent variable. If a pattern similar to the one in Figure 9-1 occurs, unequal variation is a problem. Solutions to both require an estimation technique other than ordinary least squares.[7]

Measurement error in either the independent or dependent variable (assumption 6) also poses problems for deriving accurate estimates of the population. Measures can be invalid or unreliable (See Chapter 3). If a measure is invalid, the regression coefficient is meaningless because it is unclear what

---

[7]These techniques are not the subject of a basic text in methods. If either autocorrelation or heteroscedasticity exist, it is best to secure the counsel of a statistician or a colleague who is familiar with the problems and knows how to deal with them.

FIGURE 9-1   Unequal Error Variation

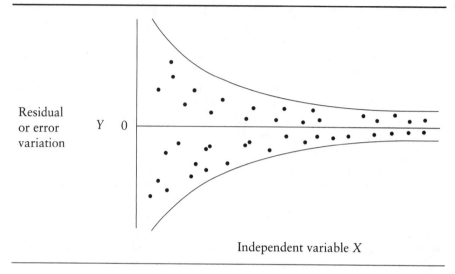

variable is being measured. Unreliability results from an inadequate measurement process that fails to capture an accurate reading of a variable. Measurement error in the dependent variable is simply attached to the error terms, reducing goodness of fit. Error variation also affects the standard error of b, leading to faulty inferences. When error variation increases, the standard error will be larger, and thus more difficult for coefficients to achieve statistical significance.[8] Similarly, measurement error in the independent variable can lead to distortion. If a measure of an independent variable includes a sizable error component, the regression estimate will be off in proportion to the magnitude of the error. The answer to measurement error, as observed in Chapter 3, is to minimize it. Procedures for doing so are discussed there.

Another problem in multiple regression analysis is **multicollinearity**, the inclusion of one or more perfectly or highly correlated independent variables. When multicollinearity exists, the partial regression coefficients of the correlated variables will have artificially elevated standard errors. That makes it difficult to estimate the population regression coefficients accurately. Whether or not multicollinearity is a problem can be determined by correlating each independent variable with the others or regressing each independent variable on the

---

[8]This formula below is for a bivariate regression, but reveals how the magnitude of error variation, $\Sigma(Y_i - Y_p)^2$, affects the size of the standard error. As the error variation increases, the numerator increases, increasing the size of the standard error. For multiple regression, the formula is a bit more complicated.

$$SE_b = \sqrt{\frac{\Sigma(Y_i - Y_p)^2 / N - 2}{(X_i - \overline{X})^2}}$$

others. In general, if correlations among the independent variables (individually or in combination) exceed .7, the standard errors are likely to be affected. Symptoms of multicollinearity include the following:

a. Two highly inter-correlated independent variables, each having large standardized regression coefficients (betas) but with opposite signs.
b. Unstandardized regression coefficients with extremely large standard errors.
c. Standardized regression coefficients larger than 1.0.

Once you detect multicollinearity, what do you do about it? One cure is to combine variables. If, for example, your regression equation included median income, mean years of education, and proportion of white-collar workers as independent variables and you find multicollinearity among them, you might combine them into a single index reflecting the socio-economic character of a city. Because of the different measurement units, you would need to standardize the variables, perhaps converting them to Z scores. If the variables are highly inter-correlated at .8 or above, another solution to multicollinearity is simply to drop some from the regression equation. High correlations are often a sign that variables are measuring the same thing. If so, only one variable needs to be retained. High correlations, however, do not always signal the same variable. If median income was highly correlated with the proportion of black population, one would hesitate to drop one of the variables on the grounds that they are measuring the same thing. In some instances, there may be nothing that one can do to secure accurate and reliable estimates of the population coefficients with both variables in the equation.

A strategy, if not a solution, to multicollinearity when nothing else suffices, is to ignore the regression coefficients and focus on R^2. Here you are giving up on assessing the individual effect of each variable in favor of assessing their combined effect. One might report, for example, that the three socio-economic measures of income, education and proportion white-collar employees, explain 33 percent of the variation in the crime rate. This may be an acceptable solution if the three variables are in fact measuring the same thing. It is unlikely to be acceptable when the variables are measuring different things and the researcher wants to know their individual effects on the dependent variable. Entering the variables in a step-wise procedure will not work either because the R^2 increment will vary depending on which variables are entered first. Thus, if one enters income first it will capture not only the variation it explains by itself but also the variation it shares with education and the proportion of white-collar employees. The coefficients of both will be less than they would be if either was entered before income. So what appears to be a solution is only a strategy that may or may not be desirable depending on the purpose and goals of one's research.

Although not related to the assumptions of regression analysis, **missing data** can be a problem in multiple regression, as it can be in contingency analysis or with any statistical procedure. Generally the default option of the software that performs statistical analyses omits all cases with missing variables. The actual analysis may only treat a subset of the entire number of cases, that is, those cases where information on each variable is complete. You cannot assume that the results from the subset will be the same as from the entire data set; indeed they may be quite different. So one needs to be aware of the actual number of cases that are processed in any particular analysis. This will be obvious in contingency table analysis where the numbers are clearly visible, but less so in regression where only the coefficients are reproduced. The ANOVA table in Table 9-2 identifies degrees of freedom associated with total sums of squares and can be used to insure that a sufficient number of cases have been included in the analysis. This will always be one minus the number of cases or ten in this example.

The answer to missing data is to do everything possible to secure complete information on each variable for every case. There will, however, always be some survey respondents who will not answer particular questions, some countries where certain information is unavailable, and some situations where one is analyzing data gathered by someone else who was less concerned with missing data. If missing data are likely to be a problem where information is generated from a survey, one might increase the number of people surveyed. However, this is an expensive option.

A less expensive and less satisfactory option is recoding missing data to the mean of the variable, if interval data. This strategy may work if the number of cases missing on a variable is not correlated with the dependent variable. But sometimes missing data is correlated with the dependent variable; for example, failure to respond to questions in a survey may be correlated with education. Recoding the missing cases in this instance to the mean or median may significantly alter the findings. Another option is to combine several variables into a scale, where missing information on one variable comprising the scale would not result in dropping a case if information existed on at least one other variable in the scale.

Still another option to correct for missing data is to utilize multiple regression to predict values for cases where variables are missing. This assumes that one has a regression equation—a set of independent variables—with sufficient predictive power, one with a sufficiently high R square, to predict values for the cases with missing information.

Nominal and ordinal data present a problem for regression but not an insurmountable one. Technically speaking, regression requires an interval level of measurement. However, it is often employed with ordinal data by simply assigning numbers 1, 2, 3, and so on to the ordered categories. Of course, when this is done, the betas are probably more meaningful than the unstandardized coefficients since a one unit change in an ordinal independent variable may not make much sense.

With nominal variables, one cannot simply assign numbers to categories of variables. One can, however, incorporate them into a regression by creating **dummy variables**, always one less than the number of values in the nominal variable. For example, four values means three dummy variables, six values means five. Consider the nominal variable *region* with the values East, West, Midwest and South. The regression equation is:

$$Y = a + D_1X_1 + D_2X_2 + D_3X_3 + e$$

where D represents the partial regression coefficients for each dummy variable and X represents three of the regions, East, West, and Midwest. X_1 is coded one if East, zero if West, Midwest or South. X_2 is coded one if West, zero if East, Midwest or South, and X_3 is coded one if Midwest, zero if East, West or South. The South, which is represented by zeros on each of the dummy variables, is captured in the intercept value, a. If the dependent variable Y is the number of teen arrests, D_1 is the influence on arrests of being a city in the East compared to the South, D_2 the influence of a city in the West compared to the South and D_3 the influence of a city in the Midwest compared to the South. The choice of the South as the comparison category to be represented by the intercept is entirely arbitrary, although a researcher may have reasons for choosing one value as opposed to another. The prediction equation for a city in the East is

$$Y = a + D_1(1) + D_2(0) + D_3(0) + e$$

but reduces to

$$Y = a + D_1(1) + e$$

as D_2 and D_3 drop out. D_1 represents the difference in the predicted number of teen arrests between eastern cities and southern cities. The intercept a represents the predicted number of teen arrests for southern cities, $a + D_1$ the predicted number for eastern cities, $a + D_2$ the predicted number for western cities, and $a + D_3$ the predicted number for midwestern cities.

Typically, there will be variables in addition to the dummy variables in a regression equation. Consider the equation where teen unemployment is included along with the three dummy variables for region.

$$Y = a = b_1 (\text{Unemployment}) + D_1X_1 + D_2X_2 + D_3X_3 + e$$

The intercept a is no longer the rate for southern cities but southern cities with zero teen unemployment. Thus, while D_1 would still represent the difference between southern and eastern cities, the number of arrests for eastern cities could no longer be obtained by adding $a + D_1$. The relevant comparison now is between eastern and southern cities where unemployment is zero.

It is very important to remember that the number of dummy variables is always one less than the number of values in the independent variable. Creating a dummy variable for each value is likely to lead to high standard errors, betas over 1.0, and other symptoms of multicollinearity.

Interactions pose a problem for multiple regression. Regression assumes that the pattern of relationship between an independent and dependent

Research in Practice 9C

USING DUMMY VARIABLES

As we discussed in Chapter 2, many state legislatures are examining school finance systems in order to provide more equity and rationality in per pupil spending across local districts.

In an attempt to explore the logic behind existing levels of spending across districts, one evaluator regressed per pupil spending on a variety of conditions thought to influence such spending. She was interested in determining the relevance of resource factors, such as the income level of the district and its property value. She also wanted to explore the influence of demand for education, which she measured as the proportion of the population who were children and the proportion who had college degrees (assuming that highly educated people will value education more than others). And she was interested in cost factors too, assuming that it costs more to educate children who have special needs and children in rural districts where children must be transported to school, for example.

Because she was particularly interested in spending levels in different sized districts, she created a series of five dummy variables measuring school enrollments. One measured districts with 200 or fewer pupils, another from 201 to 400, and so on up to a category marking those with over 10,000 pupils. In her multiple regression, she omitted the category of schools with 2,001 to 10,000 pupils. She did not indicate why this category was omitted. This is not a criticism; any of the five dummy variables could have been omitted, though usually the highest or lowest category is.

Overall, this model explained over 70 percent of the variation in per pupil spending across districts, as measured by R^2. This means that the model is fairly well specified, and that the evaluator had identified the most important factors that influence local school spending. In interpreting the dummy variables, the evaluator found that, controlling for the other factors mentioned, districts with the smallest enrollments did spend significantly more per pupil than those with higher enrollments. The highest spending was done by districts with 200 or fewer pupils. The only deviation from a linear pattern was that districts with more than 10,000 pupils spent slightly more than those with 2,001-10,000.

This information confirmed the suspicion on the part of state legislators that, taking into account resources and demand, small districts have to stretch more to provide the same per pupil spending as their bigger counterparts. Their attempt to give extra aid to small districts was therefore founded in the reality of school funding needs.

SOURCE: Jocelyn M. Johnston, "Changing State-Local Fiscal Relations and School Finance in Kansas: Pursuing 'Equity,'" *State and Local Government Review* 30 (Winter, 1998): 26–41.

variable does not change at different levels of a control or other independent variable. In other words, it assumes that variables do not interact with each other. For example, the relationship between teen arrests and teen unemployment may differ depending on the region of the country. The hypothetical relationship may be strongly positive in eastern cities, modestly positive in western and midwestern cities, and slightly negative in southern cities. These patterns are shown in Figure 9-2. Regressing the number of arrests on teen unemployment for all cities would reveal a modest, positive regression coefficient. But that would obscure the negative relationship for southern cities and the strong positive association for eastern cities.

One way to deal with interactions is to run four separate regressions, one for each region. But reducing the number of cities in each regression could be a problem. It would make it more difficult to achieve a statistically significant outcome because of the smaller number of cases in each regression, but this might not be a problem if one was only interested in drawing conclusions about the cities in the study. Another way to deal with interactions is to create a set of variables reflecting the interactions. One could, for example, multiply each city's percent of unemployment by the regional dummy variables. So along with unemployment and the regional dummy variables, the equation would include an expression for each interaction variable.

The interaction regression coefficients are evaluated by their impact on R^2 by of course, the t test. Again, one explores interactions when there is reason to believe there is an interaction effect. Check for interactions, and if insignificant, return to the regression without the interaction variables.

At the risk of stating the obvious, **nonlinear relationships** cannot be described with the linear multiple regression technique. Figure 9-3 illustrates two nonlinear relationships. One, line *a*, reveals teen arrests increasing sharply at low levels of unemployment, stabilizing at middle levels, and declining sharply at higher levels. The other, line *b*, shows teen arrests increasing gradually through low and middle levels of unemployment and then increasing sharply at higher levels. Mapping these relationships with linear regression would lead to

FIGURE 9-2   Interaction Effects between Teen Unemployment and Region

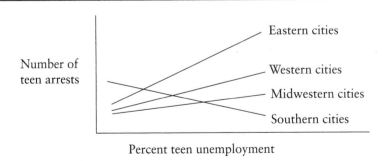

a conclusion that no relationship exists in the case of *a*, and that a modest positive one exists in the case of *b*. Both would be wrong.

The possibility that a relationship is nonlinear is again reason to examine the scatter plot of data points before any statistical analysis begins. Construct a bivariate plot of the dependent variable with each independent variable in order to detect nonlinear relationships. You can also examine the plot of residuals, the variation unexplained by the regression. If the residuals increase with increasing or decreasing values of the independent variable, it may indicate nonlinearity. It also means unequal variation in the error terms discussed earlier. These procedures are generally available in statistical software packages.

There are two options if you observe a nonlinear pattern in the scatter of points: transforming the data to satisfy the linear requirement or fitting a nonlinear regression. The log transformation is often used with a nonlinear pattern. One or more variables can be transformed, including the dependent variable. The goodness of fit can be evaluated by observing R^2. Compared to the non-transformed values, one would expect R^2 to improve. Fitting a nonlinear regression is not particularly difficult with available software, but it may be more than most policy researchers can handle. Here too, consultation with an expert or a colleague is a good idea.

The discussion of the assumptions and potential problems of regression discussed in this chapter will not make you a regression expert, but it should aid in using the technique properly. Minimally, it should allow you to evaluate the reliability of results generated by others rather than simply accept them without question. As policy researchers with influence on policymakers, managers, and the public, it is important not to accept uncritically what the computer cranks out. Remember that the computer always generates results. Whether or not the results are meaningful depends on the knowledge and awareness of the researcher. The computer is oblivious to problems in the data. It is up to the researcher to recognize and know how to deal with them.

FIGURE 9-3   Nonlinear Patterns of Relationships

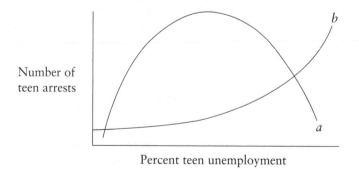

TABLE 9-3   Potential Problems in Multiple Regression: Definitions, Symptoms, Remedies and Detection

PROBLEM	DEFINITION AND SYMPTOMS	DETECTION AND REMEDY
1. Specification error	Wrong variables included in the equation. Estimates will be distorted.	Rethink regression: exclude irrelevant variables; include relevant ones.
2. Autocorrelation	Correlated errors. Large standard error renders population estimates unreliable.	Durbin-Watson will be close to 0 or 4. See Chapter 10. May require advice of an expert.
3. Heteroscedasticity	Unequal variation in errors. Large standard error renders population estimates unreliable.	Examine the scatter plots. May require advice of an expert.
4. Measurement error	Coefficients will be off or meaningless depending on the nature of the error. No visible symptoms.	Perform tests of reliability and validity and make adjustments if needed.
5. Multicollinearity	High intercorrelates among independent variables. Two highly intercorrelated independent variables have large standardized regression coefficients with opposite signs. Regression coefficients with extremely high standard errors. Betas larger than 1.0.	Check intercorrelations among the independent variables and regress each independent variable on the others. Remove or combine some independent variables. Check any dummy variables for proper coding and number. Limit interpretation to R square.
6. Missing data	Variables with incomplete information. Compare the number of cases processed in the particular analysis with the number of cases in the study.	Strive for complete information on each variable for each case. Combine variables into scale where a single missing variable will not result in loss of case. Recode missing data to mean, median or mode of the variable.
7. Nominal and ordinal variables	Values represent a classification or non-metric order.	Create dummy variables for nominal classifications and pin numbers on ordered variables. Use a technique other than regression.
8. Interactions	Pattern of relationship between two variables changes over values of a third. No visible symptoms.	Run regressions within values of the control variable. Create interaction variables.
9. Nonlinear relationships	Direction of relationship changes with values of independent variable. Little or no linear relationship.	Plot indicates nonlinear regression is appropriate. Transform variables or fit a nonlinear regression. For the latter may need advice of an expert.

EXERCISES

9-4

a. A researcher in the state department of labor has been asked to determine the effect of countywide unemployment rates on starting blue-collar industrial salaries in counties in his state. He generates the regression analysis in the table below. Can he conclude that unemployment has a large negative effect on entry salary levels? Why or why not? What, if any, potential problems exist in the analysis, and if any, what solutions are available?

Multiple regression output

Dependent variable:	Mean entry level salary for blue-collar workers (in 10s)
Independent variables:	Percent employed in the county
	Percent of industrial workers unionized in county
	Percent of urban population in the county
	Median years of education adult population
Multiple R	= .52
Multiple R Square	= .27
Standard Error of Estimate	= 60.0
N	= 112

INDEPENDENT VARIABLES	b	BETA	STANDARD ERROR OF b	t
Percent employed in the county	−600.9	−.98	5000.3	−.12
Percent of industrial workers unionized in county	10.8	.19	3.2	3.37
Percent of urban population in the county	493.4	.83	1297.5	0.38
Median years of education adult population	23.2	.25	11.1	2.09

b. A math counselor at a large state university is interested in whether or not a self-paced learning experiment has an effect on students' ability to master calculus. The data are below. Are there any potential problems in this analysis?

Multiple regression output

Dependent variable:	Posttest score on calculus examination
Independent variables:	Pretest score on calculus examination
	Year in college (1 = freshman, 2 sophomore, 3 junior, 4 senior)
	Year of high school mathematics
	Participation in the self-paced experiment (1= yes, 0 = no)

Multiple R	= .80			
Multiple R Square	= .64			
Standard Error of Estimate	= 13.2			
N	= 2,112			

INDEPENDENT VARIABLES	b	BETA	STANDARD ERROR OF b	t
Pretest score on calculus examination	.72	.51	.16	4.5
Year in college	−.05	−.07	.23	−.22
Year of high school mathematics	10.5	.36	4.1	2.56
Participation in the self-paced experiment	1.9	.11	2.0	0.95

Hint: Assume the counselor examined each group of students by class and found the following:

Gain from pre- to posttest score

STUDENTS	EXPERIMENTAL GROUP	CONTROL GROUP
Freshman	15	25
Sophomore	21	23
Junior	24	20
Senior	27	18

What does the above pattern suggest?

c. A researcher concerned with voting turnout in local elections wishes to predict voter turnout by precinct based on factors found to be important in previous elections. These variables are: Dependent variable: turnout; Independent variables: percent registered voters under thirty in each precinct; location of the precinct in the city (east, west, north and south); percent of voters voting in last election; whether or not there is a city council race in the precinct; and campaign activity on behalf of candidates where there is a race (high, medium, and low). Show how you would code each variable and write a multiple regression equation incorporating the above variables. Do you anticipate any problems in executing a regression analysis?

ANALYSIS OF VARIANCE: A RELATED TECHNIQUE

Analysis of variance (ANOVA) is a technique similar to regression. In the analysis of variance, the independent variable is generally a nominal classification; the dependent variable must be interval. ANOVA is not used as widely by policy researchers as regression, but there are situations where it is appropriate, particularly those where the researcher has greater control and can manipulate exposure to the independent variable as in an experimental design.

If one is simply interested in describing the relationship between two variables, without drawing inferences to some population, ANOVA, like regression, generates a measure of explained variation. When the task is drawing inferences and generalizing to a population, more is involved. Assume you are interested in evaluating the impact of several different approaches to work scheduling on productivity: the usual five eight-hour days, four ten-hour days, and flextime where individuals work forty hours when they choose. Productivity is an interval measure, work scheduling nominal. The null hypothesis is that there are no differences in productivity among the three approaches, that is $\bar{u}_1 = \bar{u}_2 = \bar{u}_3 = 0$ where each $\bar{u}$ stands for the mean level of productivity of the population of employees working under each schedule. Assuming employees have been assigned at random to each of the three schedules, we can employ the analysis of variance and evaluate the null hypothesis with the F test.

The logic of the analysis of variance is simple. If scheduling is important to productivity, there should be a great deal of variation among the three groups and relatively little variation within the groups. On the other hand if scheduling is unrelated to productivity, there will be little variation among the groups and a great deal of variation within each group. While the null hypothesis is stated in terms of population means, the technique and the F test involve a comparison of within and between group variation.

The technique can be demonstrated graphically. If one were to plot the productivity scores of, for example thirty employees in groups of ten, each operating under one of the three work schedules, it might look something like Figure 9-4.

One can get some idea of the effect of work schedules by simply examining the mean level of productivity for each group. In this illustration, the means

FIGURE 9-4 **An Example of a Nonlinear Relationship**

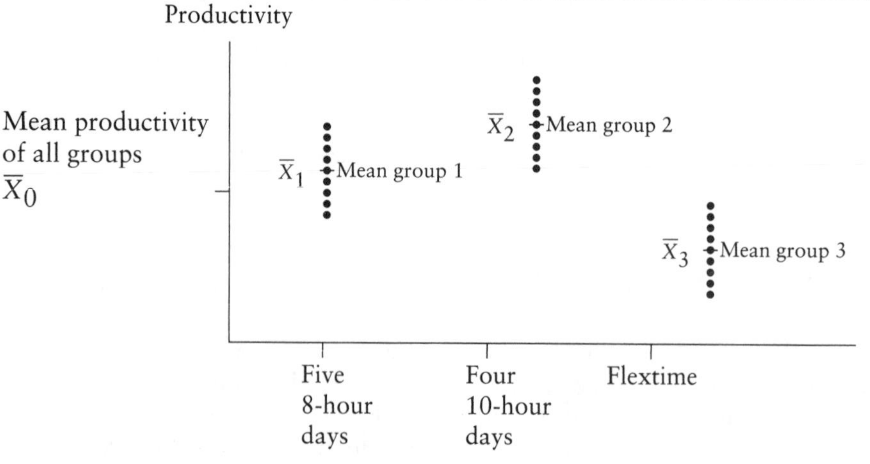

do vary, but is the variation sufficient to conclude that work scheduling makes a significant difference in the unobserved populations of workers who operate under each schedule?

The technique assumes that variation in productivity results from two factors: work scheduling and a random component that results from the randomness involved in assigning employees to one of the three groups and from the influence of other unknown factors or variables. Like regression, the analysis of variance decomposes variation into two components. Total variation in productivity scores is the difference between each employee's productivity score and the overall or grand mean $(X_i - \overline{X}_{gm})$ where gm stands for grand mean. Squaring each difference or deviation and summing over all employees gives, similar to regression, total sums of squares, $\Sigma(X_i - \overline{X}_{gm})^2$.

Within group or error variation is the difference between the individual scores in each group and the group mean $(X_i - \overline{X}_{gp})$ where gp stands for group mean. Squared and summed over each individual gives the within sums of squares $(X_i - \overline{X}_{gp})^2$. Between group or treatment variation is the difference between the individual group means and the overall mean $(\overline{X}_{gp} - \overline{X}_{gm})$. Squared and summed over each group and multiplied by the number in each group gives the between group sums of squares $N \Sigma (\overline{X}_{gp} - \overline{X}_{gm})^2$. Dividing the within and between sums of squares by the appropriate degrees of freedom (the number of individuals minus the number of groups and the number of groups minus one) yields two estimates of the population variance, called mean square treatment and mean square error. The F value is the ratio of these two estimates.

$$F = \frac{\text{Mean square treatment (between groups)}}{\text{Mean square error (within groups)}}$$

The probability of F can be determined by consulting the F table included in most statistics books, including this one, or observed directly from the ANOVA software output.

In order to work through an example, assume the following productivity scores for employees working under the three schedules.

Group 1

Score	(Score − Group mean)²	(Score − Overall mean)²
57	9	0
57	9	0
58	4	1
59	1	4
60	0	9
61	1	16
61	1	16
62	4	25
62	4	25
63	9	36
600	42	132

$\overline{X}_1 = 60$ (group mean)
$\overline{X}_0 = 57$ (grand mean)

Group 2

SCORE	(SCORE – GROUP MEAN)^2	(SCORE – OVERALL MEAN)^2
62	16	25
63	9	36
64	4	49
65	1	64
65	1	64
66	0	81
67	1	100
69	9	144
69	9	144
70	16	169
660	66	876

$\overline{X}_2 = 66$

Group 3

SCORE	(SCORE – GROUP MEAN)^2	(SCORE – OVERALL MEAN)^2
39	36	324
42	9	225
43	4	196
44	1	169
45	0	144
45	0	144
46	1	121
47	4	100
49	16	64
50	25	49
450	96	1,536

$\overline{X}_3 = 45$

Total sums of squares = 132 + 876 + 1,536 = 2,544
Within sums of squares = 42 + 66 + 96 = 204
Between sums of squares = Total – Within = 2,340

TABLE 9-4   Analysis of Variance Table

SOURCE OF VARIATION	SUMS OF SQUARES	DEGREES OF FREEDOM	MEAN SQUARE	F
Between	2,340	2	1,170	153.9
Within	204	27	7.6	
Total	2,544	29		

Analysis of variance information is generally presented in a table like Table 9-4.

Examining the F table (See Appendix) at the .05 level with 2 and 27 degrees of freedom, one observes the value 3.35. Because the F of 153.9 exceeds this, the null hypothesis is rejected. Work scheduling does indeed influence productivity and the differences are far too great to assume that they occurred by random influences. Therefore, we conclude that u1 ≠ u2 ≠ u3 ≠ 0 in the population. An examination of the group means shows, however, that employees under flextime are the least productive, and those under four ten-hour days are the most productive.

The similarity between ANOVA and regression should be clear at this point. Explained variation in ANOVA is the difference between each group mean and the overall or grand mean of the dependent variable. In regression, it is the difference between the predicted values of the regression line and the overall mean of the dependent variables.

As with regression, the analysis of variance is not limited to examining the influence of a single variable. It too can be extended to a number of variables, including interactions. The effect of each variable can be tested. With two independent variables, there are two group or treatment effects and one interaction effect. However, increasing the number of independent variables and trying to evaluate interactions is not a task for the novice researcher.

Eta (the correlation ratio) is a measure of association applicable to the analysis of variance. It is computed by dividing the between sums of squares by the total. If the groups or treatments account for all the variation in the dependent variable, the between sums of squares will equal the total, and eta will equal one. Eta is a nonlinear measure. Eta squared is analogous to r^2 in that it represents the proportion of variation explained in the dependent variable by the independent variable. From the example,

$$\text{Eta} = \frac{2,340}{2,544} = .92$$

$$\text{Eta}^2 = .84$$

Scheduling explains 84 percent of the variation in productivity.

EXERCISE

9-4 The public works department of a city has responsibility for planting trees. They are considering the purchase of special equipment to do the job. The city council thinks the usual two or possibly three-person crew can do the job as fast. They recommended a trial period of two weeks during which all three methods were tried. Below are the data from fifteen work crews assigned at random to each method. Using ANOVA, what do the data show?

Number of Trees Planted

SPECIAL EQUIPMENT	TWO-PERSON CREW	THREE-PERSON CREW
43	35	40
40	42	43
52	38	36
44	29	34
37	37	40

KEY TERMS

Multiple regression analysis
T test
F ratio
Partial correlation
Partial regression coefficient (beta)
Standardized regression coefficient
Unstandardized regression coefficient
Standard error of estimate
Standard error of *b*
Multiple correlation coefficient (*r*)
Multiple *r* squared
Degrees of freedom
Specification
Specification error

Heteroscedasticity
Autocorrelation
Multicollinearity
Missing data
Dummy variables
Statistical interactions
Nonlinear relationship
Analysis of variance (ANOVA)
Sums of squares error
Sums of squares regression
Between sums of squares
Within sums of squares
Eta
Eta squared

FOR FURTHER HELP

Achen, Christopher H. *Interpreting and Using Regression.* Sage University Paper Series on Quantitative Applications in the Social Sciences. Beverly Hills, Calif.: Sage Publications, 1982.

Berry, William D., and Stanley Feldman. *Multiple Regression in Practice.* Sage University Paper Series on Quantitative Applications in the Social Sciences. Beverly Hills, Calif.: Sage Publications, 1985.

Berry, William D. *Understanding Regression Assumptions.* Sage University Paper Series on Quantitative Applications in the Social Sciences. Beverly Hills, Calif.: Sage Publications, 1993.

Fox, John, *Regression Diagnostics.* Sage University Paper Series on Quantitative Applications in the Social Sciences. Beverly Hills, Calif.: Sage Publications, 1991.

Hary, Melissa A. *Regression with Dummy Variables.* Sage University Paper Series on Quantitative Applications in the Social Sciences. Beverly Hills, Calif.: Sage Publications, 1993.

Jaccard, James, Robert Turrisi, and Choi K. Wan. *Interaction Effects in Multiple Regression.* Sage University Paper Series on Quantitative Applications in the Social Sciences. Beverly Hills, Calif.: Sage Publications, 1990.

Lewis-Beck, Michael S. *Applied Regression: An Introduction.* Sage University Paper Series on Quantitative Applications in the Social Sciences. Beverly Hills, Calif.: Sage Publications, 1986.

Schroeder, Larry D., David L Sjoquist, and Paula E. Stephan, *Understanding Regression Analysis: An Introductory Guide.* Sage University Paper Series on Quantitative Applications in the Social Sciences. Beverly Hills, Calif.: Sage Publications, 1986.

10

OTHER MULTIVARIATE TECHNIQUES

Regression is an extremely flexible tool. In this chapter we will discuss its use in developing and testing causal models and in analyzing longitudinal data, called time series. If you understand the logic of multiple regression, you should have no problem understanding either technique.

We will then turn to methods of multivariate analysis where some of the assumptions of multiple regression are not satisfied. In particular, we will examine alternatives to regression when the dependent variable is not interval, such as when it has only two to five categories. These situations are fairly common in policy research. Examples include passing a test or not passing, agreeing or disagreeing with a statement, contracting a disease or not, and so forth. We will devote most of our discussion to a technique called probit analysis, and we briefly discuss a related topic, logistic regression.

Policy analysts also sometimes need to examine when events occur in addition to whether they occur. In other words, to determine how effective a school based sex education program is would involve knowing at what age young women became pregnant as well as if they did. Exploring the deterrent effect of imprisonment versus other types of punishments for crime would involve knowing how long the ex-prisoners stayed crime free as well as if they did. Event history analysis is often used to explore these questions, and we will examine that technique here.

CAUSAL MODELING

THE LOGIC OF CAUSAL ANALYSIS

Suppose you are examining the effect of gender on whether legislators vote for legislation expanding women's rights. Are women legislators more supportive of women's issues than men legislators? In doing such a study, we need to take into account certain factors other than gender that we know affect voting behavior: the party identification of the legislator and some characteristics of the legislator's constituency (for example, whether he or she represents an urban or rural community, as well as the racial, ethnic, religious, and social class composition of the district).

We can begin by generating a scale of voting on women's issues and regressing it on the above independent variables. The causal diagram appears in Figure 10-1. All the variables are hypothesized to influence voting directly. With these controls, we find that the gender of a legislator has no impact on voting. Can we be satisfied with this conclusion?

The answer is "probably not." That is because of the likely relationships among the independent variables. In particular, gender may influence voting through party identification. Women are somewhat more likely to be Democrats than men. In controlling for party identification, we are also controlling away this gender difference. If sex influences party identification, measurement of its influence is lost in the effect shown for party itself.

In some cases, therefore, the researcher can make a plausible argument that some independent variables in the model are caused by other independent variables in the model. These independent variables "caused" by others are referred to as **endogenous variables.** Variables hypothesized to be independent of other variables in the model are called **exogenous variables.**

Let us look at a set of hypothesized relationships that illustrate these points. For example, we can modify the causal diagram in Figure 10-1. In Figure 10-2, we are hypothesizing that sex has a **direct effect** on voting (path *a*), but also that sex has an **indirect effect** on voting through its influence on

FIGURE 10-1   Independent Variables with Direct Effects on the Dependent Variable*

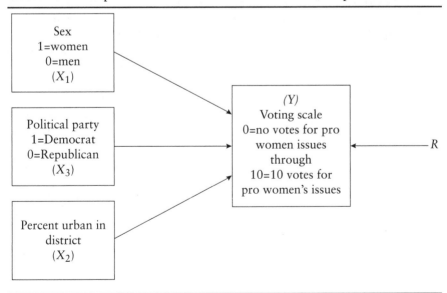

*This figure illustrates the regression equation:

$$Y = a + b_1 x_1 + b_2 x_2 + b_3 x_3 + e$$

Figure 10-2   A Model Illustrating Direct and Indirect Effects on a Dependent Variable*

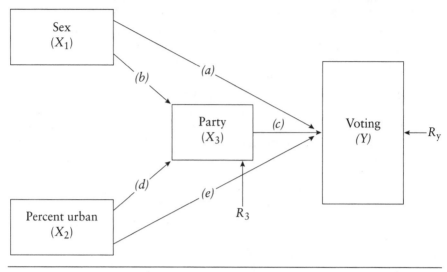

*This model illustrates the equations:

$$Y = a + b_1x_1 + b_2x_2 + b_3x_3 + e$$
$$x_3 = a + b_1x_1 + b_2x_2 + e$$

party identification (paths b and c). A direct effect, then, is a path in a causal model that runs directly between two variables (other direct effects in this model are between sex and party, percent urban and party, percent urban and voting, and party and voting). Indirect effects are paths in causal models that link two variables through one or more additional variables. In addition to the indirect effect of sex on voting through party, percent urban also has an indirect effect on voting through party.

Sex and percent urban are exogenous variables; they are unaffected by other variables in the model. Party identification and voting are endogenous variables, since they are hypothesized to be at least partially caused by other variables in the model.

Whereas a single regression equation describes the relationships in Figure 10-1, to describe all the relationships in Figure 10-2, we need two equations. One describes the direct effects of each variable on voting, and the other describes the effects of sex and percent urban on party identification. These equations are shown at the bottom of Figure 10-2.

Constructing Causal Models

The mechanics of drawing a causal model are straightforward. The dependent variable is always at the right. A variable hypothesized to have an effect on

FIGURE 10-3   Path Coefficients in a Causal Model

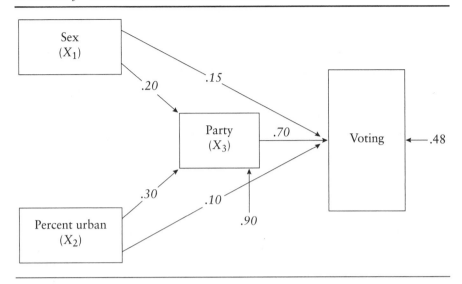

another variable is linked with a straight arrow pointing in the hypothesized direction, called a **path** (for example, a path links sex and voting in Figure 10-2). Variables hypothesized to be correlated, where no causal relationship is implied, are linked with a curved double-headed arrow. In Figure 10-2, sex and percent urban are unlinked. We did not hypothesize that they were correlated. If, however, we thought that women legislators were more or less likely than men to come from urban districts, we could link the two variables with a curved arrow. The additional arrows leading from R to each endogenous variable in the model illustrate the effects of other variables not included in the model. The R's represent residual or error terms.

The theory underlying causal modeling is more complex than the physical methods of creating them. Causal models cannot *prove* causality. The conditions for asserting causality that we discussed in earlier chapters still apply. Just because you hypothesize that sex affects party identification, and through your analysis you find a link between them, you have not proved that the causal direction is as you hypothesize. In this case, you would probably have a pretty good argument that your hypothesis is correct, since it is unlikely that party identification contributes to a person's gender (unless promoting sex change operations becomes a plank of one or the other party). In some cases, however, the causal direction of the links between variables is less clear.

Before using causal modeling, you should have confidence in the model you are testing. Each link should be carefully thought out and justified.

When the path coefficients are computed (see below), they are placed in the model, as in Figure 10-3. R values are often, though not always, included too.

COMPUTING EFFECTS IN A CAUSAL MODEL

Assume we have demonstrated the plausibility of our hypothesized model in Figure 10-2. We have shown that sex is causally antecedent to party and that the proportion of the district living in urban areas affects the party identification of the representative, with women and urban legislators tending to be Democrats. In order to estimate the effects, direct and indirect, we compute the regression equations at the bottom of Figure 10-2. That is, to estimate paths *a*, *c*, and *e*, we regress voting on sex, percent urban and party. To estimate paths and *d*, we regress party on sex and percent urban. The beta coefficients for each relationship are shown in Figure 10-3.

We can see that sex and percent urban are moderately related to party and slightly related to voting. Party, on the other hand, is strongly related to voting. In this hypothetical case, Democrats are much more likely to vote in support of women's issues than Republicans. The magnitude of the beta (.70) leaves little room for voting to be affected by other factors, such as sex or percent urban.

If we had limited ourselves to the regression model, regressing voting on sex, urbanization, and party, we would conclude that sex and urbanization have very limited effects on voting. But the use of a causal model allows us to assess the indirect as well as direct effects of these two factors. We calculate the indirect effects by multiplying the beta values of the path from sex to party (.20) times the path from party to voting (.70). This equals .14. We can then say that sex has an indirect effect of .14 on voting through party, in addition to its direct effect of .15. Similarly, we can calculate that urbanization has an indirect effect of .21 through party (.30 × .70 = .21), in addition to its direct

TABLE 10-1   Direct, Indirect, and Total Effects on Voting for Women's Issues

	Effects		
	DIRECT	INDIRECT	TOTAL
Sex	.15	.14	.29
Percent urban	.10	.21	.31
Party identification	.70		.70
$R^2 = .52$			

TABLE 10-2   A Test of the Fit of the Causal Model

	EFFECTS PREDICTED FROM MODEL	OBSERVED CORRELATION
Sex	.29	.31
Percent urban	.31	.33
Party identification	.70	.71

effect of .10. For both sex and urbanization, then, their indirect effect is about as large or larger than their direct effects.

We can then compute the total effects of each of the three variables on voting. The total effect for each variable is the sum of its direct and indirect effects. It is sometimes useful to prepare a summary table, such as Table 10-1. As a test of the model, the correlation between any two variables should approximate the sum of the direct and indirect paths linking them together. Table 10-2 contains the bivariate correlation of each variable with voting and demonstrates a reasonably good fit.

If the direct effects predicted from the model deviate substantially from the observed correlations, it means that the model is not the correct one. Most likely, an important variable or variables have been left out of the model. These variables need to be brought into the model and all paths estimated again.

The use of the causal model allows us to modify our conclusions about the impact of sex and percent urban on voting for women's issues. Instead of having a minor effect, they can be seen to have an important effect as they affect party identification, which in turn affects voting behavior.

OTHER ASPECTS OF CAUSAL MODELING

Analysts debate whether standardized or unstandardized regression coefficients are preferred as estimates of path coefficients. Here we have used betas, but some analysts argue that unstandardized coefficients are more appropriate. Betas, however, are more commonly used, and you will be on safe ground if you use them.

In some models, the causal flow from one variable to another is not unidimensional (one way). Instead, some variables influence each other. Such models are said to be **nonrecursive.** Models where all the causal links flow in one direction (such as in our example) are called **recursive.** An example of a nonrecursive model is shown in Figure 10-4.

FIGURE 10-4   Explaining a Legislator's Constituency Service (A Nonrecursive Model)

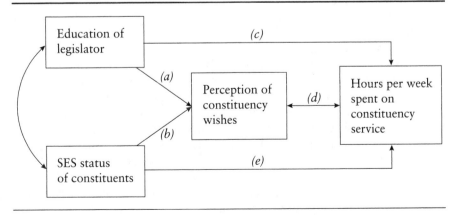

A bi-directional link (two-way) is shown by a double-headed arrow, path *d*. Here, nonrecursiveness enters in deciding how the hours per week spent on constituency service is related to a legislator's perception of how much constituency service the constituents want. One assumes that when legislators perceive how much service their constituents want, they modify their behavior. If constituents want more personal service, legislators provide more in order to improve their chances of reelection. However, you might also expect that the hours a legislator spends on constituency service would influence his perception of what constituents want. A legislator who enjoys serving constituents and spends a lot of time doing it may come to believe that constituency service is something his constituents want. Another legislator, who enjoys policymaking more then constituency service, and thus spends less time on service, may begin to believe that her constituency does not want increased service. Thus, behavior may influence perception.

Two-way relationships greatly complicate estimation procedures in causal models. Techniques for estimating such relationships, such as two-stage least squares, are beyond the scope of this book. But you should be aware that not all causal models are neat unidirectional ones.

Indirect effects in causal models can be more complex than those illustrated in our initial example. There may be, for example, three or more independent variables in a causal chain. Furthermore, an independent variable can have more than one indirect link, as shown in Figure 10-5.

Here, sex has indirect effects on voting through ideology alone ($c \times h$), through ideology and party ($c \times g \times i$), and through party alone ($b \times i$). A similar pattern exists for percent urban. In these situations, the total indirect effect of sex is the sum of the different paths from sex to voting through ideology and party. The total effect is the sum of the total indirect effects plus the direct effect. It is easy to see how causal models can quickly become very complex as more variables are added to the model.

Simple models are the easiest to compute and to interpret. However, more complex models may be a better reflection of the set of relationships you are trying to understand.

Frequently, analysts will drop paths from their final model which are not significant. In most cases this is done to simplify the model. Of course, if you drop any variable linked directly to the dependent variable, all indirect paths to the dependent variable through the variable also disappear. This is not as serious as it sounds. If the path between an independent variable and a dependent variable is so small as to be insignificant, any indirect effects through that path are likely to be small too. Purists cringe at dropping paths because the model is no longer being fully reported. Some call the practice "theory trimming." If your theory suggests that links should be present, they argue, then they should be reported. Despite this, these truncated models are often found in the literature. At the least, the model should be recomputed without the missing links. One point that all can agree on is that you should report all variables that were initially run in the model, even if some are dropped in the graphic presentation.

FIGURE 10-5   **More Complex Indirect Paths***

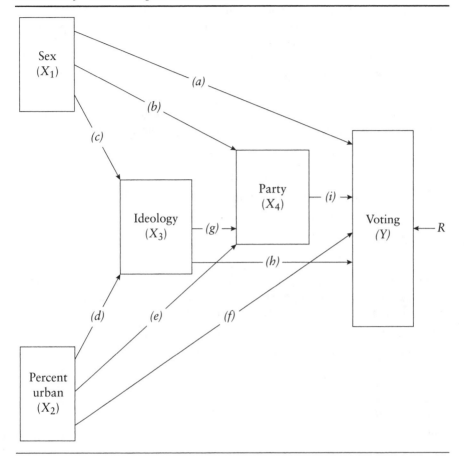

*This model illustrates the equations:

$$Y = a + b_1x_1 + b_2x_2 + b_3x_3 + b_4x_4 + e$$
$$x_3 = a + b_1x_1 + b_2x_2 + e$$
$$x_4 = a + b_1x_1 + b_2x_2 + b_3x_3 + e$$

EXERCISES

10-1 Construct a plausible causal model predicting citizen attitudes toward privatization of local garbage services. Assume the dependent variable is an interval scale. The variables used to predict attitudes include:

x_1 = Household income level

x_2 = Current evaluation of garbage services provided the city

x_3 = Party affiliation

x_4 = Individual level of education

a. Express your causal model in a set of equations.
b. Draw a path diagram illustrating your model.
c. Give a letter designation to each path in your model (*a, b, c, d...*).Which paths indicate direct effects of independent variables on the dependent variable? Using these designations, show the computation for each indirect effect in the model.
d. Using these designations, show the computations for the total effects of each independent variable on the dependent variable.

10-2 Based on data from 100 cities, an analyst uses the following set of variables to estimate the volume of garbage to be dumped yearly in a sanitary landfill.

y = Average volume of garbage dumped this year

x_1 = Average volume of garbage dumped last year

x_2 = Population of the community served by the landfill

x_3 = Percent of waste estimated to be recycled rather than dumped

x_4 = Charge for dumping last year

x_5 = Charge for dumping this year

Assume that the amount of garbage dumped the previous year is a function of the charge the previous year, the population, and the recycling percent. Also assume all variables have direct effects on the volume.

a. Express the causal model in a set of equations.
b. Draw a causal diagram illustrating your model.

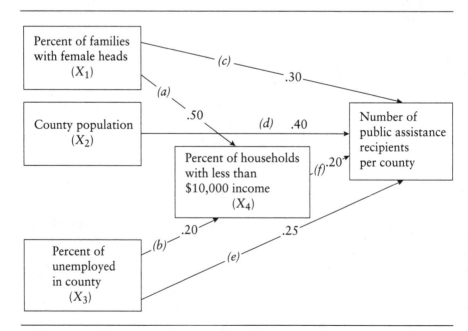

c. Give a letter designation to each path in your model (*a*, *b*, *c*, *d*...).
d. Which paths indicate direct effects of independent variables on the dependent variables? Using these designations, show the computation for each indirect effect in the model.
e. Using these designations, show the computations for the total effect of each independent variable on the dependent variable.

10-3 Regression analysis reveals the following standardized regression weights for paths in a causal diagram.

a. Which paths indicate direct relationships between the independent variable and the dependent variable?
b. Calculate the indirect effects of percent female-headed households and percent unemployed on the number of public assistance recipients in the county.
c. Calculate the total effects of each independent variable on the dependent variable. Present these effects in a well-labeled table.

TIME SERIES

In Chapter 2 we described a time series design. We noted that by collecting information on a dependent variable at several time points before and after a policy innovation we could assess the impact of the innovation. In order to eliminate various threats to internal validity, however, we need to control for factors other than the policy change that might affect the dependent variable.

In time series, we can use basic multiple regression procedures learned in the preceding two chapters. However, there are a few special techniques to use when examining changes over time. These techniques are sometimes referred to as time series or interrupted time series analyses. Interrupted time series simply means that we expect the policy innovation being examined to interrupt or in some way change the over time trends in the dependent variable.

INTERRUPTED TIME SERIES

Suppose we wish to assess the impact of state tax exemptions for industry moving into a state on growth in manufacturing in a state. Economic development and the policies that should be implemented to increase it are important issues in state politics. The kind of analyses described here would allow you to test their impact. What we want to find out is the impact of these policies on growth in manufacturing, independent of other factors. In particular, in time series we need to be aware of two factors that might contaminate our findings. The **trend** is one such factor. It might be that manufacturing growth is greater after the introduction of state tax exemptions than before; however, this growth might be part of a long-term trend toward manufacturing growth. Such a pattern is shown in Figure 10-6A. Our time series procedure must allow us to take into account these long-term trends.

Another factor is **seasonality,** or cycles in the pattern of economic growth. Perhaps economic growth fluctuates on a regular cycle, with a few boom years, followed by a few years of a slow economy, then a few boom years again. We must also consider such cyclical patterns in determining the impact of our particular policy. If the policy intervention occurs at the bottom of the cycle, it could appear to have positive effects when in reality it does not. If it occurs at the top of the cycle, it might seem to have negative effects. In Figure 10-6B, we sketch one potential impact of seasonality.

With these general concepts in mind, let us set up such an analysis. Our unit of analysis will be the year. That is, we obtain data for several years before the introduction of the tax exemption policy and several years after the policy was adopted. The dependent variable is the amount of manufacturing value added (a statistic collected annually by the Bureau of Census), which measures the growth or decline of manufacturing in the state.

Let's say a state adopted the policy in 1980. We are able to collect data for fifteen years after the policy was adopted (there is always some time lag in the publication of these kinds of statistics), so we decide to collect data for fifteen years before the policy adoption, too. Our time series, then, runs from 1965 to 1995. If the state had adopted the policy in 1990 and you were only able to have five post-policy data points, that does not mean you should only examine five pre-policy data points: symmetry is not essential. As a general rule, you should try to include as long a time series as possible, except that you do not want the time series to extend too far back (or forward) so that it includes periods when conditions were totally different. For example, it would not be useful to extend our time series back into the 1950s, when the post-war economic conditions may have been unique.

For each year, we collect data on manufacturing value added in the state. Because of inflation that, over time, erodes the value of a dollar, we must then adjust the data to reflect the fact that a dollar of manufacturing value added in

FIGURE 10-6   **Trends and Cycles**

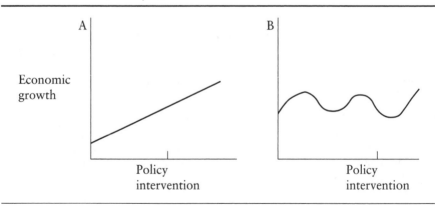

1965 is not worth the same as a dollar added in 1995. A standard adjustment in time series analysis is to transform all dollar values into standard dollars, whether this adjustment is based on a 1970 dollar, a 1965 dollar, or a 1995 one. It does not matter what year you standardize on, as long as all have been standardized in the same way. You can standardize by the consumer price index measure that is found in each year's *Statistical Abstract of the United States*. By a standard measure, it tells you what the dollar has been worth for the past forty years.

Our first independent variable is a dummy variable where 1 = the presence of a policy, 0 = the absence of the policy. All years before 1980 would be coded 0, 1980 and after would be coded 1. The regression coefficient for this variable will give the average change in the manufacturing value added after the policy was adopted. In other words, the dummy variable is like a difference of means score: it gives the difference in the mean size of manufacturing value added before and after the adoption of the policy.

To conduct a basic interrupted time series we need two more variables. First we code a counter variable, also called a linear trend variable. The value of this variable is 1 for the first year in our time series, 2 for the second, and so on. Thus, the value for 1965 = 1, 1966 = 2, all the way to 1995 = 31. This variable allows you to take into account long-term trends in manufacturing value added. We would expect the state's economy to grow each year, even without the policy; by including the trend variable, we take into account this or other trends. This coefficient tells us the average yearly level of growth when computed for the entire thirty-one year period. This is an important feature of most time series, a baseline that we expect to be changing (in this case, growing) rather than static.

Another variable is a post-policy intervention counter variable scored 0 for each year before the policy was adopted, and 1, 2, 3 . . . for each year after the policy. Thus, 1965 = 0, 1966 = 0 . . . 1979 = 0, 1980 = 1, 1981 = 2, 1982 = 3 . . . 1995 = 16. This coefficient allows us to measure the change that has occurred after the introduction of the policy. We now have our basic set of time series variables, reflected in the following regression equation:

$$y = a + b_d x_d + b_t x_t + b_p x_p + e$$

where:

x_d = The dummy variable before and after the policy adoption

x_t = Counter variables from 1965 (=1) to 1995 (=31)

x_p = Post-policy counter variable, equal to 0 before policy adoption, 1 through 16 afterward

INTERPRETED INTERRUPTED TIME SERIES COEFFICIENTS

Assume that we computed our regression and found the following regression coefficients (*t* values in parentheses):

TABLE 10-3   Values of Variables for the Time Series Regression

YEAR	DUMMY VARIABLE (d)	COUNTER VARIABLE (t)	POST-POLICY VARIABLE (p)
1965	0	1	0
1966	0	2	0
1967	0	3	0
1968	0	4	0
......	...	...	...
1979	0	15	0
1980	1	16	1
1981	1	17	2
1982	1	18	3
1983	1	19	4
......	...	...	...
1995	1	31	16

$$y = 100 + 200x_t + 50x_d + 1x_p + e$$
$$\quad\quad\;\; (4.24)\quad (1.23)\quad (0.63)$$

(*y* coded in millions of dollars)

We can interpret these coefficients as follows. The dummy variable coded 0 before the policy innovation and 1 afterward represents the immediate shift in the regression line after the policy was adopted. In this case it means there was a short-term impact of $50 million. The counter variable beginning with 1 in 1965 reflects the slope of the regression line before the policy was adopted. This indicates an increase in manufacturing value added of about $200 million per year. The sum of this counter variable plus the post-policy counter variable (where all years before 1970 are coded 0) indicates the slope of the coefficient after the policy innovation, or about $201 million per year (200 + 1). Thus, the dummy variable reflects the short-term impact of the policy and the counter variables allow a comparison of the slopes before and after the innovation. The significance level of the post-policy counter reveals whether the shift following the innovation was significant.

Figure 10-7, illustrating the expected effect of the policy, shows a small short-term effect and a change in the slope reflecting economic growth. Whereas economic growth was slow before the policy, after the policy, growth increased.

Figure 10-8 illustrates the regression equation just described. The intercept is 100, indicating that the manufacturing value added amount when all terms in our equation equaled 0 was $100 million, the pre-1965 value. Between 1965

FIGURE 10-7   The Expected Pattern

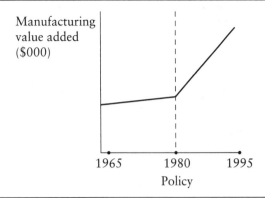

FIGURE 10-8   The Pattern Based on the Regression Equation

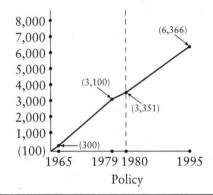

and 1980, the value of our dummy variable x_d, and our post-policy counter variable x_p are both 0. Thus, in those years the predicted y equals $100 + 200 \times x_t$. Remember that $x_t = 1$ in 1965, 2 in 1966 through 15 in 1979 (see Table 10-3). Thus, in 1965, $y = 100 + 200 = 300$; in 1966, $y = 100 + 400$, and so forth. In the final pre-policy year, $y = 100 + 200 \times 15 = 3,100$. This line indicates the pre-policy slope (see Figure 10-8).

If there were no policy intervention in 1980, we would predict the value of y in that year to equal $100 + 200 \times 16$, or $3,300$. However, the policy innovation changes our computation of y, because we must now consider our x_d and x_p terms. They are no longer 0. In 1980 both x_d and x_p equal 1. The value of x_d remains 1 in each post-policy year, but x_p increases in value each year. Let's compute the value of y for 1980, 1981, 1982, and for 1995, the end of our series:

$$y + 100 + (200 \times 16) + (50 \times 1) + (1 \times 1) = 3,351 \ (1980)$$
$$y + 100 + (200 \times 17) + (50 \times 1) + (1 \times 2) = 3,552 \ (1981)$$
$$y + 100 + (200 \times 18) + (50 \times 1) + (1 \times 3) = 3,753 \ (1982)$$
$$y + 100 + (200 \times 31) + (50 \times 1) + (1 \times 16) = 6,366 \ (1995)$$

Whereas before the intervention, manufacturing value added increased $200 million per year (as indicated by the x_t coefficient of 200), after the intervention it increased $201 million per year (as indicated by $x_t + x_p = 200 + 1$). The additional increment was not significant, as indicated by the t value in the previous equation. There was a short-term jump in manufacturing value added after the policy began, as indicated by the x_d value of $50 million, but it, too, was not significant.

Was the program a success? After all, an extra $1 million growth each year is not something to ignore. The success would depend on comparing the extra manufacturing activity with the other costs and benefits of the program. For example, how much tax revenue is being lost to provide these tax breaks? What is the program's impact on the public and business community's attitudes? Is the public losing confidence in the tax system? Do business people believe that this is an indication the state is friendly to business? All of these factors would need to be assessed in light of the findings of the lack of significant impact on manufacturing value added.[1]

Before any firm conclusion can be reached, we also need to assess other control variables. For example, the ups and downs of any particular state's economy reflect the national economy. Thus, national gains in manufacturing value added should be added as a control. Some studies have shown that spending on higher education affects growth in the economy, so this variable too should be entered. Additional control variables are entered into the time series regression equation just as in other regressions. For each case (in this instance, each year), we could enter variables measuring the national economic value added and state spending on higher education, for example.

If policymakers also implemented other policies that might affect the economy that should also be considered in measuring the effect of our economic development policies. For example, during the post-policy years, the state might have adopted policies subsidizing businesses to hire the hardcore unemployed, or to provide an accelerated depreciation for machinery. These other policies could be treated as further dummy variables in the regression. Adding controls might show that the states policy had more, or even less, impact than indicated above. You can examine the R^2 to see whether or not the equation is well specified, and whether the independent variables explain most of the variation in the dependent variable. If they do, then further controls are not necessary.

---

[1] Although this example is hypothetical, such policies have generally shown limited impact on economic development.

SPECIAL PROBLEMS WITH TIME SERIES

Multicollinearity

A time series equation, interrupted or not, will usually have a small number of cases, such as our example ($N = 31$). This makes multicollinearity problems likely. For example, if a series of economic development policies were adopted at about the same time, then it would be nearly impossible to disentangle their effects. Controlling for the adoption of one policy while examining the effects of another would produce high correlations (perfect if both were adopted the same year). One opportunity for disentanglement could occur if the different policies had different anticipated effects. For example, if the tax break for new businesses was designed to have its immediate impact on increasing manufacturing and the subsidy for hiring the hardcore unemployed was designed to affect unemployment most immediately, one could use different dependent variables to test the effect of each. However, one would expect (and hope) that business expansion would affect unemployment, and decreasing unemployment would affect business expansion, leaving a still intractable problem. Another strategy would be to examine the effects of a similar policy in another state that had not also adopted other economic development policies at the same time.

Autocorrelation

As you may recall from Chapter 9, the regression model requires that the error terms not be correlated. The term **autocorrelation** is used to describe the correlation of these error terms. In most cross-sectional regression analyses, the autocorrelation is not a problem, as the error terms are not likely to be highly correlated. But in time series analysis, autocorrelation is difficult to ignore or to avoid. The reason is fairly straightforward. If our model falls short of predicting manufacturing value added in 1995, it likely falls short of predicting it in 1994 and 1996 for the same reason. Thus, the error terms, which reflect the variation we have not explained, are correlated. For example, if we used our basic model without adding controls, we probably failed to predict manufacturing value added because we did not take into account national economic trends. National economic trends would shape manufacturing value added in 1995, in 1996, and in each other year before or after. Omitting this variable or any others that predict state manufacturing value added will produce autocorrelation.

Autocorrelation tends to make the regression coefficients appear statistically significant when they are not, and leads to inflated R^2s.[2] Thus the

---

[2] A very good, brief non-technical discussion of autocorrelation is found on pages 229–38 of the Lewis-Beck article cited at the end of the chapter.

uninformed analyst is likely to commit a type I error, rejecting the null hypothesis when it is true.

The most common way of diagnosing possible autocorrelation is to check the **Durbin-Watson (D-W) statistic**. This statistic, provided with most sophisticated regression programs, divides the summed square of each residual minus the residual of the case before by the summed square of each residual.

$$D\text{-}W = \frac{\sum\limits_{t=2}^{N} (e_t - e_{t-1})^2}{\sum\limits_{t=1}^{N} e_t^2}$$

The D-W statistic can vary from 0 to 4. The closer its value is to 2, the less likely autocorrelation is affecting the results. Usually, the statistic will be between 0 and 2, since a near zero value indicates positive autocorrelation (error terms are usually positively correlated). Negative autocorrelation occurs when a large positive error term in one year lies between large negative autocorrelations the previous and following years.

Unlike looking up a t value in a table and finding out whether it is significant at the .05 level, there is no certain test for finding out whether a particular Durbin-Watson value means that there is autocorrelation. Econometrics texts provide Durbin-Watson tables. By knowing the number of independent variables and your sample size, you can look up a range of D-W values. If your D-W statistic falls outside that range, you can be sure you have an autocorrelation problem. If it falls inside the range, though, you cannot be sure you do not have a problem. "Around 2" as an acceptable value is the advice a novice time series analyst is likely to get.

If you are so unlucky as to find a significant autocorrelation in your estimates, then you will have to take corrective action. This action involves transformations of the variables used in the equation followed by reestimation of the equation. Some regression programs have this transformation option. You should consult an econometrics text, such as those listed at the end of this chapter, for detailed information on this procedure.

There are also a whole series of sophisticated time series procedures, called ARIMA, Box-Jenkins, or Box-Tiao models that allow estimations of trends independent of autocorrelation. The McDowell et al. volume cited at the end of this chapter introduces you to this procedure.

PROBLEM OF SELECTING POLICY INTERVENTION TIME

Although in our example we assumed that the policy went into effect at the time it was adopted, that is not always a reasonable assumption. Sometimes a law is adopted in one year, but implemented the next. In doing time series, you need to think about the time at which it is reasonable to assume your policy

Research in Practice 10A

AN INTERRUPTED TIME SERIES

The 1978 Supreme Court decision, *Regents of the University of California v. Bakke* (438 U.S. 265), forbade universities to use racial quota systems in admission, but it did authorize the use of affirmative action. That meant that race and ethnicity could be considered in the admission decision. Although the *Bakke* decision was one of the most controversial Court decisions of the last thirty years, there has been little attention to its actual effects.

Thus two analysts decided to explore the impact of the decision on African American and Latino admissions to medical and law school (the *Bakke* decision involved a medical school admission). They used an interrupted time series methodology to estimate the long and short-term effects of the decision, and to disentangle the effects from random variation and changes in minority admissions that might be caused by other factors.

They collected data on African American and Latino applications to, and first year enrollments in, medical and law school each year beginning five years before the decision and continuing through a decade after the decision. They also collected information on total applications (assuming that minority applications would be affected by national trends in student interest in medical and law school) and amount of federal student aid (assuming that applications and enrollments will increase as aid becomes more generous). Using a dummy variable to indicate whether the enrollment or applications were before or after the decision, a counter variable beginning in 1973, and a second counter variable beginning in 1979, the first year after *Bakke*, they were able to estimate whether the decision had a short-term, long-term, or no effect on these applications and enrollments.

In general, they found few effects. They speculated that patterns of minority enrollments were set before *Bakke*. Institutions that had made a commitment to minority recruitment before the decision continued to do so afterward (and this interpretation was confirmed in another part of their analysis that examined enrollment institution by institution). The real growth in minority enrollments came before *Bakke* and then again a decade after *Bakke*.

SOURCE: Susan Welch and John Gruhl, *Affirmative Action and Minority Enrollments,* Ann Arbor: University of Michigan Press, 1998.

has been implemented or can be thought to exhibit measurable effects. If it is midyear, then that year should be coded as 1. If there is any doubt, you can experiment with two or more years as the intervention year to see what effect that has on your model.

LAGGED EFFECTS

In our example, we assumed that the economic development policy would have an immediate effect. Sometimes, however, the effect of policy interventions is delayed rather than immediate. For example, although the NCAA increased the academic requirements for eligibility for newly recruited athletes in 1986, any policy effect on graduation rates of athletes could not take effect until 1990 (or in the schools where most athletes are red-shirted, until 1991 or 1992).[3] If that is the case, then instead of coding 1986, the year of intervention, as 1 in the post-policy counter variable (which we called x_p), we would code 1990 as 1, 1991 as 2, and so on. The dummy variable should also be coded 0 before 1990 and 1 after. In dealing with lagged effects, consider how long before an effect might reasonably take place, and set up your equations accordingly.

Another use of lagging in time series is to estimate the effect of an independent variable on the dependent variable at $t + 1$. For example, if one is predicting the impact of unemployment on college enrollment of low-income students, one might want to lag the enrollment variable, so that the model predicts that unemployment in year one affects enrollment in year two, unemployment in year two affects enrollment in year three, and so on. Of course, variables could be lagged more than one year (or other unit).

Lagging is also used to model the effect of a variable in one year on its value in the next; for example, what impact does economic growth in one year have on economic growth in the next? The ARIMA models mentioned previously are designed to estimate these impacts.

EXERCISES

10-4 You are interested in determining the impact of the seatbelt law on traffic fatalities in your state. You have data on traffic fatalities for twenty years before and ten years after the adoption of the seatbelt law so you decide to do an interrupted time series analysis.

a. Show the basic equation for this analysis.
b. What do each of the terms of the equation mean in interpreting changes in traffic fatalities due to the seatbelt law?
c. What control variables would be necessary to use to eliminate obvious threats to internal validity?

---

[3] Red-shirted athletes take five years to use their four years of eligibility.

10-5 Assume you have an interrupted time series analysis. The policy intervention was in 1990. Your time series begins in 1982 and ends in 1997. The hypothesized effect of the policy intervention takes place immediately. What are the values for the pre-post policy dummy variable (x_d), the post-policy counter variable (x_p), and the over time counter variable (x_t) for the following years:

a. 1982.
b. 1989.
c. 1991.
d. 1997.

10-6 Assume you have an interrupted time series analysis. The policy was adopted in 1990. Your time series begins in 1980 and ends in 2000. The hypothesized effect of the policy intervention takes place two years after the policy is adopted. What are the values for the pre-post policy dummy variable (x_d), the post-policy counter variable (x_t), and the over time counter variable (x_t) for the following years:

a. 1985.
b. 1990.
c. 1995.
d. 2000.

10-7 Assume an analysis of the adoption of a state handgun control law adopted in 1985 led to the following regression findings:

$$Y = 10 + 5x_t - .01x_d - 5x_p = e$$

Y = Number of murders per 100,000 population.

x_t = Over time counter where 1969 = 1 . . . 2001 = 33.

x_d = Dummy variable equaling 1 after intervention, 0 before.

x_p = Post-intervention counter, 0 before policy adoption, 1 . . . N after.

a. What was the annual pre-handgun control change in the murder rate?
b. What was the annual post-handgun control change in the murder rate?
c. What was the short-term change in the murder rate brought about by the handgun law?
d. Write a paragraph describing the effect of the handgun law on murder rates as measured by this equation.
e. What other variables should be controlled in examining the impact of handgun laws on murder rates within a given state?

10-8 Assume you have an interrupted time series analysis as described in Exercise 10-5. The dependent variable is traffic fatalities per 100,000 miles driven. The policy intervention is a new law with a mandatory jail term for those convicted of drunk driving, passed in early 1990.

a. Using a computer program designed for multiple regression, calculate the long-term and short-term effects of the policy, using the data on traffic fatalities shown below.
b. Write a paragraph describing the long-term and short-term effects of the new drunk driving law.

Research in Practice 10B

POOLED TIME SERIES

Traffic safety experts disagree about the effect of the 65 mile per hour speed limit on interstate highways. In 1974, the federal government mandated a maximum 55 miles per hour speed limit, largely in response to the oil shortage. In 1987, federal legislation permitted states to raise speed limits on rural interstate highways to 65 (interstates in urban areas were to continue to have a 55 mile per hour limit), and in 1995, additional legislation gave control of speed limits back to the states entirely.

Some experts argue that reduced speeds reduce fatalities, and thus the consequence of raising the speed limits from 55 to 65 would be to increase fatalities. Others argue that the 65 mile per hour speed limit on interstates will reduce fatalities by encouraging faster moving traffic to travel on interstates and consequently making other roads safer.

An evaluator decided to test these differing perspectives by doing a time series analysis. The dependent variable was the number of traffic fatalities per billion miles driven in the state. The key independent variable was whether or not the state had raised its limit to 65 mile per hour on rural interstates. The analysis also included controls for population density, the presence of a seatbelt law, the minimum legal drinking age, police and safety expenditures, the proportion of the adult population who are in the higher risk eighteen to twenty-four age group, alcohol consumption per capita, income, and average temperature.

Traffic Fatalities per 100,000 Miles Driven

1982	3.2	1990	6.2
1983	4.1	1991	6.7
1984	5.5	1992	6.9
1985	4.9	1993	6.5
1986	5.7	1994	7.0
1987	6.2	1995	6.3
1988	6.0	1996	6.8
1989	6.8	1997	6.7

POOLED TIME SERIES

A special kind of time series is when you have data not just on one case over time, but several. For example, you might collect data on every state after implementation of a policy to determine the overall effect of that policy. Research in Practice 10B is an example of pooled time series.

The investigator collected data on each state for each year between 1981 to 1995, inclusive. This is called a pooled time series because the fifteen cases per state (each year being a case) are pooled across all fifty states, producing a total of 750 cases.

Alcohol consumption significantly increased fatalities, and seatbelt laws significantly decreased them. The 65 mile per hour speed limit had somewhat mixed effects. The higher speed limit increased fatality rates on the interstate highways compared with states that continued the 55 mile per hour limit. However, having the 65 mile limit on the interstate highways caused a significant reduction in fatalities on other types of roads (non interstates, urban interstates) suggesting that faster or more risk prone drivers did move to the rural interstates. The net result is that the adoption of the 65 mile per hour speed limit on the rural interstates produced an overall drop in traffic fatalities.

The evaluator commented that although this policy change had beneficial effects, further study would be necessary to determine whether raising speed limits on all interstate and many other types of highways, as several states have done, would cancel this positive effect. Nor did the study indicate whether raising the limits beyond 65, as some states have done, would increase or decrease fatalities. Nonetheless, this evaluation study provided strong evidence on the effects of one controversial policy change.

SOURCE: David Houston, "Implications of the 65-MPH Speed Limit for Traffic Safety," *Evaluation Review* 23 (June 1999): 304–313.

USING TIME SERIES IN FORECASTING

We have seen how time series is used to estimate the impact of a policy intervention. Another use of time series is for forecasting. Here we have no policy intervention or "interruption."

In public bureaucracies, a good deal of time is spent forecasting and planning. How many children will be in the public schools by 2010, and how many schools will need to be opened or closed? What will be the effect of changes in eligibility requirements for welfare on state spending? How will changes in the social security laws affect employment among those over sixty? How will the population and area growth in the community affect the need for police personnel five years from now? And so on. Often plans and projections are tossed aside with each new change in leadership or policy focus.[4] But despite the

---

[4] We are not arguing that the plans of bureaucrats should not be responsive to elected decision makers and to the public. Obviously the bureaucracy needs to be responsive, although how to make it so is another topic. Our comments are, however, based on the observation that too often low or middle-level managers must jump through hoops making plans and justifying them to suit the whims of top-level management and political leaders whose attention span for following through is limited, to say the least.

consignment of many plans and forecasts to dusty files, planning based on reasonable estimates of future conditions and thoughtful analysis of them, can be useful. And sound forecasting and projections increase the possibility that someone may actually pay attention to the plans.

Suppose your supervisor told you to make estimates of public school enrollments in your state ten years hence. How would you go about it? This is a relatively common type of projection that a research analyst might be asked to make, and it certainly should not be a cause for panic. First, ask yourself what factors influence public school enrollments? You might make a preliminary list such as:

1. The age distributions of the state's population.
2. Dropout rate of children who are over minimum school-leaving age.
3. Proportion of children attending private schools.

In projecting to the future, you start out by examining trends from the past. You can plot on a chart the enrollment for as many past years as you think appropriate.

In a trend line you would look for seasonality as well as long-term fluctuation. Do short-term fluctuations mask a long term? If a graph looked like Figure 10-9, you would try to determine the length of each short-term fluctuation and calculate an average. Here each short-term fluctuation appears to persist over about five years, with shifts downward at the end of a five-year period. Calculations of average values for each five years gives you a notion of the overall trend. The data will display a smoother line. Averaging several data points (years, months, or whatever your unit is) is called a **moving average.**

You could also plot on the same graph the estimated number of children age six to eighteen in your state (see Figure 10-10). This will give you some indication of the relationship of school enrollments to births. You can see that the two are linked. The differences between the two lines are due to children

FIGURE 10-9   **School Enrollment**

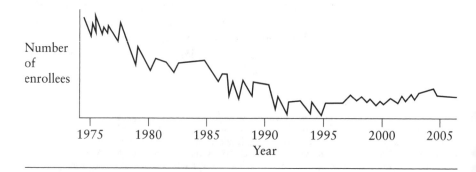

attending private schools, those who drop out, and presumably simple misestimations of school-age population.

Suppose you would like to estimate more accurately the effect of total school-age population on enrollment. Here a regression is appropriate. The unit of analysis is the year. For each past year, you can code school-age population and enrollment. Assume you coded data for each year from 1975 to 2001. You then regress the dependent variable (enrollment) on the independent variable (school-age population):

$$y = a + b_1x_1 + e$$

where

$$y = \text{Enrollment}$$
$$x_1 = \text{School-age population (000s)}$$

Assume you get this outcome:

$$y = 10 + .85x$$

If you estimated the age eighteen population in 2006 at 500,000, then you would estimate that public school enrollment would be 435,000 [(.85 × 500) + 10 = 435]. This estimate would be based on the average relationship of enrollment and school-age population over the time period you examined. But assume that relationship is changing. For example, assume that the proportion of school-age children attending public school increased from 1975 to 2001 due to closing of parochial schools and a decreased dropout rate. An estimate of enrollments in 2003 and beyond would want to take this into account. You would want to include *time* as a factor.

FIGURE 10-10   **Enrollment and Population Trends**

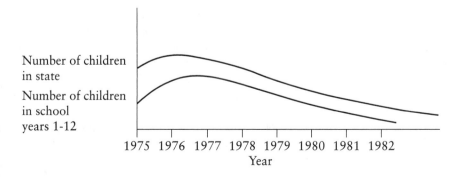

Number of children
in state

Number of children
in school
years 1-12

1975 1976 1977 1978 1979 1980 1981 1982
Year

We do this in the same way we did the interrupted time series. We construct a counter variable where the first year of our time series = 1, the next year = 2, and so forth. An equation might look like this:

$$y = 10 + .30\,x_1 + 2\,x_2$$

where

y = Enrollment

x_1 = School-age population, in thousands

x_2 = Time, where 1975 = 1, 1976 = 2, 1977 = 3, . . . 2003 = 29

Again assuming the estimated school-age population in 2003 was 500,000, the enrollment would be estimated at 468,000.

$$y = 10 + (.80 \times 500) + (2 \times 29) = 468 \text{ or } 468,000$$

The coefficient for time, x_2, indicates that the proportion of school-age children enrolling has increased as time has passed.

You must be cautious in using this kind of time series analysis because you are projecting trends from the past to the future. Obviously the rate of increase suggested by this equation could not continue, or by year 46 (2021) the predicted enrollment would exceed the estimated population. Your projections are likely to be quite a bit more accurate in the short run than in the long run.

You also need to examine whether or not the model you have proposed fits the data. In other words, if school-age population plus time explains only 30 percent of the variation in enrollment, estimates of future enrollment based on school-age population are likely to have very large errors. On the other hand, if your predictor variables explain 95 percent of the variation, as they often do in time series, then you can have more confidence in your estimates of future behavior.

Change rates or growth patterns can take many different forms. You should look carefully at your data to see which kind of growth pattern is evident. Rarely will they appear as in Figure 10-11, Panel A—a linear trend. More likely they will resemble Panel B, where a sharp increase is followed by a leveling off. Sometimes Panel C is more accurate. The growth in demand for oil in the first seventy years of the 20th century, for example, might resemble Panel C.

While the logic of time series is important, always keep in mind that rates of change will undoubtedly fluctuate and that estimations based on the past will be only partially valid.

FIGURE 10-11   **Three Change Rates**

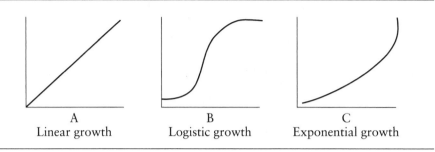

| A | B | C |
| Linear growth | Logistic growth | Exponential growth |

Reporting a Forecast

In writing your report, make sure that you make explicit the basis of your projections. Where did you get your data? What assumptions did you make about birthrates? Mortality rates? Migration flows? The effect of the economy on school dropout rate? If you made your assumptions explicit, your report will be useful because, even if others might disagree with the assumptions, they can see what the effect of their preferred assumptions might be on the trends shown. If you do not make your assumptions explicit, your report will be of very limited value because its underlying premises cannot be evaluated.

Your report should outline and discuss the implications of alternate policy choices. That is, policymakers cannot do much to affect birthrates, death rates, or in-migration in a large and direct way. Their decisions, however, could have a major impact on the public school enrollment through the choices they make to reduce the dropout rate or about how to treat private school children. These kinds of potential impacts should be discussed if they are at all on the policy agenda.

You should also mention possible external effects on school population that you did not take into account in your projections. For example, the occurrence of a steep economic downturn, a war, or the influx of new industry may affect the projections dramatically. These kinds of factors need not be dwelt on unless you think there is a strong possibility of their occurrence.

A forecaster always needs to be cautious about projecting past trends into the future. For years, utility companies projected future energy needs on the basis of ever-rising rates of demand. Now that rates of demand are decreasing (and demand itself is decreasing in some areas), their projections are proving to be far too generous (and expensive). Likewise some communities overbuilt schools in the 1960s and 1970s because they assumed that the birthrate would continue at the high levels of the late 1940s and early 1950s. Obviously we cannot always anticipate future trends. But we should be cautious, especially when the trends of the recent past have been out of line with long-term historical patterns.

PROBIT ANALYSIS

Suppose you wish to examine whether a job training program was successful in placing people in fulltime employment. The dependent variable is a simple dichotomy: whether or not a person is employed. A sample of men unemployed a year ago is used to test the effect of the job training program. In the past year, some enrolled in the program, others did not. In order to separate the impact of the training program from other characteristics of the sample, you plan to control for their years of formal education and previous employment history. Given the need for a multivariate analysis technique, what do you use?

Probit and logitistic regression (similar to probit), are commonly used analytic techniques that are useful when your dependent variable is ordinal rather than interval. Probit was developed for use with a dichotomous dependent variable, but it can also be used with dependent variables of three or more ordered categories. Because many analyses use dichotomous or trichotomous dependent variables, a technique like probit is extremely useful. If your dependent variable has more than five ordered categories, you would use ordinary regression techniques.

In this section, we will first examine why multiple regression is suspect when your dependent variable leaves only a few categories, then we will turn to the question of how to use and interpret probit. Finally, we will examine an application of probit that increases its usefulness to policy researchers.

PROBLEMS WITH MULTIPLE REGRESSION USING A DICHOTOMOUS DEPENDENT VARIABLE

In the study we suggested above, where the dependent variable is dichotomous, social scientists traditionally used multiple regression. In those circumstances, an unstandardized regression coefficient could be interpreted as a probability. For example, if, after you controlled for education and prior employment history, completion of a job training program had an unstandardized coefficient of .10, you could say that participation increased the probability of employment by 10 percent. This is a reasonable interpretation for a dichotomous dependent variable, and you will still find it in policy literature.

However, there are some problems in using multiple regression in such circumstances. We will illustrate these problems using the example of a dichotomous dependent variable, though the problems also exist with threefold and larger dependent variables. Let's assume that months of participation in job training is related to gaining employment. If so, we might find a scattergram similar to that in Figure 10-12. Note first that the values of x (job training participation) can only predict to two values of the dependent employed or not employed. The scattergram does not look like a scattergram between two

FIGURE 10-12   Scattergram of Employment and Job Training

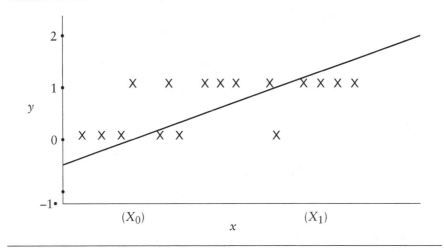

interval variables. In calculating the regression line, the following problems emerge:[5]

1. Some predictions are nonsensical. For example, x values larger than x_1 predict that the value of the dependent variable will be greater than 1. That is impossible; values on the y variable can only be 0 and 1. Similarly, x values smaller than x_0 predict that the value of the dependent variable will be less than 0, again impossible. Thus, the regression model generates predictions about the dependent variable that do not make sense.

2. Errors in predictions are all related to the value of x. That is, above the value of x_1 all errors in prediction are negative. That means that the x variable predicts scores higher than actually occur. Below x_0 all errors are positive. In those cases the x variable predicts values below 0 when the real values are 0. The relationship of the value of x to the direction of the error violates one of the assumptions of regression, which is that errors are randomly distributed around each category of the independent variable.

3. Adding new cases of ever higher values of x combined with success in obtaining employment would cause the line to flatten out, indicating less relationship when in fact the relationship would be growing stronger.

---

[5] This discussion relies heavily on Morris Fiorina, *Retrospective Voting in American National Elections,* New Haven: Yale University Press, 1978. Although only a minor footnote to the work as a whole, Appendix A of this book has one of the clearest discussions of the limitations of regression in the case of a dichotomous variable.

Probit and Its Interpretation

These problems indicate the need for a model other than linear regression to describe the relationship between *x* and *y*. One model is a sigmoid curve illustrated in Figure 10-13. Instead of being represented as a straight line as in ordinary least squares regression, the relationship between *x* and *y* is represented by an S-shaped curve that fits the data much better. No matter how far you extend the ends of the curve, it never goes beyond 1 (in our example) or drops below 0. Probit is the technique represented by that kind of curve.

Probit analysis yields coefficients, called maximum likelihood estimates (MLE), that look somewhat like regression coefficients. Associated with each MLE is a standard error. Dividing the MLE by its standard error yields a *t* value that enables you to estimate the level of statistical significance of the coefficient (by using a *t* table).

However, MLEs do not have quite as simple an interpretation as regression coefficients. While a regression equation *y* = .4 + .05*x* indicates that for every unit change in *x*, *y* increases by .05, a probit equation with the same coefficients has a different interpretation. The probit interpretation is that for every unit change in *x*, there is a .05 change in the *Z* score of *y*. *Z* scores, of course, allow you to measure probabilities. Thus, probit yields probabilities; the word probit is derived from the term "probability unit."

Some computer programs generate an estimated R^2 for the probit equation. The R^2 is not calculated the same way as in regression, and different programs use different estimation procedures. You can estimate R^2 by dividing the chi-square value of the equation by the chi-square plus the number of cases. The chi-square of the equation is almost always provided in probit computer routines.

In most uses of probit, you will see a presentation of the MLEs and the MLE/se. Discussion of findings will focus on which coefficients are significant

FIGURE 10-13   A Probit Model

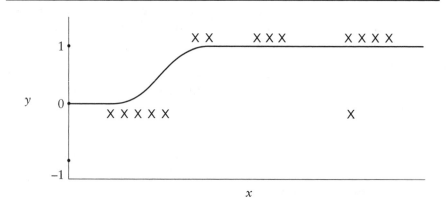

and on the relative size of the coefficients. Few analysts use the properties of probit to translate their findings into probabilities. But doing so is often useful. You can illustrate more correctly the impact of a particular independent variable on the dependent variable.

TRANSLATING PROBIT COEFFICIENTS INTO PROBABILITIES

Because probit coefficients represent change in the Z score of the dependent variable, rather than in the value of the dependent variable itself, the amount of real change in the dependent variable depends on the actual value of the Z score. This can be illustrated by examining a Z score table (see Appendix B). Here are three changes of .10 in Z scores:

ORIGINAL Z SCORE	Z SCORE AFTER + .10	CHANGE IN PROBABILITY	CALCULATION*
0.00	0.10	.0398	.0398 − 0
1.00	1.10	.0230	.3643 − .3413
2.50	2.60	.0015	.4953 − .4938

*From Appendix B, areas of the standard normal distribution. The Z score value for .1, for example, is .0398, for 0 is 0.

In the first case, moving from 0 to .1, a Z score change of .10 represents a probability of nearly .04; in the second case, moving from 1.0 to 1.1, a probability of around .02; and in the third case, moving from 2.5 to 2.6, of nearly 0. Thus, knowing the change in the Z score alone cannot tell you about the magnitude of change in the dependent variable brought about by your independent variable. Instead, we need to know the magnitude of the Z score as well as its change.

We would like to make an estimate analogous to that which a regression allows us: for example, other things being equal, job training increases the probability of employment by 10 percent. In the preceding statement, the phrase "other things being equal" conveys to the reader that the independent variable affects the dependent variable in a particular way after other variables have been controlled. In this case the control variables are education and employment history. In probit, we cannot exactly say this. Because the probability associated with a particular change in the Z score depends on the actual value of the Z score, we must find out what the value of the Z score is. We do this by holding constant the values of all of our independent variables except the one we are most interested in, in this case, job training.

Thus, we can make the following types of statements on the basis of a probit analysis: If a member of the sample has an average education and an average job history, completing job training increases his probability of employment by so much. Or, if a member of our sample has an education and job history that exceeds the mean by one standard deviation, completing job

TABLE 10-4   Some Probit Statistics

	MEAN	MLE	MLE/SE
Years of education	12.0	.40	4.3
Longest number of months of continuous employment	8.0	.20	2.5
Completed job training	0.4	.30	2.0
Constant		−5.5	
Percent who have a job		84.2	

training increases her probability of employment by so much. The change brought about by job training will not be the same for these two cases. Specifying the values that the control variables take (mean education, for example) allows us to determine the magnitude of the Z score under specific assumptions.

How do we go about calculating the change in the dependent variable? The steps are numerous, but straightforward. Assume we have certain statistics from a probit run (see Table 10-4).

We can see that all three independent variables have significant effects on the ability of a member of the sample to find a job. Completion of job training is the least significant variable. Exactly what effect does job training have? To translate these coefficients into probabilities that someone completing job training will find a job, follow these steps:

1. Multiply the sample mean of each independent variable by its MLE. Sum. Add the constant. In this case, the sum is 1.02 ((12.0*.40) + (8.0*.20) + (.4*.30) − 5.5 = 4.8 + 1.6 + .12 − 5.5 = 1.02). This is the Z score for the dependent variable when all independent variables have mean values.

2. Multiply the sample means of each independent variable except job training by its MLE (as in step 1). Sum. To calculate the job training term, multiply its MLE by the value of the variable when job training is completed, 1 (.30 × 1 = .30). Add to the sum of the other independent variables. Add the constant. This equals 1.2 (4.8 + 1.6 + .3 − 5.5).

3. Repeat step 2, but replace the job training term by the MLE times the value of the job training variable when it is not completed, 0 (.30 × 0 = 0). This equals .90 (4.8 + 1.6 + 0 − 5.5). Note that the Z score difference between the value of those completing job training (1.2) and those not (.9) equals .30, the value of the MLE for the job training variable.

4. Optionally, to help you visualize the next two steps, draw a normal curve and locate the 0 point in the middle. The area to the right of the 0 point are positive values, to the left, negative ones. The entries in a Z score table are areas of the normal curve on one side of the 0 point,

ranging from 0 to .4999999. Each side of the 0 point includes (obviously) .50 of the total area.

5. Get out your Z score table (Appendix B). Look up the area between the value for those who did not complete job training (.9) and 0. That value is .3159. Plot that on the right side of your normal curve.

   Look up the area between the value for those who did complete job training (1.2) and 0. That value is .3849. Plot that on the right side of your normal curve.

   Look up the area between the mean value of 1.01 and 0. That value is .3438. Plot that.

6. Translate these figures into proportions. Since all these points are on the right side of the normal curve, add .50 to each to include the area to the left of the 0 point. The result indicates that for those without job training .82 have jobs (.3159 + .50). For those with job training, .88 have jobs (.3849 + .50). In the total sample, .84 have jobs (.50 + .3438). As a check on your work, compare this total sample mean with the sample mean in Table 10-4. Small differences (in this case .2) are acceptable because they can result from rounding error.

   What do these calculations tell us? They allow us to make the following statement, "For those in the sample with an average education and previous job experience, completion of job training increased employment from 82 percent to 88 percent. Thus, for these men typical of our sample, those with job training are 6 percent more likely to be employed than those who did not complete the program." While such a statement is more limited than we can make using regression, it nonetheless allows us to translate MLEs into probabilities and numbers that a lay reader can understand. An MLE of .30 does not mean much to most people, but the difference between 82 percent and 88 percent is quite understandable.

   Using the above procedure, we can calculate several kinds of differences. Suppose we were interested in the impact of the job training program on those with eight years of education and those with twelve. To make this calculation, we would again assume a mean level of prior employment, letting this value assume 8.0. We are interested in those who completed the program, so we let the job training variable equal 1. We can now do steps 2 and 3. In step 2, we let the value for education equal 8, in step 3 we let it equal 12. The differences found in step 6 reflect the differential impact of the job training program on those with different levels of education.

WHEN TO USE PROBIT

Probit is most useful in cases of dichotomous or trichotomous dependent variables. As the number of categories in the dependent variable increases, the need

Research in Practice 10C

USING PROBIT

In the nuclear age, the problem grows of what to do with the waste products of nuclear medicine, nuclear power generation, and other uses of radioactivity. To deal with the problem of low level radioactive waste (such as that produced in medical uses of radioactivity), Congress in 1980 enacted legislation encouraging states to enter into interstate compacts. These interstate compacts would, in theory, allow several states located in a particular region to cooperatively designate one or a few locations for waste, then work together to construct and run the facilities to handle it. Congress saw this as a much more desirable alternative than, on the one hand, allowing each state or locality to deal with its own waste, with attendant problems of safety and expense, or on the other, creating one or two national repositories for all waste.

Unfortunately, not all states have moved to join such compacts. Problems in identifying new waste sites (the NIMBY problem—"not in my backyard!") and getting regional agreement have led to foot dragging on the part of many states. In order to find ways to facilitate states to move to address this serious problem, evaluators undertook an analysis to determine what conditions have promoted states to join compacts addressing this issue.

To assess this, evaluators used probit analysis. The unit of analysis was each state, each year since 1980 (the data was collected in 1995) up to the time when the state joined the compact. Thus a state not having joined at all would be part of fifteen cases, one joining in 1981 would have only one case. The dependent variable in the analysis was whether or not the state joined the compact in that year.

The authors speculated that states already located in a region with a waste facility would be more likely to join a compact, as would states

for probit diminishes and ordinary regression can be used. Most people would choose regression over probit once the number of categories in the dependent variable reaches 5.

Some scholars argue that it is all right to use regression analysis even with a dichotomous dependent variable as long as its distribution is not skewed. In practice, a 25–75 rule of thumb is used. In other words, as long as one category of a dichotomous variable has at least 25 percent of the cases and no more than 75 percent of the cases, the estimates provided by regression are probably not too severely biased, or so these advocates of regression say. When the sample is small, however, even an unskewed distribution on the dependent variable can cause regression estimates to be biased. It is true, however, that you are on producing much waste, and states that already had begun to address the waste problem. The evaluators also speculated that states with more highly educated citizens would be less likely to join compacts because more citizens would be aware of the NIMBY problem. They also believed that rural states would be less likely to join because their citizens would not view this issue as such a problem as states with highly urbanized populations. Finally, the evaluators speculated that states with higher capabilities (more professional legislatures and governors with more power, for example) and states governed by Republicans would be more like to join compacts.

The authors found three factors significantly related to a state's joining a compact. As expected, states in areas with an existing waste facility were more likely to join. But counter to the evaluators' expectations, more urban and less capable states were *less* likely to join compacts. None of the other variables had a significant effect.

The authors concluded that less capable states, those with smaller, less professional legislatures, probably studied the issue less and thus aroused less opposition. They also may have been more willing to join with other states, using other states' expertise, to solve this problem. Rural states may have been more willing to join, the authors conclude, because they produce less waste and have less concern than those in more urban areas.

Though its findings were largely contrary to the author's expectation, this study illustrates the use of probit analysis in examining determinants of policies or outcomes that are dichotomous. Often policy researchers do want to know the factors influencing whether something did or did not happen, and a probit analysis provides a convenient tool to do so.

SOURCE: Anthony Dodson, "Interstate Compacts to Bury Radioactive Waste: A Useful Tool for Environmental Policy?" *State and Local Government Review* (Spring, 1998): 118–128.

safer ground using multiple regression with a dichotomous dependent variable when you have both a large sample and a non-skewed distribution.

Still, if a probit program is available to you, from a technical perspective you should use it.

EXERCISES

10-9 Assess the appropriateness of probit with the following dependent variables (should definitely be used, may be used, should definitely not be used). Assume you are assessing the impact of five independent variables.

a. The mental ability of a person, measured in IQ points.

b. Whether or not an individual has ever been arrested for a felony. About 5 percent of the sample had.

c. The response to a Likert Scale item with five possible options (strongly agree, agree, neutral, disagree, strongly disagree).

d. Whether or not the individual had heard of the citizen review board that investigates citizen complaints about the police. About 40 percent of the sample had.

e. A woman's age at the birth of her first child, ranging in the sample from thirteen to forty-three.

f. Whether or not a person passed a driver's test on the first try. About 85 percent of the sample did.

10-10 Write a paragraph interpreting the following probit results. Assume you are examining the impact of several variables on whether or not drivers arrested for drunk driving in 1999 had been rearrested by January 1, 2001. The dependent variable is 1 = rearrested 0 = not rearrested.

VARIABLE	MEAN	MLE	MLE/SE
Served time in jail (1 = yes, 0 = no)	.15	−.40	−6.50
Over 35 (1 = yes, 0 = no)	.30	−.20	−2.25
Amount of fine paid at first offense	$500	.08	.62
Years of formal education	11.9	.10	1.53
Participated in program for drunk driver	.10	−.25	−2.44
Constant		−40.5	
Estimated R^2		.45	

10-11 Using the probit results used in the text to illustrate the impact of job training, estimate the effect of prior employment on the employment of those with job training. Compare those with zero months of prior employment to those with eight months.

10-12 Using the probit coefficients above, estimate the probability that someone who had served time in jail would be rearrested compared to someone who had not. Make clear your assumptions about the other variables.

LOGISTIC REGRESSION

Logistic regression is similar to probit. Like probit, it is used when the dependent variable has two or three values,[6] and assumes that a relationship

---

[6] Logistic regression may also be used with four values, but with more than this it is standard practice to simply identify the values as one, two, three, . . . N, and analyze using ordinary least squares.

between an independent and dependent variable conforms to an S-shaped rather than a linear distribution. It differs, however, in that the relationship is expressed in terms of log odds rather than Z scores. In a linear regression equation, $y = a + 4x$, where $b = 4$, for every unit change in the independent variable, the dependent variable changes by 4. If this were a logistic regression, for every unit change in the independent variable, the log odds of the dependent variable would increase by four. The log of the odds is referred to as a logit and is a logistic regression coefficient. These are derived like probit analysis using a technique called maximum likelihood estimation.

Logistic regression coefficients can also be expressed in terms of **odds ratios**. Odds ratios are more easily interpreted than the logistic coefficients and can be compared with each other, as partial standardized coefficients can be compared in ordinary least squares. Moreover odds ratios can be translated into probabilities. You can then assess the likelihood that something will occur given certain values on an independent variable or set of independent variables.

Consider the following example where the dependent variable is teenage drinking, coded 1 if a teenager drinks and 0 if not, and the independent variable friends who drink, coded 1 if yes and 0 if not. Assume the following breakdown:

	Teenage Drinking	
FRIENDS WHO DRINK	YES	NO
Yes	72	157
No	48	185

The numbers represent frequencies. To understand odds ratios, one first needs to understand odds. Odds represent the number of events (usually coded 1) to nonevents (usually coded 0), and thus, are themselves ratios. The odds of drinking are 72/157 or .46 for teenagers with friends who drink and 48/185 or .26 for those with friends who do not drink. The odds ratio is the ratio of these two odds. Thus, teenagers with friends who drink are .46/.26 or 1.76 times more likely to drink than those with friends who do not drink. And teenagers with friends who do not drink are .26/.46 or .56 as likely to drink than those with friends who drink. Odds ratios of less than one indicate that as values of the independent variable increase, the odds of the dependent variable occurring decrease. Odds ratios greater than 1 indicate that as values of the independent variable increase, the odds of the dependent variable occurring increase. The logistic regression can be expressed in terms of odds ratios:

$$Y = a * b^{N \text{ of friends who drink}}$$

or

$$Y = .26 * 1.76^{N \text{ of friends who drink}}$$

where *a* is constant value,[7] 1.76 the odds ratio, and the number of friends who drink is the power to which the odds ratio is raised to produce the estimate for those who drink, in this case zero or one. The equation can be transformed by taking the natural logarithm of each side.

$$Ln\ (Y) = -1.34 + (.56*N \text{ of friends who drink})$$

In the equation, .56 is the logistic regression coefficient. While this equation is linear in form, the coefficients lack an easily understood metric. Is an increase in the log of the odds of the dependent variable of .56 for every a unit change in the log of the odds of the independent variable large? The sign indicates that the log of the odds increases with a change in the independent variable, but the amount of increase remains something of a mystery.

As with probit, we can also calculate probabilities, which do provide a readily understood interpretation. In the above example, the odds of someone drinking who has friends who drink is

$$.26*1.76^{(1)} = .46$$

The odds of someone drinking whose friends do not drink is[8]

$$.26*1.76^{(0)} = .26$$
$$.26*1 = .26$$

The probability of drinking when friends drink is

$$\frac{\text{Odds of drinking}}{1 + \text{Odds of drinking}}$$

or

$$.46 / (1 + .46) = .32$$

The probability of drinking when one's friends drink is .32. The probability of drinking when one's friends do not drink is .21 (the latter calculation is .26/1 + .26).

In addition to the regression coefficient and odds ratio, most logistic regression software produces the Wald coefficient. This is a measure of statistical significance for each independent variable (analogous to *t*). The Wald coefficient (W) is equal to the logistic regression coefficient divided by the standard error, and is distributed as the standard normal distribution, and evaluated

---

[7] Note that the constant is the odds of drinking for those with friends who do not drink.

[8] Recall that a number to the zero power equals 1 ($N^0 = 1$), a number to the first power equals itself ($N^1 = N$).

using the Z test. Sometimes Wald's is presented as W^2, in which case it is distributed as a chi-square distribution.

Another measure associated with both logistic (and probit) analysis is -2 times the log of the likelihood or sometimes labeled -2 log L or 2LL. This is a measure of the goodness of fit of the logistic equation. In other words, it's a measure of how well the independent variables, as a group, predict the dependent variable. The reason -2 is multiplied by the log of the likelihood is because the distribution then approximates chi-square distribution, allowing chi-square to be used to evaluate its significance. Minus 2LL is equivalent to the error sums of squares in a ordinary least squares regression, and thus, is an indicator of poor fit. One would not want it to be statistically significant if the goal is for the model to fit well. In other words, the smaller, the better.

EVENT HISTORY ANALYSIS

Event history analysis is useful when one is interested in the factors that explain when an event has occurred. For example, an analyst might be interested in when a state adopts a law or when an individual who has been in prison commits another felony or when a teenager gets pregnant. In each of these, of course, it is possible that the event never occurs: a state may never adopt the law, the ex-prisoner may never be arrested for another crime, or the young woman may not get pregnant during her teens. And if the event happens, that is, the state adopts the law, the ex-prisoner commits a crime, or the young woman gets pregnant, the time at which this occurs varies greatly. Some states will be innovators and adopt a very new law early, others years later. Some ex-prisoners will be arrested for crimes shortly after leaving prison, others not until years later. And some young women will get pregnant at thirteen or fourteen, others not until eighteen or nineteen.

Assume an interest in how long, if ever, it is before an ex-prisoner is arrested again. We could use the standard regression analysis. For each ex-prisoner, one could measure the time until he was arrested. As independent variables, one might gather information on how long he was in prison, the type of crime for which he was convicted, his education, occupational skills, and so forth. We then have the usual regression equation: $y = a + bXi + e$ where y equals the elapsed time to arrest, Xi represents the independent variables, and e the error term.

A problem with the standard regression analysis in this case is **censoring** the dependent variable. Assume three ex-prisoners, Joe who is arrested for a crime one year after being released, Steve three years after being released, and Jack who has not been arrested by the time of the study, ten years after release. It would be easy enough to code t as one for Joe and three for Steve, but how does one code Jack? Should he be coded at ten? If so, that implies he was arrested in year ten, but he wasn't. In other words, the dependent variable is censored because some cases do not fall within the time period being examined.

We could eliminate Jack from the study. But this is a bad idea, because the study is presumably interested in why some ex-prisoners are never arrested again. Eliminating Jack undermines the purpose of the study.

Another problem is that some of the independent variables will vary across the time period. Perhaps Jack goes back to school after leaving prison and earns a degree or Steve gets a better paying job his second year out of prison than his first. So the values for education and income increase with time. The standard regression analysis does not allow for that unless one takes the average of Steve's income or Jack's education over the years.

Event history analysis provides techniques to handle these problems. There are different event history methods, but the focus here is on the discrete-time method, a relatively simple technique that will provide an introduction.

A key concept in event history analysis is **risk set.** The risk set refers to the set of cases (individuals or states, for example) who are "at risk" of the event occurring (adoption of a law, getting arrested, getting pregnant) at a particular point in time. Those cases that have experienced the event, that is, the law adopted or an arrest, are no longer at risk.

Another important concept in event history analysis is the **hazard rate.** This is the probability that an event will occur at a particular time to a particular individual, given that the individual is still at risk. In the example, this is the ex-prisoners who have not been arrested. The hazard rate is the probability that a case in the risk set will experience the event at a particular time, that an ex-prisoner will be arrested in a particular year. In the case of the three persons, 1 of 3 was arrested the first year, so the hazard rate was 1/3, or .33. None were arrested in year two so the hazard rate was 0. One of the two remaining was arrested in year three, so the hazard rate was 1/2 or .5. Note that the hazard rate increased even though the same number (1) of men were arrested in year three as in year one when the hazard rate was only .33. That is because the risk set was larger in year one (3 instead of 2).

The hazard rate is estimated by setting up the analysis with one case per individual for each time period they are at risk. So in the example, there is one case for each person for each year they are in the risk set. The dependent variable is coded 0 if the person did not commit a crime and 1 if the person did during that year.

Note there are fourteen cases in the three-person example. In year one, we have three cases because all three are at risk, that is, in the risk set. In years two and three we have two cases because only two of the original three are at risk. In years four through ten we have one case each year because only Jack is still at risk. Research in Practice 10C illustrates an event history data set. States are represented with varying numbers of cases depending on when they entered a compact.

---

[9] Other types include those where we examine repeatable events, not just a single event (i.e., how many pregnancies did the teenager have). For more detailed examination of these issues see Paul D. Allison cited in bibliography, or Janet M. Box-Steffensmeier and Bradford S. Jones, "Time is of the Essence: Event History Models in Political Science," in *American Journal of Political Science* 41 *(October, 1997): pp. 1414–1461.*

TABLE 10-5   Example of a Data Set for Event History Analysis

TIME	INDIVIDUAL	DEPENDENT VARIABLE	INDEPENDENT VARIABLE
Year 1	Joe	1	Income, education, etc in year 1
Year 1	Steve	0	"
Year 1	Jack	0	_
Year 2	Steve	0	Income, education, etc in year 2
Year 2	Jack	0	
Year 3	Steve	1	Income, education, etc in year 3
Year 3	Jack	0	
Year 4	Jack	0	Income, education, etc in year 4
Year 5	Jack	0	Income, education, etc in year 5
Year 6	Jack	0	Income, education, etc in year 6
Year 7	Jack	0	Income, education, etc in year 7
Year 8	Jack	0	Income, education, etc in year 8
Year 9	Jack	0	Income, education, etc in year 9
Year 10	Jack	0	Income, education, etc in year 10

Notice also that the values of some of the independent variables vary from year to year as circumstances change. Incomes rise and fall, education increases, people marry and get divorced. Some independent variables would remain constant, such as the type of the crime for which the ex-prisoner was imprisoned initially and the length of the sentence served.

As a statistical technique, one could employ ordinary least squares, but with a dichotomous dependent variable, logistic regression would be better. A standard logistic routine could be used but there are programs designed specifically for event history analysis.

If we wish to know how the hazard rate changes, and we usually do, we include in our data set a dummy variable for time. In other words, in our example in Table 10-5, we would create 10 new variables measuring time. The first would be coded 1 for the year one cases, 0 for all others. The second would be coded 1 for year 2, 0 for all others, and so forth. Recall we would only enter nine of these variables into the equation since the tenth is perfectly predictable from the other nine (and this analysis is not likely to work well with as few cases as we have).

The coefficient for each of these dummy variables gives us the hazard rate for that year. These coefficients allow us to see how the hazards change over time. In our hypothetical example, we might expect the hazard rate for being arrested to decrease over time.

In event history analysis, the time unit being examined would not always be years. Any appropriate unit could be used. Obviously, the smaller the unit, the more cases in the analysis. In the above simple example, if we had been interested in the month that the arrest occurred rather than the year, we would have twelve times as many cases, or a total of 168 just for three people. The choice of time unit needs to be determined by the purposes of the study and the nature of the data.

EXERCISES

10-13 Assume you want to analyze the effect of three different drug regimens (which changed over time for some) on the length of time, in years, from first symptoms of AIDS to death. You have a sample of individuals who first showed symptoms (assume we have a good measure of that) in 1996 and you are doing the analysis in 2002. From the following data from seven individuals, set up the data set for an event history analysis.

YEAR	INDIVIDUAL	DEATH	DRUG REGIMEN	AGE AT ONSET
1997	1	No	Type 1	25
	2	No	Type 1	32
	3	Yes	Type 1	35
	4	No	Type 2	22
	5	No	Type 2	28
	6	No	Type 3	22
	7	No	Type 3	29
1998	1	No	Type 1	25
	2	Yes	Type 2	32
	4	No	Type 2	22
	5	No	Type 2	28
	6	No	Type 2	22
	7	Yes	Type 3	29
1999	1	Yes	Type 1	25
	4	No	Type 2	22
	5	No	Type 2	28
	6	No	Type 2	22
2000	4	No	Type 2	22
	5	No	Type 2	28
	6	No	Type 2	22

2001	4	Yes	Type 2	22
	5	Yes	Type 2	28
	6	No	Type 3	22
2002	6	No	Type 3	22

10-14 Assume, in an analysis of recidivism of former prisoners, we have the following set of results from an event history analysis. Assume the dependent variable is whether the person was arrested in a particular year. Independent variables include the seriousness of the crime, whether they are on probation, and their educational level. What is the hazard rate for each year? Write a brief paragraph interpreting the results, with a particular focus on the impact of the passage of time on the likelihood of arrest.

EXPLANATORY VARIABLES	b	t
Crime seriousness*	.50	5.30
Probation	−.10	−1.99
Years of education	−.15	−2.33
Year 1	.25	5.22
Year 2	.15	2.46
Year 3	.10	2.12
Year 4	.05	0.64

*Seriousness of crime is an interval level variable measured from one, least serious, to ten, most serious. Probation is a dummy variable, yes = 1, no = 0. The year variables are also dummy variables.

KEY TERMS

Endogenous variables
Exogenous variables
Direct effect
Indirect effect
Path
Total effects
Nonrecursive model
Recursive model
Interrupted time series
Trend
Seasonality

Autocorrelation
Durbin-Watson (D-W) statistic
Moving average
Probit
Maximum likelihood estimates (MLE)
Odds ratios
Event history analysis
Censoring
Risk set
Hazard rate

FOR FURTHER HELP

Aldrich, John H and Charles Cnudde. "Probing the Bounds of Conventional Wisdom: A Comparison of Regression, Probit, and Discriminant Analysis." *American Journal of Political Science* 19 (August, 1975): 571–608. A good introduction to probit analysis.

Aldrich, John H and Forrest Nelson. *Linear Probability, Logit and Probit Models.* Sage University Paper Series on Quantitative Applications in the Social Sciences. Beverly Hills, Calif.: Sage Publications, 1984. One of the best overviews of these techniques, though hard going for the nonsophisticated user.

Allison, Paul. *Event History Analysis.* Sage University Paper Series on Quantitative Applications in the Social Sciences. Beverly Hills, Calif: Sage Publications. An excellent, short coverage of event history analysis.

Asher, Herbert B. *Causal Modeling.* Sage University Paper Series on Quantitative Applications in the Social Sciences. Beverly Hills, Calif.: Sage Publications, 1976. A short treatment of causal modeling.

Dutta, M. *Econometric Methods.* Cincinnati: Southwestern Publishing, 1975. A clear discussion of how to do transformations to reduce autocorrelation.

Lewis-Beck, Michael. "Interrupted Time Series," in *New Tools for Social Scientists,* ed. William D. Berry and Michael Lewis-Beck. Beverly Hills, Calif.: Sage Publications, 1986. The best non-technical discussion of how to use the interrupted time series model that we have seen. This discusses the interrupted time series model we have described in this chapter.

Menard, Scott. *Applied Logistic Regression Analysis.* Sage University Paper Series on Quantitative Applications in the Social Sciences. Beverly Hills, Calif: Sage Publications, 1995.

Ostrom, Charles. *Time Series Analysis: Regression Techniques.* Sage University Paper Series on Quantitative Applications in the Social Sciences. Beverly Hills, Calif.: Sage Publications, 1978. A good overview of time series models, including discussions of autocorreletion and lagging. The use of time series models in forecasting is also discussed.

II

COST-BENEFIT ANALYSIS

When Robert McNamara brought the idea of **cost-benefit analysis** with him from the Ford Motor Company to the Department of Defense in 1961, it was heralded as a move that would save the taxpayers millions of dollars, lead to efficiency in government, and make decisions more scientific. However, in addition to its failure when applied to the Vietnam War by McNamara and other Defense Department personnel, its usefulness has been challenged in other settings. The technique has been widely used by the Army Corps of Engineers, yet the Corps usually finds dam-building projects to be of net benefit, while environmental groups using the same techniques find a net cost. Utility companies display cost-benefit analyses showing the benefits of building a nuclear power plant at a given site, while local organizations use the same techniques to show that the costs are far higher and benefits much lower than claimed by utility companies.

Cost-benefit analysis has been found useful in a wide variety of settings, yet it may be difficult to accept the credibility of a technique that seems to give each interested party the answer it wants. Nevertheless, cost-benefit analysis is widely used and here to stay. In this chapter we will examine the technique and point out its strengths and limitations. Several how-to-do-it steps will be described.

COST-BENEFIT ANALYSIS: AN OVERVIEW

Suppose you are a planning officer for a fire department in a city of 100,000. The fire chief indicates that a new fire station is needed in the northwest side of the city where substantial population growth has taken place. He believes this would enable the department to reduce the time per call in that area and thus decrease the cost of fire damage to property owners as well as reducing the risk of injury and death from fire. The chief asks you to make a systematic investigation of the costs and benefits of several alternatives: continue without the new station or build one at one of four possible sites. Following your investigation you are to make a recommendation to the department on the relative utility of each course of action. Your analysis and recommendations will be the basis of the department's recommendation to the city in its annual budget and capital construction request.

The procedure you are asked to undertake is called cost-benefit analysis. Its primary rationale is that when choosing among alternative courses of action (and remember "no action" is an alternative), you should pursue that which produces the greatest net benefit. Net benefit, of course, is the total benefit minus the total cost. This rule has been termed the Fundamental Rule of cost-benefit analysis.[1]

Let's consider a simple example. Suppose you are trying to decide whether to buy a new car and you have narrowed your choice to a family car and a sleek sports model. Assume you estimate the average costs and benefits over the next six years as shown in Table 11-1.

A cost-benefit analysis would dictate choosing to stay with your old car rather than purchasing either of the new alternatives. Although the benefits of B and C greatly exceed those of A, their costs are also greater, so their net benefit is smaller.

What if all net benefits were negative as in Table 11-2? In that instance you would choose the alternative with the smallest negative benefit, B.

The logic of cost-benefit analysis is the same for public as well as private decisions. You try to ascertain all the costs and benefits of each option and calculate the net benefit in terms of a common indicator, usually dollars. Assessing costs and benefits may be more difficult in public than in private decisions, but

TABLE 11-1   Net Benefits of Three Choices

	YEARLY COSTS	YEARLY BENEFITS	NET BENEFIT PER YEAR
Old faithful (A)	$2,300	$3,000	$700
New family car (B)	3,000	3,500	500
New sports car (C)	4,000	3,500	−500

TABLE 11-2   Negative Net Benefits

	CAR	NET BENEFIT PER YEAR
	A	$−500
	B	−300
	C	−750

[1] Edith Stokey and Richard Zeckhauser, *A Primer for Policy Analysis,* New York: W.W. Norton, 1978, p. 137.

the underlying assumption is the same: the option should be chosen that yields the greatest net benefit.

Advantages of Cost-Benefit Analysis

What is the advantage of cost-benefit analysis? Its biggest contribution may be that it forces the analyst to think about the actual costs and benefits of alternative choices. In doing so, costs and benefits that have not been part of the discussion may come to light. Or one alternative may be found to have such high costs that it can be rejected out of hand. Cost-benefit analysis forces you to make explicit the foreseeable costs and benefits. Ultimately any decision is based on some sort of calculation of costs and benefits. Sometimes the calculation is unconscious. Other times it is explicit but not very well thought out. In consciously applying cost-benefit techniques, the aim is to bring to light all the costs and benefits that can be foreseen and try to assess their relative weights.

Some Limitations of Cost-Benefit Analysis

As E. S. Quade commented, with what we assume was not deliberate irony, "The great disadvantage of cost-benefit analysis is that it is very hard to perform satisfactorily."[2]

Cost-benefit analysis has a certain simplicity on its face. It sounds scientific; it tries to compare apples and apples and not apples and oranges. But even the simple example illustrated above brings some questions to mind. Just how do you calculate and translate costs and benefits into dollars? When you are choosing whether or not to buy a new car, certain costs and benefits are relatively easy to calculate. In this example, costs seem easy to estimate: the price of the car, interest to finance it, cost of gas and repairs over the years, and license fees, for example. Some benefits are more difficult. You might be able to estimate the costs of not having a car: having to take public transportation, for example, and include it as a benefit of each of the alternatives. But how do you estimate the value of "convenience" in owning a car beyond the estimate of costs of alternative transportation? And in choosing between alternatives A, B, and C, how do you assess the dollar value of your preference, let us say for a new car over an old one or a sports car over a sedan? Or, how do you assess the dollar benefits of the convenience for your family in having a large vehicle rather than a sports car?

Obviously you can make estimates of the dollar value of such things as convenience, accessibility, and preferences. However it is easy to see that even

---

[2] Quade, *Analysis for Public Decisions*, p. 26.

in this simple example, values quickly enter into the assessment of costs and benefits. And, of course, the values placed on various kinds of costs and benefits will determine which alternative has the largest net benefit. So we can begin to see why cost-benefit analyses done on the same project by groups with different basic values might come to entirely different conclusions.

Cost-benefit analysis has been quite popular among those interested in federal regulatory reform. Those wanting to reduce the amount of regulation have advocated more use of cost-benefit procedures. Regulations that could not show a net benefit would not be implemented. However, cost-benefit analyses of regulations suffer the difficulties just mentioned. Cost of regulations are relatively concrete and more easily calculated than the benefits, which often are difficult to put into dollar terms. How do you quantify saving human lives? If a particular rule saves five lives per year at a cost of $1 million, does the regulation offer a net cost or a net benefit? It ultimately depends on a judgment of the value of a human life. Of course, those who have pushed for doing cost-benefit analyses of regulation have tended to be those who oppose regulations, so there is perhaps a built-in bias.

Another limitation is that some cost-benefit analyses only consider one's own costs and benefits, and not the costs and benefits a decision may impose on others. These are called **externalities.** In the case of a decision whether or not to buy a new car, the cost-benefit analysis indicated that keeping "old faithful" maximized net benefits. However, it may be that old faithful is an environmental disaster, creating much more air and noise pollution than cars B or C. In that case, the total costs of alternative A are higher than what you yourself are bearing. Others pay the cost too (in terms of health as well as cleanup) for your old faithful.

Public as well as private decisions have externalities. For example, an externality of our nuclear testing has been borne by those contracting leukemia and other forms of cancer from the radiation. Government can make externalities part of the cost, however. Suppose your locality levied an annual fine of $300 on any vehicle not meeting air and noise pollution standards. This would change the net benefit of old faithful to only $400 ($700 − $300 tax) and make car B the most beneficial choice.

A third limitation of cost-benefit analysis is that it cannot deal with distributional questions. In both public and private decisions, the benefits and costs of each alternative option may not be distributed equally among different segments of the community because of different values, physical locations, needs, and resources. For example, assume you are a planner in the public roads department considering two possible routes for a cross-town arterial highway. The figures in Table 11-3 are the total costs and benefits you have calculated.

This simple cost-benefit calculation indicates that route B will yield the greatest benefit. But further analysis in Table 11-4 indicates that the net benefit to each of three income groups in the city is very different for each alternative.

Table 11-3   Costs and Benefits of Alternative Routes ($000)

	Costs	Benefits	Net benefit
North route (A)	$5,000	$6,000	$1,000
South route (B)	6,000	8,000	2,000

Table 11-4   Distribution of Benefits of Alternative Routes ($000) to Income Groups

	Low-income	Middle-income	Upper-income
North route (A)	$200	$ 400	$ 400
South route (B)	−500	1,500	1,000

Each group benefits from alternative A, though the lower-income group benefits less than the other two. But for alternative B most of the benefit is for the middle-income group, and the lower-income group actually has a negative net benefit. In other words, the lower-income group is bearing more costs than the benefits it will receive from the road. While this example is hypothetical, it is probably typical to find benefits distributed unevenly. In this example, it may be that the south route goes predominantly through lower-income neighborhoods so that the costs of relocation are disproportionately borne by this group. Or, alternatively, it could be that the benefits received by the low-income group are disproportionately small because they have ample public transportation available or because few of them live in the area served by the new street.

This simple example should alert you to the problems in using cost-benefit analysis without a detailed examination of who benefits and who pays the cost. Once you find that the most cost-beneficial alternative (B) is also the most inequitable among various income groups, then as a policymaker you are left to make a choice based on other criteria in addition to a simple (or not so simple) cost-benefit calculation.

One criterion that can be used is called **Pareto optimality.** A Pareto optimum solution states that any change would make someone worse off. In other words, if you reach a Pareto optimum solution, no change can be made to improve the benefits of any one party without decreasing the benefits of another. In solutions to public problems, a Pareto optimum is obviously not always (or even often) achievable, as our highway example indicated. Instead, decision makers have to consider tradeoffs in the distribution of costs and benefits to different individuals and groups. How these tradeoffs are made depends on political choices and the philosophical values that underpin them (what do we really mean by equality, for example? Equality of treatment or equality of results?). Usually what is best for one group will not be best for others. There is no sure way to combine individual or group preferences to produce a ranking for society as a whole, as Kenneth Arrow has demonstrated.[3]

Cost-benefit analysis is only a tool, and the decision maker must realize that the bottom line in a cost-benefit analysis may or may not be the "right" decision when taking into account political, social, and other factors. Values as well as dollars contribute to the cost and benefit estimates. But if analysts and policymakers accept the notion of cost-benefit analysis for what it is, a potentially useful tool, then it can be used to think through the pros and cons of alternative decisions. What cost-benefit analysis must not lead to is a "... decision maker who ... knows the cost of everything and the value of nothing."[4]

POINTERS ON CALCULATING COSTS AND BENEFITS

To make the best cost-benefit estimates, one must identify as many costs and benefits as possible and to assign them reasonable dollar values. This of course is very difficult in many situations. For example, assume the options being considered are alternative locations of state regional mental health centers.

1. **Costs of acquisition and construction.** These are obvious and can usually be easily estimated. If land is already owned by the state, then the land acquisition cost for that site should not be considered. Since the land is already owned, it represents a **sunk cost.** What should be considered, however, are alternate uses of the land (see 3 below). The cost of buying land includes not only the purchase price, but also interest

---

[3] See Kenneth Arrow, *Social Choice and Individual Values,* New York: John Wiley & Sons. 1963. One way to try to estimate a societal preference ranking is by majority rule. But consider the outcome (discovered and described by the Marquis de Condorcet over 200 years ago) of a modern example:

For simplicity's sake, assume we have a three-person society: Susan, Jack, and Bob, and a choice of one book from among three: *Public Administration: Boon or Bane*; *Our Friend Public Administration*; or *Having Fun with Public Administration*. The three individuals have preferences as follows:

	Susan	Jack	Bob
First choice	*Boon or Bane*	*Our Friend*	*Having Fun*
Second choice	*Our Friend*	*Having Fun*	*Boon or Bane*
Third choice	*Having Fun*	*Boon or Bane*	*Our Friend*

If we use the majority rule to choose among any pair of these choices, we find the following outcomes: *Boon or Bane* is preferred to *Our Friend* (Susan and Bob outvote Jack); *Our Friend* is preferred to *Having Fun* (Susan and Jack outvote Bob); and *Having Fun* is preferred to *Boon or Bane* (Jack and Bob outvote Susan). Paradoxically, then, no stable ordering of these three alternatives exists: *Boon or Bane* is preferred to *Our Friend* which is preferred to *Having Fun* which is preferred to *Boon or Bane*. Thus, even at this elementary level, and with only a three-person "society," there is no satisfactory way to rank the preferences of society as a whole.

[4] Quotation from a House Armed Services Committee report on the Defense Department, 1960, in E. S. Quade, *Analysis for Public Decisions,* New York: Elsevier North-Holland, 1975, p. 102.

paid on bonds that the state must issue and other costs involved in the purchase. Similarly, construction costs would include any interest paid.

2. **Operating costs.** How much will it cost to operate each proposed site each year? Operating costs may be higher at some sites than at others because of differences in wage scales, costs of supplies, and so forth.

3. **Costs of alternative uses of the land (or other capital).** Even if the state already owns the land on which one or more of the proposed centers are to be built, any reasonable cost-benefit analyst must consider as a cost the potential benefit of other uses of the land. For example, suppose the state could lease some of its land holdings and receive a substantial income yielding (after costs are considered) a net benefit of $20 million over twenty years. Or suppose Disney wants to buy the land for a new theme park and is willing to pay $10 million now. If the land is instead used for a mental health center, then these potential alternative revenues must be included as a cost for that particular site. This is called an **opportunity cost.** For some land holdings, there may be few alternative uses. Then the opportunity cost would be near $0. But where purchased or already-held land has other potential uses, the benefits of alternative uses must be added into the cost calculation. Failure to do so will artificially deflate the projected costs of a project and make it seem more beneficial than it really is. The same holds true of alternative uses of personnel, machinery, buildings, or other capital used for the project.

4. **Future costs and benefits.** In calculating costs and benefits accruing in the future (such as operating costs or income from the center), consider the complicated subject of discount rates.[5] It should be clear upon reflection that a net benefit of $5 million in 2001 is not the same in present value as a net benefit of $5 million in 2010. You must take that fact into account when comparing two or more alternatives with benefits and costs stretching over time. In comparing three mental health center sites, for example, it may be that the net benefits are similar to the figures in Table 11-5.

Assuming that a four-year life span is all we are interested in, how do you decide which has the greatest net benefit? Simply adding up the pluses and minuses for each alternative does not go far enough. It shows site 1 with a net benefit of 0, site 2 with $6 million, site 3 with $5 million. Does this indicate site 2 has the greatest net benefit? Before answering this, we must consider how to compare, for example, the 8, 12, and 5 in year 3. We would like to assess how much each is worth in present value so we can make a judgment comparing like things.

---

[5] For a fuller but still brief discussion, but one which does not deal at all with the effects of inflation on valuation into the future, see Chapter 10 of Stokey and Zeckhauser.

TABLE 11-5   Net Benefits of Three Sites

Year	Site 1	Site 2	Site 3
0	$-8	$-15	$-3
1	-4	-1	-2
2	4	10	5
3	8	12	5
	0	6	5

Note: Figures are in $ millions.

Two competing forces are at work to influence the **present values** (PV) of these future benefits. On the one hand, we know that a given sum today can be invested to yield a larger sum a year from now. For example, if we invested $1,000 today at 10 percent simple interest, in one year we would have $1,100. Investing that sum at 10 percent would yield $1,210 in a second year, and so forth. With compound interest rates, we would accrue an even greater yield. And, of course, investments at lower or higher interest rates would yield lesser or greater sums. So in terms of interest alone, the value of a $1,000 benefit a year from now is worth less in present terms because we can take a lesser sum today, invest it, and have $1,000 in a year. How much less is the present value of $1,000 a year from now? This depends on the rate at which we might hypothetically invest it. These rates, when used in cost-benefit analysis, are called **discount rates.** Assume three different discount rates for the $1,000 benefit a year from now: 5, 10, and 15 percent. To calculate the present value, we need to know what sum plus interest will yield $1,000, or at:

$$
\begin{aligned}
5 \text{ percent:} \quad & PV \times (1 + .05) & = & \quad \$1,000 \\
& PV \times (1.05) & = & \quad 1,000 \\
& PV & = & \quad 1,000/1.05 = \$952.38 \\
10 \text{ percent:} \quad & PV \times (1 + .10) & = & \quad \$1,000 \\
& PV & = & \quad 1,000/1.10 = \$909.09 \\
15 \text{ percent:} \quad & PV \times (1 + .15) & = & \quad \$1,000 \\
& PV & = & \quad 1,000/1.15 = \$869.57
\end{aligned}
$$

In other words, the higher the assumed discount rate, the less the present value of a future benefit. Thus if the state could safely invest its money at 15 percent, then it would only need $869.57 today to have $1,000 in a year. But if it could only invest at 5 percent, it would need $952.38 today to create $1,000 in a year. It can be seen from this simple example that depending on the discount rate applied, the present value of a future benefit varies, introducing another element of uncertainty into the cost-benefit calculus.[6]

---

[6] When calculating over more than one year, the formula: Present value (N years) = $1,000/(1 + discount rate)^N is appropriate. If calculating the present value of a benefit of $1,000 over two years at a discount rate of 10 percent, the formula is PV = $1,000/(1 + .10)^2 = 1,000/1.21 = \$826.45$.

Inflation counteracts the effect of discount rates. While the idea of a discount rate assumes that $1 today will be worth more next year since it can be invested, inflation means that $1 will be worth less next year in terms of purchasing power. When comparing two or more alternatives with differing cost-benefit streams over time, you should consider inflation as well as discounting.[7] Obviously, projecting inflation is as uncertain, or even more so, than projecting interest rates. In times when inflation was low and consistent, it could be ignored. In other times, such as the late 1970s, for example, inflation reaches such high rates that it cannot be ignored. If inflation and interest rates are equal, their effects cancel each other; thus a future benefit of $1,000 would have a present value of $1,000. If, however, inflation is projected to be higher than discount rates, then a future benefit of $1,000 will have a present value higher than $1,000. If discount rates are assumed to be higher than inflation, then a future benefit of $1,000 would have a present value lower than $1,000, as we saw above.

Because most policy analysts do not have psychic powers, it is difficult to argue that a cost-benefit analysis based on one set of projections is accurate. Before giving up these projections as hopeless, however, you could plot net present value benefits based on several different values for discount rate-inflation. This kind of procedure is called **sensitivity analysis:** varying a component of the cost-benefit estimate to see what different outcomes are created. You might discover that project A yields more net benefits than project B except when inflation exceeds interest rates by more than 8 percent. You may reasonably argue that this condition is unlikely and opt for project A. Or you may find that project C yields more net benefits than project D when interest rates exceed inflation by any amount. To decide whether that is likely, you would then have to examine the relationship of interest to inflation in the past.

Let's try this sensitivity analysis on our three benefit streams for alternative mental health centers. Start by assuming five different values for the discount rate less inflation: 10, 5, 3, 0, and −3 percent.

The total benefit from site 1 is equal to the following if we assume a 5 percent discount rate minus inflation margin (refer to the net benefits for site 1 listed in Table 11-5):[8]

$$-8 + (-4/[1 + .05]) + 4/(1 + .05)^2 + 8/(1 + .05)^3 =$$
$$-8 + (-3.81) + 3.64 + 6.91 = -1.26$$

---

[7] Two treatments of cost-benefit analysis that consider inflation are Mark S. Thompson, *Benefit-Cost Analysis for Program Evaluation,* New York: Russell Sage Foundation, 1980, pp. 162–65, and John K. Gohagen, *Quantitative Analysis for Public Policy,* New York: McGraw-Hill, 1980.

[8] This is the formula presented in footnote 6. Substitute for $1,000 the value (benefit) for each year (−8 in year 0, −4 in year 1, 4 in year 2, 8 in year 3) in the formula. Use .05 as the discount rate. Substitute the year specified (0, 1, 2, 3) for N. The calculation adds all years together to calculate the summed discounted benefit for each site.

If we calculate for each site the benefits based on each of our four values of discount rate less inflation we have the sets of values in Table 11-6. We could also plot these points on a graph to get a better picture of the relative changes in the net benefits as discount and inflation rates change (Figure 11-1).

It seems clear that site 1 is the least desirable alternative no matter how the discount and inflation rates vary (except perhaps at astronomically high inflation rates). That is because the net benefits are negative until inflation exceeds the discount rate, and even then the benefits are lower than for the other sites. Site 2 has the largest benefit as long as the inflation rate exceeds the discount rate by about 3 percent or more. But when the discount rate exceeds inflation (the most likely condition), site 3 produces the highest net benefit.

Doing computations like those in Table 11-6 allows the analyst to see just what future benefits are likely to be under changing economic conditions. In the end, however, it is guesswork to decide which of these economic trends is likely to happen, but at least some alternatives may be discarded.

The importance of estimating discount rates should not be understated just because it is a difficult problem. For example, one reason that Army Corps of Engineers estimates nearly always have shown projected benefits is that they tend to use very small discount rates (4 percent even when interest rates are much higher, for example). Opponents of Corps projects have been able to seriously embarrass and effectively challenge the Corps by pointing to this factor in their estimates. Thus discount rates, while a technical issue, have also served as the basis for hot political battles.

EXERCISE

11-1

a. Calculate the present value of a benefit of $5,000 received each year for three years. Assume a discount minus inflation rate of 1 percent, 2 percent, and 5 percent.

b. Calculate the present value of a benefit of $10,000 received each year for five years. Assume a discount minus inflation rate of 10 percent.

TABLE 11-6   Comparing Benefits by Discount Rates

DISCOUNT RATE LESS INFLATION (PERCENT)	SITE 1	SITE 2	SITE 3
10%	−$2.31	$1.37	$3.07
5	− 1 .26	3.49	3.94
3	− .79	4.44	4.35
0	0	6.00	5.00
−3	.89	7.75	5.73

Note: Figures for the sites are in $ millions.

Figure 11-1   Sensitivity Analysis of Differing Inflation and Discount Rates

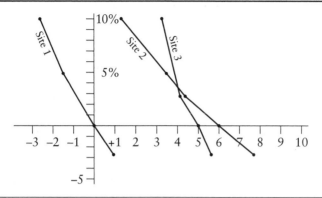

*Horizontal axis = Benefit levels.
Vertical axis = Discount rate less inflation rate.

5. **Costs borne by others (externalities).** If you are an analyst for a public agency, you have an ethical and in most cases legal obligation to examine costs borne by others. Environmental impact statements, for example, are legally mandated requirements that assess some of these externalities. Costs borne by others may include such things as health care costs, damage to historical or otherwise valuable sites, damage to the environment, inconveniences from relocation, including destruction of community, neighborhood ties, and identity. How do you quantify these values?

One way cost-benefit analysts deal with these hard-to-quantify concepts is through a "willingness-to-pay" idea. That is, how much are people willing to pay to avoid a highway project that would destroy their community, or how much would people be willing to pay to save the snail darter? Willingness to pay to avoid the impact of a project then becomes a measure of one kind of cost (or a negative benefit) of a particular project. If the residents of one neighborhood are willing to pay $1 million to save their community from a proposed mental health site, but the residents near another site would only be willing to pay $100,000, then a measure of those relative alternatives should be included in a cost-benefit calculation.

The practical problem is how we measure this willingness to pay. It must not be "can afford to pay." But still willingness to pay is a slippery concept. You could survey appropriate neighborhood residents. In our opinion, however, the kinds of responses you would get are not easily quantifiable. And whose views does one assess when discussing the preservation of a snail darter? All citizens of the United

States? All biologists? Those in the area benefiting from a dam project that will eradicate the snail darter? Differing degrees of willingness to pay will emerge, depending on the group sampled, and it is not clear which is the appropriate group. If the public does not value the snail darter or a historical site, does that mean they should not be preserved? Again these questions quickly return to the area of values rather then quantification.

Still, doing cost-benefit analysis should at least alert you to the interests involved in alternative choices. The analyst can present in descriptive, non-quantified terms the additional costs of alternative projects. If one site for a proposed mental health center will lead to the destruction of a historic old building, this should be indicated and its implications discussed even if a dollar figure cannot be placed on its value.

6. **Revenues as benefits.** It should be relatively easy to estimate revenues for alternative sites. In this example, you would want to calculate the likely patient load for each site as well as any difference in charges that each site might be able to levy. In other instances revenues might include service fees, admission charges, tuition, sales, and so on.

7. **Other benefits.** The calculation of benefits might be as difficult as calculating costs. Here you might want to examine the relative impact of each potential site in relieving patient loads at residential mental institutions. Then, too, you would want to consider relative benefits brought about by improved mental health to each alternative community. You should also consider the relative economic benefit of building and opening state institutions in each alternative community. As with costs, some benefits may, in the end, not really be quantifiable but can be carried along in descriptive form. For an example of a cost-benefit analysis, see Research in Practice 11A.

Benefits, Costs, and Risk

Assessing risk is an additional complication of cost-benefit analysis. Some analyses will include a risk factor in calculating costs and benefits. This means that there is formal consideration of the probabilities that a potential cost or benefit will occur. For a simple example, in estimating patient revenue at a mental health facility, suppose the anticipated income is $5 million but that the figure is uncertain. An analyst estimates there is a 70 percent chance of the income being $5 million a year, a 25 percent chance of it being $4 million, and a 5 percent chance of it being $6 million. Therefore it would be somewhat daring to include $5 million per year as a net benefit. There is a risk that it could be substantially less. One way to handle this is through sensitivity analysis discussed above. Another way is to estimate probable income by multiplying each projected income by its probability and summing:

$5 million × 70% = $3.5 million

$4 million × 25% = $1.0 million

$6 million × 5% = $ .3 million

= $4.8 million

Thus a conservative estimate of the patient revenue would not be $5 million but rather $4.8 million. Even though $5 million is the most likely outcome, $4.8 million takes into account the substantial probability that the income will be less and the small probability it will be more.

Thus risk assessment is another of the reasons that cost-benefit analysis can yield widely varying results. Even though estimates of probabilities of events can differ greatly, you should include an estimation of risk. For example, estimates of the net benefits of nuclear power plants that did not take into account the risks and costs of shutdown and the reluctance of investors to invest in nuclear power plants greatly overestimated the net benefits of those operations.

Cost and Benefit Figures— What Do You Do with Them?

Assume you have calculated the costs and benefits for three alternative sites. What you do now depends on the problem at hand. Assume your calculations resulted in something like Table 11-7.

Remember that, other things being equal, you should choose the site with the greatest net benefit, in this case site 3. But what if there were constraints on costs, as there usually are? Assume you could not go ahead with any project whose costs were more than $1 million. This eliminates site 3 and leads to a choice between sites 1 and 2. Site 2 is the obvious choice. Let's assume that the cost limits were $.5 million. In this case only site 1 would qualify. However, site 1 has a negative net benefit, so doing nothing (net benefit of 0) would be preferable to choosing site 1.

TABLE 11-7   **Comparing Net Benefits**

	SITE 1	SITE 2	SITE 3
Costs	$.5	$1.0	$1.5
Benefits	.25	1.5	3.0
Net benefit	−.25	.5	1.5

Note: Figures are in $ millions.

Research in Practice 11A

Cost-Benefit Analysis

Most communities offer generous financial incentives to businesses considering locating in the community. They do so because they believe that these businesses will bring considerable financial benefit to the community. Two researchers were concerned that overzealous politicians and city administrators often overestimate the benefits and underestimate the costs of such programs. They use a hypothetical example to illustrate how net benefits can be grossly exaggerated in such a situation.

Their hypothetical, albeit typical, situation illustrates the case of a financial incentive package to lure a new hotel chain into the community. In this scenario, the city estimated costs to be $2.9 million in improvements to the site and $1.8 million for a ten-year abatement of property taxes. Those supporting the project estimated that the present value of the net benefits exceeded present value of net costs by a whopping $232 million because of new jobs and tax revenue!

The authors argue that this estimate of net benefits was greatly exaggerated. Why? Because nine critical components were not considered or were mis-estimated.

1. How do the proposed tax incentives relate to broader economic development strategies?

If the hotel project is a stand-alone deal and there is no attempt at broader economic development, the net benefits could be much less than expected.

2. How important is the tax incentive to the firm's investment?

The benefits may be over-estimated because the financial incentives might purely be a gift to a business already planning on coming into the community. Calculation of the benefits should include a probability that the incentive led to a decision to locate. If the hotel already planned to move to the city, the benefits of the city's financial incentive is zero. We would rarely know for certain if the hotel had planned to move (it is in the hotel's interest not to reveal their plans if they want the financial incentives). But if the plan increased the probability that the business would locate from 50 to 100 percent, then costs and benefits should be multiplied by .5, reducing net benefits in this case from $234 million to $109.585 million.

3. Will the financial incentives generate new jobs or income for the region or redistribute jobs or income within the region?

Not all new employment or income by the hotel is net new employment or income to the community. For example, the hotel might draw business from existing hotels. This might cause job displacement so that the actual number of jobs created would be much less. The authors estimated that it would likely be 480, not the city's estimate of 600.

4. Will the incentive generate new jobs for local residents or for in-migrants?

Generally new businesses bring in employees from outside. These new employees and their families will bring new costs to the city, e.g., increased school enrollment. To the extent that new migrants come to the community, the costs of public services to them must be balanced against the new revenue they bring.

5. To what extent will the new jobs generate net income for workers?

Many workers for the hotel would already be employed. The city calculated the net income increase as though all people were previously unemployed. The authors' calculations reduced income benefits from $14.550 million to $1.527 million.

6. What is the duration of the tax incentive compared to the likely duration of the investment?

Sometimes the business may not last beyond the ten-year tax abatement period so the city will never collect taxes from the business as originally expected. The analyst must consider the probabilities of the business folding or leaving before ten years.

7. Are the proper multiplier and discounting numbers being used?

A consideration of the multiplier effect, i.e., the impact of the business on suppliers and service providers, generally expands employment and income benefits. The authors recommend a conservative multiplier that takes into consideration special circumstances such as the size and location of the city, as bigger cities tend to have a larger multiplier effect.

8. How will commitments associated with incentives be enforced?

The city must expend resources (and thus incur costs) to insure that the business lives up to its bargain.

9. How does the proposed project compare with possible alternatives?

It is important to consider how the tax money could have been used elsewhere to serve the same public goals. This is an opportunity cost.

After considering all of these questions in their cost-benefit analysis, and making appropriate adjustments in the estimates, the authors estimated that there would only be $5.352 million in present value net benefits instead of the original $238 million, a huge difference.

Source: Michael D. Oden and Elizabeth Mueller, "Distinguishing Development Incentives from Developer Giveaways: A Critical Guide for Development Practitioners and Citizens," *Policy Studies Journal* (1999): 147–164.

There are other ways of using cost-benefit analysis to make choices. Suppose the state could absorb costs of $5 million and your task was to maximize the net benefits accruing from these costs. Assume the choices in Table 11-8.

At which site or sites would you build given the $5 million cost limitation? We want to maximize net benefits while not exceeding $5 million. We can choose site 4 and site 6, the two with maximum net benefits and with costs totaling $4.5 million. After that, the two projects with the next greatest net benefit (3 and 5) both exceed the $.5 million cost allowance remaining. Only projects 1 and 2 each fall within the necessary cost range. Since project 1 has a

TABLE 11-8   Comparing Net Benefits with Cost Limitation

Site	Benefit	Cost	Net benefit
1	$ .25	$ .5	$−.25
2	.75	.5	.25
3	1.50	1.0	.50
4	3.00	1.5	1.50
5	2.00	1.5	.50
6	6.00	3.0	3.00

Note: Figures are in $ millions.

TABLE 11-9   Costs and Benefits of Different Project Scales

Number of beds	Cost ($ millions)	Benefit ($ millions)	Net Benefit
25	$ 4	$ 3.5	−$ .5
50	7	8.0	1.0
75	10	12.0	2.0
100	13	16.0	3.0
150	16	20.0	4.0
200	20	23.0	3.0
250	24	26.5	2.5

negative benefit, project 2 is chosen. Thus we can build sites 2, 4, and 6 and have a net benefit of $4.75 million. You can examine other possible combinations and see that none exceed $4.75 million net benefit while staying within the $5 million cost limit.

Sometimes you may want to use cost-benefit analysis to examine the net benefits of different project scales. Suppose you were considering building a cancer treatment hospital of different sizes. Assume further that the cost was not an important factor. Given the figures in Table 11-9, which size would you build?

The net benefit increases until it peaks at 150 beds, where the net benefit is $4 million. It then decreases as the number of beds continues to increase. A graphic illustration of this process is sometimes useful.

Figure 11-2 shows that the net benefits are curvilinear; that is, they increase up to 150 beds, then fall after that. Even though the total benefits keep increasing, their payoff in terms of increasing net benefits diminishes as costs increase faster than benefits. Perhaps after 150 beds, the capacity of the hospital has exceeded the demand, or the scale of operation becomes more expensive. These outcomes are intuitively plausible and are captured by the idea of "diminishing returns."

Whether you are assessing the possibility of multiple sites or the possibilities of different scales of projects, remember you are trying to maximize the net benefit, either with or without constraints on the cost level.[9]

AND BACK TO THE FIRE DEPARTMENT PLANNER

In pursuing his directive to make recommendations for a fire station based on cost-benefit and other appropriate criteria, the fire department planner has collected the information in Table 11-10.

FIGURE 11-2   **Benefits and Costs of Different Project Scales**

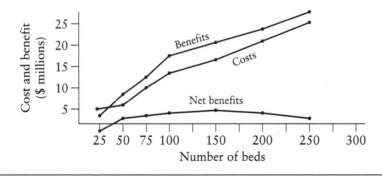

[9] Sometimes cost-benefit analysis is discussed in terms of cost-benefit ratios, but that is incorrect. The ratio is highly dependent on whether you label certain factors as "negative benefits" or "costs." You should choose the alternative with the highest net benefit regardless of cost-benefit ratios. See Stokey and Zeckhauser, *A Primer,* p. 146.

Research in Practice 11B

COST-BENEFIT ESTIMATES WITH SENSITIVITY ANALYSES

Several researchers undertook a cost-benefit analysis of the Voyageurs National Park. The analysis was designed to assess the impact of the park on the local community, the state of Minnesota, and the rest of the nation. Their study focused specifically on the economic impact and the impact on regional development rather than on environmental quality or social well being.

In order to construct an economic analysis, the researchers used a model whereby travel costs to the park were used as a proxy for the market price of the recreation experience at the park. That is, the amount people would pay to travel to the park was a surrogate measure of the benefits to them. So the benefits were estimated taking into account projected visitors to the park and their costs to arrive there (driving costs, food, and lodging). Benefits also included spending by tourists and by new park employees.

The researchers estimated the costs in the cost-benefit question directly; these consisted of the purchase and development costs for the park, operation and management costs, and some proportion of highway improvement costs on those highways serving the park (they estimated only one-third of that cost was due to the park itself). Other costs included additional police, sewer, and health facilities in the adjacent communities caused by increased tourism and the additional transportation costs to local lumber processors having to bring in lumber from greater distances.

The fire department planner figures the benefits as being property saved from fire destruction by the location of a fire station at each particular site. This figure could depend on the value of property near the site, the distance of the fire equipment from other sites (which would allow some measure of response time), and the fire proneness of each area, based on past experience and the age and condition of the buildings. The planner also did a similar calculation for the value of human life saved.

TABLE 11-10   Costs and Benefits of Alternative Sites ($ millions)

STATION SITE	CONSTRUCTION	OPERATION	LAND ACQUISITION AND RELOCATION	BENEFITS	NET BENEFITS
1	3	4	6	15	2
2	4	4	3	17	6
3	3	4	10	20	3
4	5	4	4	18	5

The analysis was based on projected thirty-year costs and benefits. A discount rate of 6.9 was used, the cost of federal borrowing in 1974. The researchers also calculated projected costs and benefits at discount rates of 3.4 and 10.3. We can see, however, that some of these rates were unrealistic in light of the high interest rates of the late 1970s and early 1980s. Such is the benefit of hindsight.

The researchers calculated net benefits at three different projected attendance levels, and for each attendance level, net benefits were computed for each of the three discount rates. The overall effects were positive in each case, with the highest net benefits under conditions of low discount rates and high attendance. When a decreased projection of visitors from other parts of the nation relative to local visitors was assumed in combination with assumptions of low attendance overall and high discount rates, a small negative benefit resulted. In all other cases, benefits were positive. The importance of the discount rate can be noted by the fact that at a given assumed attendance level, net benefits varied by as much as $500 million, depending on the discount rate assumed. Of course if more realistic discount rates had been used, the variation would have been even greater.

A strong point of the paper is that it made very explicit the assumptions on which the benefits and costs were calculated and presented alternative scenarios based on changes in the assumptions.

SOURCE: Allan S. Mills, Joseph G. Massey, Hans M. Gregersen, "Benefit-Cost Analysis of Voyageurs National Park," *Evaluation Review*, December 1980, pp. 715–38.

The planner calculated that site 2 had the greatest net benefits—$6 million. Site 4, with a net benefit of 5, was second. Before recommending site 2, the planner made the following observations: neither site 2 nor site 4 had a disproportionately negative impact on various ethnic or income groups in the area, the community resistance to locating a fire station at either site 2 or 4 was minimal since neither was in the immediate vicinity of a residential area, and there would be no exceptionally negative environmental impacts (beyond those normally associated with a fire station) at either location. The planner therefore recommended site 2 as being the best bargain for the city.

SUMMARY

You have gleaned an overview of the problems and possibilities of cost-benefit analysis. Remember that while cost-benefit analysis can be a useful tool, it is not the only way of examining a problem. Remember, too, that the seemingly

Research in Practice 11C

COSTS AND BENEFITS OF ERADICATING MEASLES

How much has the United States benefited from the eradication of measles (rubella) compared to the cost of an eradication program conducted by the U.S. Public Health Service? This question was asked by a researcher evaluating the effect of this vaccination program.

The costs of the program included the cost of each vaccination, estimated to be around $3 per dose. This included the costs of production, distribution, and administration of the vaccine, as well as costs of publicizing the program. Over a nine-year period, the total cost to the federal government was around $108.2 million.

Benefits included lives saved, cases of retardation averted, school days saved, physical and hospital days saved, years of normal and productive life saved from premature death and retardation. The researchers estimated cost savings for each of these aspects of disease prevention. Benefits for each averted case of measles were estimated at about $73. Unfortunately, however, no detail was provided as to the savings from each separate aspect of prevention of the disease.

Multiplying the estimated cost savings per case averted by the estimated number of cases averted yielded a total benefit of over $1.1 billion for the program. Thus benefits exceeded costs by around $900 million.

SOURCE: Robert Albritton, "Cost-Benefits of Measles Eradication: Effects of Federal Intervention," *Policy Analysis* 4 (Winter 1978) pp. 1–21.

"hard data" of cost-benefit analyses are based on very slippery estimates of the value of everything from human lives to interest rates. In examining and evaluating cost-benefit analysis done by others, you must discover and evaluate the value judgments that went into the estimates. What was undervalued? Overvalued? Omitted? Likewise when you are preparing your own cost-benefit analysis, be explicit about values assigned various factors. Used with care and common sense, cost-benefit analysis can be a useful tool in the policy analyst's package. It does help make explicit the kinds of costs and benefits accruing in each option under consideration. Whether it is worth the time and trouble can only be determined in each individual case. And used carelessly, cost-benefit analysis, like any other technique, can be highly misleading and even fraudulent. Because the final results (dollars of benefits) look so firm, it is incumbent on the policy analyst to exercise special care in using this form of analysis.

EXERCISES

11-2 Here are some costs and benefits of five alternative highway projects.

	COST*	BENEFIT*
Filippelli Road	5	6
Lombra Tollway	4	10
Straka Bypass	2	4
Connelly Creek Drive	1	1
Fruit and Nut Express	7	13

*In millions

a. Which project has the greatest net benefit?
b. If there is no cost ceiling, which one road should be built?
c. If the budget limit is $7 million, which road(s) should be built?
d. If the budget limit is $5 million, which road(s) should be built?

11-3 A landfill is approaching the saturation point, and a new facility for handling the city's garbage must be found. You have three choices: (1) to buy and maintain another landfill, (2) to buy and construct a plant to burn the garbage but with capabilities of using the steam from that process to furnish energy for several city-owned buildings (cogeneration), and (3) to use a composting technology for the city garbage. From the table below, calculate the costs and benefits of each alternative.

	LAND PURCHASE	CONSTRUCTION	OPERATION	SALE OF ENERGY	OTHER BENEFITS	OTHER COSTS
Traditional landfill	$2.0	0	$10	0	$14	$1.0
Garbage cogeneration	.5	$10	$20	$25	14	.5
Composting	2.0	0	8	0	14	0

Note: Figures are in $ millions.

a. What are the costs and benefits of each project? Which option would you choose if: (1) Cost was not a constraint? (2) Start-up costs (land plus construction) could not exceed $5 million?
b. What are some of the factors to be considered in calculating "other benefits?" "Other costs?"
c. What else would you like to know before making a recommendation on the basis of these overall cost and benefit figures?

KEY TERMS

Cost-benefit analysis

Externalities

Pareto optimality

Sunk costs

Opportunity cost

Discount rates

Present values

Sensitivity analysis

FOR FURTHER HELP

Bingham, Richard, and Marcus Ethridge, eds. *Reaching Decisions in Public Policy and Administration.* New York: Longman, 1982. Contains three clear examples of cost-benefit analysis.

Fischhoff, Baruch. "Cost-Benefit Analysis and the Art of Motorcycle Maintenance." *Policy Sciences* 8 (1977), pp. 177–202. A thoughtful review of the advantages of cost-benefit analysis. Several good critiques of cost-benefit studies.

Hanke, Steve, and Richard Walker. "Benefit-Cost Analysis Reconsidered. An Evaluation of the Mid-State Project." *Water Resources Research* 10, no. 5 (1974), pp. 898–908. A critique of a cost-benefit analysis done by the Army Corps of Engineers but one with wider relevance to those contemplating using cost-benefit analysis.

Mishan, E. J. *Cost-Benefit Analysis: An Informal Introduction,* 4th edition. London: Routledge, 1988.

Stokey, Edith, and Richard Zeckhauser. *A Primer for Policy Analysis.* New York: W. W. Norton, 1978, especially chaps. 9 through 10. A usable and balanced introduction to the mechanics of cost-benefit analysis.

Thompson, Mark S. *Benefit-Cost Analysis for Program Evaluation.* New York: Russell Sage Foundation, 1980. A detailed how-to-do-it discussion by a "true believer."

Weimar, Leo, Aidan Vining and Alan Vining. *Policy Analysis.* New York: Prentice-Hall, 1998. Chapter 12 contains an explanation of cost-benefit anaylsis.

12

POLICY RESEARCH AND PUBLIC ORGANIZATIONS

By now we hope you are comfortable doing and reading about quantitative policy research, whether it be surveys, regression, or cost-benefit analysis. But a public policymaker must be more than a technician familiar with computers, statistics, and other quantitative paraphernalia.

The manager must be able to use information generated by policy research wisely in helping to make decisions. Indeed it would seem that the important deficiency in contemporary public life is not the absence of information; to the contrary, especially with the growth of the Internet and wireless technology, we are deluged with information. What appears to be lacking is people in decision-making positions who can combine that information with serious and thoughtful analyses of goals and means to achieve these goals. We have no easy or quick answers. What we hope to do in this chapter, however, is to stimulate your thinking about some important value and pragmatic considerations surrounding policy research and its use. We will give particular attention to ethical issues in policy research.

ETHICAL QUESTIONS IN POLICY RESEARCH

BIAS

In doing research there are certain ethical standards you should meet. There are canons of research ethics in most professions although none specifically drawn for policy researchers.[1] Your task is to conduct your research and report your findings as impartially and completely as possible. Your biases and assumptions should be made clear: There is nothing wrong in having a bias toward honesty and assuming that one goal of a program should be that it be administered free from corruption and discrimination. But you should make clear

---

[1]Several social science professional associations, such as the American Sociological Association and the American Psychological Association, have codes of ethics.

your aims and the trade-offs necessary to achieve them. Other types of personal biases of a partisan, class, or other parochial nature are not appropriate. Most will acknowledge that it is impossible to remove all of their bias, because their own personal values affect their perceptions of the entire question with which they are dealing. Nevertheless policy researchers must strive to analyze and report their findings fairly, stressing neither those aspects that confirm their prejudices nor those that do not.

Sometimes policy researchers are pressured to obtain findings about a program that confirm the prejudices of others higher in the bureaucracy or that are in tune with the ideological prejudices of the day. Or perhaps the funders of the project have a particular point of view.[2] Someone makes it clear that a "whitewash" or "hatchet job" is expected. If you are a researcher for an independent firm, you can, of course, refuse to enter into contracts where you believe that pressure will be exerted to obtain a particular outcome. But when you are an agency employee who is asked to conduct an in-house evaluation or analysis, you have fewer options. Obviously, as an ethical person, you would not alter data or write a report deliberately misinterpreting the findings. These kinds of activities are far beyond the pale of acceptability. If discovered, they could lead to your dismissal. Even if you are not fired, your reputation and that of your program would be severely damaged.

More commonly, however, researchers are faced with more subtle dilemmas. Do you include or omit some pieces of evidence that may run counter to the findings expected by your superiors, funding agency, or to the rest of the findings of your report? It might be easy to rationalize omissions, perhaps by saying that the report can't include everything. However it is your duty to try to give as fair and complete a picture of the program or the situation as possible. If the contrary information is important to understanding the program or issue being evaluated include it. If some decision makers choose to ignore part of the evidence, that is their right, but you will have done your job by presenting as accurate a picture as possible.

This is easier said than done in some cases. After all, it is your job, not ours, that will be at stake. It is little reassurance to be told that if you are a public employee your first responsibility is to the public and not to a particular set of officeholders. Often those officeholders determine your future. However in the long run, and in many cases even in the short run, neither the public nor the political decision makers are served by decisions based on inaccurate and incomplete information.

Adhering to ethical standards in reporting your research fairly and even-handedly is ultimately protection for you as well as for the agency and the public. It is certainly possible that your report may be leaked to the press, become public through a court suit or by means of the Freedom of Information Act, or

---

[2]An interesting discussion of such a potential situation is found in Barry Popkin, "Truth-in-Funding," in the King, et al book cited in the further help section. Popkin accepted funding from Nestle to study the relative impact of breast- and bottle-feeding among infants in Africa.

be used in a legislative or other investigation of the agency. In each of these cases, you may be put in a delicate situation. Your best protection is an honest and objective report.

Finally, it should go without saying (but we'll say it anyway) that you should avoid being put in a position of evaluating or analyzing programs where you have a conflict of interest. You should not attempt to evaluate programs run by a relative, friend, or close associate, or a program competing with that run by such associates. Having a financial interest at stake is also surely a conflict of interest. Even if you think you can be impartial (and maybe you can), the appearance of conflict of interest will discredit both your report and the program itself.

HUMAN SUBJECTS

If you are working from information on individuals (such as client records), carrying out surveys or interviews, or working with animals, you must consider ethical questions concerning the use of these subjects. We would hope that any policy researcher using human subjects or individual records would consider the issues raised in the Rivlin and Timpane, King, and Weisstub books listed at the end of this chapter. We will only highlight what we consider to be the major ethical and legal considerations in policy research with human subjects.

While codes of ethics for medical and biological research have been developed over a long period of time, the subject of ethics in social research is of more recent vintage. Within the past two decades, federal and many state agencies have adopted standards that must be met if researchers are to receive government research funding. In most reputable research institutions, including universities, similar standards are also applied to non-government funded research. These standards affect policy researchers as well as those in the biomedical fields. In accordance with federal regulations, all universities whose faculties submit research grants to the federal government have committees that review proposed procedures for dealing with human (and animal) subjects in research projects. These **human subjects reviews** give careful scrutiny to all research, federally funded or not, based on subjects.

While some object to these federal guidelines, the standards have come about partly because of the scientific community's past shameful abuses of human subjects. For example, in one research project persons infected with syphilis were not treated but put into a control group. Yet these men were led to believe they were receiving treatment or did not need treatment. It is generally assumed that these persons were treated this way because they were poor African Americans living in the South at a time when human rights for African Americans was not a subject of widespread concern.[3] In another study, women

---

[3]The examples here were drawn from Rivlin and Timpane, p. 2, cited at the end of the chapter. A book has been written on the syphilis experiment, James Jones, *Bad Blood: The Tuskegee Syphilis Experiment,* (New York: Free Press, 1981).

were led to believe they were receiving birth control pills, when in fact they were only taking placebos. Consequently, many became pregnant when they did not wish to do so. So even flagrant abuses of human subjects are not events that occur only in other, less democratic countries.

While the most shameful examples are those of biomedical researchers, where the probabilities of creating harm are great, some social scientists have also used questionable methods in treating human subjects. Stanley Milgram's studies (which demonstrated the obedience of most people to authority by showing that people are willing to administer electric "shocks" to other human subjects when told to do so by an authority figure) are one example of a widely criticized social science study. The fact that the "shocks" were not really given and the supposedly agonized victim was a confederate of the researcher did little to diminish criticism that the subjects (those encouraged to give the "shocks") were treated badly.

A second example of a widely criticized study is Laud Humphrey's identification and later interviewing of men engaged in homosexual activities in a public washroom. In this case Humphrey took down the car license numbers of men entering the washroom and obtained identification through that means. In a somewhat different vein, the issue of confidentiality surfaced in what has come to be called the "Springdale" case. Arthur Vidich, part of a larger research team at Cornell University, was assigned as a participant observer to an upstate New York community (Springdale, a pseudonym). Vidich lived in the community for two and a half years making and recording observations on the people in the town. He later published a book, *Small Town in Mass Society*; and although he did not identify individuals in the community by name, it was possible to identify the individuals. This violated a pledge to the community of anonymity. Also, unflattering references to individuals and what has been described as a particular "tone" to the book has had, according to some townspeople, an upsetting and disturbing effect. The issues generated quite an exchange among those involved and other research professionals.[4]

A final example concerns an American anthropologist doing field work in China in the early 1980s. After leaving China he published without consent pictures of Chinese women having abortions, thus violating their rights of privacy and possibly even exposing them to retribution or punishment by the Chinese government.

Federal regulations regarding the use of human subjects are not very stringent when the subjects are being used for most kinds of surveys or interviews, when they are being observed in their public behavior, or when the social scientist is using already published data. With survey or document research, the researcher must make special assurances of confidentiality when individual responses can be detected, when the subjects' responses might place them in

---

[4]Arthur Vidich and Joseph Bensman, *Small Town in Mass Society*, Princeton, N.J.: Princeton University Press, especially Chap. 14

jeopardy of criminal or civil liability, or when the research focuses on particularly sensitive areas of behavior (sexual behavior, drug and alcohol abuse, or deviant behavior). In those situations assurances of confidentiality must pass a human subjects' review.

The major consideration in dealing with human subjects is that they must have the right of **informed consent**. That is, subjects in your policy research must be able to choose whether they want to participate or not, and they must be able to do so on the basis of a good knowledge of the benefits and costs of participation. This does not mean that you must tell a potential subject every detail about your project. But he or she does have the right to know what possible harm or benefit can come from your project and the probability of this harm or benefit occurring. Obviously this was sadly lacking in the extreme examples above. In many cases little harm can come to your subjects: most public opinion surveys, if they are done by professionals, yield little risk. Yet they usually offer little gain for those who are participating. Sometimes these subjects are paid if the questionnaire is lengthy. Most often there is only the promise of some vague public benefit if the researcher can find out more about health needs, crime rates, and so forth. In survey research, therefore, you should assure the individual of the confidentiality of the response and tell them in general what you are trying to accomplish.

In experimental research there may be more possibility of both risk and benefit. This should be clearly outlined. Furthermore, in both survey and experimental research, it must be made clear to the participant that he or she has a right to withdraw from the research at any time, and the conditions of the withdrawal should be explained (that is, if money is involved, how much if any will be paid, assurances of no retribution, and so forth). The respondent should also be told of the responsibility that the researcher will take if harm does occur. In other words, the respondent should have the information that a reasonable person would need in making an informed judgment about the potential benefits and risks of participation.

There are further complications when the potential participants are children, or of low intelligence, or are institutionalized. Special care is necessary in these cases so that the researcher does not take unfair advantage of those not fully capable of protecting themselves. Previously, prison populations were used for experiments that threatened their health and well being,[5] and notorious cases of experimenting on residents of homes for retarded children brought about calls for strict regulation of experiments on children.[6] Federal regulations place stricter guidelines on using these groups of people in research than is the case with noninstitutionalized adults of normal intelligence.

---

[5]Allan Hornblum, *Acres of Skin*, New York: Routledge, 1998.

[6]Jeremy Sugarman, *Beyond Consent*, New York: Oxford University Press, 1998. See especially the article by Robert Nelson, "Children as Research Subjects," pp. 47–66.

Another consideration is confidentiality. You must not only promise to protect confidentiality, you must do so. Staff must be trained to respect the confidentiality of any records or interviews they see. The violation of confidentiality must be treated as a serious offense, subjecting the offender to dismissal from the project. It is important to make clear to those handling individual records that confidentiality is to be protected, and therefore individual responses are never linked to any information that might reveal the person's identity. Confidentiality is a particular problem when you are collecting data that in some way can be used in court and thus be subject to subpoena. Behavior involving crimes is one example, and collections of data on divorced people are another. One way to protect confidentiality is to remove identifying information from your data file so no link can be made between information and specific people. In a longitudinal study where you wish to reinterview subjects and add information to the file, you will need to maintain some identifying particulars, but those should be kept in a secure place with only a code number to link them to the data file.

A final ethical problem concerns those people who are not your subjects yet who are affected by your research. These people have rights, too, so consider carefully whether your research might have adverse affects on others besides the immediate subjects of your study who are covered by the guidelines referred to above. If so, these others must be given the right to consent or to refuse consent. Certainly the nuclear testing done in the 1940s and 1950s affected many people who lived near the sites of the nuclear explosions. But they were never given information that would have allowed them to make an informed judgment about the risks of staying in the affected areas. (Some of the risks were not even realized at the time.) Consequently, cancer caused an abnormally high percentage of deaths of those residents. While social science research does not have the same impact as nuclear blasts, you should carefully consider the possible impact of your research on others beyond your sample.

COMPETENCE

If you are not competent to undertake some part of a research task, get help and consultation from someone who is. There is no disgrace in being ignorant of some portions of the research enterprise. Complex research projects require people with many different specialized skills. It's a waste of time and money to plunge ahead in ignorance hoping that things will come out all right. They usually don't. A survey based on a poor sample is worthless. Poorly designed questionnaires will not obtain needed information. Incomplete or misguided statistical analysis may lead to spurious and erroneous results. So it is incumbent on you to recognize your limitations and seek help where needed. If you are concerned (as you must be) about the quality of the final product, the end result will justify the extra expense.

Similarly, if you are hiring an individual or group to undertake policy analysis or evaluation, examine their credentials carefully. Beware of the many people and firms who claim to be policy researchers but who are trained in (for example) mechanical engineering with little record of training or expertise in policy analysis. In contracting policy research to an outside firm, examine very carefully the training and qualifications of each of their professional staff. Get the names of all those clients (or a large subset) for whom they have done policy research. Then contact those former clients to obtain an assessment of the quality and timeliness of their work. Get copies of previous reports so you and your staff can evaluate them too. There are a lot of quacks in this field, and as of now, there are few means aside from buyer caution and education to regulate them. So caveat emptor.

REPORTING YOUR RESEARCH

CONTENTS OF A RESEARCH REPORT

Writing a report is the most difficult part of research for some people. Yet, you can make the task simpler and perhaps make it seem more "doable" if you think of the report in terms of several separate pieces, each of them fairly small but essential to the overall report. Whether you are reporting on a policy or program evaluation, or another kind of policy analysis, your report should contain the following information:

1. **Executive summary.** Provide a one- or two-page summary of the major procedures, findings, and recommendations of your project written for executives or legislators who may never get past this brief synopsis.
2. **Introduction.** What is the problem or issue you are addressing, and why is it significant? A sentence or two may briefly describe your project in its most general form. For example: In 1999 this state passed a seatbelt law. Opponents have argued that the law has had little impact on traffic fatality rates, while advocates of the new law disagree. Responding to criticisms of the law, the 2001 session of the Legislature commissioned an impact study to determine just what the effect of the seatbelt law has been. This report of that study uses information on traffic fatalities and miles driven in this state since 1985 to assess the impact of seatbelt laws.
3. **Program description and literature review.** In a policy analysis or evaluation, you will want to describe thoroughly the main features of the program or policy being evaluated at an early point in the study. This will give your readers a clear (though brief) picture of the history and workings of the program. In describing the seatbelt policy, for example, you would want to note when it was passed, how it is being enforced, how many people have been arrested or cited for violating it, estimates of compliance with the law, and other features useful to readers in understanding the program.

It may be that you will want to summarize briefly other research on programs like the one you are evaluating. A review of impact studies in other states would help set the stage for your study. You will also want to summarize any previous research on the specific program you are evaluating. Thus, if anyone else has examined the impact of seatbelt use in your state, describe the study and its findings. Policy research that focuses on a general problem, for example, "What can we do to reduce the use of cocaine among young people?" should definitely summarize the earlier research and then show how your work goes beyond it or extends it to your specific setting.

If appropriate, you may wish to present formal hypotheses in this section. If no formal hypotheses are being tested, you may want to suggest what your expectations are in terms of the important questions being analyzed.

4. **Data and methods.** In this section describe the nature of your study. Elements such as the units of analysis, the time the study was done, the nature of the data and from where it was obtained, the variables used in the study and how they were measured, and the statistical procedures employed should be clearly described. If regression or other multivariate analyses were done, you should report on how each variable was coded (e.g., age is measured in years; income is coded in $1,000 dollar increments; religion is measured by a series of dummy variables, including Protestant, Catholic, Jewish, and others, with other the omitted category). You should also outline how missing data were handled. If scales are used, discuss how they were created, and append a list of items used in the scales.

5. **Findings.** What are the major findings of your study? Show the results of the test of your major hypotheses or issues. Present the research results and public organizations in well-chosen and well-designed tables with proper labels. Do not present cross-tabulations of every variable by every other variable, but focus on the relationships that are central to your study. Usually this means the relationships of key independent variables to your dependent variables, rather than relationships among independent variables.

The findings section should proceed logically from the statement of the problem and the hypotheses in the earlier section. You should not overburden the reader with tables; instead present only those revealing your most important findings. The major findings from the tables should be discussed in the text, so that a reader who is table-shy can understand your findings without reading the tables. However, it is not necessary to explain every detail of each table in the text. This is a cure for insomnia, and will send your readers to dreamland or to the wastebasket. Describe the major patterns, and let those who enjoy examining tables for minutiae do so.

6. **Conclusions and recommendations.** In this section, briefly summarize your key findings, and proceed to recommendations that might be derived from these findings. Each recommendation should be linked to the evidence from which it flows, so that the reader can see how you arrived at your judgments. It is often a good idea to explore alternative recommendations rather than advocating one set. You could phrase these recommendations in an "if-then" form: "If the Legislature directs the governor to enforce the seatbelt law more strictly, then we can expect the following:" Or, "If the seatbelt law is rescinded, these are the likely consequences." You are using the empirical data you have analyzed to provide evidence for likely outcomes of alternative policy changes.

WRITING THE REPORT

In writing a research report, indeed any report, you should strive to make your writing both clear and lively. Clarity is achieved by axing redundant words and phrases, and eliminating words and phrases with little meaning. Instead of saying "It can be seen that seatbelts are effective," say "Seatbelts are effective." Instead of "And now let us move to our second point which is . . . " say "Our second point is. . . ." While it is essential to use "although," "but," or "however" to provide exceptions to generalizations, an overabundance of such words makes for a wearisome journey through your prose. Careful editing of several drafts with an eye toward chopping excess words can greatly improve your writing.

Eliminate "bureaucratese" wherever possible. We mean verbs made from nouns or adjectives, such as "the study impacted" or "the researchers finalized." Do not add "wise" to a word to mean "regarding" for example, "genderwise, no differences were found." Purge yourself of these ugly habits (and amuse yourselves by finding where we have slipped up in this book). Effective organization will also add to clarity. One idea should be fully developed before others are introduced. Sentences and paragraphs should flow logically one from the other without jumping among topics. The introduction of the report should set out guideposts, alerting the reader to what is coming. Make a conscious effort to make your writing lively. It will be so if you use examples and anecdotes to illustrate your points. Well-chosen anecdotes focus the reader's attention. The active voice (I interviewed all employees of the battered women's shelter) usually makes for a livelier style than the passive voice (all employees of the battered women's shelter were interviewed by me), and usually is less wordy. Unfortunately, the academic prose style tends heavily toward the passive, but if you are conscious of the distinction you can construct many active sentences. Both clarity and liveliness can be improved by avoiding technical jargon in your paper. Explain statistical techniques in clear English, not in a way that only another expert can understand. Remember that you want your report to be read and understood by administrators or policymakers who are not specialists in your field.

Beyond being clear and lively, a good report should be trustworthy. Facts should be backed up with evidence or citations to other work. You should not withhold evidence or analyses that do not agree with your overall argument or major points. Acknowledge alternative views about the program or issue. And finally, acknowledge the limitations of your study: evidence that couldn't be found, documents that you were not allowed to see, time and resource limitations that diminished your sample size, area studied, longitudinal perspective, or whatever.

USING POLICY RESEARCH IN POLICYMAKING

Jerome Murphy has provided a summary of the questions that policy researchers should ask themselves as the research is completed.[7]

The first four summarize our discussion so far:

1. Is the research valid?
2. Is the research trustworthy?
3. Is the research fair? Does it protect subjects and clients and conform to high ethical standards?
4. Is the report well-written?
5. Is the report useful? Is it timely and responsive to the needs of the intended audience?

It is to these questions of usefulness that we will now turn.

POLICYMAKING AS POLITICS

Ultimately public decision making is a political process. The research and reports, the analyses and options discussed at the lower- and middle-levels of agencies eventually work themselves up, in some form, to those responsible for making decisions. This is often a frustrating process for the policy researchers because the information put together at one level becomes simplified or distorted at another. Perhaps the most rational (from the point of view of the researcher) options for dealing with a problem are discarded, and others are emphasized. Or perhaps policy research done for one purpose is being used for another, possibly less relevant one.

But in a democracy (indeed in most any complex society), decision making is based on give and take, on compromise, and on the basis of an evaluation of what can be adopted and what will work. Thus, policy analysis—collection

---

[7]Murphy is cited at the end of the chapter.

and analysis of information, the discussion and analysis of alternatives—is only a starting point in policymaking, not an ending point. Well-done policy analysis should influence the course of debate over an issue, but it cannot determine the outcome of that debate. Nor would most of us want it to. We often look with disdain on policymakers or politicians with their shortsighted emphasis on surviving the next election by pandering to the lowest common denominator of public opinion. But what is the alternative? Do we want important policy decisions made by managers in public bureaucracies based on the latest policy research and technology? We think most would say no. Politicians may be shortsighted, but there is no guarantee that omnipotent bureaucrats would be any less so. And politicians can be retired more easily than bureaucrats.

INFLUENCING THE PROCESS

So, given a situation where decisions are made in the political arena, the policy researcher can only hope to have a positive influence on these decisions. While there is no sure procedure for ensuring that the analyst will be influential, he or she can proceed in a way to maximize that influence.

First, the analyst should work with those who have commissioned the study to find out what kind of information is being sought. What kinds of information and analysis are most useful? Sometimes this will be made clear when the contract is signed or the work assignment given, but that is not always the case. Even if it is, the analyst should keep in touch so that the persons who will utilize the study are made aware of the procedures used, have input at appropriate points, and are kept informed as to what the outcomes of the study are likely to be. For example, if a survey is being conducted, those commissioning the study should be given a chance to say what kinds of questions should be asked to provide information most useful to them.

Second, the report should be written clearly, in jargon-free language, as we have noted. If it is too technical or poorly written, it is guaranteed a fast and permanent trip to the filing cabinet.

Third, the report should contain a discussion of possible solutions to problems found. The pros and cons of each solution should be fully discussed, even when the analyst knows that the group commissioning the study already favors one particular solution. A full and balanced discussion is necessary even under those circumstances because, for example, it may be that certain other alternatives have not yet been considered, or it may be that the presentation of pros and cons of other alternatives would help in future debate. The feasibility of adoption and implementation should be considered in these pros and cons.

It is important to produce a preliminary report and to discuss it with those people most likely to use the final report. At the early stage the analyst can determine if there are important questions not dealt with. Is there additional information or interpretative material that could make the report more useful to the likely users?

Fourth, the analyst should try to make the final report in person to individuals or groups rather than just mailing it. By a personal summary, the analyst can answer questions, defend conclusions, and discuss questions of feasibility. Further, the analyst can help educate the users of the report about the general techniques used and why they are appropriate. A personal report and follow-up make it more difficult to simply relegate the report to a file. They also make it possible for clarifications to be requested, and given where necessary. Thus the process becomes one of give and take, with the analyst trying to produce a report that will actually be used.

Of course there is no guarantee that the report will be used or taken seriously despite the best efforts of the policy researcher. All too often, however, some of the fault for this neglect lies with the researcher: In many cases the researcher considers the work done when the final report is mailed, and then devotes little effort to follow-up. Likewise, the user should realize that if a draft report does not contain information expected or information that will be useful, he or she should negotiate with the analyst to get what is needed and not simply shrug in resignation and write off the expense of producing the study.

Our suggestions are based on our own experiences and those of others. But some researchers have tried to examine systematically how to facilitate the use of policy research. One such study found that there were certain conditions that did seem to promote its use by policymakers.[8] These include:

1. In-house research is more likely to be used than contracted research or research by independent firms.
2. Projects guided by a steering committee of researchers, sponsors, and research consumers tended to be utilized more than those without such a committee.
3. Research where the researcher plays a larger role in formulating the problem is more used than where the researcher is just a data collector.
4. Research that sheds some light on underlying causes of a problem was more used than that merely describing a problem.
5. Research that is timely from the user's point of view, that is presented in brief and non-technical language, and that is presented to a variety of decision makers at different points in the research process (as we have discussed) also was used more than work not meeting these requirements.

These findings buttress our own recommendations about the necessity of working closely with those who are contracting and using the research so as to maximize its impact. Doing all of this will not guarantee success in making policy

---

[8]The following is summarized from Mark van de Vall and Cheryl Bolas, "The Utilization of Social Policy Research: An Empirical Analysis of its Structure and Contents" (Paper presented at the seventy-fourth annual meeting of the American Sociological Association, 1979, Boston).

analysis part of the decision process. But it will go a long way with decision makers who sincerely want and need information about policy alternatives.

RESEARCH AND THE RESEARCH ENTERPRISE: A NOTE ON PERSPECTIVE

Before closing this chapter, we want to place the research enterprise (statistical analyses and decision-making strategies) in perspective. Both can be useful tools for arriving at answers to important questions. However they do not guarantee answers, let alone correct answers. Public managers, particularly those recruited from nonacademic backgrounds or those with little research experience, introduced to research for the first time, may forget this. Ours is a call not to be overly enamored with the research enterprise. Guard against being taken in or overwhelmed by the language and procedures of research or decision-making schemes. While research performed by reputable scholars is to be taken seriously, the mere fact of reputation is not justification for abandoning a questioning and skeptical mind. We would also encourage a more reasoned response to your own research. Don't be so parochial as to believe your own research is infallible, covering all the issues and providing all the answers. Here, too, we need a thoughtful and reasoned approach. Managers and analysts should balance respect for what research can do with recognition of its limitations.

AND FINALLY

As we noted in the beginning, some of you are current and future policy evaluators and analysts. We hope that by now you have become familiar with the basic techniques we have discussed as well as aware of where you might need further assistance in carrying out a research project. Others of you will be direct consumers of quantitative policy analysis, supervising or contracting with those who do it. We hope that by now you are better-informed consumers, able to evaluate the quality of research proposals and reports submitted to you. Still others of you are less direct consumers, perhaps reading about policy studies, public opinion polls, and other quantitative reports in the newspapers and trying to analyze the reliability of these reports. We hope that you, too, are more sophisticated consumers than before, able to raise the right questions and challenge invalid conclusions. Whatever your role, we believe that the ability to understand quantitative methods will be even more important than before to a wide variety of people. We say this not because we believe people should rely solely on the answers quantitative methods provide, but because the understanding will permit more thoughtful and knowledgeable criticism of information based on poor methods and assumptions and wiser use of research that is well done.

EXERCISES

12-1 Joe Sloe is hired to conduct an evaluation of a rape victim counseling program. He decides to use a quasi-experimental design. His experimental group includes women who have been raped and who use the rape counseling service. He measures their mental health, attitudes toward men, and other indicators of emotional well being when they first arrive at the counseling service, then after they complete the counseling. As a control group, Sloe obtains police records of reported rapes and the women filing complaints. He compiles a list of these names and interviews them one week after the rape and twelve weeks later in order to match the interval that occurs in pre- and post-test information of the women who go through the counseling service. In order that those in the control group not be suspicious of the interview, he does not inform them that he is evaluating the success of a rape counseling program or even that he knows they were raped. Rather, he leads them to believe that they are part of a random community survey on some other issue. Nevertheless he obtains the same sort of health information on them as he does on his experimental group.

What issues in research ethics are involved here? If you were to review this research plan, how would you respond? What suggestions might you make to improve the plan?

12-2 Ruth Less is conducting a large-scale evaluation of an experimental chemotherapy and psychotherapy treatment for disturbed children. The treatment has been shown to be very effective in limited previous evaluations. In order to measure the program's effectiveness, she decides to use an experimental design. She randomly divides children who come into the treatment center into experimental and control groups. The control groups do not get the new treatment but get placebo medication and traditional counseling. Parents and children are not informed that a new treatment is available for fear they may demand access to it. Some parents find out anyway and complain.

If you were the administrator of the treatment center, how would you respond to complaining parents? What are the issues here? What suggestions might you make to Ms. Less?

12-3 Diane Rigdon is hired by a state agency to conduct an evaluation of a local poverty program funded largely by state funds. In her evaluation she finds a substantial amount of waste and mismanagement. However the program has had some success, and Rigdon believes the program has great potential and that the current leadership is working hard to correct the management deficiencies. Because she knows that high officials in the state agency are out to "get" local poverty programs, she decides not to report to the state agency the waste and mismanagement fit because of the overall value of the program. Instead she provides these findings only to the officials of the local program.

What are the issues here? If you were Ms. Rigdon, how would you handle this issue? If you were her supervisor in the consulting firm, how would you deal with this problem?

KEY TERMS

Human subjects review

Informed consent

Executive summary

FOR FURTHER HELP

Caplovitz, David. *The Stages of Social Research*. New York: John Wiley & Sons, 1983.

King, Nancy M.P., Gail Henderson, and Jane Stein. *Beyond Regulations*. Chapel Hill: University of North Carolina Press, 1999.

Murphy, Jerome T. *Getting the Facts*. Santa Monica, Calif.: Goodyear Publishing, 1980, especially chap. 7.

Patton, Michael Q. *Utilization Focused Evaluation*. Beverly Hills, Calif.: Sage Publications, 1978.

Rivlin Alice M., and R Michael Timpane, eds. *Ethical and Legal Issues of Social Experimentation*. Washington, D.C.: Brookings Institution, 1975.

Rothman, Jack. *Using Research in Organizations*. Beverly Hills, Calif.: Sage Publications, 1978.

Sieber, Joan. *Planning Ethically Responsible Research*. Sage Publications, 1992.

Weisstub, David. *Research on Human Subjects: Ethics, Law, and Social Policy*. Oxford: Pergamon Press, 1998.

APPENDIXES

APPENDIX A
Random numbers

10097	32533	76520	13586	34673	54876	80959	09117	39292	74945
37542	04805	64894	74296	24805	24037	20636	10402	00822	91665
08422	68953	19645	09303	23209	02560	15953	34764	35080	33606
99019	02529	09376	70715	38311	31165	88676	74397	04436	27659
12807	99970	80157	36147	64032	36653	98951	16877	12171	76833
66065	74717	34072	76850	36697	36170	65813	39885	11199	29170
31060	10805	45571	82406	35303	42614	86799	07439	23403	09732
85269	77602	02051	65692	68665	74818	73053	85247	18623	88579
63573	32135	05325	47048	90553	57548	28468	28709	83491	25624
73796	45753	03529	64778	35808	34282	60935	20344	35273	88435
98520	17767	14905	68607	22109	40558	60970	93433	50500	73998
11805	05431	39808	27732	50725	68248	29405	24201	52775	67851
83452	99634	06288	98033	13746	70078	18475	40610	68711	77817
88685	40200	86507	58401	36766	67951	90364	76493	29609	11062
99594	67348	87517	64969	91826	08928	93785	61368	23478	34113
65481	17674	17468	50950	58047	76974	73039	57186	40218	16544
80124	35635	17727	08015	45318	22374	21115	78253	14385	53763
74350	99817	77402	77214	43236	00210	45521	64237	96286	02655
69916	26803	66252	29148	36936	87203	76621	13990	94400	56418
09893	20505	14225	68514	46427	56788	96297	78822	54382	14598
91499	14523	68479	27686	46162	83554	94750	89923	37089	20048
80336	94598	26940	36858	70297	34135	53140	33340	42050	82341
44104	81949	85157	47954	32979	26575	57600	40881	22222	06413
12550	73742	11100	02040	12860	74697	96644	89439	28707	25815
63606	49329	16505	34484	40219	52563	43651	77082	07207	31790
61196	90446	26457	47774	51924	33729	65394	59593	42582	60527
15474	45266	95270	79953	59367	83848	82396	10118	33211	59466
94557	28573	67897	54387	54622	44431	91190	42592	92927	45973
42481	16213	97344	08721	16868	48767	03071	12059	25701	46670
23523	78317	73208	89837	68935	91416	26252	29663	05522	82562
04493	52494	75246	33824	45862	51025	61962	79335	65337	12472
00549	97654	64051	88159	96119	63896	54692	82391	23287	29529
35963	15307	26898	09354	33351	35462	77974	50024	90103	39333
59808	08391	45427	26842	83609	49700	13021	24892	78565	20106
46058	85236	01390	92286	77281	44077	93910	83647	70617	42941
32179	00597	87379	25241	05567	07007	86743	17157	85394	11838
69234	61406	20117	45204	15956	60000	18743	92423	97118	96338
19565	41430	01758	75379	40419	21585	66674	36806	84962	85207
45155	14938	19476	07246	43667	94543	59047	90033	20826	69541
94864	31994	36768	10851	34888	81553	01540	35456	05014	51176

The statistical tables for the Z and F were generated using the computational algorithms found in the following references:

APPENDIX A (concluded)

98086	24826	45240	28404	44999	08896	39094	73407	35441	31880
33185	16232	41941	50949	89435	48581	88695	41994	37548	73043
80951	00406	96382	70774	20151	23387	25016	25298	94624	61171
79752	49140	71961	28296	69861	02591	74852	20539	00387	59579
18633	32537	98145	06571	31010	24674	05455	61427	77938	91936
74029	43902	77557	32270	97790	17119	52527	58021	80814	51748
54178	45611	80993	37143	05335	12969	56127	19255	36040	90324
11664	49883	52079	84827	59381	71539	09973	33440	88461	23356
48324	77928	31249	64710	02295	36870	32307	57546	15020	09994
69074	94138	87637	91976	35584	04401	10518	21615	01848	76938
09188	20097	32825	39527	04220	86304	83389	87374	64278	58044
90045	85497	51981	50654	94938	81997	91870	76150	68476	64659
73189	50207	47677	26269	62290	64464	27124	67018	41361	82760
75768	76490	20971	87749	90429	12272	95375	05871	93823	43178
54016	44056	66281	31003	00682	27398	20714	53295	07706	17813
08358	69910	78542	42785	13661	58873	04618	97553	31223	08420
28306	03264	81333	10591	40510	07893	32604	60475	94119	01840
53840	86233	81594	13628	51215	90290	28466	68795	77762	20791
91757	53741	61613	62669	50263	90212	55781	76514	83483	47055
89415	92694	00397	58391	12607	17646	48949	72306	94541	37408
77513	03820	86864	29901	68414	82774	51908	13980	72893	55507
19502	37174	69979	20288	55210	29773	74287	75251	65344	67415
21818	59313	93278	81757	05686	73156	07082	85046	31853	38452
51474	66499	68107	23621	94049	91345	42836	09191	08007	45449
99559	68331	62535	24170	69777	12830	74819	78142	43860	72834
33713	48007	93584	72869	51926	64721	58303	29822	93174	93972
85274	86893	11303	22970	28834	34137	73515	90400	71148	43643
84133	89640	44035	52166	73852	70091	61222	60561	62327	18423
56732	16234	17395	96131	10123	91622	85496	57560	81604	18880
65138	56806	87648	85261	34313	65861	45875	21069	85644	47277
38001	02176	81719	11711	71602	92937	74219	64049	65584	49698
37402	96397	01304	77586	56271	10086	47324	62605	40030	37438
97125	40348	87083	31417	21815	39250	75237	62047	15501	29578
21826	41134	47143	34072	64638	85902	49139	06441	03856	54552
73135	42742	95719	09035	85794	74296	08789	88156	64691	19202
07638	77929	03061	18072	96207	44156	23821	99538	04713	66994
60528	83441	07954	19814	59175	20695	05533	52139	61212	06455
83596	35655	06958	92983	05128	09719	77433	53783	92301	50498
10850	62746	99599	10507	13499	06319	53075	71839	06410	19362
39820	98952	43622	63147	64421	80814	43800	09351	31024	73167

APPENDIX B

Normal Curve Table *(Area between Z = 0 and Z)*

	0.00	0.01	0.02	0.03	0.04	0.05	0.06	0.07	0.08	0.09
0.0	0.0001	0.0040	0.0080	0.0120	0.0160	0.0200	0.0240	0.0280	0.0319	0.0359
0.1	0.0399	0.0438	0.0478	0.0518	0.0557	0.0597	0.0636	0.0675	0.0715	0.0754
0.2	0.0793	0.0832	0.0871	0.0910	0.0949	0.0988	0.1026	0.1065	0.1103	0.1141
0.3	0.1180	0.1218	0.1256	0.1293	0.1331	0.1369	0.1406	0.1444	0.1481	0.1518
0.4	0.1555	0.1591	0.1628	0.1664	0.1701	0.1737	0.1773	0.1809	0.1844	0.1880
0.5	0.1915	0.1950	0.1985	0.2020	0.2054	0.2089	0.2123	0.2157	0.2191	0.2224
0.6	0.2258	0.2291	0.2324	0.2357	0.2389	0.2422	0.2454	0.2486	0.2518	0.2549
0.7	0.2581	0.2612	0.2643	0.2673	0.2704	0.2734	0.2764	0.2794	0.2823	0.2852
0.8	0.2882	0.2910	0.2939	0.2967	0.2995	0.3023	0.3051	0.3078	0.3106	0.3133
0.9	0.3159	0.3186	0.3212	0.3238	0.3264	0.3289	0.3314	0.3339	0.3364	0.3389
1.0	0.3413	0.3437	0.3461	0.3484	0.3508	0.3531	0.3554	0.3576	0.3599	0.3621
1.1	0.3643	0.3664	0.3686	0.3707	0.3728	0.3748	0.3769	0.3789	0.3809	0.3829
1.2	0.3850	0.3869	0.3888	0.3907	0.3926	0.3944	0.3962	0.3980	0.3998	0.4015
1.3	0.4032	0.4049	0.4066	0.4083	0.4099	0.4115	0.4131	0.4147	0.4162	0.4177
1.4	0.4192	0.4207	0.4222	0.4236	0.4251	0.4265	0.4278	0.4292	0.4305	0.4319
1.5	0.4332	0.4344	0.4357	0.4369	0.4382	0.4394	0.4406	0.4417	0.4429	0.4440
1.6	0.4451	0.4462	0.4473	0.4484	0.4494	0.4504	0.4515	0.4524	0.4534	0.4544
1.7	0.4553	0.4563	0.4572	0.4581	0.4590	0.4598	0.4607	0.4615	0.4623	0.4632
1.8	0.4639	0.4647	0.4655	0.4662	0.4670	0.4677	0.4684	0.4691	0.4698	0.4705
1.9	0.4711	0.4718	0.4724	0.4731	0.4737	0.4743	0.4749	0.4754	0.4760	0.4766
2.0	0.4771	0.4776	0.4792	0.4797	0.4792	0.4797	0.4802	0.4806	0.4811	0.4816
2.1	0.4820	0.4824	0.4829	0.4833	0.4837	0.4841	0.4845	0.4849	0.4852	0.4856
2.2	0.4860	0.4863	0.4867	0.4870	0.4873	0.4877	0.4880	0.4883	0.4886	0.4889
2.3	0.4892	0.4895	0.4897	0.4900	0.4903	0.4905	0.4908	0.4910	0.4913	0.4915
2.4	0.4917	0.4919	0.4922	0.4924	0.4926	0.4928	0.4930	0.4932	0.4934	0.4936
2.5	0.4937	0.4939	0.4941	0.4943	0.4944	0.4946	0.4947	0.4949	0.4950	0.4952
2.6	0.4953	0.4955	0.4956	0.4957	0.4958	0.4960	0.4961	0.4962	0.4963	0.4964
2.7	0.4965	0.4966	0.4968	0.4969	0.4969	0.4970	0.4971	0.4972	0.4973	0.4974
2.8	0.4973	0.4974	0.4974	0.4975	0.4976	0.4977	0.4977	0.4978	0.4979	0.4979
2.9	0.4980	0.4981	0.4981	0.4982	0.4982	0.4983	0.4983	0.4984	0.4984	0.4985
3.0	0.4985	0.4986	0.4986	0.4987	0.4987	0.4988	0.4988	0.4988	0.4989	0.4989
3.1	0.4990	0.4990	0.4990	0.4991	0.4991	0.4991	0.4991	0.4992	0.4992	0.4992
3.2	0.4993	0.4993	0.4993	0.4993	0.4994	0.4994	0.4994	0.4994	0.4994	0.4995
3.3	0.4995	0.4995	0.4995	0.4995	0.4996	0.4996	0.4996	0.4996	0.4996	0.4996
3.4	0.4996	0.4997	0.4997	0.4997	0.4997	0.4997	0.4997	0.4997	0.4997	0.4998

SOURCE: F. N. Kerlinger and H. B. Lee, Foundations of Behavioral Research, 4th ed. Copyright © 2000 by Harcourt College publishers. Reprinted by permission.

APPENDIX C
Distribution of chi square (χ^2)

	Probability.												
	.99	.98	.95	.90	.80	.70	.50	.30	.20	.10	.05	.02	.01	.001
1	.0²157	.0²628	.00393	.0158	.0642	.148	.455	1.074	1.642	2.706	3.841	5.412	6.635	10.827
2	.0201	.0404	.103	.211	.446	.713	1.386	2.408	3.219	4.605	5.991	7.824	9.210	13.815
3	.115	.185	.352	.584	1.005	1.424	2.366	3.665	4.642	6.251	7.815	9.837	11.345	16.266
4	.297	.429	.711	1.064	1.649	2.195	3.357	4.878	5.989	7.779	9.488	11.668	13.277	18.467
5	.554	.752	1.145	1.610	2.343	3.000	4.351	6.064	7.289	9.236	11.070	13.388	15.086	20.515
6	.872	1.134	1.635	2.204	3.070	3.828	5.348	7.231	8.558	10.645	12.592	15.033	16.812	22.457
7	1.239	1.564	2.167	2.833	3.822	4.671	6.346	8.383	9.803	12.017	14.067	16.622	18.475	24.322
8	1.646	2.032	2.733	3.490	4.594	5.527	7.344	9.524	11.030	13.362	15.507	18.168	20.090	26.125
9	2.088	2.532	3.325	4.168	5.380	6.393	8.343	10.656	12.242	14.684	16.919	19.679	21.666	27.877
10	2.558	3.059	3.940	4.865	6.179	7.267	9.342	11.781	13.442	15.987	18.307	21.161	23.209	29.588
11	3.053	3.609	4.575	5.578	6.989	8.148	10.341	12.899	14.631	17.275	19.675	22.618	24.725	32.264
12	3.571	4.178	5.226	6.304	7.807	9.034	11.340	14.011	15.812	18.549	21.026	24.054	26.217	32.909
13	4.107	4.765	5.892	7.042	8.634	9.926	12.340	15.119	16.985	19.812	22.362	25.472	27.688	34.528
14	4.660	5.368	6.571	7.790	9.467	10.821	13.339	16.222	18.151	21.064	23.685	26.873	29.141	36.123
15	5.229	5.985	7.261	8.547	10.307	11.721	14.339	17.322	19.311	22.307	24.996	28.259	30.578	37.697
16	5.812	6.614	7.962	9.312	11.152	12.624	15.338	18.418	20.465	23.542	26.296	29.633	32.000	39.252
17	6.408	7.255	8.672	10.085	12.002	13.531	16.338	19.511	21.615	24.769	27.587	30.995	33.409	40.790
18	7.015	7.906	9.390	10.865	12.857	14.440	17.338	20.601	22.760	25.989	28.869	32.346	34.805	42.312
19	7.633	8.567	10.117	11.651	13.716	15.352	18.338	21.689	23.900	27.204	30.144	33.687	36.191	43.820
20	8.260	9.237	10.851	12.443	14.578	16.266	19.337	22.775	25.038	28.412	31.410	35.020	37.566	45.315
21	8.897	9.915	11.591	13.240	15.445	17.182	20.337	23.858	26.171	29.615	32.671	36.343	38.932	46.797
22	9.542	10.600	12.338	14.041	16.314	18.101	21.337	24.939	27.301	30.813	33.924	37.659	40.289	48.268
23	10.196	11.293	13.091	14.848	17.187	19.021	22.337	26.018	28.429	32.007	35.172	38.968	41.638	49.728
24	10.856	11.992	13.848	15.659	18.062	19.943	23.337	27.096	29.553	33.196	36.415	40.270	42.980	51.179
25	11.524	12.697	14.611	16.473	18.940	20.867	24.337	28.172	30.675	34.382	37.652	41.566	44.314	52.620
26	12.198	13.409	15.379	17.292	19.820	21.792	25.336	29.246	31.795	35.563	38.885	42.856	45.642	54.052
27	12.879	14.125	16.151	18.114	20.703	22.719	26.336	30.319	32.912	36.741	40.113	44.140	46.963	55.476
28	13.565	14.847	16.928	18.939	21.588	23.647	27.336	31.391	34.027	37.916	41.337	45.419	48.278	56.893
29	14.256	15.574	17.708	19.768	22.475	24.577	28.336	32.461	35.139	39.087	42.557	46.693	49.588	58.302
30	14.953	16.306	18.493	20.599	23.364	25.508	29.336	33.530	36.250	40.256	43.773	47.962	50.892	59.703

SOURCE: Appendix C is taken from Table IV of Fisher & Yates' *Statistical Tables for Biological, Agricultural, and Medical Research*, published by Longman Group UK Ltd. London (previously published by Oliver and Boyd Ltd., Edinburgh) and by permission of the authors and publishers.

© 1963 R. A. Fisher and F. Yates

Reprinted by permission of Addison Wesley Longman Limited.

Reprinted by permission of Pearson Education Limited.

APPENDIX D
Distribution of t

df	Level of significance for one-tailed test					
	.10	.05	.025	.01	.005	.0005
	Level of significance for two-tailed test					
	.20	.10	.05	.02	.01	.001
1	3.078	6.314	12.706	31.821	63.657	636.619
2	1.886	2.920	4.303	6.965	9.925	31.598
3	1.638	2.353	3.182	4.541	5.841	12.941
4	1.533	2.132	2.776	3.747	4.604	8.610
5	1.476	2.015	2.571	3.365	4.032	6.859
6	1.440	1.943	2.447	3.143	3.707	5.959
7	1.415	1.895	2.365	2.998	3.499	5.405
8	1.397	1.860	2.306	2.896	3.355	5.041
9	1.383	1.833	2.262	2.821	3.250	4.781
10	1.372	1.812	2.228	2.764	3.169	4.587
11	1.363	1.796	2.201	2.718	3.106	4.437
12	1.356	1.782	2.179	2.681	3.055	4.318
13	1.350	1.771	2.160	2.650	3.012	4.221
14	1.345	1.761	2.145	2.624	2.977	4.140
15	1.341	1.753	2.131	2.602	2.947	4.073
16	1.337	1.746	2.120	2.583	2.921	4.015
17	1.333	1.740	2.110	2.567	2.898	3.965
18	1.330	1.734	2.101	2.552	2.878	3.922
19	1.328	1.729	2.093	2.539	2.861	3.883
20	1.325	1.725	2.086	2.528	2.845	3.850
21	1.323	1.721	2.080	2.518	2.831	3.819
22	1.321	1.717	2.074	2.508	2.819	3.792
23	1.319	1.714	2.069	2.500	2.807	3.767
24	1.318	1.711	2.064	2.492	2.797	3.745
25	1.316	1.708	2.060	2.485	2.787	3.725
26	1.315	1.706	2.056	2.479	2.779	3.707
27	1.314	1.703	2.052	2.473	2.771	3.690
28	1.313	1.701	2.048	2.467	2.763	3.674
29	1.311	1.699	2.045	2.462	2.756	3.659
30	1.310	1.697	2.042	2.457	2.750	3.646
40	1.303	1.684	2.021	2.423	2.704	3.551
60	1.296	1.671	2.000	2.390	2.660	3.460
120	1.289	1.658	1.980	2.358	2.617	3.373
∞	1.282	1.645	1.960	2.326	2.576	3.291
	0.80	0.90	0.95	0.98	0.99	0.999

SOURCE: Appendix D is taken from Table III of Fisher & Yates' *Statistical Tables for Biological, Agricultural, and Medical Research,* published by Longman Group UK Ltd. London (previously published by Oliver and Boyd Ltd., Edinburgh) and by permission of the authors and publishers.

© 1963 R. A. Fisher and F. Yates

Reprinted by permission of Addison Wesley Longman Limited.
Reprinted by permission of Pearson Education Limited.

APPENDIX E

Critical Values *of* F *(0.05 level in medium type, 0.01 level in boldface type)* *

		Degrees of Freedom (Numerator)									
		1	2	3	4	5	6	7	8	9	10
Degrees of Freedom (Denominator)	1	161.00	200.00	216.00	225.00	230.00	234.00	237.00	239.00	241.00	242.00
		4052.0	**4999.0**	**5403.0**	**5625.0**	**5764.0**	**5859.0**	**5928.0**	**5981.0**	**6022.0**	**6056.0**
	2	18.51	19.00	19.16	19.25	19.30	19.33	19.36	19.37	19.38	19.39
		98.49	**99.00**	**99.17**	**99.25**	**99.30**	**99.33**	**99.36**	**99.37**	**99.39**	**99.40**
	3	10.13	9.55	9.28	9.12	9.01	8.94	8.88	8.84	8.81	8.78
		34.12	**30.82**	**29.46**	**28.71**	**28.24**	**27.91**	**27.67**	**27.49**	**27.34**	**27.23**
	4	7.71	6.94	6.59	6.39	6.26	6.16	6.09	6.04	6.00	5.96
		21.20	**18.00**	**16.69**	**15.98**	**15.52**	**15.21**	**14.91**	**14.80**	**14.66**	**14.54**
	5	6.61	5.79	5.41	5.19	5.05	4.95	4.88	4.82	4.78	4.74
		16.26	**13.27**	**12.06**	**11.39**	**10.97**	**10.67**	**10.45**	**10.29**	**10.15**	**10.05**
	6	5.99	5.14	4.76	4.53	4.39	4.28	4.21	4.15	4.10	4.06
		33.74	**10.92**	**9.78**	**9.15**	**8.75**	**8.47**	**8.26**	**8.10**	**7.98**	**7.87**
	7	5.59	4.74	4.35	4.12	3.97	3.87	3.79	3.73	3.68	3.63
		12.25	**9.55**	**8.45**	**7.85**	**7.46**	**7.19**	**7.00**	**6.84**	**6.71**	**6.62**
	8	5.32	4.46	4.07	3.84	3.69	3.58	3.50	3.44	3.39	3.34
		11.26	**8.65**	**7.59**	**7.01**	**6.63**	**6.37**	**6.19**	**6.03**	**5.91**	**5.82**
	9	5.12	4.26	3.86	3.63	3.48	3.37	3.29	3.23	3.18	3.13
		10.56	**8.02**	**6.99**	**6.42**	**6.06**	**5.80**	**5.62**	**5.47**	**5.35**	**5.26**
	10	4.96	4.10	3.71	3.48	3.33	3.22	3.14	3.07	3.02	2.97
		10.04	**7.56**	**6.55**	**5.99**	**5.64**	**5.39**	**5.21**	**5.06**	**4.95**	**4.85**
	11	4.84	3.98	3.59	3.36	3.20	3.09	3.01	2.95	2.90	2.86
		9.65	**7.20**	**6.22**	**5.67**	**5.32**	**5.07**	**4.88**	**4.74**	**4.63**	**4.54**
	12	4.75	3.88	3.49	3.26	3.11	3.00	2.92	2.85	2.80	2.76
		9.33	**6.93**	**5.95**	**5.41**	**5.06**	**4.82**	**4.65**	**4.50**	**4.39**	**4.30**
	13	4.67	3.80	3.41	3.18	3.02	2.92	2.84	2.77	2.72	2.67
		9.07	**6.70**	**5.74**	**5.20**	**4.86**	**4.62**	**4.44**	**4.30**	**4.19**	**4.10**
	14	4.60	3.74	3.34	3.11	2.96	2.85	2.77	2.70	2.65	2.60
		8.86	**6.51**	**5.56**	**5.03**	**4.69**	**4.46**	**4.28**	**4.14**	**4.03**	**3.94**
	15	4.54	3.68	3.29	3.06	2.90	2.79	2.70	2.64	2.59	2.55
		8.68	**6.36**	**5.42**	**4.89**	**4.56**	**4.32**	**4.14**	**4.00**	**3.89**	**3.80**
	16	4.49	3.63	3.24	3.01	2.85	2.74	2.66	2.59	2.54	2.49
		8.53	**6.23**	**5.29**	**4.77**	**4.44**	**4.20**	**4.03**	**3.89**	**3.78**	**3.69**
	17	4.45	3.59	3.20	2.96	2.81	2.70	2.62	2.55	2.50	2.45
		8.40	**6.11**	**5.18**	**4.67**	**4.34**	**4.10**	**3.93**	**3.79**	**3.68**	**3.59**
	18	4.41	3.55	3.16	2.93	2.77	2.66	2.58	2.51	2.46	2.41
		8.28	**6.01**	**5.09**	**4.58**	**4.25**	**4.01**	**3.85**	**3.71**	**3.60**	**3.51**
	19	4.38	3.52	3.13	2.90	2.74	2.63	2.55	2.48	2.43	2.38
		8.18	**5.93**	**5.01**	**4.50**	**4.17**	**3.94**	**3.77**	**3.63**	**3.52**	**3.43**

APPENDIX E *(continued)*

20	4.35	3.49	3.10	2.87	2.72	2.60	2.52	2.45	2.40	2.35
	8.10	5.85	4.94	4.43	4.10	3.87	3.71	3.56	3.45	3.37
22	4.30	3.44	3.05	2.82	2.66	2.55	2.47	2.40	2.35	2.30
	7.94	5.72	4.82	4.31	3.99	3.76	3.59	3.45	3.35	3.26
23	4.28	3.42	3.03	2.80	2.64	2.53	2.45	2.38	2.32	2.28
	7.88	S.66	4.76	4.26	3.94	3.71	3.54	3.41	3.30	3.21
25	4.24	3.38	2.99	2.76	2.60	2.49	2.41	2.34	2.28	2.24
	7.77	5.57	4.61	4.18	3.86	3.63	3.46	3.32	3.21	3.13
26	4.22	3.37	2.98	2.74	2.59	2.47	2.39	2.32	2.27	2.22
	7.72	5.53	4.64	4.14	3.82	3.59	3.42	3.29	3.27	3.09
28	4.20	3.34	2.95	2.72	2.56	2.44	2.36	2.29	2.24	2.29
	7.64	5.45	4.57	4.07	3.76	3.53	3.36	3.23	3.12	3.03
29	4.18	3.33	2.93	2.70	2.54	2.43	2.35	2.28	2.22	2.18
	7.60	5.42	4.54	4.04	3.73	3.50	3.33	3.20	3.08	3.00
30	4.27	3.32	2.92	2.69	2.53	2.42	2.34	2.27	2.21	2.16
	7.56	5.39	4.51	4.02	3.70	3.47	3.30	3.17	3.06	2.98
34	4.13	3.29	2.88	2.65	2.49	2.38	2.30	2.23	2.27	2.12
	7.44	5.29	4.42	3.93	3.61	3.38	3.21	3.08	2.97	2.89
38	4.20	3.25	2.85	2.62	2.46	2.35	2.26	2.29	2.14	2.09
	7.35	5.21	4.34	3.86	3.54	3.32	3.15	3.02	2.91	2.82
40	4.08	3.23	2.84	2.62	2.45	2.34	2.25	2.28	2.22	2.07
	7.31	5.18	4.31	3.83	3.51	3.29	3.12	2.99	2.88	2.80
46	4.65	3.20	2.81	2.57	2.42	2.30	2.22	2.14	2.09	2.04
	7.21	5.10	4.24	3.76	3.44	3.22	3.05	2.92	2.82	2.73
50	4.03	3.18	2.79	2.56	2.40	2.29	2.20	2.13	2.07	2.02
	7.17	5.06	4.20	3.72	3.41	3.11	3.02	2.83	2.78	2.70
60	4.00	3.15	2.76	2.52	2.37	2.25	2.57	2.10	2.04	1.99
	7.08	4.98	4.13	3.65	3.34	3.12	2.95	2.82	2.72	2.63
70	3.98	3.13	2.74	2.50	2.35	2.23	2.14	2.07	2.01	1.97
	7.01	4.92	4.08	3.60	3.29	3.07	2.91	2.77	2.67	2.59
80	3.96	3.11	2.72	2.48	2.33	2.21	2.12	2.05	1.99	1.95
	6.96	4.88	4.04	3.56	3.25	3.04	2.87	2.74	2.64	2.55
100	3.94	3.09	2.70	2.46	2.30	2.19	2.10	2.03	5.97	5.92
	6.90	4.82	3.98	3.51	3.20	2.99	2.82	2.69	2.59	2.51

*5 percent (roman type) and 1 percent (bold face type) points for the distribution of F.

Source: P. G. Hoel, *Elementary Statistics,* 2nd ed. (New York: John Wiley & Sons, 1966). Copyright © 1966 by John Wiley & Sons. Reprinted by permission of John Wiley & Sons.

Source: F. N. Kerlinger and H. B. Lee, *Foundations of Behavioral Research,* 4th ed. Copyright © 2000 by Harcourt College Publishers. Reprinted by permission.

Name Index

Achen, Christopher, 235, 266
Aldrich, John, 310
Allison, Paul, 306, 312
Arrow, Kenneth, 316
Asher, Herbert, 310

Babbie, Earl, 37, 86, 210
Bachstrom, Charles, 186
Bader, Genia, 86
Bausman, Kent, 243
Bensman, Joseph, 336
Berry, William, 266, 267
Bingham, Richard, 332
Blalock, H.M., 207
Bloomquist, Leonard, 243
Bolas, Cheryl, 344
Booth, Alan, 173
Box-Steffensmeier, Janet, 306

Campbell, Donald, 25, 29, 37
Cantarero, Rodrigo, 141
Caplovitz, David, 347
Castellan, John, 207, 211
Chiricios, Theodore, 23
Cnudde, Charles, 310
Converse, Jean, 86
Cook, Thomas, 37
Couper, Mick, 210

Dearing, Brian, 134
Dinger, Mark, 208
Dodson, Anthony, 301
Dutta, M., 310

Ethridge, Marcus, 332

Feldman, Stanley, 266
Fischoff, Baruch, 332
Fowler, Floyd, 86
Fox, John, 235, 267

Gaber, Sharon, 141
Groves, Robert, 177
Grube, John, 179
Gruhl, John, 285

Haddon, William, 35
Hagle, Timothy, 134
Hanke, Steve, 332
Hartwig, Frederick, 134
Hary, Melissa, 267
Hatry, Harry, 64, 81, 82-85, 86, 210
Hebert, F. Ted, 48
Henderson, Gail, 347
Henkel, R. 221
Hornblum, Allan, 337
Houston, David, 189
Humphrey, S. Laud, 336
Hursh-Cesar, Gerald, 186

Jaccard, James, 267
Jacobs, Marilyn, 229
Johnston, Jocelyn, 31, 256
Jones, Bradford, 306
Jones, James H. 335

SUBJECT INDEX